650

TUTANKHAMUN

THE
UNTOLD STORY

by Thomas Hoving

A TOUCHSTONE BOOK
Published by SIMON & SCHUSTER, INC.
NEW YORK

To my wife, Nancy

A Touchstone Book
Published by Simon & Schuster, Inc.
Simon & Schuster Building
Rockefeller Center
1230 Avenue of the Americas
New York, New York 10020

TOUCHSTONE and colophon are registered trademarks
of Simon & Schuster, Inc.

Designed by Eve Metz

Photo Editor: Vincent Virga

Manufactured in the United States of America

10 9 8 7 6 5 4 3 2 1 Pbk.

Library of Congress Cataloging in Publication Data

Hoving, Thomas Pearsall Field, Date.
    Tutankhamun—The Untold Story
    Includes Index.
    1. Tutankhamun, King of Egypt—Tomb. 2. Excavations
(Archaeology)—Egypt. 3. Egypt—Antiquities. I. Title.
DT87.5.H68   932   78-17751

ISBN 0-671-24370-5 Pbk.

Acknowledgments

To all those who have dealt with Tutankhamun, the most fascinating archaeological adventure in history, and helped in the preparation of this book on the subject, I owe profound thanks:

The members of the Egyptian Department of the Metropolitan Museum of Art for invaluable leads and discussions on the subject—in particular, Thomas Logan, Associate Curator.

I.E.S. Edwards, former Curator of Egyptology at the British Museum, for his interest, his expertise, his recollections and splendid anecdotes.

Bernard Bothmer, Curator of the Egyptian Department of the Brooklyn Museum.

John Cooney, Curator of Ancient Art at the Cleveland Museum of Art, for his help in informing me of the whereabouts of a number of objects in the United States originally from the tomb and for his invaluable assistance in rooting out errors in this book.

Robert Keedick, President of the Keedick Lecture Bureau, for supplying me with fascinating unpublished material about Howard Carter, compiled by his father, who had arranged Carter's American lecture tour.

Lord Carnarvon of Highclere for his gracious permission to quote from certain unpublished letters and notes of his father, the patron of the excavation.

Ashton Hawkins, Secretary of the Metropolitan Museum of Art, for his permission to quote from Metropolitan Museum sources.

Sir Denis Hamilton, Publisher of the London *Times*, for his interest in the book and his forthright suggestion that I probe the Tutankhamun files in the archives of the *Times*.

Gordon Phillips, Archivist of the London *Times*, for his warm hospitality and keen humor and for his permission to quote from letters and documents in his well-tended archives.

Alice E. Mayhew, Editor at Simon and Schuster, for her dynamic help in so many things regarding the publication of this book.

Vera Schneider for her sensitive copy editing of the final manuscript.

Mary Doherty, of the Metropolitan Museum, for her unstinting aid in tracking down slides and photographs.

Cecilia Mescall, Executive Administrator of Hoving Associates, Inc., for her constant help in preparing the manuscript.

Nancy Hoving for research, critical judgment and constant support.

Robert Lescher, Literary Agent, without whose unremitting interest, professional skills in editing the many manuscripts and sage advice, this book would never have emerged.

THOMAS HOVING

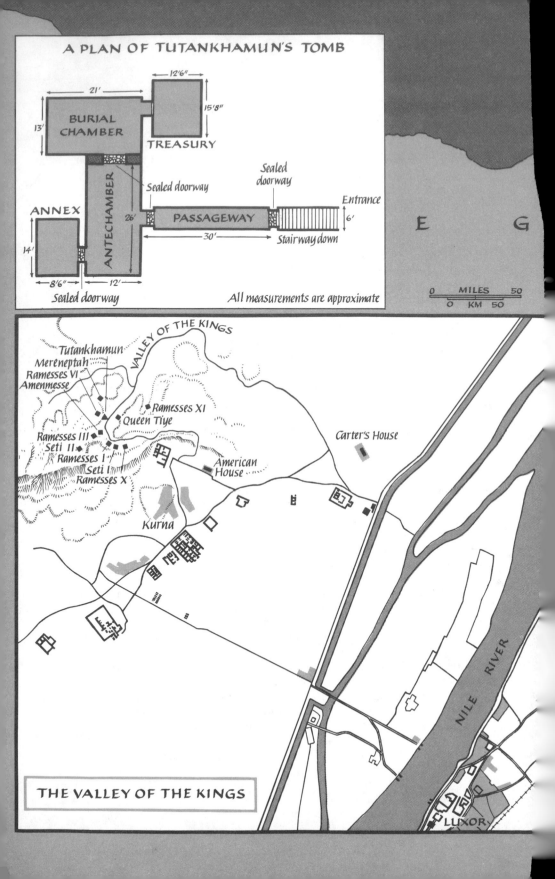

A PLAN OF TUTANKHAMUN'S TOMB

21'

BURIAL
CHAMBER

13'

12'6"

15'8"

TREASURY

Sealed doorway

Sealed
doorway

Entrance

6'

ANNEX

ANTECHAMBER

26'

PASSAGEWAY

30'

Stairway down

14'

8'6"   12'

Sealed doorway

All measurements are approximate

E   G

0   MILES   50

0   KM   50

THE VALLEY OF THE KINGS

VALLEY OF THE KINGS

Tutankhamun
Mereneptah
Ramesses VI
Amenmesse

Ramesses XI
Queen Tiye

Carter's House

Ramesses III
Seti II
Ramesses I
Seti I
Ramesses X

American
House

Kurna

NILE RIVER

LUXOR

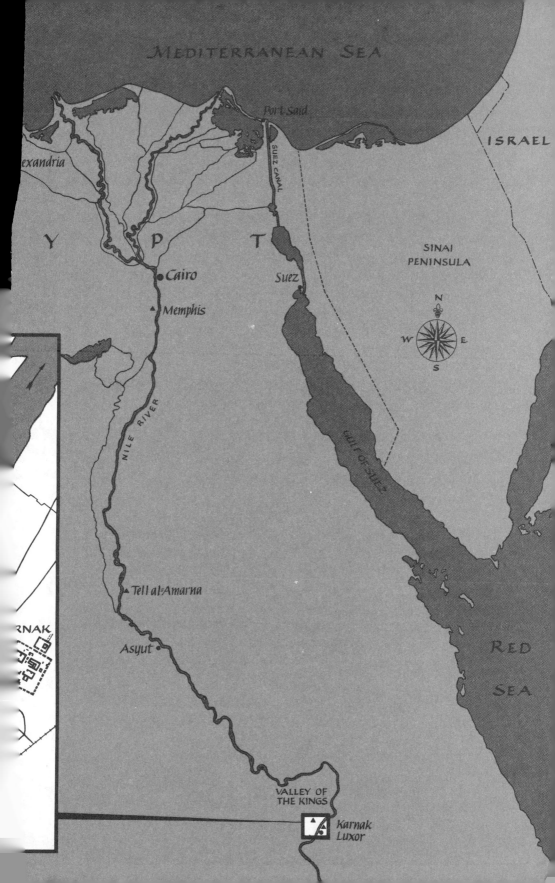

Contents

INTRODUCTION 11

1 • Dramatis Personae 17
2 • The Stage: The Valley of the Kings 30
3 • Forty Kings and the Thieves from Kurna 40
4 • First Clues of Tutankhamun 47
5 • The First Years of Search 55
6 • Deep Doubts 63
7 • "The Tomb of the Golden Bird" 75
8 • "Wonderful Things" 83
9 • The Long Night 90
10 • Revelations 104
11 • The Limelight 108
12 • "Discovery Colossal and Need Every Assistance" 114
13 • The Affair of the Three Princesses 127
14 • The Metropolitan Museum Makes a Coup 138
15 • "Tutankhamun Ltd." 146
16 • A "Renegade" Speaks Out 158
17 • "Strong Bull, Beautiful of Birth" 166
18 • Carnarvon Returns to the Tomb 176
19 • The Sealed Doorway 191
20 • The Queen's Visit 201
21 • Closing Down the Tomb 213
22 • Sudden Tragedy 219

23 • The Curse   226
24 • The Season Ends   231
25 • Collision Course   236
26 • The Bastion of Bureaucracy   253
27 • Dismantling the Shrines   263
28 • "The Public Domain"   270
29 • Strike!   283
30 • "Bandits!"   297
31 • "A Malignant Influence"   307
32 • "Much *Kalaam*"   318
33 • Carter in America   326
34 • Surrender   338
35 • The Secret Division   349
     Sources   370
     Index   377

Introduction

THE DISCOVERY in the late evening of November 26, 1922, of the tomb of King Tutankhamun in Egypt's romantic Valley of the Kings, and the removal from it, over ten years, of nearly five thousand dazzling works of art caused a sensation throughout the world. It was, and remains, the richest discovery in the history of archaeology.

Tutankhamun, a shadowy pharaoh who lived over three thousand years ago and died under mysterious circumstances at the age of eighteen or nineteen around 1350 B.C., instantly became a prime celebrity of the 1920s. The discoverers of the tomb—Howard Carter, who was a British Egyptologist, and his wealthy patron, George Edward Stanhope Molyneux Herbert, Lord Carnarvon—became unwilling celebrities at the same time.

After the shattering years of the Great War, the unearthing of the only pharaoh's tomb in the valley that had not been totally pillaged by ancient tomb robbers was extraordinarily appealing. The two excavators had been told by all the experts that the ancient City of the Dead had been completely excavated, yet they pressed on doggedly. For years they found nothing. But over the years they persistently assembled clues that led them to the inescapable conclusion that the valley held

11

one more royal tomb, which other archaeologists had ignored. Then, in the very last season that the patron would support, in the last minute area of the valley where they guessed no earlier excavator had plumbed to the bedrock, there came the splendid discovery. Suddenly before them lay thousands of works of art of such serene beauty that certain visitors to the tomb literally felt faint when they looked upon them.

Word of this phenomenal discovery spread throughout the world, speeded along by techniques that had barely existed before, the miracle of modern communications, including telegraph and telephones at the tomb itself, and the first minute-by-minute photographs and moving film footage ever undertaken in the history of archaeology. The following year, a mummy's curse which was said to have killed Lord Carnarvon ignited a conflagration of public excitement.

Since the startling day of the discovery just over a half century ago, the treasures of King Tutankhamun have continued to capture the public imagination. No exhibition of works of art has been more popular in world history than "The Treasures of Tutankhamun," which has traveled outside Egypt—to Paris in 1967, to the British Museum in 1972, to four cities in the Soviet Union in 1973, and to seven cities in the United States. Because of this exhibition, a madness for King Tut seems to have taken hold. When the fifty-five masterpieces were at the National Gallery of Art in Washington, D.C., nearly a million visitors viewed them in sixteen weeks. At the Field Museum in Chicago the million mark had been reached in just ten weeks. No doubt over seven million individuals will have paid homage to the youthful Pharaoh by the end of the three-year tour that was sent to the United States in honor of the Bicentennial by the government of Egypt.

In the fifty-six years that have passed since the discovery, dozens of books and exhibition catalogues have been published, and hundreds, even thousands, of news stories have appeared. One would think there would be little new to relate about Tutankhamun and the events surrounding the dramatic find. Not so. As a matter of fact, in all the accounts published up to now—including the three-volume history written by Howard Carter and a colleague, A. C. Mace of the Metropolitan Museum of Art in New York—some of the most important facts regarding the discovery and its aftermath were not revealed, deliberately on the part of some, unconsciously by others. These facts, overlooked or suppressed, substantially change the official and up to now unquestioned story and impart to it a human interest far beyond simply the obvious nature of its archaeological significance.

How was the true story of the discovery unearthed? By intuition, a bit of searching and some serendipity.

As head of the team from the Metropolitan Museum that organized the exhibition "The Treasures of Tutankhamun" for its American tour, I have been, since 1975, immersed in all things relating to that mysterious boy King. I read virtually every piece of the literature, popular and scholarly. I examined the one hundred eighty-odd pages of the volume of the "Journal of Entry" in Carter's own handwriting in the Egyptian Museum of Antiquities at Cairo and studied every one of nearly five thousand objects on display in the galleries. I became fascinated with Howard Carter and his patron, Lord Carnarvon—their characters, their working methods, their relationships with the members of the Egyptian Department of the Metropolitan Museum, their dealings with the Egyptian Service des Antiquités. I even helped dream up the general philosophy of the show. I picked objects from all four chambers and placed them as much as possible in the order in which they were discovered and removed, so as to recreate as far as possible what Carter and his colleagues had experienced in those exciting years of discovery.

I was involved in the myriad administrative details of bringing such an undertaking across the ocean. This entailed hundreds of hours of tense and complex negotiations with the Egyptian authorities. The work was carried out in an office in Cairo crowded with representatives of a variety of countries— England, France, East Germany, Poland, West Germany, not to mention the United States—all waiting their turn in the same room, eavesdropping on everyone else. They took up with the president of today's Organization of Antiquities subjects ranging in significance from the right to conduct a massive new dig to a permit to sleep alone deep in the burial chamber of the Great Pyramid. One even asked permission to embrace the statue of Pharaoh Chephren outside its glass case in the Egyptian Museum, to test the power of the life-giving rays that "most assuredly emanated from the ancient divinity-being and would beyond doubt cure most, if not all, maladies of mankind's oppressed and enfeebled bodies."

I participated in an unorthodox method of bringing electricity into the darkened section of the Egyptian Museum where I was to supervise the building of a temporary photo studio and a small factory for making casts and molds for reproduction. Weeks before my arrival I had been told that the electricity would "surely be working." When I arrived with a team of eight specialists, I was assured that the lights would indeed function—perhaps in a month or two! So two hundred meters of cable were promptly borrowed from the sound-and-light extravaganza at the Great Pyramid. A street light near the museum was tapped. The cable was hauled up the side of the building, across the roof and down through a broken pane of glass into the studio. There, accompanied by the first and no doubt last sounds of the music of Bach, Mozart and Vivaldi heard in the Egyptian Museum, the work was begun.

Then, months later, when every detail of the complex agreement for the exhibition had been thrashed out, a problem concerning transportation arose that threatened to cancel the show. After agreeing, or seeming to agree, to send the objects by commercial air freight, the Egyptians suddenly demanded the hiring of charter cargo flights at an additional half million dollars' expense to the exhibitors. I rushed to the American Embassy to discuss the grave difficulty with Ambassador Herman Eilts. When I pointed out to the ambassador that, shortly after World War II, the American Navy had brought an exhibition from Europe to the United States, the ambassador said, "I think I shall cable Henry Kissinger and my old school friend

Jim Holloway about that particular technique of transportation." Holloway? The Chief of Naval Operations. And so the Navy saved the show for America by sending the great treasures over on the U.S.S. *Sacramento*—for free.

But amusing as these episodes were, they were extraneous to Tutankhamun, his treasures, Carnarvon, and Howard Carter, whose three volumes, *The Tomb of Tut-ank-Amen*, I must have read half a dozen times. I am not sure exactly when I became baffled, then suspicious, then skeptical of Carter's account of the noble discovery. I began to wonder how Carter could simply have looked into the tomb the first night, resealed it and then retired. That was not human nature. At any rate it was totally different from the impulses I had experienced as an excavator of a Greek city in Sicily. For me to see the barest tip of the nose of a terra-cotta head appear in the caked soil of the trench was a monumental temptation to cast aside restraint, patience and method and tear away at the soil with my bare fingers. Perhaps it was when I could find no mention in Carter's first volume of one of the most beautiful objects, a wooden portrait head of the boy King on lotus leaves, that I began to say to myself, "What really went on?" Perhaps it was when I tried to recreate the precise order in which Carter removed the objects from the four chambers, and found curious discrepancies between his text and the series of more than eighteen hundred photographs made on the spot by the Metropolitan's photographer Harry Burton, that I began to question the total veracity of his recounting of the events.

Routinely I examined the archives of the Metropolitan Museum regarding Tutankhamun and the "partnership" between the museum and Howard Carter. There was nothing of interest, save for a few references—curious, to say the least—to the effect that the American Secretary of State, Charles Evans Hughes, was pressuring the Egyptian government on behalf of the museum and Lord Carnarvon. The museum *and* Lord Carnarvon? An intriguing little note stated that the prime aide of the Secretary of State in the museum's Egyptian affairs of 1922–1924 had been doing "splendidly." The aide was a young man by the name of Allen Dulles. Allen Dulles?

But nothing more. There was not even a "hush-hush section" in the archives for those years of the 1920s.

Again, routinely, I inquired of the museum's Egyptian Department what it had in its files. Nothing, beyond copies of some of the material in Archives. Then, by chance, I asked a member of the department who has an office adjacent to the space where twenty-seven bound volumes of the prints of the original Tutankhamun photos were stored if there were materials or files regarding the episode. There were. Nothing put away in a special place, nothing marked "Confidential"—just there. The materials were described as things relating to "the mummy's curse," with standard forms for handling that particular Egyptological annoyance—"junk like that." I looked, and saw hundreds of original documents, letters, drawings, notes, observations, parts of diaries in the handwriting of Howard Carter and Lord Carnarvon and many of the members of the Egyptian Department who labored for years on the excavation—all in precise chronological order, with a host of clippings from a number of newspapers.

It is through these materials that the full and true story of that most amazing of archaeological discoveries makes itself manifest. And the full story is not altogether the noble, waxen, proper and triumphant tale so familiar to us. The truth is also full of intrigue, secret deals and private arrangements, covert political activities, skullduggery, self-interest, arrogance, lies, dashed hopes, poignance and sorrow—a series of events disfigured by human frailties that led to a fundamental and enduring change in the conduct of archaeology in Egypt.

THOMAS HOVING

New York
April 1978

CHAPTER ONE

Dramatis Personae

TUTANKHAMUN IS one of the most famous and, at the same time, least known rulers of the ancient world. Or, as Howard Carter put it, "We might say with truth that the one outstanding feature of his life was that he died and was buried." In 1907, when Howard Carter was introduced to George Herbert, Earl of Carnarvon, by the director general of the Egyptian Service of Antiquities, Sir Gaston Maspero, an enormously entertaining French archaeologist much revered by European and American Egyptologists owing to his immutable support for their right to dig in Egypt, very few people either knew or cared about even that accomplishment of Tutankhamun.

Specialists knew that he had two names—a given name, Tutankhamun, blessed of Amun, the all-powerful god, and a throne name, Nebkheperura. His cartouche, the elliptical emblem surrounding the hieroglyphs, appeared on a number of monuments. A few experts in dynastic records and royal genealogy knew that a king by that name had existed in the second half of the Eighteenth Dynasty, which had produced some of the greatest rulers Egypt had known—Thutmose I, Thutmose III, Queen Hatshepsut—and one of the worst, Akhenaton, the heretic Pharaoh who had brought the New Empire into chaos. But no one could say for sure just where Tutankhamun fitted in, although it was generally agreed that the shadowy monarch belonged among a confusing number of minor rulers who emerged after the death of the "monotheist" Akhenaton and before the ascendancy of Ramesses the Great. Some Egyptologists suggested that Tutankhamun had been the son-in-law of Akhenaton, had himself once been sympathetic to the Aton heresy, yet had at some point in his reign moved from Akhenaton's sacred city, the present Tell al-Amarna, back to Thebes, the city of Amun, and helped restore the old religion.

Certain monuments did proclaim him—in a muted way. There was a nearly life-sized seated statue of Tutankhamun, carved in a dark, rather unpleasant-looking stone, in the Egyptian Museum of Antiquities in Cairo. It showed a youth whom some looked upon as frail but confident and others as weak, almost sickly. And there were fragments of a partly obliterated relief sculpture at Karnak depicting his solar boat. There were also references to him in a tomb of one of his officials stating that certain tribes in Syria and in the Sudan were subject to him and brought him tribute.

And in 1907 a French archaeologist, Georges Legrain, published his discovery of a stele at the base of the temple at Karnak in ancient Thebes. Its inscription referred to Tutankhamun's coming to the throne and, roughly translated, read:

This land was overriden with ills. The shrine of the Gods ran to destruction. The Gods neglected the land. I appealed to the Gods and Goddesses for assistance, but they shunned me. To win them back I labored mightily. I found the temples fallen into ruin, with their holy places overthrown, and their courts overgrown with weeds. I reconstructed their sanctuaries, I re-endowed the temples, and made them gifts of all precious things. I cast statues of the Gods in gold and electrum, decorated with lapis lazuli and all fine stones.

The proclamation goes on to say that Tutankhamun made laws for the land every day without ceasing, and built new ships to ply the waters, and covered them with gold so that they illuminated the Nile. It says that he was benevolent as a ruler and as a judge. For this everyone, everywhere, exulted and praised him and danced for gladness.

But nothing more was known of Tutankhamun than that. Compared to the masses of historical data, inscriptions, sculpture and paintings referring to other kings, it was meager. Since history seemed not to care enough about him to leave an extensive record—even an enigmatic record—the archaeologists who flourished during the early part of the twentieth century must have felt they had somehow been spared the necessity of finding out where he had been buried. There were other pharaohs to investigate, particularly the intriguing heretic Akhenaton. It was Akhenaton whose brooding, troubled visage, with its strange, distended features almost like a caricature, captured contemporary imagination. Tutankhamun was hardly a likely candidate in 1907 for the most extraordinary discovery of the entire history of Egyptian archaeology.

In 1907 very few people outside his own special social set had ever heard of George Edward Stanhope Molyneux Herbert, former Viscount Porchester, the fifth Earl of Carnarvon. If they had bothered to find out, they would have discovered that Lord Carnarvon was a wealthy member of the English landed aristocracy who had, in the forty-one years since his birth on June 26, 1866, accomplished virtually nothing at all. He appeared to be merely a titled ne'er-do-well, an individual whose achievements were so slim and erratic that—except in sporting activities—he did not even deserve the title of dilettante. But he was a most charming and witty ne'er-do-well. In his youth, Lord Carnarvon had been trim, elegant, a bit dashing. He had sandy hair and a devastating profile, the kind that silhouette cutters of the Victorian epoch would have found a splendid challenge to cut out of their thin black papers, preserving perfectly the snub-nose, the neat mustache, the deceptively subtle angle of the forehead and the mildly strong chin. But by 1907 Lord Carnarvon's face was haggard, his body thin and frail. His bones seemed to protrude from the impeccably tailored yet rumpled tweeds he invariably wore, even in

Egypt. Contemporary photographs show him with a cane in one hand and the other hand thrust in a pocket of his jacket, holding himself as if he had just been wounded.

His father, the fourth Earl of Carnarvon, was a noted politician. At one time a member of Disraeli's Cabinet, he was once described by a relative as a "statesman who never allowed ambition to deflect him by a hair's breadth from the path mapped out by a meticulous conscience." To other observers, less adulatory, the fourth Earl was such a statesman because he was rich enough to be independent of any position. He was also, however, a superb scholar of the classics, capable of reading, writing and even speaking both Latin and classical Greek.

None of these talents seems to have been handed down to his young son, Viscount Porchester, or "Porchey." Teachers at the various schools he attended, and his private tutors, considered Porchey to be very bright, able to concentrate at times, but "idle" in matters of scholastic achievement. He first attended a public school near the country seat of the Carnarvon family, the magnificent Highclere, which, even when matched against the many stately homes of England, connoisseurs agreed, was certainly a domain of rare beauty. Soon he dropped out of that school, was tutored at home, and eventually enrolled in Eton. There he fared badly, and he left. It was, according to his aunt, who reared him after his mother had died when he was but nine years old, "most unfortunate that Eton had not done much for the formation of methodical habits in a boy with an exceptionally fine memory and unusual quickness of mind."

If Lord Carnarvon had not been titled, wealthy and living in the most glorious epoch of English aristocracy, he would perhaps have been a drifter—certainly a young man who would have been described as someone still searching for an identity. After Eton he went back to a local school and then enthusiastically entered "cram" schools in London and in Germany, with a view to entering the military. Soon, however, the notion of an Army career paled. Somehow he was able to enroll in Trinity College, Cambridge. There he stayed but two years, never graduating. His single noteworthy effort there appears to have been an attempt to persuade the authorities to remove from his room at his expense the many coats of paint that, to him at least, disfigured the fine wooden paneling. The offer was refused. In his two years at Cambridge he began to collect works of art, primarily French prints, for which he gradually developed a fine eye; he also developed an obsession for exceptional bargains. But his real passion was sports.

After the brief sojourn at college, Porchey traveled for seven years. His itinerary, even in terms of today's air age, was phenomenal. He first sailed three quarters of the way around the world, then went to South Africa, following that with trips to Australia and, successively, Japan, France, Turkey, Sweden, Italy, Germany and the United States, which he covered coast to coast before setting out for South America. During all these peregrinations, Porchey, who became an earl when he was twenty-three, would return frequently to Highclere, then suddenly dash off to Paris or Hannover or Constantinople, and just as abruptly return.

He affected a rather allusive style of communication and would drop such lines as "When I saw the chief of the Mafia in Naples . . ." or "On being refused an audience in Constantinople by Abdul the Damned, I was given one of Turkey's highest honors." He relished what were then known as "quaint people" and acquired numerous friends in callings far removed from his exalted station—herdsmen, jockeys, hair cutters, railroad brakemen.

Lord Carnarvon might appear to have been the most superficial of men at a time in history when superficiality was considered by some to be a high calling. But well hidden beneath the surface of his frivolous behavior and picturesque talk were a steely seriousness, a brilliant mind and a deadly shrewdness. Carnarvon seems to have been one of those "disguisers," the type of man who, when discovered intensely studying a serious book, would exclaim, "Oh, I just picked it up and, having done *that*, I supposed I should simply turn the pages to the end."

21

The reality is that, despite the camouflage, Lord Carnarvon was a brilliant man—possibly even a genius.

He was also resourceful. His Aunt Winifred told a story about him that perfectly illustrates this side of his character. On his way to California he paused in New York City, where he had promised a friend he would try to obtain some privileged information about a certain business. He gained it by first asking his barber about the president of the company in question. Amazingly, the barber knew a lot about the tycoon. Porchey contrived to meet the particular captain of industry, asked him for his advice on a certain stock, and was told on no account to touch the securities. Carnarvon looked hard at him, thanked him, and went quickly to a telegraph office, where he cabled instructions to his broker—to buy. When he returned from California, he dropped in to thank the magnate for the advice that had been so profitable. The industrialist burst out, "But, Lord Carnarvon, I advised you *against* buying." To which Porchey replied, "Oh, yes, I know you said that, but of course I saw that you wished me to understand the reverse."

On his twenty-ninth birthday, Carnarvon married Almina Wombwell, an extraordinarily pretty and highly intelligent girl. In four years they had two children—a son, Henry, Viscount Porchester, today the spry, somewhat garrulous octogenarian sixth Earl of Carnarvon, and a daughter, Lady Evelyn Herbert, who was destined to become her father's dearest friend and close companion, particularly in Egypt.

A few years later Lord Carnarvon suffered an automobile accident that completely changed his life, his outlook and his destiny. He was fortunate to have survived, and if his chauffeur had not pulled him out of the mud into which the car had fallen and dashed a bucket of cold water into his face to start his heart beating, it would have been all over. He was a shattered young man: he had sustained a severe concussion and was temporarily blinded; his chest had been crushed, his legs badly burned, his jaws broken, and his arms dislocated. From that moment, he was never well again and was frequently in pain. But he bore his wounds with great courage and emerged, as some people do under such circumstances, mellowed, thoughtful, determined. At the same time he appeared to be slightly saddened by the realization that he had wasted so much of his life.

Carnarvon thought about trying to enter politics, even began to consider an academic life, but nothing really worked. It seemed to be too late. After all, what future was there for a partially crippled young lord, uneducated in a formal way, peripatetic, and passionate for sports? Apparently, nothing. On his physician's recommendation, however, he went to Egypt in 1903, and was at once enchanted by the majestic age and the immemorial serenity of that ancient civilization. He soon became captivated by "digging."

Carnarvon had in fact been interested in archaeology for some years, but his frenetic travels had prevented any involvement. However, once in Egypt, where he now went each winter, he took it up as a hobby with, as he said, "the idea of keeping me out of mischief, as well as keeping me employed." He obtained a concession in 1906 from the Ministry of Public Works and its Service of Antiquities to work a part of the pyramid-shaped promontory high above the Theban hills, west of the modern city of Luxor, in the vicinity of the fabled Valley of the Tombs of the Kings. There he started digging enthusiastically and in a highly undisciplined manner.

Today, the idea that an English "lordy" (as he was known to the local Egyptians, or natives as they were called in those days) could descend upon Egypt and almost at once obtain official permission to flail away in the sacred precincts of the pharaonic age without training or proper supervision is not only bewildering but appalling. But to say that at the turn of the century the rules and guidelines for such activities in Egypt—and elsewhere—were lackadaisical is to be generous. Then a private citizen had only to be rich and alert enough to find an "in" with the appropriate Frenchman in the Antiquities Service to obtain a license to dig. The French had almost exclusive control over all matters concerning antiquities on behalf of the Egyptian government, and had maintained that control since the turn of the nineteenth century, as an out-growth of Napoleon Bonaparte's occupation of Egypt of 1798 to 1801. The French primacy in archaeological affairs in Egypt was reinforced in 1904 when England and France banded together against Germany and partitioned North Africa into two spheres of interest. The French took Morocco; the British assumed control of Egypt. But in Egypt, as far as archaeology was concerned, France retained the right to rule the roost. As the first clause of the agreement of 1904 states: "It is agreed that the post of Director General of Antiquities in Egypt shall continue, as in the past, to be entrusted to a French savant."

At that time the license or concession to excavate was a simple, rather routine piece of "boiler-plate." It had a preamble and a list of thirteen conditions.

Authorization to Excavate
I, the undersigned, Director-General of the Antiquities Service, acting in virtue of the powers delegated to me, hereby authorize _____, residing at _____ to carry out scientific excavation in _____, on lands belonging to the State, free, unbuilt upon, uncultivated, not included within the Military Zone, nor comprising any cemeteries, quarries, etc., and in general, not devoted to any public use, and this on the following conditions . . .

Those conditions of any significance at all involved, primarily, having the work carried out at the expense, risk and peril of the concessionaire. The undertakings had to be conducted under the control and supervision of the Antiquities Service—a condition that was only casually enforced. If the digger found a tomb, he was required to give instant notice to Antiquities. But the discoverer did have the right to enter the tomb first, provided he was accompanied by an inspector of antiquities. Notes, drawings and data, when completed, could be delivered to Antiquities anytime within two years. Mummies, together with coffins and sarcophagi, were to remain the property of the State, but objects in tombs found not intact—that is, tombs which had already been "searched in ancient

24

times"—would be divided. The Antiquities Service would take all works of art of capital importance from the point of view of archaeology and history and would share the remainder with the permittee.

The critical issue, having to do with the division of the spoils, was handled in an exceedingly offhand manner. The unwritten rule, forged by precedent, was that the digger and the Antiquities Service should share the objects evenly. The admonition in the concession form to the effect that treasures from an intact royal or noble tomb would all revert to the State had never really been an issue. For no one in history had ever found a tomb that had not been substantially plundered by ancient robbers.

So in 1906 Lord Carnarvon obtained a concession and started his digging. Because of his noble status, apparently, the authorities did not even bother to insist that an archaeologist or qualified expert accompany him. And he really did flail away. Years later, in reminiscing about his first season as an archaeologist, he recalled, "We suddenly struck what seemed to be an untouched burial pit." This had given rise to much excitement, "which soon simmered down when the pit was found to be unfinished." There, for six weeks, enveloped in clouds of dust, Lord Carnarvon stuck to it day after day. Beyond finding a large mummified cat, nothing whatsoever rewarded his "strenuous and very dusty endeavours."

But the more dust clouds he sent up, the more Lord Carnarvon became convinced that he did need, after all, an expert to assist him. That expert was to be a curious individual named Howard Carter.

In 1907, Carter, like the other members of the cast of characters, was wholly unrecognized outside his field. His origins, unlike those of the others, were humble. He was born on May 9, 1873, in Kensington, Norfolk, a hamlet of no more than twenty-five hundred inhabitants. His father, Samuel John Carter, a draftsman and watercolorist whose specialty was painting portraits of the animals belonging to the landed aristocracy, was too poor to send the boy to school. So Carter was tutored at home and never obtained formal schooling of any kind, including either archaeology or Egyptology. Taught by his father, Carter became a watercolorist. He seemed fated to continue, like his parent, the unpromising career of a portrait painter of animals, village scenes and landscapes in a style of uncompromising rectitude and banality.

But in the summer of 1890 his life totally changed. Professor Percy E. Newberry, who was on the staff of the Egyptian Museum of Antiquities and a lecturer in Egyptology at the university in Cairo, happened to visit an old acquaintance, Lady Amherst of Hackney. Her husband was a devotee of ancient Egypt and had in his extensive rare-book collection a famous ancient papyrus that showed in line drawing the layout of a royal tomb in the Valley of the Kings. Newberry told his hostess of his recent work in Egypt recording by pencil tracing the hieroglyphs of a number of ancient monuments at Beni Hasan in Middle Egypt, and expressed his desire to find someone to help finish the drawings. Lady Amherst suggested Howard Carter, then seventeen, who lived in the neighboring village. His father had done occasional work for her ladyship, and she had been impressed with Carter's early efforts.

Professor Newberry interviewed the young man and hired him. Carter worked at the British Museum for three months; then, in the fall, he became the most junior member of the staff of the Egyptian Exploration Fund, a private organization linked to the museum that carried out excavations in the land of the Nile for "the further elucidation of the history and arts of Ancient Egypt, and to the illustration of the Old Testament narrative."

Carter eventually became an assistant to one of the greatest Egyptologists who ever lived, Sir William Flinders Petrie, a gaunt, leathery sage with an impressive white beard. Petrie can be justly credited with bringing system, sense and order to a field that up to that time was not known for its methodical character. From 1890 to 1898 Howard Carter worked under the tutelage of Newberry, Petrie and a Swiss Egyptologist,

Édouard Naville, patiently recording in watercolor the paintings, reliefs, and inscriptions from the walls of the imposing funerary temple at Deir al-Bahri, which had been constructed by order of ancient Egypt's most powerful Queen, Hatshepsut. It was she who, when she eventually became pharaoh, for twenty years guided the land of the Nile to one of the highest moments in its long history.

Howard Carter was the perfect man for the job. Quiet, retiring, awkward in the presence of anyone who seemed to have been blessed with greater privileges in life, he was a loner, and an utterly dedicated worker. The very fact that his watercolors gave no hint of inner spirit, or demonstrated any sort of creative spark, made them perfect for the task at hand. He made his eyes and his fingers totally subservient to the process of recording the precise shape and outline, and the exact colors, of his subject matter. A number of watercolors by Howard Carter are on exhibit in the Egyptian Department of the Metropolitan Museum. They display punctiliousness, verisimilitude and no life at all.

Carter, a short, stocky man of great physical strength, with ample dark hair and mustache and an egg-shaped expressionless face with brooding dark eyes, kept fairly well to himself during his apprenticeship in Egypt. He was a humorless, rather dour individual of driving energy. Despite his lack of formal schooling, Carter learned archaeology and Egyptology quickly, teaching himself the basics of hieroglyphics with the guidance of Petrie and Newberry. His mind was keen and his powers of deductive reasoning were extraordinarily acute. His dedication and enthusiasm eventually won him the respect of his superiors, and in 1899, at the age of twenty-five—only nine years after his arrival in Egypt—he was appointed by Sir Gaston Maspero to the post of inspector of monuments in Upper Egypt and Nubia, with headquarters in Luxor, the site of ancient Thebes. While he was inspector, he worked a number of seasons for Theodore M. Davis, an American millionaire who had amassed his fortune from law and finance and who had become obsessed with Egyptian archaeology. Although

Davis was thoroughly pleased with Howard Carter's work, they never really became friends. Perhaps it was because at times Carter tended to become aggressive, or in turn highly defensive, at even an implied criticism, or perhaps because of his obstinacy, his impetuousness or his explosive temper, which occasionally suggested the possibility of physical violence.

Carter's career in Egypt in the Antiquities Service flourished until 1903, when it suddenly ended forever. Sir Flinders Petrie, accompanied by his wife and three young women apprentices, had been recording hieroglyphs in a tomb at Saqqara, one of the most important sites of ancient Egypt's Old Kingdom. According to Petrie, several drunken Frenchmen entered their camp one evening, demanded a special guided tour of one of the mastabas, or table-shaped tombs, and then attempted a forced entry into the women's quarters. Petrie sent word to Inspector Howard Carter, who arrived as soon as he could with a squad of Egyptian guardians attached to the Antiquities Service. There was a struggle in which one of the Frenchmen was knocked to the ground by an Antiquities guard. Later the French complained bitterly to Sir Gaston Maspero and lodged a formal complaint against the guard and Carter. The French consul general demanded a formal apology, but Carter refused on the grounds that he was doing his duty and that it was the group of Frenchmen that ought to do the apologizing. Maspero tried to persuade him that the issue was an insignificant one blown up into a political squall by several stupid Frenchmen who were momentarily injured by their own pride and sense of guilt. He urged him to make a routine apology for the sake of Anglo-Gallic amity, and advised him that the incident would be utterly forgotten. But Carter, a man completely insensitive to the exigencies of petty politics and apparently blind to the subtle demands of human and public relations, staunchly refused. Maspero, the genial Frenchman, who was director general of the Service of Antiquities and had great affection for the headstrong Howard Carter, continually begged his stubborn subordinate to change his mind. Carter would have none of it. Sorrowfully, Maspero, who fully recognized who controlled the power structure in Egyptian archaeology, dismissed him from the service.

For the next four years Carter barely survived. He conducted guided tours, sold his watercolors to tourists, and apparently also dealt occasionally in antiquities—*antikas*, as they were called by the natives. When he was introduced to Lord Carnarvon by a solicitous Sir Gaston Maspero and was asked to become his archaeological expert, he readily accepted. It was an excellent arrangement for both, for Howard Carter was a professional, and eminently and cheaply available.

CHAPTER TWO

The Stage:
The Valley of the Kings

THE STAGE FOR THE extraordinary and troubled drama that would involve Tutankhamun, Lord Carnarvon and Howard Carter is an awesome one—the Valley of the Tombs of the Kings.

The very name is full of romance. But one cannot imagine a more remote, unpleasant, hot, dried-out, lonely place anywhere in the world. In this valley head, far from every sound of life, once lay buried, for their sleep of a million years times infinity, thirty of the greatest kings ancient Egypt had known.

In ancient days, as now, one traveled to the valley from Thebes, today the modern city of Luxor, situated about four hundred miles south of Cairo on the east bank of the great Nile. Across the river, stretching for three or more miles to the west, was the lush green plain made incredibly fertile by the seasonal flooding of the Nile. At a certain point fields, palms and vegetation would abruptly cease, becoming sand, rock, boulders and desolation. The point of transition from the life and humanity of the arable land to the deathly precincts of the desert has not varied more than a few yards in countless thousands of years. From that point the wasteland rises up, at first gradually and then in a dynamic crescendo, to a great cliff at a place known as Deir al-Bahri. Beyond that, stretching out in what to the ancient Egyptians must have seemed infinite space, lay the great deserts.

At the very base of the towering cliffs which face the open plain and the rising sun is the Valley of the Kings, known in Arabic as the Wady Biban al-Maluk. It was there, in one ancient dried-out valley tributary, that one of the greatest rulers of one of the highest moments of ancient Egyptian history unexpectedly broke with a precedent forged over thousands of years and constructed an innovative tomb. This King was Thutmose I, a great military pharaoh of the Eighteenth Dynasty, in which Tutankhamun also reigned. Thutmose I was one of the most vigorous, dynamic and inventive pharaohs of all of Egyptian history. As such he had fascinated Howard Carter. The place where he chose to ensure his afterlife, called by the ancients the "Place of Truth," was to Howard Carter a magical and, at times, frightening locality. It was dominated by a peak called the Horn, the highest in the Theban hills, standing sentinel like a natural pyramid above the sleeping Thutmose and his successors.

Carter would explain Thutmose's achievement to those whom he conducted on guided tours of the valley, during the lean years after he had been cashiered from the Antiquities Service and the beginning of his association with Lord Carnarvon. To understand how profound a change from tradition was Thutmose's tomb, one had to know something about the funerary beliefs of the ancient Egyptians and the nature of tomb design before the innovative Pharaoh.

To the ancient Egyptian it was vital that his body should be fully equipped for every need in the afterlife and should rest inviolate in the place constructed for it. The pharaohs "were luxurious and display-loving Oriental monarchs," Carter would say, and the equipment for their needs after death naturally involved a lavish use of gold and other treasure. The earliest kings of Egypt, who ruled a thousand years before

Thutmose I, sought to ensure their ultimate security by erecting pyramids over their bodies, veritable mountains of stone. But, far from guaranteeing protection, the very massiveness and magnificence of the pyramid attracted the tomb robbers. Always within a few generations at most, the mummy was disturbed and the treasure stolen.

Everything that ingenuity could suggest or wealth could buy was tried in the pyramids. The entrance was plugged with granite monoliths weighing tons. False passages were constructed. Secret doors were contrived. It was all in vain. For in that timeless struggle between those who sought to conceal their incalculable treasures for eternity and those who sought them for themselves, those who yearned for secrecy were inevitably vanquished.

After the age of the pyramid had passed, the kings of Egypt built more modest tomb structures above the ground, adjacent to temples dedicated to them where priests would carry out various rituals pertaining to their afterlife. But the plundering continued, and by the beginning of the Eighteenth Dynasty there was hardly a tomb in the whole of Egypt that had not been rifled—which, as Carter explained to the tourists, was "a somewhat unsettling and grisly thought to Thutmose I, who was choosing the site for his last resting place." In a drastic break with tradition, Thutmose I finally decided to construct a totally hidden burial chamber. He selected one of the valleys beneath the great cliff that loomed up across the Nile from his capital city, Thebes. It was, Carter would say, the perfect place. Eons before, when time was but a spirit, before man had lived in Egypt, powerful waters had cut into the Eocene limestone and flint bedrock and had formed the valley. So violent were the primeval torrents that wide furrows seem to have been cut through the region, as if by the talons of some grotesque prehistoric creature. These floods caused innumerable faults and fissures, eminently suited for the construction of a hidden tomb. There, tucked away in a corner at the extreme western end of the valley, half concealed by a projecting bastion of rock, Thutmose I placed his secret burial sanctuary.

It was difficult to find, easy to overlook and infrequently visited by tourists. "But," Carter would say, "it is a very special place, since it is the very first tomb ever constructed in the valley." Thutmose I had no doubt hesitated long before he made his decision. His pride must surely have suffered, for "love of ostentation was ingrained in every Egyptian monarch, and in his tomb more than anywhere else he was accustomed to show it." Thutmose's decision must also have caused a certain inconvenience to the priests charged with the enactment of funerary rituals. But Thutmose had traded pride and ritual for secrecy as the only chance of escaping the fate of his predecessors.

Surprisingly enough, even the architect involved in Thutmose I's startling innovation was known. His name was Ineni, and on the walls of his own funerary chapel he had carved the story of his accomplishments in life. Foremost among them had been the tomb for his King. "I, Ineni, superintended the excavation of the cliff tomb of his Majesty, Thutmose I, alone, no one seeing, no one hearing." Ineni omitted to relate what had happened to the workmen he employed to cut out of the flint the tons of living rock. In some manner they were prevented from ever speaking about the hidden chambers. There is no doubt that secrecy was the primary reason for Thutmose's and Ineni's remarkable invention. His royal tomb and all those which followed were constructed in out-of-the-way places. The prodigious amount of debris from each one was carefully removed and deposited a long distance away. Neither the sanctuary of Thutmose I nor any other had any external mark or monument to show its existence.

Thutmose I's brilliant idea set the pattern for centuries. All the succeeding monarchs of the great Eighteenth Dynasty followed his lead, and during the first part of the New Empire very few robberies were known. But the secret did not last forever. Later on, in the Nineteenth and Twentieth Dynasties, a period of history when order and discipline broke down under a series of feeble rulers, tomb plundering became a plague. In time, all the great monarchs had been defiled.

Carter had fallen in love with the solitary character of the

33

valley, its history and what he called a "religious feeling emanating from it so profoundly that it appears almost imbued
with a life of its own." He had always been impressed with
the "savage rocks which rise rugged and barren" on both of
its sides, "rounding off to bare summits gilded by the rising
and setting sun." He often liked to ride up, alone, on the back
of a donkey, and as he passed over the endless stones covering
the valley bed he would be moved by the solemn, almost
gloomy character of the silent desert chasms. All was dead and
mute. The footsteps of his beast would be interrupted by an
occasional and frightening howl of a jackal or the sudden somber boom of a desert "eagle" owl. It was sometimes almost
terrifying to pass through the winding, trackless desert's rocky
defiles to the tombs themselves, called in ancient times the
"Great Seats" of eternal silence. At those moments nature
seemed to be standing before him "naked in all her majesty."
All was "stationary, fixed, immutable, as for eternal duration."
In such moments, Carter felt himself "participating in the full
tranquillity of nature."

Carter would invariably take the touring group first to the
tomb of Thutmose and point out how beautifully Ineni had
camouflaged it among the rugged cliffs. Its entrance was visible only when the visitors were on the very brink of the top
step sunk into the flint bedrock. From the humble, tentative
scheme of this first burial chamber the design gradually became more grandiose during the New Empire, culminating in
breathtaking man-made caves of startling complexity in the
Nineteenth and Twentieth Dynasties. The entrances to the
later tombs were enormous. Their architecture was rectilinear,
sharp. The brilliant surfaces and fresh vivid colors of their wall
paintings provided a magnificent contrast to the rugged sun-
burned rock of the valley walls. These particular tombs appeared to Carter almost like friendly human presences in the
lifeless terrain.

As Howard Carter guided visitors through the largest of the
New Empire tombs, those of Seti I or Ramesses II, he spoke
poetically of their shapes, their "emanations," the serene spir-

its that seemed to exist within them. One would enter the tiny entrance and penetrate into long, straight corridors, past a profusion of bays sculpted from the limestone, past a succession of rooms that coursed deeper and deeper into the cliffs. The walls were beautifully carved and painted with innumerable scenes of the Underworld, known as Amenti to the ancient Egyptians. The king was portrayed countless times, standing before his gods, invoking prayers for his future, justifying the conduct of his earthly life. The peace that would come to the justified was depicted on one side, the punishment for the wicked on the other.

Carter was particularly fond of one of the paintings in the tomb of Seti I. There the goddess of heaven, Mother Nût, was depicted extended lengthwise on the ceiling, her great attenuated body painted blue, her back supporting like a table the imperishable stars, which themselves issued forth from her womb. The symbols of every hour of the day and night were painted and carved on the walls. According to the ancient Egyptians, each one exerted enormous influence over man. All scenes—as rich and complex as the illustrations in the stained glass of a Gothic cathedral—would be elucidated by hieroglyphic texts carved from the surface of the rock. "These are not, of course," Carter would say disdainfully, "as some fools have actually *suggested* to me, the creations of crazed brains, but symbols with a dignified and recondite meaning, for which only the ancient colleges of priests could furnish the true key." He would point to some of the virtually thousands of hieroglyphic texts covering the walls and translate some of them: a psalm to Ra, the Sun God; a book of hours; a book explaining the various portals to the Underworld.

The number and complexity of the writings were bewildering. As the Eighteenth Dynasty progressed, the underground tombs had become larger and larger, carved with more and more surfaces for the specific purpose of carrying the profusion of incantations. At some time in the Eighteenth Dynasty, a deep pessimism about the future had set in. The dead king was suddenly thought to be beset with innumerable and terrifying dangers in the next world. Magical formulas were evolved to protect him. Guidebooks to conduct the ruler through the hereafter proliferated. An elaborate network of chambers, passages and cells was constructed to carry the literature and contain the profusion of objects required to protect the king against his foes in the Underworld.

The farther the visitors progressed into the chain of subterranean caverns, the deeper they became involved in endless but marvelous depictions of gods, genii and thousands upon thousands of painted and engraved cobras in every possible attitude and form—human-headed, human-legged, crowned, uncrowned, lying down, rising up, curled back, even upside down. This was the royal serpent.

The visitors would at last enter into a great vaulted chamber of pillars, the "Golden Hall," more spacious and splendid than all the rest. A stone sarcophagus usually dominated the space, enclosing the royal mummy conceived as the descendant of Ra, the Sun, and the "Eternal Horizon." This chamber was the "Holy of Holies," the eternal dwelling of a pharaoh. In every tomb discovered in modern times this room was, but for the stone coffin, barren, plundered. All the finery, the treasures, had been stripped, hacked away as if a band of madmen had scratched and clawed their way, taking everything, leaving only wisps of linen mummy wrappings and broken shards of stone and pottery.

An intact Holy of Holies must have been magnificent. And, although no one in the history of archaeology had ever discovered an intact or even only partially plundered royal burial chamber, it was possible to imagine one in its full glory. This could be done from surviving tomb paintings, descriptive texts and several ancient papyri, scrolls made of paper fashioned from papyrus plants, which showed actual ground plans of royal tombs and described the contents of their chambers. Some of the dozens of rooms and storage areas of the royal tomb would have been outfitted with an array of objects: mummified food—dressed duck, haunches of mutton; jugs for beer and wine. For the king's mummy had to have sustenance for eternity. There would have been hundreds of caskets packed with clothes of all sorts, and thousands of containers for precious oils, unguents and perfumes. There might have been a full armory of weapons—bows, arrows, harpoons, boomerangs, spears. And throughout would be countless little statues in wood, faience and gold, depicting the king in all his many forms, to serve as substitutes for him if anything went awry with his mummy. There would have been regiments of little wooden figures of servants—in Egyptian, *shawabtis*, "answerers"—to respond to his every request and fulfill his every need. And the eye would surely have been beguiled by gold— mountains, rivers, cascades of gold in leaf, plate, bulk.

The Amherst Papyrus, an important source, is quite explicit about the nature of the Holy of Holies. In the ancient drawing, five rectangles are to be seen around the sarcophagus. These signified, most probably, a series of gilded wooden shrines. Each one would have been carved or painted with thousands of texts warding off evils and describing the safe way through the Underworld.

On virtually every door, box, casket, and shrine a curious and powerful device would appear: the seal of the royal City of the Dead. A number of examples had previously been found. It is remarkable and beautiful in itself. It depicts the jackal Anubis, who is the god of embalming and the god of the valley itself, where even today living jackals abound. On the seal the jackal lies prone, stately, with his elegant long neck and pointed nose held at a majestic angle. Below him nine prisoners or slaves kneel, cruelly bound by their elbows, with their arms held so tightly back that it was a form of execution as well as bondage. The seal is unique to the valley and to the Eighteenth, Nineteenth and Twentieth Dynasties. No one knows exactly what it signified. But since Egyptians had always feared foreign powers, one can presume that the prisoners were intended to signify alien forces of any kind dominated, crushed, vanquished by the god of the eternal afterlife. If one were to find this seal on the outer doorway of a tomb, one could be sure that one might be about to experience the most awe-inspiring sight of all time—an intact royal tomb.

Carter would inform his listeners that one had a fairly good idea of what would be inside a royal sarcophagus. This information, too, had been culled from a variety of ancient writings. Most important among them was a poetic fragment from the Middle Kingdom referring to "the night devoted to oils and bandages when thou art reunited with the earth in the mummy case of gold with a head of pure lapis lazuli." And, from the Nineteenth Dynasty, there was a startlingly fresh and human account of eight thieves which describes the royal mummy and its trappings. The names of some of these vandals are even known: the stonecutter Hapi, the artisan Iramne, the peasant Amenemkab, the water-carrier Kemmese and the Negro slave Ehenefer. They were apprehended during the reign of Ramesses IX and brought up on the charge of having desecrated a royal tomb. An almost full account of their trial has been preserved. It began, according to custom, by "beating the prisoners with a double rod, smiting their feet and their hands," to assist their memories. They made full confession. The thieves had tunneled through the rock to the burial chamber and had found a king and a queen in their sarcophagi. The papyrus recounts that the thieves penetrated them all, opened their coffins and the coverings in which they lay, to discover the mummy of the "August King." Amulets and ornaments of gold adorned its neck. The head of the King was covered with a mask of solid gold. The mummy was overlaid with coverings of gold and silver, inlaid with every costly stone and jewel. The thieves told how they stripped off the gold and all of the precious amulets and ornaments. After they had stripped the King they did the same to the Queen. And they told of setting fire to the linen wrappings. Not content with that, the thieves had stolen the furniture and all else they found there—vases of gold, silver and bronze. Finally they had left and had divided everything into eight parts.

What eventually happened to them is not known. But they were declared guilty and were removed to the house of detention until the Pharaoh Ramesses IX himself could determine their punishment, which, one can assume, was appropriately severe.

In the Nineteenth and Twentieth Dynasties this macabre and lugubrious testimony was repeated with increasing frequency. The tombs of the greatest kings of all—Seti I, Amenhotep III and Ramesses the Great—are mentioned in court records as having been defiled. In the Twentieth Dynasty all attempts to guard the sepulchers were abandoned. The guardians resorted to a curious expedient. They would pick up the mummies of the kings and drag them from sepulcher to sepulcher in a desperate effort to stay one step ahead of the robbers. Ramesses III was disturbed and reburied at least three times—and even Ramesses the Great was disinterred and buried at least once.

With the passing of the Twentieth Dynasty the history of the valley came to an end. Five hundred years had passed since Thutmose I and his architect Ineni had built his innovative little tomb. "Surely, in the whole world's history," Carter would say, "there is no small plot of ground that had half a millennium of more romantic story to tell."

From that time onward the valley was deserted, spirit-haunted to the Egyptian. Its cavernous galleries, plundered, remained empty. The entrances to many of them, left open, became the home of living jackals, desert owls or colonies of bats. In the early Christian period, when thousands forsook the world and adopted the contemplative life, such a perfect spot as the valley did not pass unnoticed. In the second and fourth centuries A.D. a large colony of anchorites and hermits came into full possession. The open tombs were used as monk's cells; in one case a chapel was constructed within the chambers.

And, as Carter would point out in concluding his intriguing tour, this final glimpse of the valley in ancient times presented a fascinating incongruity. For great luxury and kingly pride, rank poverty had been substituted. The "precious habitation of the Pharaoh has narrowed to a hermit's cell."

CHAPTER THREE

Forty Kings and the Thieves from Kurna

OVER THE YEARS, working with Sir Flinders Petrie and for the Service of Antiquities, Howard Carter had compiled extensive notes on the ancient history and records of the valley, and records of who had gone there in modern times. He kept careful track of every archaeological discovery, no matter how insignificant, and accounted for every king's tomb or mummy that had been exposed. He began to believe, early in his career, that the valley had not given up all its secrets. He was convinced that earlier investigators had failed to examine it properly, owing to their unsystematic techniques. And Howard Carter revered system.

He had identified the earliest travelers and treasure seekers, where they had gone in the valley, what they had observed, and voraciously consumed their books and journals. He admired, for its extraordinary accuracy, the account of Richard Pococke, an English traveler who published a story of a visit to the valley in his *A Description of the East* in 1743. Pococke wrote of entering such tombs as were accessible in those days and mentioned fourteen in all. He started to make plans of a number of them, but was stopped from further researches because of the dangerous hordes of bandits which had taken over from the anchorites and the hermits. By the middle of the eighteenth century the valley had become an extremely dangerous place in which to linger. The bandits who dwelt in the village of Kurna, situated among the foothills leading to the valley, terrorized the entire countryside. No scientist interested in ancient Egypt could explore the valley in safety for long; as Carter was fond of pointing out, not even the magic of Napoleon's name was a deterrent to the greedy and arrogant bandits of the Theban hills. The members of his scientific commission who visited Thebes in the last days of the century were molested and even fired upon. But Napoleon's specialists, even under attack, had been able to make a complete survey of all the tombs then open, and their lists had been dissected by Howard Carter.

During his researches on the early visitors to the area, Carter, this orderly, precise, inwardly directed, retiring, yet tempestuous individual, became fascinated with one of the most flamboyant, undisciplined, picaresque and quarrelsome self-made adventurers in the history of Egyptian archaeology—or pure treasure hunting, for that is what it really was at the time. This man was Giovanni Belzoni, whom Carter would describe as "the most remarkable man in the whole history of Egyptology." In his first volume on the tomb of Tutankhamun, Carter devoted more pages to him than to any other archaeologist, even his mentors Petrie and Newberry. Perhaps as a self-made man with humble origins he felt an invigorating kinship with Belzoni. He wrote:

In the early years of the century, a young Italian giant, Belzoni by name, was earning a precarious income in England by performing feats of strength at fairs and circuses. Born in Padua, of a respectable family of Roman extraction, he had been intended for the priesthood, but a roving disposition . . . had driven him to seek his fortune abroad. In the intervals of circus work Belzoni seems to have studied engineering, and in 1815 he thought he saw a chance of making his fortune by introducing into Egypt a hydraulic wheel which would, he claimed, do four times the work of the ordinary native appliance.

The wheel didn't work; although Belzoni exuberantly claimed it a superior success, Mohammed Ali, the great leader of Egypt, refused to have anything to do with it, and Belzoni was stranded in Egypt without anything to do. But not for long; for he turned to "archaeology."

Carter then touched on Belzoni's early excavations. The Italian "archaeologist" had managed an introduction to the British consul general in Egypt and contracted with him to bring the "colossal Memnion bust" (Ramesses II, now in the British Museum) from Luxor to Alexandria. Belzoni had remained for half a decade, excavating throughout Egypt, assembling hoards of antiquities for the British consular officials and for himself. He contended with other excavators, arguing and quarreling. His chief rival was the archaeologist Drovetti, who was allied with the French consul and who detested anyone working for the British. And here one can pick up, not for the first time and, for Howard Carter, certainly not the last, reference in his publications to the Anglo–Gallic rivalry. Then Carter added: "Those were the great days of collecting. Anything to which a fancy was taken, from a scarab to an obelisk, was just appropriated, and if there was a difference of opinion with a brother excavator one laid for him with a gun."

Giovanni Belzoni roamed Egypt, and his published diary—*Narrative of the Operations and Recent Discoveries . . . in Egypt and Nubia* (London, 1820)—was, to Howard Carter, one of the most intriguing pieces of literature on Egypt and early archaeology ever written. Carter used to regale his friends, over and over, with the incredible escapades of the restless, energetic Belzoni; how he dropped an obelisk weighing hundreds of tons into the Nile through a monumental miscalculation of engineering and then quickly "fished it out again." Carter was greatly amused by the unending series of squabbles Belzoni managed to have with practically everyone he met. In this regard, too, Howard Carter must have felt a secret kinship with the outrageous Italian.

Carter studied with avid interest Belzoni's account of his excavations in the Valley of the Kings. The Italian had been the first man in history to carry out large-scale investigations of the tombs. Apparently this "strong man," who thought nothing of cranking off a barrage of rifle fire at anyone who stood in the way of his work, thoroughly cowed even the vicious bandits of the Theban hills and Kurna. Carter compiled a special list of the tombs Belzoni had found and the finds within them.

Carter gave effusive credit to Belzoni for the highly systematic manner in which he had carried out his work, and admired the lavish scale of his undertakings—hundreds of fellahin laboring often seven days a week. Carter admitted, however, that there were incidents that were shocking in terms of modern excavating. Particularly bizarre was Belzoni's favorite technique of dealing with the sealed doors of tombs: he simply slammed right through with battering rams. Yet, when examined in its entirety, Belzoni's accomplishments were to Carter extraordinarily good.

Carter was particularly intrigued by the fact that Belzoni, like all others who followed him in succeeding years in the valley, was convinced that he had totally investigated the area.

It is my firm opinion [Belzoni wrote in his *Narrative*] that in the Valley of Beban el Malook there are no more [tombs] than are now known, in consequence of my late discoveries; for, previously to my quitting that place, I exerted all my humble abilities in endeavouring to find another tomb, but could not succeed, and what is still a greater proof, independent of my own research, after I quitted the place, Mr. Salt, the British Consul, resided there for four months and laboured in like manner in vain to find another.

For twenty years after Belzoni had departed the valley in 1819, it was plumbed by literally dozens of real scientists, would-be scientists and treasure seekers. Carter absorbed every single one of the accounts. Every time someone had stated that the valley was finished, Carter made a note of it. In 1844, one of the greatest archaeologists of all time, the German

Karl Richard Lepsius, did extensive work, and since all others believed that the meticulous scholar had finally unearthed the last bits and pieces, no other work of any serious nature was carried on.

Then in 1875 the most curious discoveries of all took place— not in the valley, but just on its edge in the cliffs at Deir al-Bahri. There a family of professional tomb robbers from the village of Kurna by the name of Abd-al-Rasul discovered a cleft filled with treasure. The village of Kurna may have the distinction of possessing the longest-lasting tradition of high thievery of any human habitation in world history. The citizenry of that place had become adept thieves as early as the thirteenth century B.C. and had carried on highly successful thefts right down to 1875 and beyond—more than three thousand years of the pilfering trade! A member of the Abd-al-Rasul clan had found a rock-cut chamber in the cliffs containing the mummies of no fewer than forty kings of the Eighteenth through the Twenty-first Dynasties who had been gathered up throughout the valley and put away in one common chamber in a last frantic attempt to foil the thieves of antiquity.

The leader of the Abd-al-Rasul family, seeing that the treasure was unprecedented, swore all members to secrecy. He drew upon the breathtaking jewelry, gold amulets and ornaments found within the wrappings of the royal mummies like the contents of a savings bank—only when the clan was in pressing need of cash. Eventually greed got the best of him. And soon the authorities began to see exceedingly rich and diverse royal discoveries coming on the *antika* market. Sooner or later these objects were traced to the Kurna vicinity and thereupon by a cool trail to the Abd-al-Rasul family.

It was virtually impossible to find factual evidence or proof of any discovery. The eldest member of the clan was apprehended and examined by the governor of the province of Kena, a certain Daoud Pasha. The patriarch fulsomely denied any knowledge of ancient treasure. All the citizens of Kurna flocked to the defense of the Abd-al-Rasul family, its chieftain and the community as a whole, proclaiming self-righteously the integrity and the honesty of everyone. In time the leader of the Abd-al-Rasul family was released for lack of hard evidence, but his questioning by the unrelenting Daoud Pasha appears to have unsettled him.

Daoud had a unique system of examination; he simply riveted the suspect with a pair of the coldest and most malevolent eyes in the interrogation business. One of Carter's workmen who had been a chief in his youth had once been dragged before him. Daoud was sitting up to his neck in a large jar filled with water. To see only a great bullet head cut off by the water, and a pair of cruel black eyes, was upsetting right at the start. Then, as Carter described the scene:

. . . from this unconventional seat of judgment the Mudir had looked at him—just looked at him—"and as his eyes went through me I felt my bones turning to water within me . . . Then very quietly he said to me: this is the first time you have appeared before me. You are dismissed, but—be very, very careful that you do not appear a second time, and I was so terrified that I changed my trade and never did."

Not too long after this episode the unique mudir gazed at one of the members of the Abd-al-Rasul family, who made a full confession and led the authorities to the ancient chamber in the cliff. There, bunched together in a rude, shallow grave, lay, tattered but intact just the same, the remains of the most powerful monarchs of ancient Egypt. They had lain in a sort of involuntary royal conclave ever since the priests had secretly and in desperation plucked them from their own half-plundered sanctuaries. On their wooden coffins (the rich trappings had long since been stolen) and on the linen wrappings on the mummies themselves, the priests had composed a precise travelogue of their wanderings. Some of the kings had been rewrapped several times in the course of their peregrinations, yet each king was specifically identified, a point of particular interest to Carter, who many years later retained the knowledge of just who was still missing in the royal succession.

The mummies were gathered up by the officials from Antiquities and the tomb was cleared in just two days—an unbelievable haste for archaeological material of such magnitude. The earthly remains were loaded onto a barge belonging to the museum and in a week arrived in Cairo. As the barge floated down the Nile the men in villages on the river banks fired guns as they would do for a modern funeral, while bands of women walked slowly, tearing their hair and giving forth that distinctive Arab high, ululating cry—a form of lamentation that had no doubt been passed down directly from ancient times.

This phenomenal discovery convinced all historians of ancient Egypt that this time the valley really had been exhausted. After all, fifty or more individuals had excavated it since the eighteenth century—some more seriously and vigorously than others, but it had been probed well nevertheless. What foreign archaeologists and savants had not found in modern times, no doubt the villagers at Kurna probably had.

But if the Valley of the Kings were a living creature, one of its characteristics would certainly be mischievousness. For when it became conventional wisdom that the valley was "finally empty," almost on schedule something else turned up. Less than twenty-five years after the episode of the forty kings and the thieves from Kurna, the director general of the Antiquities Service discovered and opened five royal tombs that had escaped earlier attention. They included those of Thutmose III, Amenhotep II and the inventive King who had first gone to the valley, Thutmose I, whose relatively tiny chamber was radiant with superb wall paintings in deep rust reds, startling blues and snapping greens, depicting a profusion of scenes from the various guides to the hereafter. In the tomb of Amenhotep II no fewer than thirteen royal mummies were found. "Their wealth," wrote Carter, "which in their power they had lavished on their funerals, had long since vanished, but at least they had been spared the last indignity. The tomb had been entered, it is true, . . . but it had escaped wholesale destruction. . . . and the mummies remained intact."

CHAPTER FOUR

First Clues of Tutankhamun

BY 1900, NO SERIOUS archaeologist except possibly Howard Carter believed that a concession for the Valley of the Kings would produce anything of special interest at all. And Carter was not in a position to do anything about it, since he was still in his apprentice years and, at any rate, had no money to bankroll the costly process. To conduct a dig of substance, requiring several hundred workers, the workers alone would cost upward of five thousand pounds sterling for just one season. Roughly translated, that amount would be several hundred thousand dollars at today's purchasing power.

The Antiquities Service had few funds for exploration. It restricted its activities to the general upkeep of existing monuments and encouraged foreigners to participate by promising they could take from Egypt half of what they discovered. At the turn of the century, the idea that the average Egyptian would ever become interested in excavations or in what was discovered, other than a mummy, had never seriously entered anyone's mind. So the work was carried out by foreign archaeological teams from museums or universities, or by individual

American or English millionaires. The work of these private entrepreneurs, however, was suspect. As one archaeologist (quoted by Arnold Brackman in *The Search for the Gold of Tutankhamen*) put it just before the beginning of the First World War:

For many years European and American millionaires, bored with life's mild adventures, have obtained excavating concessions in Egypt and have dallied with the relics of bygone ages in the hope of receiving some thrill to stimulate their sluggard imaginations. They call it "treasure-hunting," and their hope is to find a King lying in state with his jewelled crown upon his head. With this romantic desire for excitement one feels a kind of sympathy; but, nevertheless, it is a tendency which requires to be checked. The records of the past are not ours to play with: in the manner of the big game of Uganda, they have to be carefully preserved; and the tombs, like elephants, should only be disturbed by those provided with a strictly-worded license.

These words might well have been directed at the American millionaire Theodore Davis, who, although by no means irresponsible, was by his own admission far more interested in the discovery of works of art of rare beauty than in turning up common shards, fragments, bits and pieces of sculpture, or inscriptions that are often more valuable to the scientist than the most magnificent treasures, which may be unmarked or whose provenance may be unknown. And for Lord Carnarvon and Howard Carter, it turned out to be a stroke of luck that Davis nurtured the dream of treasure, not information. In 1902, Theodore Davis obtained the concession for the Valley of the Kings; he held it for twelve years, and he worked in a manner that Carter characterized as wholly unsystematic.

While Davis carried on his examination of the valley, Lord Carnarvon and Carter, starting in 1907, investigated a number of sites elsewhere—the area on the east side of the Nile around the ancient city of Thebes, including Karnak, Luxor and a few places on the west bank of the Nile. They worked for four years; except for two or three important finds, the work, in their words, was "barren." In a joint publication entitled *Five Years' Explorations at Thebes*, appearing in 1912, Lord Carnarvon described their thwarted hopes and despair:

Open and half-filled mummy pits, heaps of rubbish, great mounds of rock debris with, here and there, fragments of coffins and shreds of linen mummy wrappings protruding from the sand. . . . The necropolis itself extends for some five miles along the desert edge and evidence of the explorers and robbers present themselves at every turn.

Despite Carter's misgivings, Theodore Davis had one success after another. His discoveries included the tombs of Thutmose IV, Queen Hatshepsut and King Siptah—all empty; a chamber with a number of pieces of furniture and two great coffins containing the well-preserved remains of the high noble Yuya and his wife Tuya; the tomb of General Haremhab (who would later be known as one of Tutankhamun's generals and would eventually become a king on his own); and a vault, not a real tomb, that Davis thought had been used for the transfer of the burial of Akhenaton from its original tomb at Tell al-Amarna. The cache supposedly contained the mummy and coffin of the heretic King, a minute part of his funerary equipment, and fragments of one of the burial shrines of his mother, Queen Teye.

Starting in 1906, Davis came across a number of items that pointed directly to the presence of King Tutankhamun. They are published in a volume co-authored by experts associated with his undertakings, Gaston Maspero, Georges Daressy and Lancelot Crane. Entitled *The Tombs of Harmhabi and Touatankhamanou* (the accepted spellings of the kings' names at that time), the volume describes some of Davis' discoveries: "While digging near the foot of a high hill in the Valley . . . my attention was attracted to a large rock tilted to one side, and for some mysterious reason, I felt interested [in] it." Under the rock he discovered a small, beautifully shaped cup in light-blue faience which carried the royal cartouche contain-

ing the hieroglyphs of Nebkheperura, the throne name of Tutankhamun. He made a note of it, gave it to the Egyptian Museum and forgot about it.

The first week of the following season of 1907–1908, Davis
and his assistants came across the unmistakable signs of a
tomb. "At the depth of twenty-five feet we found a room filled
almost to the top with dried mud, showing that water had
entered it." Then they found what Davis described as "a broken box containing several pieces of gold leaf stamped with
the names of Touatankhamanon and his wife Ankhousana-
manon," and an alabaster statue of an unidentified man a little
less than two feet in height. The gold foil, when partially
pieced together, showed Tutankhamun hunting in his chariot;
on another fragment, the King was depicted slaughtering a
bound prisoner while his Queen, Ankhesenamun, eagerly
urged him on. Hieroglyphs adjacent to her proclaim: "All protection of life is behind him, like the sun."

A few days later, Davis came across a crude pit on a hill just
above the tomb of Seti II and about one hundred thirty yards
from the entrance to the tomb of Ramesses VI. The pit measured about four by four by seven feet. There were no mark-
ings of any sort on it, and the contents were, to Davis at least,
completely disappointing. They included about forty crude
pottery jars filled with linen, a number of clay cups, fragments
of the bones of animals and birds, wreaths fashioned from
leaves and flowers, a couple of small hand brooms, "some bags
containing a powdered substance," and, in one of the jars, the
only object of note to Davis—a miniature funerary mask
painted bright yellow. That these unprepossessing leavings
had something to do with Tutankhamun Davis had no doubt.
He had found that "the cover of one of these jars had been
broken and wrapped around it was a cloth on which was inscribed the name of Touatankhamanon." But he misread their
importance. The leavings were of such modest character that
neither Davis nor anyone else in 1908 gave them much
thought.

At this moment, into the first act of the drama of the discovery of the tomb of Tutankhamun enters a most delightful,

whimsical, modest and confident individual, who would have, next to Howard Carter himself, the most extraordinary impact upon archaeological events in Egypt for nearly twenty years. His name was Herbert E. Winlock, and he was then an associate curator of Egyptology at the Metropolitan Museum of Art and a member of one of its Egyptian expeditions near Luxor. Short in stature, slightly roly-poly in physique, with short legs and splayed-out feet, Winlock gave the impression of a balding, mature Kewpie doll. His body always seemed to move in abrupt, agitated bursts. Extraordinarily articulate, and a brilliant archaeologist, Winlock was highly respected for his scientific ability and adored for his sunny disposition, sparkling wit and high sense of humor. His wit, like his character, was almost always benevolent, even when he was going after a stuffy and jealous colleague. At one point, writing about the Harvard Egyptologist George Reisner and speaking of his total disinterest in bothering to come from Giza, where he was working fruitlessly, to Luxor to see the tomb of Tutankhamun, Winlock said that the magnificent discovery was considered not worthwhile "by him—the finder of those Ethiopian heroes, Asphalta and Concreta!"

It is entirely possible that Herbert Winlock, who became the director of the Metropolitan in 1932, was the finest writer who has ever been involved in Egyptology. His 1920 description (in a museum publication) of the discovery of a hoard of statuettes and models of boats, farms, wineries and shops belonging to a character named Meketra stands as some of the finest prose ever composed on archaeology and the magical significance of the passage of time.

The beam of light shot in to a little world of four thousand years ago, and I was gazing down into the midst of brightly painted little men going this way and that. A tall, slender girl gazed across at me perfectly composed; a gang of little men with sticks in their upraised hands drove spotted oxen; rowers tugged at their oars on a fleet of boats, while one ship seemed floundering right in front of me with its bow balanced precariously in the air. And all of this busy going and coming was in uncanny silence, as though the distance back over the forty centuries I looked across was too great for even an echo to reach my ears. . . .

Four thousand years is an eternity. Just saying it over and over again gives no conception of the ages that have gone by since that funeral [Meketra's]. Stop and think of how far off William the Conqueror seems. That takes you only a quarter of the way back. Julius Caesar takes you halfway back. With Saul and David you are three-fourths of the way, but there remains another thousand years to bridge with your imagination. Yet in that dry, still, dark little chamber those boats and statues had stood indifferent to all that went on in the outer world, as ancient in the days of Caesar as Caesar is to us, but so little changed that even the fingerprints of the men who put them there were still fresh upon them. Not only fingerprints, but even flyspecks, cobwebs, and dead spiders remained from the time when these models were stored in some empty room in the noble's house waiting for his day of death and burial. I even suspect that some of his grandchildren had sneaked in and played with them while they were at that house in ancient Thebes. . . .

Winlock—outgoing, serene, amusing—was the exact opposite of Howard Carter. True to the adage that opposites attract, they became the closest of friends, making innumerable visits to each other's sites. Indeed, over the years, Carter was to say that Winlock was his only true friend. How sad it was to be that, years later, Carter, in an act of typical insensitivity to another human being, betrayed even his "only" friend.

Winlock visited Theodore Davis' headquarters in 1909 and observed the contents of the crude pit stacked casually around the yard. Davis expressed his thorough disinterest in the pieces, and Winlock asked him whether he could have them for the Metropolitan Museum for "scientific reasons," thereby giving Davis a typically gentle twist of the knife. Davis willingly handed them over. At the time, the jars, the pieces of linen and the bags of a dried-out substance were really of no great immediate interest to Winlock either. His reason for wanting them was primarily a purely practical one—acquisitions.

The major share of the funding for the museum's digs in Egypt in those days came out of the income of a munificent and surprising bequest from Jacob Rogers, who once held controlling interest in a vast locomotive factory in Paterson, New Jersey. Rogers had developed the habit of dropping in at the Metropolitan every so often over the years to chat with the various directors of the museum about matters of no great import or significance. He didn't seem to have a great appreciation for art or archaeology, but liked the museum as a whole. His visits had been so casual and the discussions so general in nature that it came as one of the greatest and most pleasant surprises in the history of the Metropolitan to learn upon Rogers' death that he had made the museum his major beneficiary—to the tune of ten million dollars, the income from which was "*solely* for the purpose of adding to its collections." The Metropolitan had been unable to raise the full funds for excavations, so the trustees decided that Rogers' acquisition funds could legally be used, owing to the standard arrangement in Egypt that the excavators could retain half of what they found. The board decided that the division system was a far better means of forming a great collection than relying upon the inventories of art dealers, whose offerings were often obscure, at best, as to provenance. This decision enabled the Metropolitan to gather together a vast and unique collection of Egyptian antiquities, the prime significance of which is that the great majority of the works of art and the objects have an absolutely known place of origin.

Winlock had apparently experienced a lean season in 1909 and 1910, and thus wanted the Davis discoveries. They were shipped home. For eleven years Winlock paid them no attention at all.

By 1912, Theodore Davis had become frustrated and bored in the valley. He didn't do much work there, but he wouldn't leave and give up his concession. Howard Carter observed his sporadic comings and goings somewhat sourly. For by this time Carter, who often would say that had he not been an archaeologist he would have been a detective, had become

53

convinced that the tomb of one more pharaoh still lay in the Valley of the Tombs of the Kings, and that this pharaoh was Tutankhamun.

Yet when Theodore Davis published his "considered opinion" that the chamber in which he had found the cache of gold foil was probably the tomb of Tutankhamun, Carter found fault. He considered Davis' conclusion to be ludicrous. The pit was too small, too insignificant for a royal burial of the powerful Eighteenth Dynasty. Carter was thoroughly convinced that the material that seemed to belong to Tutankhamun had been deposited in the pit at some late date and that the chamber itself had no connection with a bona fide tomb.

Finally, even Davis proclaimed the valley exhausted and relinquished his rights, so Lord Carnarvon and Howard Carter received their "long-coveted" concession at last. It was granted in 1914, signed in 1915 by the acting director general, Georges Daressy, and approved by Sir Gaston Maspero himself. At the time the concession was signed, Maspero told the pair that he didn't consider that the number of finds they would unearth would repay the costs of their excavations.

CHAPTER FIVE

The First Years of Search

THE CONVENTIONAL VIEW of the discovery of Tutankhamun's tomb holds that Carter simply blundered upon it in a monumental act of serendipity. It was exactly the opposite. Precise, calculating, gifted, in this case, with absolute tunnel vision, Carter had been planning for four years to unearth whatever remained of Tutankhamun. From a number of clues and some fragments of circumstantial evidence he was convinced that the tomb still lay in the valley undiscovered.

Deliberately, pedantically, Carter put the pieces together. Tutankhamun existed, had married Queen Ankhesenamun, and had clearly been the successor to Akhenaton. This latter he deduced from a number of clues. The stele found by Legrain in the temple of Karnak mentioned that the kingdom had been in great disorder on his accession to the throne. That was certainly a description of the state of affairs under the heretic King. The same stele depicted, curiously enough, the symbols of the "heretic" sun manifestation Aton. Added to that, Sir Flinders Petrie and others had discovered over the years fragments with cartouches bearing the name Tutankha-*ton*. Clearly, Tutankhamun had once been a devotee of the Aton cult but had converted or had been converted back to the religion of Amun-Ra, the god most sacred to Thebes and to the Valley of the Kings. The stele of Karnak documented the fact that the court had moved back to Thebes from Akhenaton's city of Tell al-Amarna. Therefore, the valley, the necropolis of Thebes, must have been where he was buried.

The lists Carter had carefully made of discoveries and his identifications of all the mummies found in 1875 and 1898 proved to his satisfaction that neither the tomb nor the body of Tutankhamun had yet been found. No ancient court records of robberies mentioned his tomb; no ancient documents describing the movement of kings' mummies from place to place alluded to him. All of this meant to Carter that Tutankhamun had not vanished off the face of the earth. He had, instead, never been found.

The materials pertaining to Tutankhamun discovered by Davis, all in the valley, indicated further that Tutankhamun's tomb had to be there. Carter believed that the blue faience cup and the gold foil were obvious examples of thieves' booty. Their presence *could* mean that the tomb had been entered in ancient times by thieves, who had then, somehow, successfully hidden them again. The fact that the thieves had not returned to pick up their loot suggested they had been apprehended or killed. The lack of any reference in court records to such an episode might have been due to the fragmentary nature of the records, but could also be explained by the fact that the tomb had really not been seriously disturbed. The contents of the shallow pit found by Davis were obviously not from the tomb, but the linen fragment in one of the jugs with the name Tutankhamun was at least further evidence that the King was somewhere in the area.

Carter considered that the chamber, also found by Davis, which contained what was thought to be the mummy and the sarcophagus of Akhenaton, constituted an exceedingly important clue. Carter believed that Tutankhamun was either the son or the son-in-law of Akhenaton. A number of scarabs with the cartouche of Tutankhamun had been picked up from the floor. To Carter, this meant that Tutankhamun had moved his predecessor's mummy from Tell al-Amarna. Was it not logical that he would have put it in the valley somewhere near the place he had picked for himself?

Carter even had a theory which explained why Tutankhamun's might be the only tomb that had escaped the ravages of thieves. He believed that one of those rare downpours that occasionally swept down the valley fissures could have sealed the entrance even more firmly and effectively than the closing at the original ceremonies and could have obliterated all external traces.

Howard Carter set great store by that "mischievous" character of the valley itself: every time it had been deemed barren, something turned up. Furthermore, he recognized that most of the diggers who had gone there had carried out their investigations in an unsystematic way, frequently scurrying around in nothing more promising than the dumps of their predecessors. They had all worked at the bottom of the valley, and seldom above the known line of tombs that lay in the lower areas of its small tributaries. At any rate, whether Carter found Tutankhamun or not he felt that a "systematic and exhaustive" search of the inner valley presented them with a reasonable chance of discovering fascinating materials. He and Lord Carnarvon were in the process of completing their plan for an elaborate campaign in the season of October 1914 to April 1915 when the First World War broke out. For the time being, all had to be left in abeyance.

In the fall of 1917 their campaign resumed. Carter decided that the only satisfactory thing to do to be absolutely sure they were not simply going over land already examined by others would be to ignore all earlier excavations and to penetrate right down to bedrock—for the first time in the history of Egyptian archaeology. He wrote in his description of the dig in the first of three volumes that "the difficulty was to know where to begin, for mountains of rubbish encumbered the ground in all directions, and no sort of record had ever been kept as to which areas had been properly excavated and which had not." It was a curious statement, for notes on file at the Metropolitan Museum and recollections of at least one individual indicate strongly that Carter had made a careful study of where two earlier explorers had gone and had a fairly good idea where he would find territory in the Valley where other searchers had not made a systematic probe.

Carter was reluctant to let anyone other than his most intimate friends and colleagues know his archaeological techniques. Apparently Carter had dreams of looking for the legendary tomb of Alexander the Great, for he believed at one time that he had an inkling of where the sepulcher might be found in the modern city of Alexandria. Whether it was his desire to search for Alexander's tomb that caused him to keep his working methods to himself—even those relating to the Valley of the Kings—or a natural penchant for secrecy is not known. At any rate Carter was brilliant in his powers of deduction and in the way he assembled and sifted his clues. He tracked the tomb of Tutankhamun almost as if he were able to read directions in the random stones of the Valley, laid out in a language no one else could even recognize.

Whatever the case, Carter insisted to Lord Carnarvon that they concentrate, at least at the beginning, on digging right down to the bedrock, in the triangular plot of land defined by the tombs of Ramesses II, Merenptah and Ramesses VI. It was the area where, he had decided from earlier researches, the tomb of Tutankhamun might be situated.

In order to be absolutely certain that the work would be systematic, Carter devised a grid system based upon the devastating step-by-step artillery barrages of the war. He planned to follow each square on his grid without variation.

The triangle was not large, only about two and a half acres, but the work was prodigious. The earlier dumps were piled high. Hundreds of thousands of cubic meters of sand, rock chips and boulders would have to be moved. In those days there was no mechanical equipment. Young boys and men hired for nickels a day worked with picks, hoes and small baskets, filling them and emptying them thousands of times a day. Contemporary film footage of similar work shows a gang of boys scurrying around all over each other, like an ant castle gone berserk. The boys would be paid at the end of the day, on the basis of the number of small tokens given to them by the foreman for each basketful.

In the course of the first season, Carter cleared a considerable portion of the upper layers of the triangular plot and had descended to the foot of the entrance to the tomb of Ramesses VI, a pharaoh whose sepulcher had been cut into the valley fully two hundred years after what most specialists assumed the death date of Tutankhamun to be—around 1350 B.C. Ten or fifteen yards from the entrance to the Ramesside tomb, Carter suddenly came across the ancient foundations of a series of workmen's huts, constructed above a mass of limestone boulders. The presence of these boulders was normally a sure sign, in the valley, of the proximity of a tomb, yet he abruptly stopped and instructed his work force to go to the very opposite end of the triangle.

It is monumentally puzzling that he did. Carter knew that the ancient foundations on bedrock were excellent signs. Perhaps he thought that the huts belonged to the time of Ramesses VI. A few yards away, just above the opening of that empty tomb, were other similar remains. It is more likely that Carter did not continue because of his insistence on system and his conviction that a plan, once started, *had* to be carried out religiously. For the workers' huts were lying just on the edge and a little outside the lines drawn between the points of his triangle.

The only reason Carter himself ever gave for his curious disinterest in the huts was that they were so close to the tomb of Ramesses VI that to continue their investigation would have necessitated closing it to the tourists who were beginning to flood into the valley for the winter season. The tomb of Ramesses VI contains some of the most beautiful paintings of any in the valley and was highly popular. One would think that it would have been possible to examine the almost certain clues without disturbing public access to the royal tomb. But Carter loathed large groups of people—particularly tourists—coming anywhere near his workings and bombarding him with inane questions. So he left the huts and started on the

59

other end of the triangle, proceeding square by square on his grid. In the next two months all he found was dust, sand, rocks and a few *ostraca*—potsherds and flakes of limestone used for sketching and writing purposes. By the close of the first season he had discovered—nothing. Seven long months of the most incredible labor had ensued in vile circumstances of heat, dryness, dust, and occasional sudden winds that choked one's throat and nose and left, seemingly for weeks afterward, the bitter taste of dried-out clay.

The second season, commencing in October of 1918, was little better. His thought was to clear the whole of the remaining part of the triangle. Proceeding square by square on the grid, it took six months simply to clean the top debris before they could even begin to penetrate the virgin rock. Just as Lord Carnarvon arrived with his wife, whom he was escorting on her first visit, they knew they had reached bedrock in one small area where they discovered thirteen alabaster jars with the names of Ramesses II and Merenptah. This was the nearest thing to a discovery of any significance in almost two years. It was exciting, particularly to Lady Carnarvon, who had removed the spectacular objects from the parched soil with her own hands. Other than that—nothing.

The third and fourth and fifth seasons, from 1919 to 1922, revealed no trace of the tomb of Tutankhamun and offered no startlingly beautiful proceeds of that "night devoted to oils and bandages when thou art reunited with the earth." Only months of backbreaking labor with a large and expensive crew. Even if one has not been on an unsuccessful dig, one can understand the bitter disappointment of discovering dry hole after dry hole. Both body and mind become deeply exhausted. A horrifying frustration and then resentment take over.

At some point during the fifth fruitless season, Lord Carnarvon began to lose interest in their venture. By 1921, inflation had become a burden; the pound was beginning its long slide. At home in England the wages of workmen and servants, gamekeepers and gillies who were needed to keep Highclere and its thirty-six thousand acres in the condition Lord Carnarvon expected it to be were rising rapidly. How long could he afford his lavish life style at Highclere and fund a totally unproductive dig? He recalled the pessimistic words of Sir Gaston Maspero years before, when he had warned the team that they might not find enough to compensate them for their investigations. Thirteen alabaster jars were hardly worth twenty-five thousand pounds, a sum worth more than half a million dollars today. And Carnarvon could not have been immune to the observations of other Egyptologists, even though they were known for their jealousies, who pointed out that everyone knew the valley was now exhausted. The Carnarvon-Carter enterprise became something to smile about. Carter also began to lose hope in the fourth and fifth seasons; he did, for him, what was abnormal. He left his triangle and his grid and examined a number of areas beyond it.

Then, in 1921, came a discovery which elated Carter and pleased Lord Carnarvon sufficiently to keep him going, at least a little longer. The discovery did not occur in the valley, but far away—in New York City, in the Egyptian storeroom of the Metropolitan Museum of Art—and it was the work of Herbert Winlock.

He had finally got around to examining the profusion of jars, wreaths and other unpromising objects he had received from Theodore Davis twelve years before. And when he did, he saw things no one had seen before. The jugs, the cups and some clay items actually carried a number of seals of Tutankhamun *and* the seal of the royal necropolis. That in itself was the absolute and final clue to the fact that Tutankhamun had been buried in the valley. But Winlock deduced much more than that from the evidence. Eventually he was able to prove that some of the material pertained to the actual ceremony of the mummification of Tutankhamun. Others were implements used in the final, ritual funerary banquet held within the tomb just before it was sealed for the last time.

Winlock had deduced that the dried-out substance in several linen bags was natron, a material used in embalming. And by piecing together all the evidence he deduced not only the nature of the ritual banquet but its menu, the number of guests and some of the clothes they had worn. Eight individuals, wearing floral and leaf wreaths and linen headbands, one inscribed with the last known date of Tutankhamun—the sixth year of his reign—had partaken of five ducks, a couple of plovers, and a haunch of mutton washed down with beer and wine, and had reverently, carefully swept up after themselves with two small brooms. At the end of the ceremony the eight priests or necropolis officials—for it is not known exactly who they were—gathered up their dishes, cups and pottery jars, stuffed the latter with leftovers, and buried them all in a pit dug for that purpose. To have left those remnants in a tomb symbolizing the purest manifestations of the afterlife would have rendered it unclean.

In *The Tomb of Tut-ank-Amen,* Carter dealt inaccurately with Winlock's discovery. He was of the opinion that Herbert Winlock recognized the significance of the contents of the pit as soon as he glanced at them strewn about in the courtyard of Davis' headquarters. He described how Winlock gained possession of the material and had it sent to the Metropolitan, and implied that he had made a thorough examination in 1909 or 1910 and come across his important find. According to Winlock, however, in an article discussing the material published in 1941, the objects really did not impress him all that much when he first looked at them. It was only years later that he found out what they were. And then he told Carter.

CHAPTER SIX

Deep Doubts

THE EXCAVATORS' STATE of mind at the end of the fifth season, in April of 1922, was gloomy. Despite Winlock's brilliant find, they had dug in the valley with "extremely scanty results," and it became a hotly debated question whether they should bother further with the valley or search for a more profitable site. Were they really justified in going on with it? Carter's own feeling was that so long as a single minute area of ground lay untouched on the bedrock, the risk was fully worth taking. Carter admitted to Lord Carnarvon that a digger could find less in more time—at more expense—in the Valley of the Kings than in any other place in Egypt. But, he pointed out, if one were to make a lucky strike, one would be repaid "for years and years of dull and unprofitable work."

Carter had become convinced that the area underneath the combination of flint boulders and huts near the foot of the tomb of Ramesses VI had, finally, to be investigated. He had developed a kind of superstitious feeling that it was there, in that particular corner of the valley, that he might find his missing King. "Eventually," he said, "we decided to devote a final season to the Valley, and, by making an early start, to cut off access to the tomb of Ramesses VI, if that should prove necessary, at a time when it would cause least inconvenience to visitors."

In Carter's laconic description of the period between the end of the fifth season and the start of the sixth, an extraordinary amount of fascinating human drama is left out. It can be reconstructed from notes, letters and conversations of Herbert Winlock, and from parts of an interview given to the author Leonard Cottrell in the late 1950s by the archaeologist Sir Alan Gardiner, a close acquaintance of both Lord Carnarvon and Howard Carter.

At the end of the fifth barren season, Lord Carnarvon had made up his mind not to seek the annual renewal of the concession. He was defeated by the futile and expensive operation which had cost him a small fortune. His health was fading rapidly. More and more, his friends and family observed him falling into long periods of silence. He was only forty-seven years of age, but his body was beginning to fail; he was continually fatigued in spirit and soul, and constantly in pain. Lord Carnarvon's patronage of Egyptian archaeology was about to cease.

Carnarvon's disposition had also been soured by the new mood of the Service of Antiquities—which had threatened to change the rules on him.

At this moment in the drama it is important to introduce the fourth major character, who would have the most fundamental impact upon all the undertakings surrounding Tutankhamun. This was Pierre Lacau, who had, in 1917, succeeded Sir Gaston Maspero as director general of the Service of Antiquities.

Lacau, a French savant, was a highly intelligent man, an extremely capable archaeologist with an extraordinarily handsome face and flashing eyes, who prided himself on his administrative abilities. He could discourse volubly, brilliantly, on dozens of subjects, yet was deeply fond of being so precise that it was said "he kept lists of lists."

Gaston Maspero had personally chosen Lacau to follow him because he had taken it for granted that he would espouse his extremely liberal attitudes toward foreign archaeologists. But Maspero, an easygoing individual, had grossly misjudged his younger colleague.

Maspero had been staunch in his conviction that foreign explorers had to be vigorously encouraged to come to Egypt by the promise of a division of discoveries at least amounting to one half or more. They had to be fully protected from any petty regulations and entangling bureaucracy once they had arrived and obtained their concession. Lacau utterly disagreed with him. He was of the opinion that the strictest controls ought to be placed upon excavators, whom he described privately as having "no rights." Lacau had also stated publicly that he intended to make the casual language of the standard concession a great deal more precise. He wanted the Antiquities Service to have complete control over the supervision of any dig. A member of the Antiquities Service had to be present at all times.

But what was even more ominous to foreign interests and to Carnarvon, Lacau announced in 1921 that he planned to change the Antiquities Law regarding the division of discoveries. Instead of the automatic fifty percent partage, Lacau insisted that, in all discoveries, the head of the Antiquities Service could have the full and exclusive right to pick any or all objects of any discovery he wanted for Egypt. Only then would he offer the discoverers a residue.

Privately, Lacau told acquaintances that he deeply resented the wealthy foreigners who came to Egypt, dug where and when they wished, and then took with them pretty much what *they* wanted. He would say that the existing division had been honored more in breach than in practice, and that excavators frequently placed aside what they really wanted before they even presented to Antiquities the group of objects to divide. Lacau had vowed to tighten up the loose language in the standard concession form defining an "intact" royal tomb.

Howard Carter, a proponent of a policy of total laissez-faire toward the rights of an excavator working with private funds, was contemptuous of Lacau. He looked upon him as the epitome of French petty bureaucracy and considered him an undistinguished archaeologist and scholar, a man of monumental incompetence and small mind. Carter's contempt for Pierre

Lacau would prove to be the foundation of one of the most significant mistakes he would make in his life.

Herbert Winlock didn't like Lacau personally, either, but he respected his sharp Jesuit lawyerlike mind and feared his unyielding idealistic character. Winlock advised Carter to proceed carefully with Lacau, but Carter never heeded his words. Winlock was a man who liked to cover his and his institution's flanks at all times, and he urged his superior at the Metropolitan, Albert Lythgoe, the curator of the Egyptian Department, to begin a campaign of political pressure to deal with "Lacau's importunate suggestions." Albert Lythgoe was an exceptional man, scholarly, serious. He was apparently one of those rare individuals who relish taking a behind-the-scenes position in every activity without any desire or intention to pull the strings of power. As an *éminence grise,* he was, one of his acquaintances was fond of pointing out, "pure white."

Albert Lythgoe immediately took Winlock's advice and prepared a briefing paper for Dr. J. Merton Howell, an elderly, somewhat sleepy, but amiable lawyer representing the United States. (In those days the title "ambassador" was not used, since Egypt was not technically a nation on its own but a nation under the protectorate of Great Britain.)

Facts Concerning the Proposed Change in the Law Relating to the Division of Antiquities Found in Excavation

At the end of the war, when M. Lacau first actively assumed office as Director-General of Antiquities, he immediately showed the intention of disregarding the existing law of a fair half and half division of results, and assumed the right to take practically *every good object we* had found. This was so entirely contrary to the spirit of the law and the treatment we had received for so many years, that we were obliged to insist on an equitable interpretation of our rights. This he met by repeated statements that he should use every means to effect a change in the law, and this intention has culminated in his present effort.

M. Lacau's main contentions have been as follows:

That, in his position as Director-General, he ought to have the right to take whatever he wished, without discussion.

We have always been the first to concede that objects of unique historical or archaeological importance *should* go to the Cairo Museum, but in such cases we had always previously been given other satisfactory objects as an offset. M. Lacau has not voluntarily agreed to this procedure. Such a position was never assumed by M. Maspero, as Director-General, in all the years we were working under his regime. He was a man of broad vision, and repeatedly assured us that, without in the least depriving Egypt of antiquities which should go into the Cairo collection, he wished to do everything possible to encourage the scientific and historical results which excavation produced and at the same time help to build up representative Egyptian collections in the largest European and American museums for the enlightenment and enjoyment of the people.

Unfortunately, M. Lacau is not a man of the same calibre and is not in the least interested in such a point of view.

M. Lacau has stated to us that we should be willing to carry out excavations solely for scientific ends and without *any* return in antiquities for the increase of our collections for educational purposes.

He has also said, when we pointed out to him that it would be utterly impossible to secure the large sum required for our work unless we had a fair return, that our position was untenable, and that we ought to be able to obtain support for our work regardless of returns, "just as the American Schools in Athens and Rome have obtained support." I happen to have an intimate knowledge of the pitiably inadequate support which those schools have ever been able to obtain, under the conditions in those countries which M. Lacau would wish to exist here. My father-in-law Professor R. B. Richardson was Director of the School at Athens for many years, and if the sum of $2,500. could be raised for the excavations in any year, that was the most that could be expected. Our annual Museum appropriation for our excavation here is $60,000., and in addition to that a further annual sum of more than $40,000. is now being spent on publications and other sides. Because of the laws in Greece under which no antiquities are assigned to the excavator, no really adequate excavations have ever been carried out there, except such excavations as those of the French at Delphi and those of the Germans at Olympia. These were carried out under grants from the French and German governments. British and American work in Egypt can not hope for governmental support.

In 1909, when the late J. Pierpont Morgan, then President of the Metropolitan Museum, first visited our excavations here, he assured me of his complete approval and support in the plans I submitted to him for enlarging our field-organization here to its present high state of efficiency. Before beginning the enlargement of our organization, however, I went to M. Maspero to ask his assurance as to conditions in the future, which he at once said he was only too glad to give me. His statement to me was as follows: That he had the right, on retiring, to hand to the French Minister here in Cairo the name of his successor as Director-General; that whoever his choice proved to be, he would be one who would carry out the same policies he himself had established and that we could develop and carry forward our work "without any fear as to the future." M. Lacau was afterwards designated by M. Maspero to succeed him, but when some two years ago, at the time M. Lacau asserted his intention of effecting this change in the law, I brought to his attention these very definite assurances which M. Maspero had given me, he refused to give the matter any consideration.

I maintain that we have a strong moral position, for we have built up our organization in good faith and at large expenditure; we have undertaken broad programmes of work some of which are but half finished; and we are now confronted with a situation not only ruinous to our own programmes, but, we believe, detrimental to the Cairo Museum itself and disastrous for archaeological science as a whole.

It is my firm conviction that if the proposed change in the law goes into effect, and, as is certain to be the case, the scientific organizations now working here are withdrawn, the Egyptian authorities will soon realize their mistake in having followed M. Lacau's blind policy. These various archaeological expeditions have produced many valuable antiquities for the Cairo Museum in these past years, and are employing large forces of native diggers who will lose their present lucrative employment. Our Metropolitan Expedition is employing an average force of 700 to 800 men. Very considerable sums are also being spent annually in this country for supplies of every kind, packing materials and transport, and on various other sides. Just before the war, Lord Edward Cecil, the Financial Adviser, was so impressed with the statement of our expenditures in Egypt, that he offered to see that our Expedition was especially favored in the share of antiquities assigned to us—a friendly offer which I much appreciated but felt obliged to decline.

Not only is every one of the British and American Egyptologists (whether conducting excavations or in purely disinterested capacity) united in their opposition to M. Lacau's action—as meaning the ruination of what we have all been endeavoring to accomplish in scientific results during the past twenty-five years—but also leading British archaeologists in the Service des Antiquités have expressed themselves privately as unequivocally opposed to M. Lacau's action. For obvious reasons they can not thus express themselves publicly, but I venture to state that they would welcome the opportunity of making their opinions known to Lord Allenby [Field Marshal Allenby, the British High Commissioner in Egypt].

By the summer of 1922, just after the fruitless fifth season in the Valley of the Tombs of the Kings, Lord Carnarvon had become completely discouraged by Lacau's new policy. And he had begun to look a bit "seedy," as his beloved twenty-year-old daughter Evelyn described him—lapsing into longer and longer periods of silence, lying frail and listless on a reclining chair, so fatigued that he hardly had the strength to lift the book he was reading. He hardly bothered to walk around his beautiful Highclere, and when he did, he did not appear to marvel, as he had never failed to do in the past, over the splendid vistas of his great estate.

Normally Howard Carter would look forward with the greatest pleasure to spending a lazy, long weekend at Highclere, made invigorating by hours of superb and witty talk about Egypt, archaeology, Carter's experiences, Carnarvon's collections, and their mutual dreams of finding the royal tomb, its myriad chambers filled to the ceilings with treasures. When Carnarvon had a story about his life that particularly pleased him, or heard a tale from a friend that he found particularly enchanting, he would tell it over and over again. But the retelling of his favorite stories never became dull, for Carnarvon had a gift of language that enabled him continually to renew the magic of the tales. His favorite from his own experiences recalled an episode during an attempted round-the-world cruise when he was in his early twenties. His sister mentions it in her introduction to the first volume of Carter's popular book on Tutankhamun:

69

One one occasion . . . he hired a boat to take him somewhere off the coast to his ship lying far out to sea. He was alone, steering the little bark rowed by a couple of stalwart fishermen. Suddenly, when far removed from land, and equally distant from his goal, the two ruffians gave him the choice between payment of a large sum or being pitched into the water. He listened quietly, and motioned them to pass his dressing bag. They obeyed, already in imagination fingering the English "Lord's" ransom. The situation was, however, reversed when he extracted, not a well-stuffed pocketbook, but a revolver, and pointing it at the pair sternly bade them row on, or he would shoot. The chuckle with which he recalled what was to him an eminently delectable episode, still remains with his hearer.

And of all of Carter's own fascinating stories, one involving danger and courage had especially appealed to Lord Carnarvon. This took place during the early war years when Carter was on a short holiday at Luxor and found himself suddenly implicated in an unprecedented and hazardous task.

The war had brought about a great revival of activity on the part of the local tomb robbers. The unorthodox and effective governor, old Daoud Pasha, had died long ago, and prospecting parties of thieves fanned out in all directions. News came into Kurna one afternoon that a remarkable find had been made by one family in a most unlikely spot—a virtually inaccessible area in the western side of a mountain above the valley. A rival group of Kurna thieves promptly picked up their guns and rushed to the illicit diggings. After considerable yelling, screaming and the exchange of a few shots, the first band was ousted.

Some of the notables of the village made contact with Howard Carter and begged him to take some action to avoid further trouble. Despite the fact that he had no official standing with the Antiquities Service, Carter said he would help. It was already late in the afternoon, so he quickly called the few workmen still around and took off for the scene of the crime. This involved the most unbelievably hazardous adventures. First the party had to make their way up more than eighteen hundred feet over the Kurna foothills by moonlight only. At midnight they arrived at the top of the great sheer cliff which rose up *three hundred fifty feet* from the base of the valley, and saw the end of a rope hanging down its face. They could hear the hollow, eery sounds of the robbers at work, somewhere down the sheer cliff, unknown to him, they were hacking their way into some sort of hidden chamber.

Without a second's thought, Carter cut off the thieves' rope and shinnied down his own in pitch black right into a "nestful of industrious tomb-robbers." It was, he said, "a pastime which at least does not lack excitement." He found eight at work. When he reached the bottom there was an awkward moment or two. He gave them the alternative of clearing out by means of his rope or staying where they were without a rope at all. Eventually they saw reason and departed.

Carter shinnied back up the rope, remained on the cliff top for the rest of the night and, at earliest light, went down again to take a look. He found a most remarkable tomb. Its entrance was a natural water-worn cleft so perfectly hidden that even the most acute observer could not see the slightest trace of its existence from above or below. Carter discovered a passageway which plunged straight into the cliff for about fifty feet, then turned sharply and entered a room about eighteen feet square.

The thieves had already cleared their way through the rubble-filled passage making a small entry just barely wide enough for a man to wriggle through. Carter decided to make a complete clearance of the perfectly camouflaged tomb. He was convinced that it had to be a pure, unviolated sanctuary because of the consummate skill with which it had been disguised. But, to his profound sadness, he discovered that the enormous passage and chamber were unfinished and unoccupied. All that the chamber contained was a large empty sarcophagus, also unfinished, with some inscriptions pertaining to Queen Hatshepsut. Carter believed that the grand lady had ordered the curious tomb constructed for her during the period when she had been the wife of Thutmose II. Later on, when Hatshepsut had taken over the throne and proclaimed herself pharaoh, it was imperative for her to build a proper tomb somewhere in the valley side by side with the sepulchers of all other kings of her dynasty. The cliff tomb was abandoned. Carter observed wryly that she would have been better advised to hold to her original plan. In this secret spot her mummy would have had a reasonable chance. In the valley, it had none at all. In her zeal to become a king, she spelled doom for her afterlife of eternity. Hatshepsut, the Pharaoh, was pillaged like all other kings.

But one can be sure that in the summer of 1922 the disheartened Lord Carnarvon did not want to hear again even such an extraordinary tale as this, for he faced the highly unpleasant task of informing his intimate friend and partner that he would no longer participate as funder in the search for the tomb of Tutankhamun. And without Carnarvon's prodigious wealth the work could never continue. Carter was stunned, but then, according to Sir Alan Gardiner, he made a puzzling, almost unbelievable statement. He expressed his intention, if agreeable to Lord Carnarvon, to continue the dig himself with his own funds. Lord Carnarvon, moved by such a demonstration of dedication and selflessness, immediately changed his mind and promised his friend that he would agree to underwrite the full cost of their expedition for one, and only one, more season. It was, as Gardiner stated, the "last chance" for Howard Carter.

Was it really his last chance? Unknown to Sir Alan Gardiner and to virtually everyone else then and now, Howard Carter did have the money to pursue the dig and apparently had also taken at least one step toward acquiring another financial backer.

Although he was an impetuous man who, by his abrupt resignation in 1903 from government service in Egypt, demonstrated that he had given no great thought either to his future or indeed to how he was to survive financially, Carter had become over the years a great deal more prudent. Carnarvon had encouraged him to plan for his future. The link with the wealthy lord had enabled him to meet people of stature and privilege unknown to him earlier, when he literally fled from anyone who was not in the field of archaeology. Over the years Carter had very quietly become a highly successful "gentleman dealer" in Egyptian antiquities. Not only had he assembled a small but respectable collection of fine *antikas* for himself, but he had become an adviser to collectors such as Lord Carnarvon and Edward S. Harkness, a member of the board of the Metropolitan Museum. He had even acted as the covert art dealer for the Metropolitan in one of the most important acquisitions it had ever made. Howard Carter also gave collecting advice, for a fee, to Calouste Gulbenkian, the legendarily rich oil broker of the Middle East, the famed "Mr. Five Percent."

If he had sold his collection of antiquities and cashed in all his savings, Carter could easily have raised the prodigious sum required for the continuation of the dig, at least for one additional season. But he didn't need his own investment; it appears that he believed he had the financial backing from another source. It was not Gulbenkian. There are strong indications that he had discussed the possibility with Herbert Winlock of the Metropolitan. There is no doubt at all that the museum was keenly interested in the possibility of picking up the Carnarvon concession in the valley if he let it lapse. This was especially true after Winlock's discovery of the "absolute clue" to the existence of at least an empty tomb of Tutankhamun in the valley. In his correspondence, Winlock referred twice to the possibility of expanding the museum's "expeditions into certain areas of the Valley." Yet Winlock, a scholar of utter selflessness, and the very model of scientific cooperation, had not concealed the significance of his discovery from his friend and colleague Howard Carter. He preferred, apparently, to let matters evolve naturally. If Lord Carnarvon decided to allow his concession to run out, the Metropolitan would attempt to pick it up; but if Carnarvon wanted to continue the pursuit, the museum would help in every way possible, which is what it did.

There is the possibility that Winlock's reference to the valley did not mean specifically Tutankhamun. But further support for the assumption that it was came to me in the first years I worked at the Metropolitan. James J. Rorimer, who was then the director, related to me that Winlock had told him that Carter had once talked with him about the museum's possible role as full partner with him and not merely as a participant in the search and excavation for Tutankhamun in case Lord Carnarvon left the field. That, Winlock had added, looked highly likely at one point in the game. It is hearsay, of course, but it is logical and credible and, fitted with Winlock's written words, makes a very good case. Whether or not Carter ever told Lord Carnarvon of the arrangement is not known. There is no evidence whatever that he did.

CHAPTER SEVEN

"The Tomb of the Golden Bird"

CARTER ARRIVED IN THE Valley of the Kings on October 28, 1922, for the "last" season. He spent a few days hauling in equipment, going over the work plan with his three foremen, hiring the crews, sorting out who was available from the last season and who was not for a variety of reasons ranging from the marriage of a daughter to a "completely unfounded" case of petty crime. Not all the equipment was purely archaeological in nature; there was a wealth of tinned meats, boxes of special crackers, canned sweets, a plum pudding or two, and an abundance of the finest clarets and Burgundies, carefully selected by Lord Carnarvon from Fortnum & Mason, the world-famous purveyors, caterers and vintners to the aristocracy. He would deal with no other, and he dealt with the selected vintners lavishly. A casual visitor to the area might easily have thought that what he had walked into was Fortnum & Mason on the Nile, so numerous were the distinctive wooden crates neatly bound up in bands of steel, each punctiliously identified as to its contents underneath the precise graphics proclaiming the name of that most elegant establishment.

Carter had also brought along a companion to brighten up his lonely house and add a note of gaiety and sweet song. This was a canary, which immediately became an object of great affection to the workers and the foremen, who called it the "Golden Bird," and became a symbol of great good luck and an almost sure sign that the season would bring them success.

By November 1, Carter had enrolled his full crew and was ready to dig. He began near the spot where five years before, with the highest of expectations, he had probed and then backed off: the ancient foundations that indicated workers' huts. The huts covered the whole area in front of the tomb of Ramesses VI and continued to the south to join up with a similar group of huts on the opposite side of the valley.

By the evening of the third of November, Carter had uncovered a sufficient number of them to get a clear idea of their type. He recorded them by drawing plans and taking a few photographs, and then removed the huts. Late in the evening he could see that there was still about three feet of ancient soil underneath the huts and above bedrock. That would be the place to go the following day.

When Carter arrived early the next morning, he was very much surprised by an unusual silence he noticed among the workers, who normally jabbered throughout the entire day. Instantly he realized that an unusual event had taken place. Carter recalled thinking that there had been an accident. Then one of his foremen announced to him that a step cut in the rock had been found underneath the very first hut that had been removed the previous day.

Several years later, when on a lecture tour of the United States, Carter was to tell the president of the bureau handling the bookings, Lee Keedick, that the most insignificant member of the working team had discovered the step, *not* under the hut as he stated in his book, but a bit outside the area that Carter had instructed the foremen to begin upon the evening before. According to Keedick's recollection of Carter's story:

Gloom had settled over the entire party. The incentive for achievement had almost completely vanished—except for the water boy whose stake was small but whose energy the sun could not penetrate or slacken. Like small, industrious boys emulating their elders he was carrying on, in his play, digging with sticks in the sand, when suddenly he hit a hard surface. He dug furiously and in a few moments had unearthed a stone step. His heart almost ceased to beat. Hastily he covered the step with sand, so that the rival archaeologists might not see him, and then ran as fast as his legs would carry him to tell Howard Carter of what he had found.

The step seemed to Carter too good to be true. Shortly, however, when a little more clearing had been undertaken, he could see that he was actually in the entrance to a steep cut in the rock, some thirteen feet below the entrance to the tomb of Ramesses VI. He recognized that the manner of cutting was precisely that of a sunken stairway entrance to a royal tomb, so common in the valley. He dared to hope that he had found his tomb at last.

The work continued at a fever pitch throughout the entire day of November 4 and through the morning of the fifth. By that afternoon the workmen had cleared away masses of rubbish that were heaped up over the cut, and Carter was able to discern the precise rectangular shape of all four sides of the upper edges of the stairway. It was clear to everyone present, beyond any question, that they were looking down on the rarest and most exciting thing possible in the valley—the entrance to a tomb.

The style of the steps and the fact that they led almost straight down signified a tomb entrance of the Eighteenth Dynasty, possibly the era of Tutankhamun. Whatever the entrance was, it was definitely not the direct, horizontal opening typical of the tombs of the Nineteenth or Twentieth Dynasties. Everyone was intensely excited. Some of the workmen began at that moment to speak of it as "the tomb of the Golden Bird," pointing to Carter's canary for having produced a stroke of such monumentally good fortune.

But Carter had his doubts, which he communicated to no

one else that afternoon of the fifth of November, doubts born of previous disappointments. Recalling his own experiences with promising opportunities which were all found to be empty—Amenhotep II and the unfinished chamber of Hatshepsut—Carter believed there was always the "horrible possibility" that the sanctuary would prove to be unfinished, incomplete, or never used. And of course the chances were almost one hundred percent that if finished it had been ransacked. But there was the one-in-a-million chance that it really was an untouched tomb. Barely able to contain his breathless excitement, he watched the steps, one after another, come to light.

The next four or five hours, while the workmen cleared step after step, may well have been the most exhilarating for Howard Carter in all the years he had worked in his beloved valley. At times, one can imagine the work appearing to progress incredibly slowly, in half motion, as if the men were working partially somnolent, almost as if they had taken on the dreamy movements of those who work underwater. One can be sure Carter had to suppress the desire to bark at them to go faster, had to hold himself in check, for one cannot hurry the progress of a dig. One can almost visualize him watching the next step appear, then the next, each slowly—all too slowly—being cleared away. No doubt his feelings of excitement and elation occasionally became confused, to be replaced by doubt, skepticism and even fear that he would discover nothing more than bare steps, a rubble-filled passageway and empty chambers showing only the sorrowful marks of a once resplendent monarch ripped to shreds by thieves.

The stairway, entirely rock-cut, descended at a forty-five-degree angle into a small hillock. As step after step emerged—first five, then eight, and then ten—its western edge gradually became fully roofed in and the stairs became a stepped tunnel with a horizontal roof, measuring about ten feet high and six feet wide.

Work progressed. Step succeeded step. At the level of the twelfth step, toward sunset, Carter came across the upper part of a door, constructed of large stones, plastered over and over and stamped with a number of figurative seals and hieroglyphs. My God, he thought, it was actually true!

Carter could scarcely bring himself to believe that the years of fruitless labor might be rewarded after all. His first feeling was one of self-congratulation for his faith that the valley had not indeed been exhausted. Frantically, in a fever of expectancy, he searched the seal impressions, each about the size of his hand extended, for the name or identity of the owner of the tomb. But inexplicably he could find no name. The seals— there were about a dozen—were stamped into the plaster somewhat haphazardly, some perfectly vertical, others at peculiar angles. The only impressions Carter could decipher were those of the seal of the royal necropolis, the jackal and the nine cruelly bound captives. But there was no owner's name. Carter was confused. There simply had to be the name of the owner; that was absolute and sacred procedure in the valley. The fact that there was no name led Carter to deduce that the tomb was not that of a king.

The blocked door and the necropolis seals did, however, indicate two very favorable things to Carter. The royal seal showed that the tomb had at least been used for a person of very noble standing. And whatever lay beyond had not been entered since the end of the Twentieth Dynasty—three thousand years before—since the door had been completely covered up by the workers' huts of Ramesses VI.

While examining the seals, Carter had noticed, at the very top of the doorway where some plaster had dropped down, a heavy wooden lintel. Just under the beam of wood he made a small hole barely large enough to peer through with a flashlight. The space beyond the door was filled completely with stones and rubble, further proof of the great care with which the tomb had been protected.

It was, for Howard Carter, the most thrilling moment in his long career. There he was, alone, except for his Arab workmen, on the verge of what might be a unique discovery in the history of Egyptian archaeology. In that blocked passage—beyond it in a host of chambers—could be unimaginable treasures, unbelievable discoveries. Carter had to hold himself in check with all the professional discipline he could muster to prevent himself from smashing the doorway and entering into the enticing and mysterious space.

Carter was a mercurial man, given to rapid cycles of elation and doubt. As he stared at the door, the doubts consumed him. The door was really too small for the tomb of a king. It had to be the sepulchral chamber of a noble of the Eighteenth Dynasty, buried there with royal permission. But that couldn't be; or at least if it were it would be unique. The tombs of nobles began to appear in the Nineteenth Dynasty, not the Eighteenth. Or was this "tomb" not a tomb at all? Was it nothing more than one of those royal caches or stray hiding places to which a mummy and its paraphernalia had been frantically moved to stay just one desperate step ahead of the voracious thieves? Or was it really the tomb of the king whom Howard Carter had sought for so long?

Once again he searched for seals other than those of the royal necropolis, and found nothing. If Carter had dug down just a few more inches he would have found a number of seals bearing the elliptical cartouche of Nebkheperura, the throne name of his cherished Tutankhamun—and thus, as he said, would not have tossed and turned trying to sleep that first night and would have spared himself more than three weeks of anxiety. He didn't for the practical reason that it had become late. Darkness would descend in several hours; electric lights other than flashlights were not yet readily available in that part of the valley. He needed to devote the remaining hours of light to refilling the entire cleared part of the stairway, protecting it as fully as possible. And there was a gentlemanly reason too. Carter decided not to proceed beyond the upper part of the sealed doorway until his loyal patron Lord Carnarvon could arrive on the site from England. It was only fair.

So with great reluctance he reclosed the small hole he had made just below the lintel of the doorway, and filled in the excavation. He chose a group of the most trustworthy of his workmen, established an orderly system of watches, day and night, and rode by donkey-back down the valley by moonlight to his rest house to pass a most restless night—wondering, hoping, doubting.

The next morning, November 6, at Luxor, he dispatched a cable to Lord Carnarvon at Highclere: "At last have made wonderful discovery in Valley: a magnificent tomb with seals intact; re-covered same for your arrival. Congratulations."

He also cabled A. R. "Pecky" Callender, a British archaeologist working at a site named Erment for the Egyptian Archaeological Fund, to join him at once. Callender, a low-keyed, placid man of saturnine expression, was the "perfect second man." He could do anything on a dig—string electrical wire, build a stout door of stray material and judge the precise amount of wood and packing material needed for a packing case—with easy skill. Callender had worked on special tasks for Carter a number of times over the years and was particularly well suited, for he was, as Winlock said, "one of the few colleagues who could actually be with Carter for any length of time without going clear out of his head."

Under Carter's supervision, the workmen filled the entire excavation to the surface level of the first rock-cut step and, to camouflage the site, rolled the large boulders on top of the tamped-down area. By the evening of the same day, only forty-eight hours after he had come across the first step of the staircase, the tomb had vanished. It was almost as if there never had been a tomb at all. He found it hard to persuade himself that the whole episode had not been a dream.

Lord Carnarvon cabled that he and his daughter, Lady Evelyn Herbert, would arrive at Alexandria on the twentieth of November. In the intervening two weeks, Carter prepared for their arrival and purchased in Cairo a large amount of electrical wire and numerous lamps to tap the electrical outlets in the tomb of Ramesses VI so as to illuminate the forthcoming explorations.

Everyone was in the highest state of excitement imaginable. The work went smoothly. The appropriate officials of the Antiquities Service were alerted, and the electrical equipment was easily installed. Only two things now annoyed Carter. Tourists began to show up (news travels fast in Egypt), and, within days of the discovery of the steps and the sealed doorway, a flood of cables and letters of congratulation, inquiries and offers of help descended upon him. All of them had to be answered, a task that vexed Carter.

And then something happened that was deeply disturbing to the workmen and the foremen: the yellow canary, the "Golden Bird," harbinger of the greatest good luck, perished under strange circumstances. Herbert Winlock described the event in a letter to Edward Robinson:

When Carter came out last October, alone, he got a canary bird, in Cairo, in a gilded cage to cheer up what he figured was going to be a lonely and deserted house. Carter, coming over to his house with his servant, Abdul Ali, carrying the canary behind him and the guards and the [foremen] greeting him and right off, when they see a golden bird they say: "Mabrook—it's a bird of gold that will bring luck. This year we will find inshallah (God willing) a tomb full of gold." Within a week they had made the most fabulous find of all time and at first the tomb was called "the tomb of the Golden Bird" by the natives. The canary almost had a halo around its cage.

As soon as he struck the tomb, Carter got Callender from Erment and shortly afterwards Carnarvon arrived and Carter went to Cairo to meet him. Callender was living alone in Carter's house with the bird consigned to his especial care. Suddenly, one afternoon he heard a fluttering and squeaking and went into the next room and there in the cage with the bird was a cobra just in the act of gulping the canary down, halo and all.

Now cobras had even been known around there before, and cobras, as every native knew, grow on the heads of the Old Kings. The conclusion was obvious. The King's serpent had struck at the mascot who had given away the secret of the tomb. And the sequel was equally obvious—at least to them, though I admit to have lost some links in the chain of argument—that before the winter was out someone would die. It was all very dismal. Carter didn't seem to appreciate its funestrialness quite as much as his old [foreman], however.

CHAPTER EIGHT

"Wonderful Things"

ON NOVEMBER 23, Lord Carnarvon and his daughter, Lady Evelyn Herbert, along with Howard Carter, arrived at Luxor by train from Cairo and were greeted at the station by the governor of the province. A photograph of the event shows Carnarvon looking pleased but rather fatigued and a radiant young Evelyn holding a bouquet of flowers. Twenty years old at the time, she was an extremely beautiful young woman with a firm, somewhat square face, but with delicate features nevertheless. Lively and energetic, with a sense of humor inherited no doubt from her father, she was forthright, adventurous and highly impressionable.

The group made its way at once to the Valley of the Kings, six miles away, on the backs of donkeys urged on by the constant shrieking and whippings of the dragomans. After a late lunch they inspected the entrance and the steps to the tomb, which Pecky Callender had been clearing away slowly. Despite their eagerness to proceed, everyone retired early. All agreed that sleep would be necessary for the next few days of work and the discovery—of what?

On the morning of November 24, the workers cleared the debris from the remaining steps. Only then were the excavators able to examine the entire sealed doorway. On the lower part the seal impressions were relatively clear. Without any difficulty, they could make out on several of them the name Tutankhamun. The unbelievable was true!

There was a moment of jubilation. They had, after all, grasped their most cherished dream—the actual tomb of the king they had sought for so long. Suddenly the discouraging years of digging, the disappointments, the agony of fruitless work were forgotten.

Evelyn became transfixed with the high drama of seeing the ancient past rolled back, foot after foot, and she gasped with amazement and delight whenever the workers would come across a find in the debris that filled the staircase, even if the discovery was a modest one. As they dug through the lower stratifications, they found masses of potsherds and fragments of wooden boxes scattered throughout. Evelyn was overjoyed by each discovery. But Carter was not. As he picked up piece after piece and turned them over in his fingers, he was deeply troubled. For the fragments carried partial cartouches inscribed or painted with the names of not only Tutankhamun but also Akenhaton and Smenkhkara, who Egyptologists thought was Tutankhamun's half brother. What was even more disturbing, Carter had come across a scarab inscribed with the name of Thutmose III and a fragment of pottery with the name of Amenhotep III; both kings had ruled nearly half a generation before Tutankhamun.

Why the mixture of names? To Howard Carter it could only mean—to his depression—that what they had found was not a tomb at all, but a cache filled, if indeed anything was left, with a miscellaneous collection of objects belonging to a number of kings of the Eighteenth Dynasty, brought from Tell al-Amarna by Tutankhamun and deposited here for safety.

By the next day, November 25, they had removed all the ancient debris. The stairs were dusted off and a heavy wooden grille was readied to be set up after the removal of the sealed doorway. Carter guided the chief inspector of the Service of Antiquities, Rex Engelbach, through the excavation. Pierre Lacau had insisted that a member of the Antiquities Service be present as soon as possible after the discovery of a tomb and remain on the site for the opening and entry of the chambers, despite the fact that the concession implied that the discoverer had the right to enter first. Carter had objected to Engelbach, a pinch-faced Englishman of waspish demeanor, about the issue of entry. But Engelbach (who had been codenamed "Trout" by Carter and Lord Carnarvon) informed him that Lacau's position was firm. He explained in a careful and dry manner that although one clause of the license might have stated that the entry was the right of the discoverer, the very next stated firmly that an inspector had to be there at the time. Thus the issue was moot. At the time, Carter was almost too excited to care.

As the inspection progressed, with Carter making notes and sketches of the full doorway, and Lord Carnarvon taking photographs of the seals—he had been president of the local camera club near Highclere and was justifiably proud of his endeavors—the team discovered something deeply disquieting.

There was no doubt at all that other searchers had been there before them. Evidence of at least two consecutive openings and closings of part of the door could not be denied. The seals of the necropolis, Anubis and the nine prisoners, had been stamped all over the area that had been opened and reclosed. The seals of Tutankhamun were spread over the pristine part of the door and were clearly those that had originally secured the Pharaoh's tomb or cache.

The tomb, then—if it was a tomb—was definitely not intact. Plunderers had entered it, and appeared to have conducted their evil work more than once. But the thievery could not have taken place in modern times; in fact, it could not have happened later than the construction of the tomb of Ramesses VI, some two hundred years after Tutankhamun's reign. Although Carter and Carnarvon were fearful of discovering a chamber ripped to shreds, they found some hope in the fact that the tomb had been so carefully resealed twice in ancient times. This tended to suggest that those who had come to disturb it had not rifled everything. Carter took great pains to point out to Engelbach the evidence of the ancient openings and reclosings—semicircular areas on the upper left-hand corner of the plastered doorway, just large enough to enable a man to squeeze through. Both excavators wanted to be absolutely certain that Engelbach's *procès-verbal* to the Antiquities Service emphatically brought attention to the fact that the first doorway of the tomb or cache had been penetrated illicitly in antiquity.

At midmorning of the same day, Carter instructed the foremen to remove the blocks of stone which formed the door. Once these were removed, a rather strange sight came to view. A passageway, without stairs, sloped down at an angle of about twenty-five degrees. The puzzling feature was that it was entirely filled with small white chips of flint mixed with dust. Carter figured that these chips could only have been the debris from the original cutting. But there again were traces of the thieves' penetration, evident in the upper left-hand portion of the rubble in darker flint.

As the excavators dug out the passageway, they tracked, anxiously, the irregular tunnel made by the robbers, finding within it additional bits and pieces of pottery and wooden boxes. Unlike those discovered on the stairs, none carried emblems or insignia of either Tutankhamun or earlier kings. On the bed of the passage itself, within the white flint debris, Carter found still more fragments, jar sealings, potsherds, numerous pieces of smaller articles, and the remains of leather skins. The latter had been brought as water receptacles for the job of replastering the doorway. This evidence led Carter to believe that one group of thieves had entered the tomb through the passageway before it had been filled up. Then the officials of the necropolis had caught the thieves and filled the passage with flint. After that, a second band of desecrators had entered, by hacking a winding, narrow tunnel through the fill. Then either the thieves themselves or their tunnel had been discovered and the tunnel refilled by the cemetery officials.

By nightfall the excavators had cleared the passageway a

distance of approximately twenty feet down, but had found no second door. Throughout the morning of the next day, November 26, the clearing of the rubble-filled passage went on, basket by basket. The work was agonizingly slow. Whenever they found a fragment of an object, jar or box, a piece of dried-out leather or a single faience bead, they had to stop the digging in order to record and remove each piece of jetsam. They found dozens of them.

Then, in the early afternoon, thirty feet beyond the first doorway, the party—Carnarvon, Evelyn Herbert, Carter and Callender (no longer was any representative of the Antiquities Service present, for Carter had not asked for one)—encountered a second door, almost an exact replica of the outer one. This, too, carried the seals of the necropolis and Tutankhamun's throne name. Here, too, were the familiar semicircular entries of the thieves which had been resealed. By now the excavators were convinced they had unearthed a deposit, not a tomb. The configuration of stairway, doors and passage was almost precisely similar to the layout of the "cache" of Akhenaton found in the valley by Theodore Davis years before.

Slowly—desperately slowly, it seemed to the group at the time—the last pieces of the debris blocking the passage were taken away. At last the full height of the second door was exposed before them. The unbelievable moment had arrived. Carter's hands trembled as, taking an iron rod from Callender, he made a tiny hole in the upper left-hand corner. Whatever lay beyond was empty, had not been filled in like the stairs and the passage. Carter lit a candle and brought its flame close to the small aperture in order to test for the presence of foul gases within. He widened the hole with the iron testing rod. And looked in.

Later, in one of the most dramatic and famous passages of literature in archaeological history, Carter described what happened then that fateful afternoon:

I inserted the candle and peered in, Lord Carnarvon, Lady Evelyn and Callender standing anxiously beside me to hear the verdict. At first I could see nothing, the hot air escaping from the chamber causing the candle flame to flicker, but presently, as my eyes grew accustomed to the light, details of the room within emerged slowly from the mist, strange animals, statues and gold—everywhere the glint of gold. For the moment—an eternity it must have been to the others standing by—I was struck dumb with amazement, and when Lord Carnarvon, unable to stand the suspense any longer, inquired anxiously, "Can you see anything?" it was all I could do to get out the words, "Yes, wonderful things." Then, widening the hole a little further so that both could see, we inserted an electric torch.

Carter's own published account and all the dozens, even hundreds, that have described those magical few minutes on November 26, 1922, report that the four discoverers looked into the tomb's first room, which would be called the Antechamber, flashed their light upon one magnificent object after another, and saw, too, on the north wall of the Antechamber the traces of another sealed doorway. Carter repeats emphatically that they simply looked in, eventually reclosed the hole, and left the valley, silent and subdued. He went so far as to describe how the four of them wondered how many chambers they would actually find when they eventually gained entry.

Carter and his colleagues were most intrigued about the sealed door on the north end of the first chamber. They debated long into the night what would be found beyond it. The very least they could expect would be a single room. But why not more—a long chain of rooms and galleries leading to the great burial chamber, that sacred Holy of Holies? They were preoccupied with the ancient thieves and wondered whether the plunderers had been successful in breaking through the third closed partition. From where they stood, outside the first room, it *seemed* that the door was intact. The discussions, Carter reported, went on long into the night. They could hardly sleep that enchanted night.

In fact, although Carter, Carnarvon, Lady Evelyn and Pecky Callender undoubtedly raised those questions that evening and assuredly "slept but little, all of us, that night," their lack of sleep had nothing to do with those questions, for they had already obtained the answers to most of them. Carter's published account of his first examination of the Antechamber and its contents is highly deceiving—it is a lie. What actually occurred had little of the restraint that Carter imparted to it in his official account.

They "slept but little . . . that night" because they must have spent practically the whole of it physically inside the tomb, going through every chamber, penetrating even into the Burial Chamber—the "Holy of Holies," as Carter called it— and into the so-called Treasury beyond, moving objects around, and disguising their entry, about which they would never tell anyone outside their own special circle. The actual events are revealed in unpublished materials in the Egyptian Department of the Metropolitan Museum of Art and in three obscure notes published in a scholarly journal in 1942 and 1947 by an individual who participated in the excavation. It is from these materials, from the excavators' subsequent observations and from logical conjecture that one can reconstruct what the party proceeded to do that splendid evening and night.

CHAPTER NINE

The Long Night

As HE PEERED THROUGH the small hole, Carter was at first unable to distinguish specific objects, because the pale light cast off by the candle flickered constantly. But he soon realized that he was looking, not at wall paintings, but at three-dimensional objects—they appeared to be enormous gold bars stacked against the wall opposite his entrance. Dumbfounded, transfixed, he just stood there muttering. "Wonderful, marvelous, my God, wonderful!" were among the words he finally spoke.

Lord Carnarvon, after a moment, began pulling at his arm, his patience finally exhausted. "Hey, let me have a look!" But Carter wouldn't budge; he was immobilized by what he saw. Finally he was pulled from the hole, "like a cork from a bottle," and Carnarvon took his place, then Lady Evelyn and finally Pecky Callender.

At first the excavators couldn't believe what they were looking at. They were overpowered, awestruck. And, at the same time, they felt a kind of embarrassment to have broken through into a sanctuary that had been closed with deep piety so many thousands of years before. In the presence of such antiquity that seemed so fresh, so perfect, the sense that three millennia had passed ceased to exist.

As Carter enlarged the hole, Callendar dashed up the passageway to collect some electric lamps. In all likelihood none of the party, particularly Howard Carter, thought about actually entering the first chamber at that moment. He was, after all, a professional, a man of system and order who would have restrained himself under normal conditions even without the strictures of the concession. But the effect upon Carter was dazzling, confusing and overwhelming. Neither Carter nor his patron ever formulated exactly what they expected or hoped to see. Certainly they had never dreamed they would fall upon anything of this dimension. It was a jam-packed room, looking like a whole museum of treasures some of which seemed familiar, yet others he could hardly comprehend—treasures stacked on top of each other in what appeared to be an infinity.

After the depressing years of "barren labor," to have happened upon the most magnificent and extraordinary discovery in the entire history of Egyptian archaeology brought on euphoria. It may have been Lord Carnarvon or Lady Evelyn who first suggested and then persuaded Carter that they remove a sufficient number of blocks from the doorway to enable them to climb into the tomb. One will never know. But in a draft for an article describing the first impressions and actions of the party, written by Lord Carnarvon but never published, his lordship stated that Howard Carter made an opening in the inner doorway large enough for the party to jump down with some difficulty into the Antechamber. Evelyn wriggled in through the tiny hole. Being the smallest in the party, she was the only one who could get through at first. As she flashed the light around her, she was transfixed by a forest of creamy-white alabaster vases standing upright. Soon the others followed.

One can imagine the scene. A tiny chamber, dark, haunting, filled with the air, unchanged over the millennia, that had existed from the time of those who had lain the King to rest and from the time, too, when the ancient thieves had come to plunder. Hundreds and hundreds of objects, each single one worth a whole season—seven full months—of digging.

The Antechamber was not large; it measured twelve by twenty-six feet, with unpainted walls and a low ceiling only about seven and a half feet high. The room was rectangular and had been cut into the rock of the valley so that its walls nearly faced the four cardinal points of the compass. The doorway through which they had entered was on the long east side of the room, practically at its center.

Against each wall was stacked—"in confusion, but orderly confusion," as Carter recalled—a treasure house of magnificent objects, furniture, and works of art. The floor was littered with small articles and fragments of linen, baskets and reeds. The intruders tried to be as careful as they could so as not to tread upon them. The litter lent weight to Carter's conviction that thieves had defiled the sanctuary in ancient times.

The near-embarrassment at being intruders themselves haunted the party. An eon had passed since another human being had stood where they were standing. Yet it seemed but yesterday. Everything seemed so incredibly fresh—a bowl of mortar used in the plaster for the door, a lamp seemingly just extinguished, a fingerprint still visible on the painted surface, a remarkably well-preserved bunch of flowers left at the threshold. The intimacy of it all, the penetrating sense of life still clinging to the ancient room, made them all feel like trespassers.

But they shared other feelings too: a surge of unbelievable excitement; the agony of having to hold themselves in check, having to keep themselves from ripping seals apart and impulsively tearing open boxes; the realization that they were making history and were about to solve one of the greatest problems of all archaeology; the tense excitement of treasure hunters.

There was also fear, the insistent feeling that they should keep looking over their own shoulders, lest *they* be caught. They knew they should be scientific and cautious, yet they yearned to move things around, rummage through chests, small caskets, beautiful boxes, dimly realizing how close to the feelings of the ancient thieves were *their* emotions. They were, in fact, unable to resist the temptation to pick up various objects, captured brilliantly for a second by the light, and delightedly show them off to one another. The smells of the tomb fascinated them. They were amazed to find they could distinguish the faint odors of sweet perfumes, oils and unguents and the lingering pungent aromas of a variety of woods.

Some of the objects, highlighted in the gloom by the flashing beams of their lights, terrified the searchers. On the long western wall of the rectangular room, directly opposite the door, were three phantasmagorical couches. The group had been aware of them all the while, but had not quite believed they were there. The sides of the gilded couches were carved into monstrous animals, attenuated in form. They were startling, realistic, yet unreal at the same time: strange beasts—a lion; a cow; a Typhon, part hippo, part crocodile. Their brilliant surfaces were plucked out of the darkness by the excavators' lamps, as though by limelight, their heads throwing grotesque, distorted, wildly gyrating shadows on the wall of the silent tomb, making the beasts seem to move as if they had suddenly come to life.

The searchers were finally able to get themselves under control, and with the aid of a flashlight and at least one lamp they could see clearly enough to make a cursory examination of the chamber and its contents. The lamp was a godsend to the excavators. No doubt just the existence of rays of light that were part of the modern world, part of their own day, helped to calm their nerves.

To the north, directly right from the entrance, was a wall where two magnificent statues had been placed at each corner. They were life-sized sculptures of the King in black, facing each other like sentinels, dressed in gold kilts, wearing golden sandals and carrying staffs and maces of gold. The figures were majestic, serene, and in excellent condition after thousands of years. The eyes of the figures, inlaid with glass, were remarkably lifelike. Each face resembled that of a young man, probably not older than his early twenties.

The massive gilded wooden funerary couches and the sentinels were the first things that captured the searchers' attention. Surrounding the dominant objects, piled above them, were hundreds of others—fabulous caskets, painted and inlaid; vases in creamy alabaster; peculiar black shrines, closed

93

and sealed; clusters of leaves and flowers; a haphazard group of white boxes, shaped like giant eggs; chariots overlaid in gold; and, partly hidden among them, what appeared to be a half-length figure of the Pharaoh.

The four moved from one object to another shaking their heads in disbelief, uttering cries of astonishment. One can be sure there was little order in the way they examined things. They simply darted from one treasure to the next like scavengers: to the golden couch fitted out with two lion's heads, their quartzite eyes glowing like those of a cat whenever the lamp illuminated them; to several bronze images of an ankh, the symbol of life, each holding a twisted-rope wick in its perfectly sculpted hands. Such a lamp was "unique," according to Carter. And he was to repeat that word over and over as he stood on tiptoe, crouched, or fell prone to the floor to inspect dozens of objects which no one in the past thirty-two hundred years of world history had ever seen.

On the floor toward the middle of the north wall Carter was amazed to find a large bouquet of flowers, their petals and leaves preserved. Nearby lay a painted casket about two feet long with a lid curved in a gentle arc. As he examined the casket he could not suppress a sharp gasp of astonishment and delight. The paintings depicted Tutankhamun's enemies, hundreds of them—Nubians, Hittites and Syrians—fleeing in panic before the King in his chariot, their bodies twisted and coiled into a hopeless snarl of defeat. The Pharaoh, far larger than either his enemies or his aides, stood upright, serene in his chariot of war, launching arrows at the foe. At the same time, several soldiers ceremoniously fanned him as he rolled headlong into the fray. To Carter the quality was breathtaking, far more beautiful than anything that had ever before been found in Egypt. It had all the delicacy and the humanity that one would have expected from the most accomplished artists of the Italian high Renaissance, and for a brief moment Carter was even struck by the curious thought that the casket could not be Egyptian, thirty-two hundred years old. But, of course, it was.

Someone in the party suggested they open it. And they did,

gingerly inching off the lid, and discovered a queer jumble of items: a pair of rush-and-papyrus sandals too fragile to touch and, around and below them, in a tangle, what appeared to be a linen robe decorated with thousands of beads—green, red, blue, brilliant yellow—interspersed with sequins of gold.

The utter disorder in the casket was yet another trace of ancient thieves. How much had they taken? Where had they gone? How many chambers did the tomb contain? Presently it dawned upon the excavators' bewildered brains that in all the medley of treasures before them there was no coffin or trace of a mummy, and the much debated question of whether it was a tomb or merely a cache intrigued them again. But even that question failed to quell the feverish excitement they felt. As each one of the party of four would happen upon a work of art that was particularly pleasing, a hurried call would go out for the others to share the beauty and excitement of the discovery. Lord Carnarvon became fascinated by a forest of creamy-white and golden-beige alabaster jars, standing upright, so delicate in construction that they appeared almost to be organic in nature. Lady Evelyn uttered a cry of joy when she came across a superb golden throne with the figures of Tutankhamun and his Queen, Ankhesenamun, depicted on the back, in lapis lazuli and carnelian. The image conveyed such affection—the Queen standing in front of the King seated on a throne, bending her supple young body toward him, lovingly reaching out to touch his shoulders—that the four searchers fell silent for a few moments, deeply moved. How intimate it was, how full of humanity, how full of instinct for life and feeling. Later Carter was to say, "It is the most beautiful thing that has ever been found in Egypt."

They must have spent several hours, in total awe, examining dozens of masterpieces. They came upon another throne, this one fashioned out of cedar, decorated with panels of gold plate, representing the god of eternity, Heh, kneeling upon the hieroglyph for gold. And gold there was in profusion, befitting the monarch.

Despite the fascination, Carter was looking for something far more important to him—evidence of other chambers. And

95

he found it, in the southwest corner, where he detected a tiny hole. Peering in, he saw to his great pleasure yet another room. This one was square; like the Antechamber, it was situated within the rock-cut tomb so that its four walls faced nearly toward the four points of the compass. Crammed with objects, it looked like a treasure house that had suffered an earthquake. Golden beds, gold-and-white stools, and alabaster jars were strewn about the floor and stacked in heaps against the far west wall. The floor was littered with bits and pieces of smaller articles; Carter was convinced the thieves had used this room, which he called the Annex, for their headquarters to examine the treasures and to strip the decorations of gold. The objects in the Antechamber had been left in confusion—orderly confusion—but it was clear that the guardians of the tomb had at least attempted to put things right. But here it seemed that the priests had turned away, totally discouraged by the chaos they saw.

But in that tangled mass were some dazzling works of art. There were spectacular alabaster sculptures, one in the form of a lion, paw raised in the air as if to hail the astounded Carter; another in the shape of a large boat, with a cabin amidships supported by alabaster columns in the shape of papyri, a dwarf at the helm and a tiny, beautiful princess at the bow. There was furniture of all kinds, and even games. Carter found one made of ebony and ivory, which the King had to have enjoyed when alive.

Carter rejoined the others in the Antechamber, where he and Pecky Callender began a systematic search for the traces of other holes, entrances, doorways. Where were the sarcophagus and the mummy? For now Carter was completely convinced that what he had found was Tutankhamun's tomb itself, and not merely a deposit of miscellaneous treasures belonging to a variety of kings. The style of all the material was singular and had a continuity. That uniform style was the most subtle, strong and vivacious that Carter had ever seen, wholly unlike the mannered, somewhat overripe art of the preceding period of Akhenaton. Most of the objects Carter had examined were decorated with the cartouches of the two royal names of Tutankhamun. Yet if it was the tomb, it had some curious features. It was modest in size and shape. It was *not* the long, straight, expansive tunnel of grandiose chambers leading one after another in a perfect chain directly into a great pillared sanctuary, the Holy of Holies, which contained the King's sarcophagus. Where could the Holy of Holies be?

A careful examination revealed that, apart from the entry to the Annex, there was only one other possible door. That was a plastered and sealed partition in the middle of the north wall, between the two black-and-gold sentinels. When he looked at the sealed door carefully, Carter was dismayed to discover, however, that the thieves had made a penetration. At the bottom, almost exactly in the middle, was another semicircular discoloration in the plaster similar to those apparent on the outer and inner doorways. The resealed area was perhaps three and a half feet in height. Carter observed that on the resealed part, as on the two doors, appeared a cluster of the necropolis seals, a sure sign that the priests had closed the hole after the departure of the thieves. But the plastering had been done hastily; there were large cracks on the bottom, through which irregular blocks of stone could be seen.

It took only minutes for Carter to pry a few of them away. As he pointed his flashlight into the small opening, he must have been deeply disappointed, for he could see no mound of golden objects, no stack of treasures, only a narrow corridor going straight to the north for perhaps a dozen feet, ending with a blank wall. He must have thought that the thieves had ransacked everything.

Carter was consumed by the desire to discover whether or not he was looking at a plundered, empty chamber or at a passageway leading to other rooms, bays and eventually to a burial chamber itself. He and Callender removed more stones from the bottom of the old entry until they had opened a narrow hole large enough to squeeze through. As the others watched, Carter entered, probably feet first, and inched along on his back—somewhat fearfully, one can imagine, not knowing what lay beyond.

The corridor was some three feet below the level of the Antechamber, and for a few seconds Carter simply disappeared. When he found his footing, he played the flashlight onto the west wall of the narrow passageway and discovered to his absolute joy a wall decorated with gold and blue faience of the most breathtaking beauty. But the wall did not extend from floor to ceiling. It was not a corridor at all. Instead, he found himself within a square chamber, an enormous and magnificent wooden shrine. He was thunderstruck, and quickly informed the others that he was standing in the Burial Chamber itself. As he faced west he stood before two massive doors of an outer shrine, bolted but not sealed.

After a time, both Lord Carnarvon and Evelyn Herbert managed to squeeze their way through the tiny hole. Pecky Callendar, a tall, heavyset man, could not get in. Carter apparently decided not to try to make the hole bigger. It probably occurred to them that they were about to embark upon an adventure wholly unauthorized by their concession which, if discovered, might result in the annulment of their license. But the breach had been made. There was no retreat, no possibility of turning back—no desire to do so. They examined the doors of the great blue-and-gold shrine—subdued, awed, for they realized suddenly in the silence of that chamber that they stood where no human being had trod for three thousand years. They were in the most sacred of precincts of the whole span of the ancient Egyptian world.

Should they open the doors of the shrine? They shouldn't, in a sense they had no right to do so. Perhaps the thought crossed the mind of one of the now silent party that they should leave, retrace their steps and cover up the haunting sanctuary forever. But no matter how poignant and deeply affecting was the presence of that silent protective shrine, they had to enter it, penetrate it and discover its secrets. It might enclose, Carter told his associates, a nest of other gilded shrines, shell within shell, perhaps as many as five—if it were similar to the drawings in the Amherst Papyrus. The shrines would enclose a great sarcophagus containing coffins of gold and lapis lazuli, and within them would be the King himself, sleeping, yet ready every night to pass through the Underworld, illuminating the nether darkness by his royal presence.

So the two ebony bolts were drawn back, and slowly Carter pulled, at first gently and then, when the great double door would not budge, with increasing force. Nothing. And then, with Carter exerting almost all the power he could bring to bear, there was a sudden, abrupt movement, and the door jumped on its ancient hinges and swung back. The flashlight revealed a gossamer hanging of linen, so diaphanous that it seemed to be made of the very motes in the air. Suspended on the shroud were dozens of pure-gold rosettes, each the size of a coin. As Carter touched one, it fell into his hand as if waiting three thousand years to be plucked; he put it into his pocket. Ever so cautiously, he pushed back the linen to reveal the doors of another shrine—this one magnificently gilded and covered with hieroglyphs. And there in the center, upon two large bronze staples, was a neatly coiled and braided rope stamped with a perfectly intact seal of the royal necropolis— the jackal and the nine bound slaves. So, Carter observed in a hushed voice, the King had not been disturbed after all. That moment, he was to remark later, was easily the most thrilling of his entire life.

Between the doors of the outer and second shrines was a treasure trove of marvelous objects: what looked like staves, canes and several alabaster urns including one with a lion carved on top with a bright red tongue sticking out. It was "a beautiful little thing . . . a cat with a pink tongue I could scarcely take my eyes off," Lord Carnarvon was to say later— months later—when the official opening of the shrines was carried out before a breathless group of onlookers, none of whom, but one, ever suspected that the three had been there before. Would every shrine contain such treasures? So far it seemed as if every possible nook and cranny had been gorged with works of art.

In the crowded space between the shrines, standing apart, was a curious object shaped like the letter ꟽ with two softly curving roofs. Perplexed, Carter examined the object by flash-light. It was a box about the size of his hand, in solid gold decorated with two squatting images of King Tutankhamun, one facing the other, inlaid in lapis, carnelian and obsidian, each with a single tightly bound lock of deep lustrous black hair falling down the side of his head. It was a perfume box. To look at it today it is difficult to believe that a mere human being could possibly have made a thing of such radiant beauty and vitality. It fairly shines. In diminutive scale, the facial features of the King, in profile, are fashioned without hesitation or flaw. They seem to be carved or, indeed, almost extracted from the hard semiprecious stones in some mysterious manner. It was clear to Carter that it was unique in Egyptian art. He put it in his pocket to study it at leisure.

After touching the tightly coiled rope and its intact seal, the searchers carefully replaced the great gilded doors of the shrine and returned the bolts to their original positions. They made their way northward along what Carter had first believed to be a corridor, pausing to look down the right-hand side of the shrine. A startling vision appeared. They saw nine wooden oars lying on the floor, intended, Carter explained, to help the King navigate into the world of eternity. The oars had been systematically placed, and looked like magical footprints captured on the surface of a still river.

The walls of the Burial Chamber were covered with paintings in several rows, portraying the rituals for the preparation of the mummy and a scene of the traditional "weighing of the heart" to discover the King's true honesty and worth of character. The paintings were flaccid in style, hasty in execution, the only crude note in the tomb so far. Carter was disappointed. After having seen the magnificence of the treasures, he had expected something glorious. Their banal style was another clear sign that the tomb was something uncommon, wholly unlike the great shining halls of majesty that had been hewn out of the solid stone of the valley for several of the great New Kingdom kings—Seti I, Amenhotep III, Ramesses the Great. And to Carter it was the first indication of several that Tutankhamun had in all probability died unexpectedly, making it necessary to construct and finish the tomb hurriedly.

But if Carter was momentarily disappointed, he was not to

remain so for very long. He walked directly north in the area between the front of the shrine and the east wall of the chamber. At the northeast corner of the room, facing east, was an open door. He flashed his light inside, to find another room, almost square. And there, just inside, guarding the entry, virtually blocking it, was a large sculpture in black wood of the jackal god, Anubis, lying upon an elevated pedestal. It was almost shocking in its beauty. The head of the majestic beast was held high, watchful; its ears were erect, listening. Its gaze was intense, disturbing. Around the high thin neck of the beast hung a linen shroud reaching to the floor. It was one of the most impressive works of art Howard Carter had seen in his life.

As he made his way into the room, edging his body around the jackal, he ordered Carnarvon and Evelyn Herbert to be cautious where they stepped, for the floor was littered with small articles—lamps, reed baskets and little faience jars. Just behind the jackal lay a row of caskets, and on the floor beyond was a life-sized head of a cow, the goddess Hathor, with great shining golden horns. Behind that stood the most beautiful monument that Carter had ever seen. It was so lovely that it made him cry out with wonder and admiration.

The central portion of it consisted of a large shrine-shaped chest about eight feet high, completely overlaid with gold and surmounted by a cornice carved with images of the sacred cobra. Surrounding this, free-standing, were statues of four goddesses of the dead. Each was about three feet high. They were graceful creatures, with their arms held out protectively around the shrine. Their faces were so full of compassion that the excavators experienced a feeling of sacrilege just looking at them. Each side of the shrine was guarded by one of the goddesses. The figures at the front and the back kept their gaze firmly fixed upon the side of the shrine, but the other two were looking sideways and over their shoulders toward the entrance of the room, as though watching against intrusion. There was a simple grandeur about the monument that appealed irresistibly to Carter's imagination. He said later that he was not ashamed to confess that it brought a lump to his throat.

What could the shrine possibly contain? Carter explained that it was in all likelihood the so-called canopic chest which enclosed four jars holding the mummified remains of the vital organs of the King—heart, lungs, liver and viscera. According to ancient rituals of mummification, these were always stored outside the sarcophagus.

The flashlight illuminated the rest of the square chamber, which Carter christened the Treasury. Chests, caskets and tall, thin, ominous-looking black boxes, closed and sealed, were standing against all sides of the room. And on top of them were several dozen boats, as if the room were somehow the surface of the Nile itself, with a flotilla ready to set sail. Some were simple little vessels like sampans, others full-fledged sailboats with complex rigging and sails furled, looking as if one had only to give the command and a crew of a hundred or more would prepare them for their voyage.

In the northwest corner of the room were what Carter thought to be two golden chariots, similar to those in the Antechamber. It appeared to the searchers that the thieves had not opened more than two or three of the thirty caskets that lined the walls of the Treasury. They opened one of the unsealed boxes and saw a pile of gold jewelry inlaid with semiprecious stones and glass of many colors. One of the necklaces was in the shape of a vulture flying through the air. As they touched the magnificent necklace, once again it seemed they were back thousands of years in time and fully in tune with the sanctity and reverence of a long-vanished religion. The piece was so astonishingly fresh that it seemed the King had just removed it from his neck that very day. Time had ceased to exist.

One of the tall black shrines was slightly ajar. The flashlight revealed a most astonishing sight. Inside, in diminutive form, were two nearly identical wooden, golden statuettes of the King standing upon the backs of fierce black leopards. Both were wrapped in linen sheets. What did they mean? Carter was not sure, since he had never seen anything quite like them before. But he guessed that the twin images had to have something to do with the nightly passage of the King through the Underworld.

Hours must have passed since the party of four had entered the tomb and searched through its four chambers. One can imagine their exhaustion, not only from the emotional strain but from the shock—a pleasurable yet enervating shock—following the exhilaration of the discovery. All must now have realized they had insufficient strength to go on. And they no doubt felt that they dare not examine too many of the works of art for fear that the officials from the Service of Antiquities might discover their illicit presence. So they carefully made their way through the Burial Chamber, pausing momentarily to gaze in silence at the mysterious shrine with its closed doors, then back through the tiny hole Carter and Callender had forced through the lower part of the entry made so many centuries ago by the thieves. Carter must have breathlessly described to Callender what he and the others had seen as the two of them replaced the stone blocks covered with plaster and parts of the necropolis seals. Finally, Carter picked up the lid of a large reed basket lying near one of the sentinels of the King and leaned it, along with a bundle of loose reeds, against the wall to cover *their* entry hole.

Just before climbing out of the opening in the inner doorway to leave the passageway, they might have crouched for a final few minutes saying nothing, preoccupied with their own thoughts.

On the threshold of the Antechamber, Carter looked down and found a beautiful and poetic work of art—a marvelous alabaster chalice. He translated the hieroglyphs surrounding the membrane-thin rim of the bowl which represented a white lotus, open. He called it the King's "wishing cup," for the inscription wished him "millions of years happily enjoying the cool breezes from the north and his eyes beholding felicity." Then they left, taking the magnificent "wishing cup" with them, reclosed the hole, mounted their donkeys, and rode home down the valley, strangely silent and subdued.

CHAPTER TEN

Revelations

IN THE FIRST VOLUME OF *The Tomb of Tut-ank-Amen*, published in 1923, Carter reported that on the following day, November 27, the group was at the site early in the morning, for much work had to be done. In fact there is strong likelihood that none of them had gone to bed at all, except perhaps for an hour or two of rest at most. The evening before, just before entering the Antechamber, Carter had written a hasty note to the inspector, Rex Engelbach, advising him of the final clearing of the inner doorway, and asking him to make an official inspection. The note was delivered to the local headquarters of the Service of Antiquities at Luxor too late in the evening for Engelbach to respond.

The timing was probably deliberate. On November 27 Engelbach was occupied with official duties, and around noon the local inspector of antiquities, a gentleman by the name of Ibrahim Effendi, came in his stead. By the time he had arrived, all traces of the entry and examination of the night before had been obliterated or sufficiently disguised. To read in Howard Carter's book the pages on the events of the day after their entry, one would never suspect that the party had taken affairs wholly in its own hands, just hours before, and had not indeed waited patiently for the inspector's arrival. The account is utterly convincing. Were it not for evidence in the unpublished draft of an article that Lord Carnarvon wrote for *The Times* of London, which described the breaking down of the inner-chamber doorway and the objects they saw, and two other fascinating pieces of evidence, one would have fully believed Carter's story: that he had examined with the Egyptian official the sealed door between the statues and with considerable disappointment had discovered that a small opening had been made by the thieves; and that despite his urgent desire to break through he had reluctantly but firmly decided to wait until he had cleared the Antechamber.

Except for Howard Carter, Lord Carnarvon, Lady Evelyn Herbert and Pecky Callender, and the foremen who presumably had waited outside, no one seems ever before to have been aware of their unorthodox actions and the entirely false image imparted by Carter's publication. Or if anyone outside of this group did know the facts, he or she kept it a secret. But there was one exception. This was the director of the Chemical Department of the Egyptian government, Alfred Lucas, who at the time of the discovery was taking three months' terminal leave prior to retiring from government service. Lucas joined the expedition on December 20, 1922, and worked initially for three months and then sporadically throughout the ten years that it took to remove the incredible amounts of material from the tomb. In 1947, at an advanced age, eight years after the death of Howard Carter, Alfred Lucas wrote three short notes in various editions of the official journal of the Egyptian Antiquities Service, *Annales du Service des Antiquités de l'Égypte*, regarding certain statements made by Carter in his official publication. They are extraordinarily revealing.

One note discusses the issue of the thieves' penetration into the Burial Chamber. Lucas observes that "a considerable amount of mystery was made about this robbers' hole. When I first saw the tomb about December 20th, the hole was hidden by the basketwork tray, or lid, and some rushes taken from the floor that Mr. Carter had placed before it." And Lucas observes that "Mr. Carter, Lord Carnarvon, his daughter certainly entered the Burial Chamber and the store chamber, which latter had no door, before the formal opening." The formal opening was held three days after the evening of November 26—on the twenty-ninth.

Then, in another issue of the *Annales du Service,* also of 1947, Lucas wrote again about the mysterious hole leading to the Burial Chamber:

> With reference to the robbers' hole in the door of the burial chamber I stated that "Lord Carnarvon, his daughter and Mr. Carter certainly entered the burial chamber," and that the photo mentioned earlier shows the hole closed.
>
> This leaves to the imagination the identity of the person who closed the door and the date when it was closed, and to that extent is ambiguous, an ambiguity that I now wish to remove. Carter's published statement that the hole had been filled up and re-sealed is misleading. The hole, unlike that in the outermost doorway, had not been closed and re-sealed by the cemetery officials, but by Mr. Carter. Soon after I commenced work with Mr. Carter (on December 20th) he pointed out to me the closing and re-sealing, and when I said that it did not look like old work he admitted that it was not and that he had done it.

Lucas concluded his observations about the entry by the four searchers by stating that the magnificent perfume box Carter had found in the space between the first and second shrines was definitely not found in the sarcophagus "as stated by Mr. Carter." "I saw it," Lucas wrote, "at Mr. Carter's house before the official opening . . . and evidently it was found when Lord Carnarvon and Mr. Carter first penetrated into the burial chamber."

Why none of the dozen or so writers about the tomb of Tutankhamun and its discovery since 1947 ever mentioned Alfred Lucas' observations is incomprehensible. Either they deliberately chose to overlook the damaging evidence for the sake of the reputations of Howard Carter and Lord Carnarvon or, far more plausible, they simply did not know of the existence of the comments. After all, *Annales du Service* is an obscure publication studied normally only by professional Egyptologists. Furthermore, it would have been thought highly unlikely that such things occurring in 1922 would be described by one of the participants as late as 1947.

In the existing letters between Lord Carnarvon and Howard Carter, there is no reference to their marvelous adventure. But in a letter written to Carter by Lady Evelyn on the twenty-seventh of December 1922, one month and a day from their entry into the tomb, on her return with her father to England for a brief Christmas vacation, the splendid and secret experience is revealed. In warm, affectionate words, Evelyn Herbert praises Carter and wishes him the best of everything in his life—happiness and continuing success as a man of history. She mirthfully tells him that when her father had reached the point of exhaustion, all she had to do to restore him to full vigor was to describe, over and over, their entry into the tomb and its Holy of Holies. Her thanks to Carter for allowing her to have penetrated the tomb are effusive. It was for Evelyn Herbert the single most memorable and gripping event in her life. From that letter, at least, it is evident that the young girl had developed what can only be described as a temporary infatuation for the older archaeologist.

CHAPTER ELEVEN

The Limelight

WHETHER OR NOT THE four collaborators entered the Holy of Holies and the Treasury again prior to the "official opening" of the Burial Chamber months later is not known, but it is unlikely. After Ibrahim Effendi had inspected the tomb on November 27 there would have been little opportunity to do so. From that time onward there was a member of the Service of Antiquities on the site every day. Carter would not have dared disturb the camouflage of the basket lid and the bunch of reeds, for that would have given their secret away and would have seriously and perhaps permanently jeopardized their license.

The word that an incredible discovery had been made in the "barren" and "thoroughly exhausted" Valley of the Kings spread almost instantly throughout Egypt. "All sorts of extraordinary and fanciful reports were going abroad concerning it," Carter observed, "and one story, that found considerable credence among the natives, being to the effect that three aeroplanes had landed in the Valley, and gone off to some destination unknown with loads of treasure."

To quell the disturbing rumors that the excavators had broken in and stolen some treasures, Lord Carnarvon and Carter staged an official opening of the tomb on November 29, without asking the Antiquities Service for permission. On their own they issued invitations to Lord Allenby, the British High Commissioner for Egypt; the Egyptian governor of the province, Abd-el-Aziz Bey Yehia; the *mamur*, or police chief, of the district, Mohammed Bey Fahmy; and "a number of other Egyptian notables and officials." Neither Pierre Lacau nor his second-in-command, Paul Tottenham, the adviser to the Ministry of Public Works for cultural and archaeological affairs, was asked. They came the day after and made an official inspection. It is a mystery why Carnarvon and Carter failed to consult the Antiquities Service about the public opening. It may not have occurred to them, because by that time they believed the tomb of Tutankhamun to be *their* tomb, which they had discovered and paid for. And, of course, Carter and Carnarvon had little affection for Pierre Lacau or his associates. They compounded their blunder by inviting only one member of the world press, Arthur Merton, head of the London *Times* bureau in Egypt and a personal friend of Howard Carter. Not a single member of the Egyptian press was told of the most breathtaking discovery in the history of Egyptology. No one representing Europe or America was allowed in on the exclusive "formal" discovery. The chief correspondent for *The New York Times*, a peppery man by the name of A. H. Bradstreet, was enraged when he learned of the London *Times*'s spectacular scoop. Thus, in a monumental example of bad judgment, insensitivity and thoughtlessness, Lord Carnarvon and Howard Carter alienated the very people whom they would need as friends and sympathizers in the future.

The exclusive dispatch from the London *Times*, sent "by runner from the Valley of the Kings," created a world-wide sensation and initiated one of the longest-lasting news stories in the history of journalism, one that would continue unabated almost daily and weekly for eight years, and sporadically ever since. Arthur Merton described the find as "the most sensational discovery of the century." The next day the international news agency Reuters, as well as the Egyptian newspapers and the rest of the world press, seized upon the incredible story.

The discovery was called "the most sensational in Egyptology," a treasure worth "millions of pounds sterling." And, from the outset, certain inaccuracies cropped up that would plague Carter and his patron for years. Some papers stated that "important papyri" and historical documents had been found in the tomb and that it was "intact."

From the moment the first newspaper stories appeared, the lives of Lord Carnarvon and Howard Carter and the image of Tutankhamun were to change drastically, tracked minute by minute by the intense searchlight of publicity. Under that harsh and unrelenting scrutiny, only one of the three would flourish.

To Carter the excitement was deeply puzzling, even embarrassing. He could never quite comprehend how archaeology, normally an activity of intense interest only to the specialist and something that up to that time had engendered only tepid politeness among others, could conceivably become something so enormously interesting to the entire world. Carter found it bewildering to meet highly paid correspondents every hour of the day reporting upon his every movement and "hiding round corners to surprise a secret" out of him. He figured that the interest had been brought about by the public's boredom with the news about tedious mandates, reparations, political conferences and treaties of the postwar era. But the fascination had far deeper roots. The discovery appealed to the general public as it had to Carter himself when he first gazed with disbelief at the mountain of gold in the Antechamber and worried whether or not the true prize—the mummy of the King itself—would be discovered. And of course the very name Egypt conjured up a host of mysterious, spine-tingling thoughts far removed from the annoyances of daily life. The essence of the appeal lay in its history, its magical remoteness, and the presence there of the most exotic treasure of all time.

Telegrams, letters, messages from almost every country on earth inundated the excavators. Cables and letters of congratulation came first, followed by offers of assistance, ranging from advice in tomb planning to requests to join the party as personal valets. Hundreds of requests for souvenirs—a grain of sand, a bar of gold or two—descended upon the excavators. Zany offers of money, of a small partnership arrangement, suggestions on contracts for movie rights and fashion copyrights were received. The excavators were advised how to preserve their discoveries, and how to placate the swarm of evil spirits that were no doubt "looming up on all sides." Carter would open a batch of letters and would encounter an outpouring of "would-be facetious communications," criticisms that he had committed sacrilege, and dozens of pretentions to family relationship—"surely you must be the cousin who lived in Camberwell in 1893, and whom we never heard of since." One letter solemnly inquired whether or not the discovery of the tomb would be able to throw any light upon the recent alleged Belgian atrocities in the Congo.

If the press reaction and the arrival in Luxor and in the valley itself of a horde of reporters and commentators put the excavators on edge, the tourists pushed them over the brink into near-panic. The valley had always attracted tourists, to be sure. Indeed, since the early 1900s travelers had arrived by the hundreds in the romantic precinct in the late fall and early winter. But before Tutankhamun the tourists had been fairly disciplined. They had observed the sights in the valley dutifully, faces buried in their guidebooks, following their official guides like sheep, listening, nodding, turning on cue to clamber up the next hillock and into the next tomb. Carter had known them very well. But when he had taken groups of tourists through the valley he had been "in command." He had set the pace—a very systematic pace. Now, with the discovery of Tutankhamun, Carter was overcome by an unruly throng of visitors who came at all hours, seldom with a guide—with all types of demands, backed by excuses and subterfuges of all kinds. Nobody wanted to learn about the tomb or Tutankhamun; they just wanted to say they had been there.

Visitors would start toward the valley from Luxor at five-thirty or six in the morning and arrive by horse cart, donkey cart, sand cart and even automobile just when Carter was about to begin the day's work. At times, a frightful clamor in several languages would arise about who had the right to sit on what section of the retaining wall surrounding the tomb's entrance. The tourists would remain all day in the blinding heat, reading, talking, knitting, working on crossword puzzles, vacantly staring off into the cliffs and the dried-out tributaries of the valley, waiting patiently for a dramatic event. This seldom happened. But it seemed to be sufficient reward for most just to stare down into the darkened entrance of the tomb and listen to the movements and the muffled voices of the excavators.

Whenever Carter and his associates removed an object from the tomb, a flurry of activity would ensue. Everything would be thrown aside for a glimpse. At times the stone parapet seemed about to collapse upon the excavators. The constant buzz of the tourists added to the sounds of the real insects which they already had suffered in profusion. The clicking of cameras and cries of "Turn it this way, please" became a constant, annoying and even debilitating refrain.

The special guests, armed with a wide variety of entrees, particularly bothered Howard Carter. Hundreds of letters of introduction would come in from friends or friends of friends whom Carter never realized he had possessed. Some came from individuals who had a legitimate claim upon him, others came from people with fabricated claims. They rolled in from ministers or departmental officials in Cairo, from members of clubs, fraternities or archaeological societies, or just from single individuals who bluntly insisted upon instant entry or who would arrive ingeniously disguised as telegraph boys or special messengers and then would barter for just one peek.

The urge to visit *inside* the tomb became an obsession based upon pride and social and even political status. A number of American politicians who had experienced difficulty obtaining entry expressed alarm that they would lose ground with their constituents if they could not somehow enter, even if only for two minutes. Senator Oscar W. Underwood of Alabama said, "I hope Lord Carnarvon will permit me to visit the tomb he

[has] discovered, as it would be a great disappointment to find it sealed up after traveling seventy-six hundred miles to be there." Some personages, political or otherwise, who did receive a personal tour from Carter infuriated him when he heard them exclaim afterward, well within earshot, "Well, there wasn't much to see, anyway!" He deplored the waste of time spent in guiding each visitor around and considered each of them to be a potential vandal.

As the requests grew and the hordes descended, any visitor he did not personally approve he snubbed or ignored. Carter would, in time, pay a terrible price for his attitude.

CHAPTER TWELVE

"Discovery Colossal and Need Every Assistance"

CARTER WAS TO REMARK to friends over the years that his excitement about the tomb diminished when he contemplated the condition of the Annex with its confused mound of treasures. He realized that years of the most delicate work lay before him. He was sobered and, at times, depressed by the thought. He had, in a sense, entered a new career, involving wholly new techniques of archaeology.

Despite his multiple experiences in the field, Carter had nothing really to draw upon in dealing with the tomb of Tutankhamun. Up to that time, he had invariably dealt with discoveries which were easily dispensed with in a few weeks or a quarter of a season at most. Here he had found something that he was totally unprepared for—something that he doubted any group of human beings, much less professional archaeologists, could carry out.

To repair just one royal robe embellished with hundreds of gold sequins would take two months. Just the thought of that tangled mass of gilded chariots at the southeast corner of the Antechamber numbed him. There were, in fact, countless things to be accomplished before he could remove even the smallest object from the Antechamber. Preservatives and packing materials had to be obtained, experts in conservation enlisted. He would have to find specialists in texts and inscriptions, for volumes of hieroglyphs seemed to cover every object. A laboratory had to be set up, storerooms acquired, guardhouses constructed. Electrical power had to be generated; a photographic studio and a darkroom had to be assembled. Draftsmen and cataloguers were vitally needed. Howard Carter was a single, free-lance archaeologist. Where would he get the assistance?

He dismissed the idea of calling upon the members of the Antiquities Service. Their competence was questionable and their points of view were incompatible with his. He never even considered seeking help from the British Museum or any other archaeological institution of Great Britain. The obvious choice—the only choice—was the Metropolitan Museum of Art. Its officials had been vigorous and highly effective in persuading the United States Department of State to apply pressure upon the Egyptian government not to alter the law relating to the fifty-fifty division of discoveries. The Metropolitan had an exceptional Egyptological staff. For one, there was Herbert Winlock, who had supplied Carter with an invaluable clue to the presence of the tomb in the valley in a graceful and typically selfless manner.

The best archaeological photographer in the business was also at the Metropolitan. This was Harry Burton, a sprightly, energetic man who could handle as many cameras at one time as a topflight circus juggler could balance plates. He was legendary for being able to coax out of semidarkness the most brilliant glass negatives that anybody had ever seen, carrying on all the while the most animated dialogue with himself and simultaneously flicking away flies and picking tiny pieces of sand off his plates with unerring dexterity. The genius of Harry Burton lay not only in his technical skill, nor even in his placid temperament, which was described by a colleague as "perfectly suited to archaeological affairs—you know, the isolation, the cramped quarters, the ability to work sometimes with a bunch of people who are about as fascinating as railroad ties,'' but in the fact that Burton was of the opinion that two distinct styles of photography had to be mastered in archaeology, the scientific and the aesthetic. He was able to capture the technical aspects of an object he photographed, just as he could capture its sheer beauty. Harry Burton was one of those rare human beings who sought for and achieved harmony between science and art.

The Metropolitan had other personnel who would be advantageous to Carter, too. There was A. C. Mace, a tall, gangling, introspective man who was thought by those in the profession to be a genius in conservation and who was also a nephew of Carter's mentor, Sir Flinders Petrie. And the museum had the perfect drafting team in Walter Hauser and Lindsley Hall. A friend had once jokingly observed that if the fiercest desert sandstorm in the annals of Egypt were to hit while Hauser and Hall were making line drawings of the reliefs of some temple, they would copy with verisimilitude not only the carvings but also every single grain of sand—in correct size, proportion, direction and velocity.

These professional factors aside, Carter and Carnarvon both recognized that for years they had been involved in a special financial relationship with the Metropolitan Museum of Art, which up to now has been one of the best-kept secrets in the history of the institution. This relationship surely put the two men under some obligation.

Lord Carnarvon also wanted to enlist two personal friends— Sir Alan Gardiner, a British Egyptologist, and a brilliant American from the Oriental Institute of Chicago, Professor James Henry Breasted, an indomitable Egyptologist, surely the preeminent archaeologist of his day, who combined the most profound sense of scholarship with an enticing wit. Breasted's specialty was deciphering hieroglyphs and unraveling the infinite subtleties of the ancient Egyptian language. He was so gifted in this that someone once remarked that James Breasted's only profound sorrow in life must have been that, early in puberty, he had become aware there were few others in his neighborhood who could carry on a conversation for longer than a few minutes in the language of the Middle Kingdom. Carter readily approved of both men.

Carter himself soon had what he considered to be a marvelous piece of good fortune. This came in the form of Alfred Lucas, the director of the Chemical Department of the Egyptian government, who offered his services for conservation work. The offer from Lucas was quickly accepted.

While the team was being assembled, Carter closed the tomb once more by filling it up to the first step. A detachment of Egyptian soldiers was placed on round-the-clock guard duty. To look after *them*, Carter hired his own native guardians. When Lord Carnarvon and Lady Evelyn Herbert departed from the site on the fourth of December for England to spend the Christmas holidays at Highclere, Carter journeyed to Cairo to purchase the equipment, including a gate of thick steel bars for the inner doorway. Pecky Callender remained, spending most of his time guarding the invisible entrance to the fabulous treasure with a loaded rifle on his knees.

Carter sent a telegram to Albert Lythgoe, who was in London: "Discovery colossal and need every assistance. Could you consider loan of Burton . . . ?" Lythgoe immediately cabled back that he was "only too delighted to assist in every possible way. Please call on Burton and any other members of our staff." And in a few days he followed up his immediate offer of help with a letter in which he stressed that any help he and his staff could give Carter in his "present great undertaking" would give them "the greatest pleasure and satisfaction." Lythgoe wanted it absolutely understood that there would be "no question of remuneration" for any member of the Metropolitan Museum staff engaged in work on the tomb of Tutankhamun. The trustees of the Museum had been "most anxious to demonstrate their deep appreciation in some adequate way for all Lord Carnarvon and [Carter] have done" for the institution in recent years.

The Metropolitan's plans for its own digs that season could

not possibly have fitted in more felicitously with the crisis of Carter's discovery. The major sites were to have remained at more or less of a standsill anyway, Mace and Winlock having planned to concentrate instead on some unpromising tombs of the Eleventh Dynasty near Thebes. Lythgoe encouraged Carter to make immediate arrangements to obtain Mace, Burton and Hauser, which would provide "the nucleus at least of your assisting force." He also gave Carter virtual carte blanche over every single member of the Metropolitan's Egyptological staff to use in any way he saw fit. Simultaneously, Lythgoe wired Winlock at the Continental Hotel in Cairo, instructing him to do *everything possible* for Howard Carter.

Everyone who had described the arrangement seems to have praised it as one of the most selfless and cooperative acts in the history of archaeology. At first it was just that, but later it became a firm pact of mutual self-interest, coldly calculated by both sides in order to achieve the greatest monetary and artistic gain.

In Cairo, Carter also purchased an automobile, a storehouse of special equipment, photographic material, chemicals, and packing boxes of every description, along with thirty-two bales of calico and more than a mile of wadding and two miles of surgical bandages. While he was there, the peripatetic Professor James Henry Breasted was hurrying to the valley, for he had received a letter from Lord Carnarvon inviting him to come to the excavation. With his son Charles, he rushed to the site but saw nothing particularly invigorating. All he could see was a freshly excavated pit, walled on three sides. In the middle of the area was a pile of stones surmounted by a chunk of limestone on which someone had painted the coat of arms of the house of Carnarvon. There was Callender with his rifle, sitting impassively. From time to time a tourist would look casually into the hole and "in the gleaming hot sun," Breasted observed, "would note chiefly the huge beads of perspiration upon Mr. Callender's uncovered and balding head."

Carter returned to Luxor on the fifteenth of December and went directly to the Breasteds' houseboat to tell the great archaeologist, firsthand, the story of the find. Breasted's eyes glistened with joy as Carter described the final days before the opening of the Antechamber, without speaking about his entry into all of the chambers. In the course of this conversation, according to Breasted, Carter exclaimed, "Think of it! Twice before I had come within two yards of that first stone step! The first time was years ago when I was digging for Davis, and he suggested that we shift our work to some 'more promising spot.' The second was only a few seasons ago when Lord Carnarvon and I decided to reserve clearance of this area for a time when we wouldn't interfere with visitors to the tomb of Ramesses VI."

Breasted was stirred as Carter portrayed his emotions during the first seconds of looking into the tomb, and recalled that Carter's "voice failed him." Carter pulled out an old letter from his pocket and sketched the ground plan of the tomb's Antechamber and Annex with a number of the monuments *in situ*. Breasted told him that he must have found a cache—an indescribably rich one, but a cache nevertheless. Breasted even suggested that no mummy would be found, even behind the sealed northern door. But Carter quietly told him that he simply could not agree, and he said no more.

As Carter departed, he instructed Breasted and his son Charles "to cross the river, on the third day from today, as if on a routine visit to the Theban temples, climb the mountain as if for a view—and then drop down into the valley. Plan to reach the tomb at three o'clock in the afternoon. Bring with you a complete change of underclothes—the temperature in the tomb is still such that after only a brief stay in it, one comes forth dripping with perspiration!"

On the appointed day James and Charles Breasted went to the tomb entrance and met Carter, Callender, Burton and Herbert Winlock, who was accompanied by his wife and one of his daughters. In the ten days since the Breasteds had first visited the site, the guards' shack had been finished, the stairway and the passage had been cleared of tons of debris, and chairs had been placed at the head of the stone stairway,

"Everything wore a purposeful, business-like air," as Charles Breasted observed in his memoirs.

Extraordinary tension gripped the visitors. Those who had not seen or had not even had a decent description of the tomb were nervous and stiff in the company of their old acquaintances. A perfunctory exchange of commonplaces took place, and finally Carter stepped to the head of the stairs and said, "Are we ready? Come, please."

The party descended the stairs and followed the gently sloping passageway, to arrive at the great steel gate that Carter had had erected over the inner doorway. He had draped it with a white sheet and had turned on a battery of electric lights inside the tomb. A magical glow seemed to emanate from within, passing through the white sheet, on which only the forbidding silhouettes of the steel bars could be seen. It was almost as if a membrane of time clouded infinite spaces beyond. Carter paused. Then, taking hold of the opaque sheet at the upper left-hand corner of the doorway, where, he pointed out, the robbers had forced their entry thousands of years before, he smoothly pulled the sheet aside.

The effect was shattering, wholly unlike Carter's first impression weeks earlier when a confusing medley of half-recognizable shapes and colors came slowly into his cognizance out of the mists. The shock was breathtaking, so sudden and dramatic that the observers staggered back a few paces. Carter was immensely amused to see that his *coup de théâtre* had been so successful.

To Breasted, it was an absolutely "incredible vision"—a totally impossible sight. It wasn't real; it was a fairy tale, a peculiar combination of fantasy and truth. He felt as if he had, without warning, stumbled upon the vast and wholly enchanted property room of a theater packed with opulent sets made for a wildly imaginative opera.

The onlookers cried out in amazement. Carter had given the principal objects—the couches, the great silent sentinels, the cluster of alabasters and the golden throne—full illumination. The lights had been deftly placed so that the treasures seemed to leap out from the soft brown limestone walls. The visitors were gazing at what seemed an unreal, three-dimensional mosaic made from hundreds of tesserae of sublime colors—golds, browns, yellows, blues, ambers, russets and blacks.

Carter took his time unlocking the profusion of chains with which he had secured the steel gate. The harsh rattling of the metal and the chattering sounds of the massive links being dragged through the bars failed to break the spell that had fallen upon the mesmerized spectators. Carter turned to his guests and in a quiet voice said, "Will you not enter?" The group hesitated. It seemed as though were they actually to enter the sanctuary, the treasures within would all vanish. Finally they went in, followed by Carter. Once inside, James Breasted and Herbert Winlock stood for a time, immobilized. When at last they turned and looked into Carter's eyes, the tears welled up into the eyes of all three. For a moment no one could speak. Then there was a babble of voices uttering congratulations and outbursts of laughter, while they continued to rub the tears from their eyes.

Breasted recalled that he could only shake Carter's hand repeatedly. He struggled to control his emotions and tried to replace them with the "processes of professional observation," but could not. His critical faculties were defeated, and he "surrendered to the act of just looking, without system or reason, at the profusion of majestic objects." He perceived that he was experiencing a revelation of ancient life that surpassed anything any modern man had ever seen up to that time. Before him lay a magnificence which none but the ancient Egyptian civilization could have dreamed up or achieved. Nothing in the whole range of archaeological endeavor, Breasted thought, could possibly have equaled the drama of his first view of what he recognized had to be Tutankhamun's tomb.

The chariots particularly intrigued Breasted, for although they were totally covered with gold leaf and plate, hammered into reliefs of the most accomplished style, and were encrusted with a host of semiprecious stones and inlays, the wheels bore distinct traces of use. They had clearly been driven "over the rough streets of Thebes" and were therefore not just ornamental pieces prepared for the King's afterlife, something hollow and lifeless.

The party wandered slowly—at first rather dreamily—from one great work of art to another, astounded at what they found. Nothing like it had ever been discovered before in the full course of art history! The two "sentinel" images of the King astonished them with their calm yet penetrating presences. Breasted remarked that in spite of their sumptuous gilding, oxidation had invested the royal figures with something of the "somber livery of the burnished sun" under which the King had lived.

Winlock's ten-year-old daughter, Frances, armed with a flashlight, was allowed to scurry through the hole into the Annex. She lay on her stomach with her feet peeking out of the portal, flashing the light at the staggering array of treasures and calling out, "Daddy, gold, gold, gold!" It became impossible for her mother to persuade or even order the hypnotized youngster to leave her magical station, and so finally she had to be pulled out by her heels.

As they examined the stupendous contents of the chamber, the visitors became increasingly aware of the ravages of the ancient thieves. The heavy gold openwork embellishing much of the furniture had been wrenched away. The gold plate of the chariots had been attacked with pry bars. Stoppers from the alabaster vases lay strewn all over the floor. As the thieves had made their exit they had picked up a small couch designed for common household usage and, perhaps angered to find that it was not decorated with gold plate, had apparently tossed it violently against the west wall, where it bounced back down on top of one of the animal couches. It had come to rest on one of the horns of the head of the beast, which now stuck through the plaited thongs of the couch's seat.

Carter and Lord Carnarvon had a theory about just when the robberies had taken place. Carnarvon had emphasized in a special London *Times* interview that the tomb had been entered and ransacked during the reign of Ramesses IX, a king of the Nineteenth Dynasty—hundreds of years after the great empire had passed. Carter was utterly convinced there had not been a single episode of tomb robbery of any monarch of the Eighteenth Dynasty during its evolution because the awesome power, wealth and dedication of those rulers would have prevented it. He argued that since there had been not a single allusion to tomb robbing in documents of the Eighteenth Dynasty, but many during the breakdown of discipline in the Nineteenth, Twentieth, and Twenty-first Dynasties, all break-ins had taken place after the great kings had relinquished their supreme authority. Carter also claimed that he had even discovered one seal impression dating to the specific time of Ramesses IX.

Carter's theory is inexplicable. One wonders why he ever thought he could even propose it, much less support it for long. It would appear that the statements by Carnarvon and Carter that the tomb had been violated long after the burial of the King were part of their efforts to underscore the fact that the sanctuary was definitely not intact.

The Antiquities Service generally defined a defiled royal tomb as one that had been penetrated during the disordered epoch of the enfeebled rulers of the Nineteenth through the Twenty-first Dynasties. Carter and Lord Carnarvon apparently feared what might happen if it could be proven that the tomb of Tutankhamun had been defiled during the Eighteenth Dynasty itself. The tomb might technically be defined as *intact*, with the appalling result that the standard division of treasures would be eliminated for the excavators.

Breasted, fascinated by the question, hoped to determine precisely when the thieves had done their work. In the weeks to come, he was to return to the Antechamber time and again. One day, while working alone on the deciphering of seals, he suffered a terrifying experience. Absorbed in the difficult task of attempting to piece together the plaster fragments from the resealing of the hole in the north wall, he began to hear a strange rustling, a soft whistling sound rising, falling and dying away as if a pair of bellows in some far-off world were being gently pressed inward and outward. After a while he was able to convince himself that the sounds were "melancholy changes" taking place in the ancient sepulcher. The air, undisturbed for thousands of years, was being gradually displaced by the atmosphere of the present day. And a metamorphosis was taking place, minute by minute, in the physical and chemical properties of the objects contained within the tomb. The wood in the furniture, caskets and statues was adjusting to the arrival of new, alien air, resulting in an audible rustling and an occasional muffled snap. Sitting alone, listening to the sounds of change, Breasted was saddened. He ruminated on the "inexorable manifestations of the beginning of slow death. All this meant," he realized, "that the life of the superlatively beautiful things around me was limited: a few generations more, those objects not of pottery, stone or metal would steadily deteriorate."

As he puzzled over the fragments of the seal impressions made weeks after the death of "the benign ruler who had dominated the known world in the days when the Hebrews were captives in Egypt and when their leader Moses had not yet been born," Breasted happened to look into the face of one of the two royal guardians. Suddenly one of the sentinels winked! Breasted almost fainted. At length he got the courage to get up and take a look at the statue. Only when he was close at hand did he see the reason for its frightening behavior. Attached to a virtually invisible filament hanging from the King's eyebrow was a tiny piece of dark pigment dropping off in iridescent, micalike flakes. In a gentle breeze that had momentarily passed through the entrance into the Antechamber, the minute flake of ancient paint, shivering slightly, had mirrored the light in such a way that it resembled the wink of the eye.

Breasted, in tracking the thieves, examined the seals on all doorways, for there he believed the positive evidence as to the exact historical moment when the tomb was plundered would be unearthed. Carter encouraged him. Breasted found only two types of seals on the doorways; one was Tutankhamun's, the other the standard seal of the royal necropolis. Breasted also studied the seals on the north partition. He didn't observe the hole that Carter and Callender had forced through the bottom of the thieves' penetration, simply because he was unwilling to disturb the basket lid and the reeds—which Breasted apparently never realized had been stacked there by Carter himself.

After a thorough investigation—a "Sherlock Holmes case of unusual interest"—Breasted presented his conclusion to Carter: the tomb of Tutankhamun had been penetrated once, for sure, and possibly a second time, during the Eighteenth Dynasty, when one would have expected that such an activity would be impossible, a time when powerful rulers utterly desirous and eminently capable of protecting the tombs of their ancestors held sway.

Breasted demonstrated that the seal identified by Carter to be that of Ramesses IX was actually a fragmentary one of Tutankhamun. Breasted took issue with Carter's statement that no Eighteenth-Dynasty tomb had been defiled during the New Empire, and reminded him that surely he must know that a tomb of at least one other king of the Eighteenth Dynasty, Thutmose IV, had been robbed, and restored and resealed during the empire—under one of Tutankhamun's successors, Haremhab. For this specific tomb had been discovered by none other than Howard Carter himself. Haremhab had even left a record of his pious deed on the wall of Thutmose's tomb. To this Carter exclaimed, "My God, I never thought of *that!*"

Breasted told Carter that it was highly unlikely that the thieves who had entered the tomb of Thutmose IV were the same as those who had penetrated Tutankhamun's. The former had been apprehended by the officials of the valley during the early reign of Haremhab. Breasted pointed out to Carter that the huts of the workmen who had constructed Ramesses VI's tomb lay directly across the mouth of Tutankhamun's tomb; this showed without a doubt that the latter had been covered over and forgotten long before the reign of Ramesses IX and the period of rampant robberies. To this obvious fact

Carter once again exclaimed to Breasted, "My God, I never thought of *that!*"

Neither Carter nor Lord Carnarvon ever attempted to correct their story in the London *Times* stating that they firmly believed the tomb had been defiled hundreds of years after the funeral. In the text of the first volume of *The Tomb of Tut-ank-Amen,* Carter avoided mentioning Breasted's evidence. He stated that plunderers had entered, and entered more than once, not later than the reign of Ramesses VI. But in a footnote to the main text, Carter stated without attribution or credit of any kind that he had become convinced the tomb could not have been resealed any later than a decade after the interment of the King.

But the footnote obscures the facts, for Carter must have known that *if* Haremhab had attempted to set things in order in the tomb of his predecessor, it must have been even earlier than ten to fifteen years after the burial. For, within a year or two after he became pharaoh, Haremhab had already become deeply committed to a program of obliterating all records mentioning Tutankhamun.

CHAPTER THIRTEEN

The Affair
of the Three Princesses

WHILE HOWARD CARTER BOUGHT his equipment and started to assemble his team, Lord Carnarvon and his daughter Evelyn made their way by ship to Marseilles and then by train to England. Off the volcanic island of Stromboli, Carnarvon composed a letter for Howard Carter which was warm, chatty and, on the surface, routine. Lord Carnarvon was occupied primarily with sending his best wishes for the upcoming holiday; expressing the hope that Carter's recent cold would be swiftly cured; passing on the information that a plum pudding had been left for him at his hotel in Cairo; and assuring Carter that Sir Alan Gardiner would be arriving on the site shortly after Christmas. But the communication contains two short passages of great interest, both extraordinarily revealing about the personal relationship between the two men. The letter also tips off the existence of a remarkable secret association between them and the Metropolitan Museum of Art, which has never before been revealed.

In the conclusion to his letter, Lord Carnarvon expressed the hope that everything would go off well in the discussions Carter was about to conduct with officials in the Antiquities

Service—particularly Pierre Lacau—to obtain full assurances that Carnarvon would be able to obtain his proper share of the spectacular objects from the tomb. Both men had decided that they had to pin down, in writing, that the tomb of Tutankhamun would be officially defined as a *defiled* sanctuary. Although Lord Carnarvon fully expected to be granted a generous share of the treasures, he was worried that Pierre Lacau might attempt to stall the proceedings.

In another passage, Lord Carnarvon observed dryly that he was deeply concerned that he and Carter would have no chance of obtaining something from New York that year. Yet he expressed the profound hope that more might be found of the Treasure of the Princesses.

What is the significance of these cryptic remarks?

Doubtless, the reference to New York was to the Metropolitan Museum of Art. There is also no doubt that the Princesses' Treasure referred to the most important collection of ancient Egyptian jewelry in the museum's awesome holdings.

Ever since it was triumphantly placed on view in 1926, the Treasure of the Three Princesses of the family of King Thutmose III—or, what is even more likely, the treasure of three lesser wives of the Pharaoh—has been considered by the Metropolitan as among the top works of art in the entire museum. Most Egyptologists regard this collection as one of the superb golden hoards of the entire Eighteenth Dynasty, second only to the treasures of King Tutankhamun. Although certain specialists have their doubts that all the objects come from a single tomb, they admit that the material is spectacular. The complete story, never before published, strongly indicates that the hoard is homogeneous.

The treasure is vast. In all, the fabulous material comprises over 225 pieces. Since they belonged to three women, the objects are distributed in sets of three. The most striking pieces are two splendid gold-and-faience headdresses, one decorated with antelope heads of great vivacity; three broad collars fashioned in gold; seven gold bracelets, including one with small reclining cats carved in feldspar; eight rings; six large gold pectorals in the form of vultures and hawks; thirty solid gold

The imposing entry into the remote Valley of the Kings. THE METROPOLITAN MUSEUM
OF ART

The Valley in 1907. In the left foreground a worker stands beside the pit discovered by Theodore Davis. In the background is the entrance to the tomb of Ramesses VI. THE METROPOLITAN MUSEUM OF ART, PHOTOGRAPH BY EGYPTIAN EXPEDITION

The Davis pit in which were found important clues to the presence of Tut-ankhamun in the Valley, later deciphered by Herbert Winlock. THE METROPOLITAN MUSEUM OF ART

George Herbert, fifth Earl of Carnarvon. GRIFFITH INSTITUTE, ASHMOLEAN MUSEUM, OXFORD UNIVERSITY

Howard Carter at fifty, portrait painted by his brother William in 1924.

The first step—to what? GRIFFITH INSTITUTE, ASHMOLEAN MUSEUM, OXFORD UNIVERSITY

The ancient foundations of workers' huts, which became the critical area for Carter. GRIFFITH INSTITUTE, ASHMOLEAN MUSEUM, OXFORD UNIVERSITY

Watercolor of 1899 by Howard Carter. THE METROPOLITAN MUSEUM OF ART

Above, the seal of the City of the Dead—nine bound prisoners and the jackal god, Anubis. Below, two seals of Tutankhamun. THE METROPOLITAN MUSEUM OF ART

Lord Carnarvon and Lady Evelyn Herbert are met at Luxor by Carter and the governor of the province of Kena in November 1922. GRIFFITH INSTITUTE, ASHMOLEAN MUSEUM, OXFORD UNIVERSITY

The workmen dig out the steps and the passageway. UPI

The tomb of Tutankhamun in relationship to that of Ramesses VI. THE METROPOLITAN MUSEUM OF ART

Tomb of Meses

Rameses III

Entrance to Tomb of Rameses VI
Corridors

Iron Grill

1st Sealed Door

Earlier portion constructed for

2 Chambers crowded with Royal Furniture, Statues, Etc.

1st Chamber

2nd Chamber

Steps on inclined way to entrance Door

"Everywhere the glint of gold"—the first view. THE METROPOLITAN MUSEUM OF ART,
PHOTOGRAPH BY HARRY BURTON

The north wall with the "sentinels," several caskets, one of the phantasmagorical couches and the sealed entrance to the Burial Chamber.

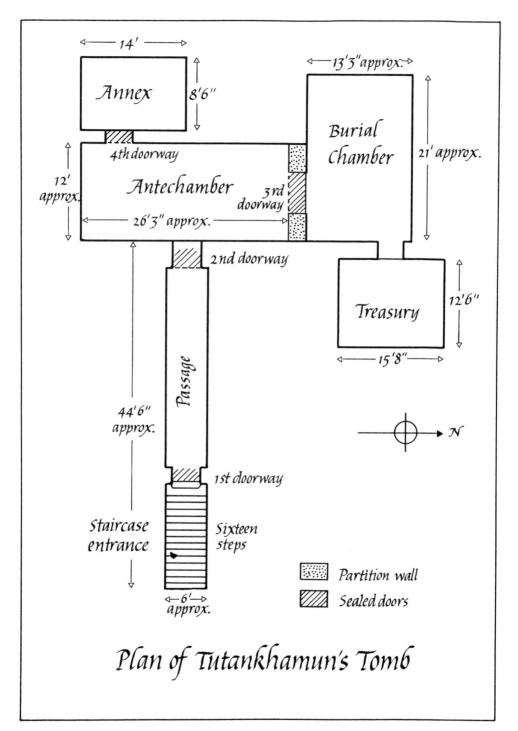

Plan of Tutankhamun's Tomb

Annex
14'
8'6"

4th doorway

Antechamber
12' approx.
26'3" approx.
3rd doorway
2nd doorway

Burial Chamber
13'3" approx.
21' approx.

Treasury
12'6"
15'8"

Passage
44'6" approx.

1st doorway

Staircase entrance
Sixteen steps
6' approx.

Partition wall
Sealed doors

N

The head of the lion on the first great couch. LEE BOLTIN

The King's "wishing cup" found by Carter on the floor of the Annex. LEE BOLTIN

The two "sentinels"—life-sized statues of the King—seem to stand guard over the baskets and reeds placed by Carter to hide the discoverers' secret entry into the Holy of Holies. THE METROPOLITAN MUSEUM OF ART, PHOTOGRAPH BY HARRY BURTON

The objects strewn on the floor of the Annex. GRIFFITH INSTITUTE, ASHMOLEAN MUSEUM, OXFORD UNIVERSITY

The perfume box that Carter removed from the Burial Chamber. LEE BOLTIN

One of the alabasters from the forest of vases. LEE BOLTIN

Walter Hauser, master draftsman. THE METROPOLITAN MUSEUM OF ART

Albert M. Lythgoe, curator of the Metropolitan's Egyptian Department, and Edward S. Harkness, member of the museum's board of trustees.

THE METROPOLITAN MUSEUM OF ART

Herbert Eustis Winlock, associate curator of Egyptology, later director of the Metropolitan Museum.

THE METROPOLITAN MUSEUM OF ART

Harry Burton of the Metropolitan, the best field photographer in the business. THE METROPOLITAN MUSEUM OF ART

Lindsley Hall, master draftsman.

THE METROPOLITAN MUSEUM OF ART

Line drawing by Hall and Hauser showing the precise placement of all objects in the Antechamber. GRIFFITH INSTITUTE, ASHMOLEAN MUSEUM, OXFORD UNIVERSITY

The little golden shrine with reliefs showing Tutankhamun and his Queen, Ankhesenamun. LEE BOLTIN

Arthur Mace and Alfred Lucas working on a chariot outside the laboratory. THE METROPOLITAN MUSEUM OF ART

Detail of the small golden shrine.
LEE BOLTIN

The mannequin of the King "walks" out of the tomb.
UPI

Detail of the throne back. LEE BOLTIN

The golden throne of Tutankhamun. LEE BOLTIN

The golden throne as drawn and annotated by Howard Carter. GRIFFITH INSTITUTE, ASH-
MOLEAN MUSEUM, OXFORD UNIVERSITY

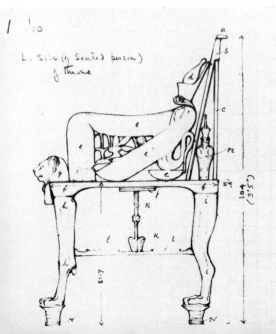

The official opening
through the sealed
partition into the Holy
of Holies. GRIFFITH
INSTITUTE, ASHMOLEAN MUSEUM,
OXFORD UNIVERSITY

The great gilded outer shrine. GRIFFITH INSTITUTE, ASHMOLEAN MUSEUM, OXFORD UNIVERSITY

Peering in: Would the shrine be intact? GRIFFITH INSTITUTE, ASHMOLEAN MUSEUM, OXFORD UNIVERSITY

The doors of the second shrine, sealed for three thousand two hundred years. THE METROPOLITAN MUSEUM OF ART

The alabaster jar described by Lord Carnarvon as "a cat with a pink tongue which I could scarcely take my eyes off." LEE BOLTIN

The King in gold on his walking staff.
LEE BOLTIN

The visit of Elisabeth, Queen of the Belgians. THE METROPOLITAN MUSEUM OF ART, PHOTOGRAPH BY HARRY BURTON

Selket, one of the four goddesses of
the underworld, protecting the
canopic shrine in the Treasury.
LEE BOLTIN

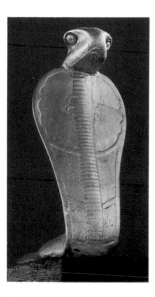

The golden snake re-
moved by Carter in the
presence of the Queen of
the Belgians. LEE BOLTIN

The doorway to the Treasury,
guarded by the jackal god, Anubis.
THE METROPOLITAN MUSEUM OF ART, PHOTOGRAPH BY

HARRY BURTON

Filling in the entrance to the tomb at the end of the first season. GRIFFITH INSTITUTE, ASHMOLEAN MUSEUM, OXFORD UNIVERSITY

Moving the objects to the Nile. GRIFFITH INSTITUTE, ASHMOLEAN MUSEUM, OXFORD UNIVERSITY

The second season begins with the wrapping of the sentinels. THE METROPOLITAN MUSEUM OF ART, PHOTOGRAPH BY HARRY BURTON

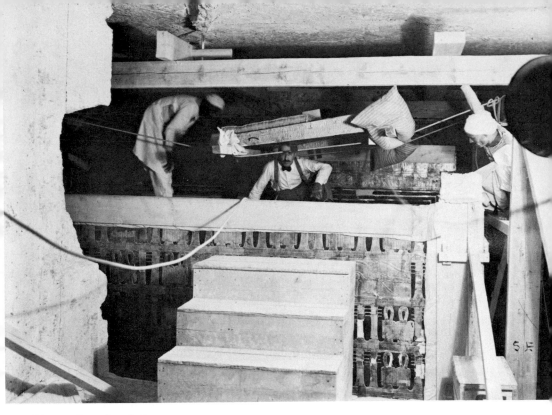

Dismantling the shrines. GRIFFITH INSTITUTE, ASHMOLEAN MUSEUM, OXFORD UNIVERSITY

Prime Minister Zaghlul Pasha
Saad. THE GRANGER COLLECTION

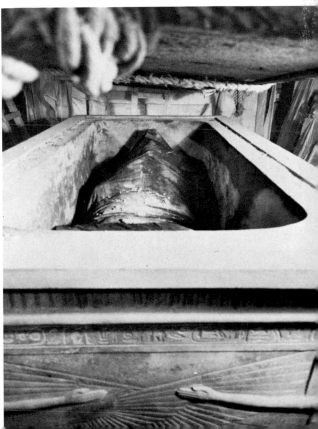

The first view into the
sarcophagus.
THE METROPOLITAN MUSEUM OF ART,
PHOTOGRAPH BY HARRY BURTON

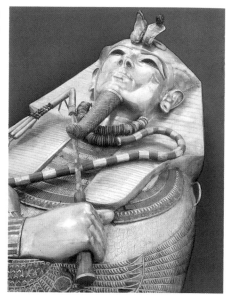

The third, solid-gold coffin.
LEE BOLTIN

The golden mask—one of the most beautiful portraits in all antiquity—which adorned the mummy inside the third coffin. LEE BOLTIN

The first look at the golden mask. The ceremonial beard had become dislodged during the unwrapping. THE METROPOLITAN MUSEUM OF ART, PHOTOGRAPH BY HARRY BURTON

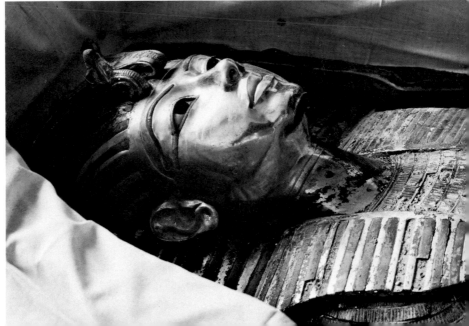

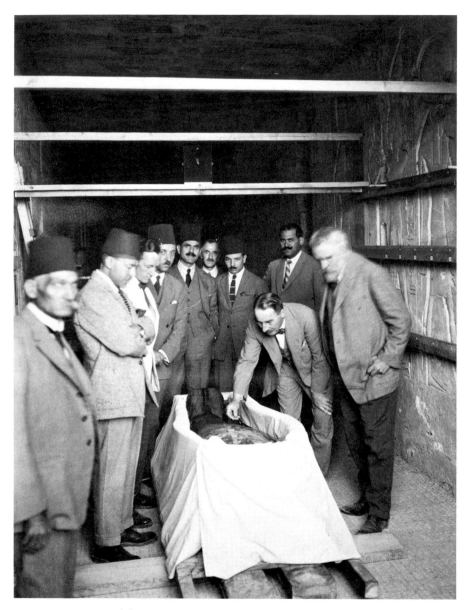

The examination of the mummy. GRIFFITH INSTITUTE, ASHMOLEAN MUSEUM, OXFORD UNIVERSITY

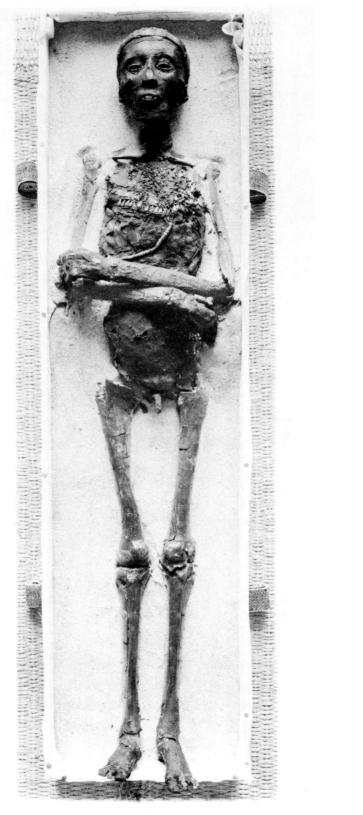

The pitiful remains of Tutankhamun. THE METROPOLITAN MUSEUM OF ART

Statuette of a girl, painted ivory.
THE BROOKLYN MUSEUM, CHARLES EDWIN
WILBOUR FUND

Toilet box in the form of a grasshopper, painted
ivory. THE GUENNOL COLLECTION, ON LOAN TO THE BROOKLYN MUSEUM

Ointment spoon, painted ivory. THE BROOKLYN MUSEUM, CHARLES EDWIN WILBOUR FUND

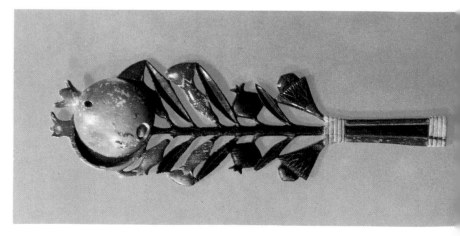

TO HAVE BEEN TAKEN BY CARTER FROM THE TOMB.

Puppy, bronze and gilt. THE
METROPOLITAN MUSEUM OF ART

Ariel (African gazelle), painted ivory.
THE METROPOLITAN MUSEUM OF ART

Horse, painted ivory, probably a handle for a whip. THE METROPOLITAN MUSEUM OF
ART

The display of the treasures of Tutankhamun in the Egyptian Museum of Antiquities, Cairo. AUTHENTICATED NEWS INTERNATIONAL

toe-stalls; three solid-gold sandals; dozens of gold rings; heart scarabs; amulets; alabaster jars banded in gold (and made for cold cream!); two gold-handled silver mirrors of exceptional beauty; a half-dozen cups and small jugs in gold; and vessels and goblets in silver, amethyst, serpentine and feldspar.

Most of the jewelry carries either the cartouche of Thutmose III or the names of either the princesses or wives—Menhet, Menwi and Merti. Every one of the objects carries the museum's acquisition number for the year 1926. But in a special publication of the 1940s Herbert Winlock states that they were purchased, in part by special acquisition funds, over "some years." And he casually mentions that a small number of the gold jars and vessels were once in the possession of Howard Carter.

But Winlock fails to give the full story. And that story is of a remarkable and fascinating collecting adventure, with tales of robbery, tense bargaining and the hair-raising process of trying to raise money before a part of the hoard got away. Even more astonishing than that, it turns out that the Metropolitan Museum clandestinely purchased all the 225 pieces of the Treasure of the Three Princesses or Wives directly through Howard Carter, who bought them from an Egyptian dealer with funds deliberately supplied by Lord Carnarvon so that Carter could profit handsomely from the direct sales and make a commission as well.

The treasure of Menhet, Menwi and Merti was discovered under circumstances which would have been considered unbelievable anywhere but in Egypt. In late July of 1914 at a place called in Arabic the Gabbanet al-Kurud, "Cemetery of the Apes," an ancient nonroyal burial ground in a valley to the south of the royal necropolis, a violent rainstorm took place. Whenever a rare downpour occurred, the local tomb robbers issued an instant call to arms. In general, they were not very industrious or particularly interested in working for loot by patiently searching throughout the crags and cliffs of the lonely valley. It was far easier and more efficient to go up and see what the floods themselves had disclosed.

After this particular storm a group of robbers from that

"world capital" of thieves, Kurna, went up to the mountain and discovered a place where the water cascaded down the sheer cliffs, disappearing into a great crack high among the crags and then emerging from a hole about forty yards away. In order to find out where the water went when it disappeared, the searchers entered the crevice by lowering into the depths an enormously heavy water-wheel rope which they dragged over the foothills.

Naturally, everything was carried out in the highest secrecy. But the results of their work surpassed any expectations the gang might have dreamed of before they began their labors. In several days it was generally known throughout Kurna, and Luxor too, that a treasure of absolute majesty had been rooted out somewhere in the Cemetery of the Apes. Even the name of the Egyptian dealer who had bought all but a minor portion was no secret to the local gossips. He was a certain Muhammed Mohassib, a canny specialist in the *antika* trade who somehow managed to learn at once about any clandestine excavation, no matter how modest. Mohassib was well respected for getting there first and paying quickly—always in golden coin.

A fortnight after the find, a British archaeologist working near Luxor, Ernest Mackay, had tracked the story down and sent word to Sir Alan Gardiner, who immediately informed Lord Carnarvon and Howard Carter. Mackay reported that he had informed the local inspector of antiquities, Tewfik Boulos Effendi, about the find and had taken off to see the place for himself. He found a modest tomb, nothing more than a gash in the cliff, situated about thirty feet up from the floor of the valley. Mackay asked the villagers of Kurna some routine questions, but discovered very little. He gained only the information that the robbers had come across a great many alabaster vessels inscribed with cartouches, and an abundance of gold ornaments. Their quality was said to be "excellent"; they included a gold belt, bracelets, a headdress, necklaces and beads and a number of gold sandals. The latter somewhat confused Mackay. He guessed that they were "probably thin plates of gold which were sometimes used in Ramesside times to cover the soles of the feet of the dead after they had been flayed."

Mackay stated that after "sifting the grain from the chaff" in the reports given to him, he concluded that the clandestine excavation had produced a fabulous return. He asked Mohassib what he knew, but that clever practitioner of the art of "fencing" denied having bought any gold or knowing anything at all about the matter. That was not unexpected. The time-honored procedure was to let some time pass before the dealer began the deliberate process of playing upon the feelings of greed and the competition among several prospective buyers. It was also common practice to divide a hoard into two or more lots, each one of which would have its equal share of superior and mediocre pieces. Then each lot would be offered to a different collector or museum. Each lot was given to one of Mohassib's relatives for safekeeping; that ensured that the authorities could never track all the items down. But more important than that, the division into more or less equal lots was critical in obtaining the highest possible price for the entire group.

The trick was to offer, at the right time, one lot to one collector or museum, and another to a second, while at the same time letting out the word to both that, of course, it would be a far better thing if the one collector or museum could acquire both lots. The price for the two would be slightly higher than the sum of the two separately, but think of the scientific value of the whole! Then, when the collector had secured the first two lots, in due time Mohassib would suddenly discover a third, and then a fourth and a fifth, which the collector or museum would be unable to resist.

Normally the Egyptian police or the officials in the Antiquities Service were the last ones to track down the thieves or any of the loot from a clandestine find. They came very close in the affair of the Three Princesses, but not close enough. One of the tomb robbers was a curious little old man named Mohammed Hammad, who told Winlock that a few hours after the treasure had been discovered he and his eight cohorts had already divided and hidden the golden coins received from Mohassib.

Mohammed's first thought upon gazing at his share of gold had been the acquisition of a new wife. The one he chose was his junior by a goodly number of years and, as Winlock describes her, was "straight as an arrow . . . with eyes that looked over the corner of her head shawl with an unmistakable invitation." After a hurried wedding, Mohammed settled into the entertaining pastime of enjoying his young wife and spending one golden coin after another.

Then, only a few weeks after the wedding, a crowd of village guards and policemen, headed by the chief himself, the *mamur*, suddenly burst into the village. Mohammed had just enough time to pack up the gold coins, throw them into a basket of corn and send them off with his nubile young wife in a basket balanced upon her pretty head. All would have gone well had she not cast one provocative look from behind her shawl at one of the government police. This was deeply resented by one of the village guards, a surly lout who had always been the butt of jokes from the girls of Kurna. He reached out and batted the basket with his club. It toppled from her head. The girl shrieked. A mixture of golden corn and golden coins spread in the dust. Winlock reported that there was an hour-long melee of villagers, police and guards in a mad, biting, scratching tangle. When the melee was over, everyone in the village was exhausted and they all filed home except for Mohammed and a few suspects who were questioned by police at headquarters. But nothing came of this, and eventually all the thieves were released with no one the loser but Mohammed Hammad.

After that, the local inspector of antiquities, Tewfik Effendi, examined the tomb carefully to see what, if anything, the thieves had left. There had been a rumor that some of the larger vases, including the four canopic jars, had been left behind and buried in a niche nearby. But before he could excavate, the hapless Tewfik had to get official permission from Cairo. The bureaucrats in Cairo told him "not to bother," since they were well assured there could not possibly be a tomb in that section of the valley, for a Frenchman had searched it years ago and had found nothing. Their instructions must have seemed a bit bizarre to Tewfik Effendi, because he was actually standing inside the sanctuary when a messenger delivered the judgment to him.

Despite a number of requests to the authorities in the Antiquities Service by both Mackay and Tewfik for permission to excavate the tomb and examine the general area around it to see if others might come to light, the persistent answer was negative. It would cost too much, the authorities claimed—a sum of about two hundred and fifty dollars!—and, anyway, if something were found, the cost of guarding the site would be far too much. Eventually, however, the hole was cursorily examined and found to be totally empty. Beyond that, nothing was ever done in the area by professionals—except for Howard Carter in 1918. Presumably the men of Kurna rejoiced.

In the spring of 1917, Ambrose Lansing, who was then the curator of the Metropolitan's Egyptian Department, met the dealer Mohassib, who had divided the treasure into three lots and planned to offer it in thirds to the Metropolitan Museum, the British Museum and Lord Carnarvon. Lansing purchased three sets of small canopic jars and several other vessels for the modest sum of three hundred pounds, examined some of the gold pieces and then backed off, primarily because the price quoted by Mohassib for the rest—eighty thousand pounds—was "horrendous."

But then Howard Carter entered the scene. In the fall of 1917 he approached Edward Robinson, the director of the Metropolitan, who was in London at the time, told him about the treasure and stressed that it was of "great importance that all these objects should, if possible, remain together, both from a scientific point of view and a 'collective' value." He offered a neat deal to the surprised and elated Robinson. Lord Carnarvon had decided to try to purchase the entire treasure with his own money. But since he wanted only a few special pieces for himself, Carnarvon suggested that the Metropolitan buy the rest from Howard Carter, who would realize a modest profit plus a commission of fifteen percent. In this manner Carter could supplement his income. No one was ever to tell the dealer Mohassib that Carnarvon was surreptitiously acting as an agent for the Metropolitan. Carter urged the museum to negotiate with Mohassib for a while, always offering a far lower price than the dealer asked for—lower even than the figure that Mohassib would come to after an Oriental bargaining exchange—and then break off the bargaining. This, Carter said, would place him in a perfect position to obtain the best price from a discouraged Mohassib, who, he pointed out, was old and sick and didn't expect to live very long anyway.

Robinson readily agreed, and put Herbert Winlock in charge of the affair. Over the next five years, the Metropolitan purchased in seven lots, always directly from or through Howard Carter, the 225 pieces of unique funerary equipment and dazzling jewelry. The negotiations were complex, at times frightening, and they often floundered just on the edge of failure. But, slowly, the Metropolitan gained the prize. The museum was frequently low on funds, and Winlock and Robinson continually had to scratch for cash, sometimes just when Carter, on behalf of Carnarvon, had paid a large sum of money to Mohassib or his grandson, Mahmoud, who entered the picture after the old man's death. They were fearful at times that if they were not able to raise enough money Carnarvon would be forced to sell the prize to someone else, or another buyer would snatch a part of the treasure. The letters from Winlock to Lythgoe and Robinson describing the five-year history of the deal are full of descriptions of agonizing moments.

On one occasion the British Museum seemed ready to step in with funds pledged by "some rich Englishman who was going to give the stuff to the B. M.," as Winlock described the event. But it happened by chance that the intended donor asked Howard Carter whether he knew anything about the material the British Museum wanted. Carter, in an absolutely amazing statement, said that he did know about it but that the stuff was "quite worthless."

Then there was the problem of whether or not Lord Carnarvon would insist on retaining some of the better objects for himself. For a while he did keep one of the crowns and five solid-gold cups for his collection at Highclere, but finally he agreed to sell them to the Metropolitan, partly because the museum had expressed its deep desire to gain the complete collection but primarily to help Howard Carter. As Winlock described the situation, Carnarvon "knew that if he took the best things, we would soon get tired of taking the second-rate ones, and thus be cutting Carter out of a chance to make something."

At times the Metropolitan staff would praise Lord Carnarvon for his true sportsmanship in giving up his pieces to the museum and for his friendly assistance. On other occasions, however, Winlock was not so certain about Carnarvon's or Carter's fundamental benevolence. At one point, Winlock wrote that his "feet froze solid" when it appeared, momentarily, that Carter interpreted a lot which he had just bought for twenty-five thousand pounds as a legal commitment on the part of the Metropolitan. But eventually all worked out: the Metropolitan was overjoyed by its superb and unique treasure trove, Lord Carnarvon was delighted to have been able to help his great friend Howard Carter, and Carter was deeply relieved to know that his financial future was almost totally secure.

The transactions started in 1917 and were concluded in 1922. The total amount the museum paid eventually reached the staggering sum of £53,397. At the 1922 rate of the pound sterling, that came to the unheard-of amount of $256,305.60! In today's values, that would be worth well over two and a half million dollars. With his profit and commission, Carter received nearly forty thousand dollars. Today it is almost impossible to comprehend what the purchasing power of that amount of money was in Egypt in the early 1920s. But it is safe to say that a single individual with a modest life style could live more than handsomely—that is, with no more than four or five servants—on three thousand dollars a year.

In March of 1922 when the Treasure-of-the-Princesses deal had been completed, no one could know that in just four years

Carter would have far greater financial security. For after the death of Lord Carnarvon, Howard Carter anonymously helped to arrange the sale of Carnarvon's distinguished collection of Egyptian antiquities, which he had helped his patron assemble, to the Metropolitan Museum of Art for the sum of forty-five thousand pounds, or $216,000. Apparently Carnarvon had decided to arrange his will so that a percentage of the proceeds would go to Carter. He seems to have made his decision in March 1922, for, as Winlock pointed out in a letter, at that time Lord Carnarvon recognized that his life was fading. He feared another operation and had decided not to go through with it.

Today the arrangement that Lord Carnarvon and Howard Carter made with the Metropolitan Museum regarding the Treasure of the Three Princesses would be impossible. Regulations in Egypt governing the purchase of antiquities and their exportation are rigid. In the period just after the First World War the situation was a great deal more flexible, and although the laws demanded that a collector obtain permission from the Egyptian Museum of Antiquities for exportation, which Winlock stated was done in the case of the golden hoard, the convention was frequently overlooked. One wonders whether or not a permit for the treasure would have been given if it had been brought to the authorities as a whole instead of in small lots. Probably not. For even among the extraordinary rich collections of Eighteenth-Dynasty jewelry in the Egyptian Museum, the objects of the princesses would be considered among the most valuable of all, both historically and aesthetically. Today it would be utterly beyond the pale for a professional archaeologist like Howard Carter, and the holder of an official governmental concession such as Lord Carnarvon, to be deeply involved in art dealing of a rather cutthroat and questionable variety. Even in the early 1920s it would have been deemed unethical had it come into the open.

Not surprisingly, it turns out that the Metropolitan, vigorous in its desire to form the greatest Egyptian collection in the world, had made similar deals with other archaeologists. Howard Carter was not alone. From a series of letters between

Albert Lythgoe and Herbert Winlock about the Three Princesses affair, one discovers, astonishingly, that the museum had even concluded a purchase agreement with none other than the legendary Egyptologist Sir Flinders Petrie.

In a letter of 1920, Lythgoe mused to Winlock that perhaps they could get something in England—from Petrie(!), who had unexpectedly found at Lahun another secret niche in the tomb where he had discovered in 1914 some unexcelled jewelry of the Middle Kingdom. Lythgoe reported that Petrie had come across a "large alabaster jar bearing a magical inscription." He asked Winlock, "Can we get that?" Lythgoe mentioned that Petrie had also found in the passage of the pyramid at Lahun the gold-and-lapis-lazuli uraeus from the crown of Senusert II. He wrote Winlock, "How about that?" Then, somewhat petulantly, Lythgoe complained that Petrie seemed to be overlooking their "written agreement," part of which had stated that if the Metropolitan purchased certain jewelry from his dig at Lahun, Petrie was obligated to "get out," in addition, a certain limestone canopic box. Lythgoe stated, "I *offered* to pay the cost of labor in getting it out!" Lythgoe urged Winlock to remind Petrie of the written agreement, and to talk to him at once about the purchase of two additional sarcophagi from Lahun.

When one reads the public and lofty protestations by the Metropolitan Museum of Art and by practically every other foreign Egyptologist against Pierre Lacau's attempts to alter the standard half-and-half division because of their concern that the "science of archaeology" would suffer deeply, and then reflects on the finaglings of Carter, Carnarvon and the Metropolitan, and the deal between Sir Flinders Petrie and the museum, there is a certain tendency to be somewhat skeptical of the merits of their arguments. Because of such deals, some of which were undoubtedly known to the Egyptian authorities, the era of free commercial enterprise in archaeology was doomed. Within a year after the discovery of Tutankhamun, the era would close forever.

CHAPTER FOURTEEN

The Metropolitan Museum Makes a Coup

LORD CARNARVON AND HIS daughter, once they had arrived in England on the twentieth of December, were greeted as national heroes. Two days after his return Carnarvon had an audience with King George V at Buckingham Palace. According to a court spokesman, the monarch listened "with great interest to a description of the important discoveries made recently by him and Mr. Carter as the culmination of the excavation which they have carried on for nearly sixteen years." The palace spokesman also reported that Lord Carnarvon had assured George V that the mummy of the Pharaoh would be found when each of the *gilded* shrines was dismantled. Oddly enough, no one at that time—and no one since—picked up the significance of his incredible remark describing precisely an event that did not take place, at least officially, until the following February. Before his King, Lord Carnarvon had almost let the cat out of the bag.

To be back in England after the discovery was one of the most thoroughly enjoyable periods in Lord Carnarvon's life. The interest created by his achievement had been "perfectly extraordinary," according to Carnarvon, and had "taken the public fancy to a quite remarkable extent"—chiefly because it "had been a private concern and . . . Englishmen had been responsible for it." He told Carter that "a poor artisan wrote offering me *Five Pounds* towards the cost of a cinema."

Despite his deep fatigue, he felt totally rejuvenated not only when Evelyn would describe their discovery of the Holy of Holies but also when he would describe to yet another incredulous listener the dramatic moments of opening the inner doorway of the tomb and the subsequent entry into the Antechamber. One can imagine the lord enthralling his audiences with speculations of what might be found deep within the burial sanctuary, choosing his words so that they would teeter delightfully just on the brink of hypothesis.

To Albert Lythgoe, too, it was the most pleasing moment of his career. He had pulled off the greatest coup in the history of the Metropolitan. He conversed with Lord Carnarvon immediately upon his return to London and cabled Edward Robinson: "Carnarvon has arrived here. Is deeply grateful for assistance we are rendering him and is relying on my advice. Would recommend your cabling him confirming our help in every possible way."

In a follow-up letter, Lythgoe exulted that his being in London had been "the most fortunate thing" for him and for the entire Metropolitan. First and foremost, he had been able to grant full assistance to Carter when he asked for it and had managed to discuss "the best lines of procedure" with A. C. Mace, who happened also to be there.

Any anxiety that Lythgoe may have had that the discoverers would turn for help to an institution other than the Metropolitan team was dispelled when Carnarvon solicited his views on the matter. At that moment in the Tutankhamun affair, one can imagine each side jockeying cleverly to form a partnership with the other, each fearful that the other might refuse a businesslike liaison. Lythgoe bluntly told Lord Carnarvon that the preservation and the conservation of the works of art were the key to every aspect of the success of the Tutankhamun undertaking. He described a firm plan of action which revolved around A. C. Mace, whose "painstaking skill and incredible patience" in conservation were "unsurpassed." Mace, working with Carter, would choose the rest of the group to repair and preserve the hundreds of delicate works of art, furniture, chests, military equipment, and robes of state.

Lythgoe had learned that Pierre Lacau had given "assurances" that Carnarvon would obtain a generous selection of the objects from the tomb, and that Carnarvon was now awaiting further confirmation from Carter, who had remained in Cairo principally to deal with that most critical of subjects. Carnarvon had told Lythgoe, "The *more work* he does on the restoration of the objects, *the more* Lacau will *give* him!" With this in mind, Lythgoe had urged Lord Carnarvon to secure an agreement from Pierre Lacau guaranteeing Carnarvon the right to undertake and carry out the "entire restoration" of all the objects even after they reached Cairo, instead of turning them over "to the tender mercies of Georges Daressy," the second-in-command of the Antiquities Service and a conservator of the Egyptian Museum.

Lythgoe wrote of his talks with Carnarvon in a letter to Edward Robinson and observed that "strictly in the family circle" he believed that Robinson could clearly "see what I am hoping for in all this—aside from what I know would be the Museum's desire in extending every assistance to Carnarvon in this tremendous emergency." Carnarvon, Lythgoe continued, "is certain, in return for all we are doing, to give us some of the things he receives."

Lythgoe was careful to point out to his superior that he had taken every precaution to ensure that the Metropolitan's own digs would go forward on an adequate scale. But, he pointed out, he personally believed "that objects which we are bound to receive from Carnarvon's 'find' would far outweigh the possibilities to be derived from the excavation of an additional number of Eleventh Dynasty tombs."

He urged Robinson to get the trustees of the Museum to ratify his actions and to persuade them to cable their official support at once to Lord Carnarvon. He stressed that Carnarvon was "really all at sea" as to how to proceed and what to do. He informed Robinson that Lord Carnarvon was "deeply touched" by the Metropolitan's assistance. When Lord Carnarvon and Carter had received Lythgoe's original assurance of "every possible assistance," they had triumphantly taken it to Evelyn's room to show it to her and were "greatly relieved."

Lythgoe sat in his room at the Burlington Hotel for several days, waiting desperately for another meeting with Lord Carnarvon, in which he hoped the museum would be offered a share of the treasures. Then, two days before Christmas, he received a cablegram from Carter that gave him another opportunity to approach Lord Carnarvon. The news was excellent. Carter had informed him that the first proofs of Harry Burton's photographs had turned out "superbly." Lythgoe knew that Lord Carnarvon would be pleased and relieved to hear about Burton's success. Lythgoe privately told Robinson that it was exceedingly lucky that Burton had been available and had done such a fine job, since the photographic efforts of Carnarvon and Carter had "failed." Burton's successes would further put Lord Carnarvon into the debt of the Metropolitan.

Lord Carnarvon was indeed delighted with the news and said that he would like to come over to Lythgoe's hotel to say goodby to him. Carnarvon arrived with Evelyn, but at once asked for a private word with Lythgoe. While Evelyn, Mrs. Lythgoe and A. C. Mace retired, Carnarvon excitedly told Lythgoe that he had just received "splendid news" from Howard Carter. Carter had just concluded a series of highly confidential meetings with Pierre Lacau regarding the division of the discovery. Lacau had reconfirmed his "full and further assurances" that Lord Carnarvon would receive an excellent choice of objects. Carter had expressed slight disappointment to Carnarvon that Lacau had told him it was unnecessary to put the "assurances" in writing, but Carter felt that, at that moment, the verbal agreement was sufficient.

Then Carnarvon lowered his voice and, according to Lythgoe, told him to "tell *no one* of what he was going to say"—not even Carter, his associates, or even his daughter Evelyn. "I'm," he informed Lythgoe, "going to give you a part of the things which I receive. Of course," he continued, "I shall have to give something to the British Museum, but I intend to see that the Metropolitan is *well taken care of!*"

That evening Lythgoe dispatched an exultant letter to Robinson, instructing him that the major news in his letter had to be taken "in the strictest secrecy," and then explaining the unbelievable news of Carnarvon's extraordinary offer. He described Lord Carnarvon as being "simply splendid" and wrote, "You can imagine that I met him more than half-way in the assurances I gave him as to the gratitude of the Museum for all he was doing—both in the present case and in the great thing he had done for [the Museum] these past years in the 'Princess' material."

Lythgoe emphasized that there were obvious and powerful reasons to maintain strict secrecy regarding Lord Carnarvon's intentions toward the Metropolitan and urged Robinson not to tell anyone but two members of the board of trustees, Edward Harkness, and Robert de Forest, the museum's president. Lythgoe stated that he did not intend to give a hint of the proposed gift to Mace or even Winlock until the right moment and told his superior that he would let him know "the earliest moment when it proves possible that you should let Carnarvon know that you are aware of his intention and can express the thanks of the Museum." It is not unreasonable to speculate that Lythgoe believed that Carnarvon would pledge a share of the Tutankhamun objects on two conditions. The first would be the use of the Metropolitan staff; the second would be the museum's continuing political pressure on the Egyptian government. With that pressure from America, nobody, Pierre Lacau or anyone else, would ever be able to change the law regarding the division of discoveries.

During their private conversation Lythgoe talked for nearly an hour with Lord Carnarvon on how he should handle the tomb. The eyes and ears of the scientific and public world were upon Carnarvon, he said, and he advised the peer to conduct the rest of the excavation and the clearing of the first two chambers with the highest possible professionalism, and with the Metropolitan team as a constant participant. He emphasized the necessity to obtain the delicate and knowledgeable hands of A. C. Mace in the laboratory and in the Egyptian Museum in Cairo.

Lythgoe also brought up the subject of how to deal with the mummy of the King "if it were discovered behind the sealed door." It would be imperative to enlist the services and the talents of Dr. Elliot Smith for the investigation and conservation of the body. Smith was a British chemist who had undertaken the first scientific study of the royal mummies in the Egyptian Museum some years before.

Carnarvon told Lythgoe that he had been assailed by requests of all kinds, by mail, by personal visitations, by bands of experts, real, imagined, would-be and charlatanic. The exhausted lord was confused and was willing, and indeed eager, to agree to all his suggestions. Lythgoe had pointed out that in the case of every other royal tomb that had ever been discovered, whatever evidence had been found had been "wantonly discarded and lost." He stressed to Lord Carnarvon that he now had in his grasp not only the most important and exciting archaeological discovery in the world's history but the most *perfect* working machine in the known course of all of Egyptian archaeology. It was critical to keep that "machine" working for Howard Carter. Only then would Lord Carnarvon be "credited with taking the fullest advantage of this greatest of opportunities" and praised for having "furnished a record of the evidence on every side, uniquely complete in every detail." Lord Carnarvon agreed with every one of Lythgoe's suggestions.

Lythgoe found himself in London not only the happiest man in the world but the busiest. He was able to meet on several occasions with James Quibell, a congenial English member of the Antiquities Service who had expressed himself totally sympathetic to the foreigners' point of view. As an old associate of Gaston Maspero, Quibell had dedicated himself to seeing that his mentor's policy of encouraging foreign exploration in Egypt would never be altered. He offered to write a special letter to Lord Allenby himself, in the hope that the High Commissioner would lend his support and massive influence. Lythgoe, deftly sensing the correct psychological moment, discussed with Quibell the touchy question of the legal exportation of the final lot of the Treasure of the Princesses and was assured by him that he would obtain the appropriate permission. For Albert Lythgoe it had been truly a magnificent fortnight in London.

The board of trustees of the Metropolitan eventually drafted a resolution confirming the action of the director and the curator of Egyptian art in extending to Lord Carnarvon, "to whatever extent may be necessary, assistance in the tasks of recording, removing and preserving the objects found in the tomb." The board expressed to "his Lordship" its appreciation of the honor "he had done the members of the Museum's staff in selecting them for assistance in this important and delicate work." A second resolution coldly informed the Egyptian government that if, as the formal notification seemed to indicate, "the authorities of the Antiquities Department really meant to change paragraph II of Law No. fourteen of 1912 relating to the fifty percent division of antiquities unearthed in Egypt by foreign excavation, the Museum would see to it that the entire work of all its Expeditions in Egypt would be brought to an end soon after the new ruling goes into effect."

A few days after Christmas *The New York Times* printed a story about the Metropolitan's role in the excavation of Tutankhamun's tomb, headlined "Americans to Dig in Tomb." The article emphasized the great compliment it was to the museum workers "to have been chosen to aid in the excavation of these exceptional treasures from among many excavators—English, French, other Americans and Egyptians."

At the same time Edward Robinson was asked by a reporter from the New York *Herald* to comment upon a rumor that the Metropolitan, in helping Carnarvon, would obtain a share of the treasures. Robinson issued a formal denial, stating that he knew "nothing about the suggested gift" to the museum of objects found in the tomb, except "what I have seen in the newspapers." Robinson stressed, in his statement, that in all the correspondence between Lord Carnarvon and the museum in which Carnarvon had asked for and had received assurance of aid, there had been no allusion of any sort to the possibility of such a gift. He went on to say that the assistance had been promised "without any expectation of such a return." The eventual disposition of "this unique and marvelous treasure" would be decided upon entirely between Lord Carnarvon and the government of Egypt. And the Metropolitan Museum of Art would have no part in those transactions.

Two days later, a flabbergasted Edward Robinson received Albert Lythgoe's letter, sent in "strictest secrecy," informing him of the "splendid news" of Carnarvon's proposed gift of a number of treasures from Tutankhamun's tomb. Thus the elegant and cool director had the double pleasure of learning that his institution had been assured a part of one of the greatest discoveries in history and knowing, because of the timing of the situation, that his conscience was entirely clear.

CHAPTER FIFTEEN

"Tutankhamun Ltd."

IN ALL OF THE BOOKS and articles dealing with the tomb of Tutankhamun, including the memoirs of James Breasted and the recollections of Sir Alan Gardiner, the impression is imparted that Lord Carnarvon eagerly sought his rightful share of Tutankhamun's treasures and that Howard Carter vigorously objected, urging his lordship to commit them all to the Egyptian Museum of Antiquities. Nothing could be further from the truth. The confusion probably arose from a number of Carter's statements to the press that it might be better to deposit the contents of the tomb in the Egyptian Museum for "archaeological interests." But an unpublished letter from Carnarvon to Carter just after the discovery makes it apparent that Carter made public utterances of the highest scientific rectitude while privately striving for an arrangement with Pierre Lacau that would ensure a share of treasures for Lord Carnarvon, in grateful compensation for his exceptional efforts in having worked sixteen barren years at his full expense before making the unparalleled discovery.

Another misconception, universally published, is that Howard Carter had opposed Lord Carnarvon's handling of the press. For Carnarvon had decided to sell to the London *Times* the world copyright on all news, photographs and drawings of the tomb. It is also generally believed that Carter objected so strongly to Lord Carnarvon's desire to make money out of the sale of news and photographs from the excavation that he eventually broke with his long-time patron and friend. But correspondence between Carter and Carnarvon demonstrates that Howard Carter was working just as hard as Lord Carnarvon to secure the "best, most bonafide, and profitable" press offers, including cinema rights and everything else they could handle.

The prevailing opinion in many of the publications was that Lord Carnarvon granted exclusivity to the London *Times* either because he was naïve or because, as a peer of the realm and a gentleman, he could not envisage any newspapers other than the distinguished *Times* having the privilege. The full story behind his decision is far more complex—and fascinating.

Even before Carnarvon left Egypt to spend Christmas in England, he and Carter had decided that they would both gather all press offers and pick the most favorable and lucrative. Carter had suggested that they ought to establish an informal auction and allow the highest bidder to take the prize. Carnarvon liked the idea at first, but early in January he had second thoughts and confided to Carter that if the auction were to go through they might be accused of *appearing* to be too commercial.

From the outset the London *Times* had a favorable position in the friendship between its correspondent in Cairo, Arthur Merton, and Howard Carter. Both the executives of *The Times* and Merton himself exploited their position vigorously. As soon as the spectacular news of the discovery splashed across the world the editors of *The Times* had instructed Merton to attempt to secure world newspaper and magazine copyrights to the interior photographs of what they described as "the Carnarvon chambers." Merton had discussed the proposition with Carter in the valley and received his promise that neither he nor Lord Carnarvon would sign a contract with any other newspaper or wire service until a definite settlement was made one way or the other with *The Times*.

Yet Carter told Merton, in confidence, that he was wholeheartedly opposed to giving *The Times* an exclusive copyright over any photos of the interiors of the tomb or the works of art themselves. When Merton stated that he supposed that was to protect the scholarly and scientific use of the material, Carter chuckled and observed that Merton was right—in a way. For "the scientific requirements swelled the cinematographic rights." Carter explained that he had received "a very favorable" offer from America for the world rights to make a motion picture about the removal of the treasures and their preparation for shipment to Cairo, and that he did not intend to lose that opportunity. He explained to Merton that if he ceded the photographic copyright to *The Times* it might make it difficult or even legally impossible for him to use them free of charge in books he hoped to write, or as lantern slides for any lectures he might give.

Merton assured Carter that the appropriate language could be drafted to protect him. He wrote his editor at *The Times* that he had been able to persuade Carter to give him a certain number of photos—adding, "and I would see that they were the best"—at least one day before *The Illustrated London News* and other competitors. Carter had sent a cable to Lord Carnarvon in which he sought permission from his patron to deal with the matter of copyright in his name. Merton wrote to his editor: "Until we can get Lord Carnarvon to leave this matter entirely in the hands of Carter it will be impossible to do anything at this end." But, he observed dryly, at the same time it was eminently desirable that Lord Carnarvon should not hand the copyright over to Carter since by doing so he might "unintentionally" commit himself to more than he really intended and trouble might "ensue" between patron and archaeologist to the disadvantage of *The Times*.

In letters to Carter from England, Lord Carnarvon revealed himself to be remarkably avid to retain all copyrights for himself. He was also eager for revenues from newspaper, magazine, book and cinema rights, and not merely to cover the massive costs of the ongoing excavation. He frankly wanted to make the largest possible amount of money he could. This was utterly in keeping with the shrewd and crafty Carnarvon who had for years rejoiced over how he had been able to cash in on the attempted deceptions of an American tycoon. And Howard Carter was eager to assist him, as was totally fitting for an individual who had relished his financially successful handling of the Treasure of the Princesses.

In his letters, Carnarvon also displayed an ability to exploit the media far more acutely than most others of his day. In a letter written to Carter on the twenty-fourth of December—which appears to ramble a bit, owing to the obvious excitement with which it was written—he suggested hiring a press agent who would return with him to Egypt and would keep careful financial track of all communications, including "bulletins gratis" and special articles to be sold to a wide variety of magazines. He mentioned having seen Geoffrey Dawson, the editor of the London *Times*, on the twenty-third of December, and said he had asked him to make an offer.

Wasting no time in getting to Lord Carnarvon, Dawson had almost jeopardized his chances. He had simply driven up to Highclere at midday in the hope of talking to the Earl. When the butler announced his presence, Carnarvon grumbled about Dawson's unscheduled arrival to his luncheon guest, Sir Alan Gardiner, the eminent Egyptologist and a personal friend, and told Gardiner that he would refuse to see Dawson. Gardiner gently advised the Earl that the editor of *The Times* was hardly the type of person to snub, and after an hour Carnarvon received him. Dawson proposed that *The Times* be the sole news agent and source for all aspects of the excavation. Carnarvon explained to Dawson that he could definitely not give all the news first to *The Times*, especially under the arrangement Dawson initially suggested to him. He added to Carter that Dawson would be "writing to me about it after thinking it over."

Lord Carnarvon asked Gardiner what he thought of the proposed news exclusive. The Egyptologist was enthusiastic and urged him to make an agreement. The arrangement, Gardiner pointed out, would save considerable time for Carter, who would have to deal with only one member of the press rather than with a horde of reporters. *The Times*, he added, was virtually the only daily newspaper in the world which had always written splendidly and accurately about archaeological subjects.

Carnarvon was particularly enthusiastic about the prospect of making a movie about the adventure. Under a special section in his letter of December 24 headed "Cinema," he wrote that Pathé and many others had applied for the rights to a film, but so far no sum had been mentioned. For his film he even sketched out a "treatment," consisting of seven essential sections. The first would deal with the dramatic approach to the haunted Valley of the Kings, from the Theban Plain stretching toward the valley from the Nile, past the great corroded "Colossi of Memnon," with a sweeping look at the magnificent terraces of the spectacular funerary temple of Hatshepsut and then up and over the cliff into the valley itself. The second part would chronicle the history of the excavation, incorporating the lean years, films which, Carnarvon explained; "we can get up"; and then, with a certain acceleration, the movie would pinpoint the final small piece of territory where all the extraordinary and dramatic circumstances took place—the first step, the stairs, the outer doorway, the cramped passageway, the inner door. The third part would deal with the chambers and their contents in a general way. Then, fourth, he would recreate on film "the official opening." Fifth, he would examine a variety of the specific objects. Sixth would be the "unrolling," as Carnarvon described it, of the mummy. And finally, seventh, there would be some sort of "strong and uplifting ending."

Carnarvon explained to Carter how he had urged Pathé to send a specialist to the site to reconnoiter site and tomb to determine the scope of the project, and to assess how much machinery they would need—"Dynamo Engines" and other electrical equipment. "There is, I imagine, a good deal of money in this," Carnarvon observed. Just how much, he said, he could not be certain, but he guessed that even with the technical difficulties the profits might eventually amount to as much as twenty thousand pounds—roughly one hundred thousand dollars.

Over the months just after the discovery, Lord Carnarvon spent considerable time thinking about the Tutankhamun film and refining its scenario. He encouraged Goldwyn Ltd. to submit a cinema concept and a contract. Goldwyn's treatment was brisk and imaginative. The first of the two parts dealt with the "essence and idea of ancient Egypt, including the Pyramid and the Sphinx with moving pictures of costumes and customs"; models of the Valley of the Kings and "why such a remote place was used for burial"; a careful reenactment of the "wonderful ceremonies attendant upon the interment of a dead Pharaoh, with living people chosen from living Egyptians looking like those from Tut's time, acted out on the 'via dolorosa' leading to the Valley"; and the re-creation of the discovery and the opening "showing the 'via dolorosa' under conditions brought about by the discovery." The anonymous author of the outline wrote to Carnarvon: "I've not the slightest doubt that a film of the character indicated, going out under the proper auspices, would be one of the biggest and most profitable events in film history." Carnarvon made a note: "I fancy this can be made one of the greatest successes ever known."

The sale of still photographs was, to Lord Carnarvon, another important part of the package. He placed this task in the hands of one of his solicitors, who "wasted little time in making a sale." Lord Carnarvon informed Carter that he had "six uninteresting negatives," two of which he planned to give away; the rest he expected to sell, "for I think *anything* sells." He instructed Carter to send all the photos he could get his hands on—"even those of the 'native' press," so that he could have "a clear run" with them in London. He mentioned that he had sold the copyright of his old pictures of the valley, done mostly two years earlier, and explained that his basic plan was to provide a certain number of pictures "gratis" and then sell the great majority, for "I don't think the Press thanks you for *getting anything for nothing.*"

In Egypt, the offers made to Carter subsequent to Arthur Merton's were not as promising as those being discussed in London. Carnarvon told him in a subsequent communication,

"What you have had in the way of offers is nothing to what rolls in here." In the same letter Carnarvon spelled out his most recent thoughts on the sale of the photos. He preferred to divide them into three groups: free prints for the press ("not very important"), "prints for Press on payment" and "prints which we reserve—the best."

Considerable thought was given by both men to what they called "The Book." Lord Carnarvon preferred to plan for two editions. One, possibly three or four volumes in length, would sell for five to eight pounds each. The other, a popular version, would have an initial press run of twenty thousand copies and be offered at a little over half a pound. Considering the "extreme and somewhat fascinating" popularity of the event, which was building all the time, Carnarvon figured that the popular version would sell very well. He suggested that Carter write The Book with Sir Alan Gardiner. "The two of you," he wrote, "can muddle it out."

In the same letter Carnarvon observed to Carter that "at the moment we sell prints we lose the copyright—but what value is it, really?; except for the book or books which, of course, *I* reserve." He informed Carter that he planned to discuss the complicated issues of the press with Gardiner, who would in turn talk to Carter about it upon his arrival in Egypt. Every newspaper in Great Britain and elsewhere seemed to be making offers, Carnarvon explained, and "neither of us having much of any experience with Press sharks, one is rather at a loss how to act for the best." He related that *The Illustrated London News* wanted to send two photographers and an artist to produce plates in color. The magazine *Outlook* desired sole rights, as did the London *Times*. In order to decide what to do, Carnarvon paid a visit to the Royal Geographic Society to obtain an insight into how that institution had handled the press regarding its abortive expedition to Mount Everest. His letter informed Carter that the expedition had sold its rights to *The Times* for "a thousand Pounds for fifteen lengthy cables." But, he pointed out, there was "much grumbling over that and eventually *The Times* supplied the Press with a shortened piece of each cable."

As an amusing aside which he entitled "An Idea," Lord Carnarvon advised Carter to "reserve the best object" for himself to paint. "Produce it in colours and you will get a lot of money. *Think this out!*"

At the beginning of January, Carnarvon believed the *Daily Mail* would offer the most money, but remarked to Carter that he was leaning to *The Times*, which was "afterall, the first newspaper in the world," with highly sophisticated services including excellent distribution facilities.

By the first week in January, interest in the tomb had become explosive. Carnarvon had been badgered incessantly by the press, and he complained to Carter that he had "a trying time since returning and the papers are the chief offenders." That had not prevented him, however, from taking part in one of his greatest pleasures, hunting. During the full height of the publicity, with daily visits to Highclere by reporters from all over the world and hundreds of phone calls, he delightedly informed Carter that he "still killed seventeen hundred head, nearly all rabbits, and five hundred next day."

In the Valley of the Kings, Howard Carter was also experiencing increasing difficulties with the press. The scene at the tomb was bedlam. A dispatch in January filed by the *Daily Telegraph* captured the drama perfectly:

The scene at the tomb awakened memories of Derby Day. The road leading to the rock-enclosed ravine . . . was packed with vehicles and animals of every conceivable variety. The guides, donkey-boys, sellers of antiquities, and hawkers of lemonade were doing a roaring trade. . . . When the last articles had been removed from the corridor today the newspaper correspondents began a spirited dash across the desert to the banks of the Nile upon donkeys, horses, camels and chariot-like sand-carts in a race to be the first to reach the telegraph offices.

The Luxor headquarters of the Eastern Telegraph Company remained completely unprepared for anything but the normal, and relatively calm, exchange of tourists' messages—the booking of guides, fellucas and rooms—and although it was feverishly attempting to expand its services, including the installation of a new set of telegraph lines to Cairo, the daily rush by reporters for the few available telegraph machines frequently touched off a rash of physical confrontations.

On the tenth of January, Lord Carnarvon made his final decision and signed an exclusive contract with the London *Times* for five thousand pounds in a direct cash payment, plus seventy-five percent of all profits from the sale of *The Times*'s articles to other world newspapers. By June 1923, the revenues had amounted to £11,600, or $55,600. It was a financial benefit, but in a short time the contract became a public-relations and political nightmare with horrendous consequences. From that time on, Tutankhamun became a never-ending public scandal.

Lord Carnarvon wrote Carter about his decision just before the public announcement:

I am afraid that you have had a very poor time with the Press. I could have settled earlier, but I wanted to consult you and have your views . . . I feel in this matter it would not do to, so to speak, auction the rights of journalistic publication, etc. I am afraid it would make the matter too common and commercial therefore I consider the *Times* offer the best thing that can be done. After all is said and done, it is the first paper in the world and even now has greater power and facilities than any other paper, which power I think very likely to increase under the new organisation and above all with Geoffrey Dawson, Editor. Even although I don't particularly care for him you are dealing with a straight gentleman.

At no time does Howard Carter appear to have raised any objection to the arrangement. He immediately wrote Arthur Merton, asking him to join the excavation team as a full-fledged member of the staff.

Merton, delighted, answered:

I beg to confirm my acceptance of your offer to join your staff in the capacity of publicity agent. As agreed between us, I shall represent you in the Valley of the Kings in all publicity matters connected with the work at the tomb of Tutankhamun, and, as regards the publication of news and data, I shall only communicate such information as you may consent to publish, to such quarters as you may, from time to time, indicate to me.

When Albert Lythgoe learned of the agreement he immediately wrote to Edward Robinson, cautioning the Metropolitan's director to be "extremely careful . . . with regard to giving out *anything* which could reach the newspapers, concerning the Tutankhamun tomb." He reported that Carnarvon had made a contract with the London *Times* under which "they became the sole news bureau for the publicity of this work. . . . Although we are doing the lion's share of the work in the tomb, the tomb *is* Carnarvon's and Carter's and the right to speak publicly of it in any *definite* way is solely theirs—at least for the present."

News of the exclusive contract with the London *Times* produced a howling storm of editorial protest from virtually every major newspaper in the world. Carnarvon and Carter were accused of "prostituting pure science to commercialism," "the sale of the profession of archaeology and world history for cash." Under the headline "Tutankhamun Ltd.," the *Daily Express* published an article that generally summed up the prevailing ire on the part of the press that had to purchase *Times* dispatches:

While we have admiration for the faith and persistence which have brought so magnificent a reward to the labours of Lord Carnarvon, it is difficult to approve the manner in which he has seen fit to exploit his discovery. . . . The tomb is not his private property. He has not dug up the bones of his ancestors in the Welsh mountains. He has stumbled upon a Pharaoh in the land of the Egyptians . . . and by making an exclusive secret of the contents of the inner tomb he has ranged against him the majority of the world's most influential newspapers.

The *Daily Express* equated Carnarvon's handing over of the journalistic rights in the valley to the sole control of *The Times* "to treating the find as his own personal property." With this shot, the paper initiated an unceasing cannonade, urging the

Egyptian government "to assert its full power and keep their kings, their treasures in Egypt."

A week after the signing of the contract, one of the correspondents for the *Morning Post,* an English-language paper published in Cairo, went directly to Pierre Lacau for information about the tomb. But the Director General of Antiquities refused to utter a word, and the *Morning Post* immediately commenced a bitter campaign of its own:

Lacau definitely stated that he would not give any information to the Press, even if he received orders directly from the Egyptian Government itself, as it was Lord Carnarvon's affair, and he could not encroach on Lord Carnarvon's preserves. He added that he had his own private views concerning Lord Carnarvon's arrangements in London, but he could not interfere . . . The statement is an illuminating sidelight whereby a French official in the Egyptian Government is willing to and can disregard an order from the Government.

Within a week of *The Times*'s contract the other correspondents had formed what Merton described as the "opposition combine." At first everyone was polite to Merton; then, as he put it, "our rivals began to get restless at getting very little news." Merton wrote home that the chief correspondent of Reuters, Valentine Williams, twice asked him if he "would be so kind as to escort Mrs. Williams back to Luxor in the evening—apparently as an excuse to try and get me out of the way." With the arrival in the valley of H. V. Morton of the enraged *Daily Express,* politeness turned to unconcealed dislike and active harassment. Morton held a meeting of all reporters but those of *The Times* in his rooms in Luxor in order to concoct a scheme "to do everything possible to break *The Times'* agreement." The group wired repeated protests to Pierre Lacau and the authorities in the Ministry of Public Works about *The Times*'s exclusivity. And, as Arthur Merton observed in his report home, "many champagne dinners were given, presided over by Mrs. Williams who was apparently becoming a sort of News Editor for the rival Press." On one occasion at the mouth of the tomb itself, Merton sensed Mrs. Williams looking over his shoulder at his writing pad. Merton didn't let on that he recognized her presence, but wrote: "It is unladylike and rude to look over my shoulder." "Exit Mrs. Valentine Williams," he observed with glee.

But the editors of *The Times* were not amused. Shocked by the violence of some of the criticism from its rivals, the paper immediately went on the offensive and fired back that "discreditable and unfounded aspersions" had "been cast on Lord Carnarvon's work." The article pointed out that the team of excavators had even been charged with creating a monopoly of news from Luxor and *even* with commercialism, but it stated, no charge could be more false. *The Times* contended that Lord Carnarvon had decided to supply the news through its services "solely because he thought it would be the best way, in fact the only practical way, of supplying it fully and independently to all newspapers throughout the world who wanted to take it," and that the "scientific character of the work compelled him to distribute news of it through the agency of its own world resources."

The logic—for scientific purposes—of Lord Carnarvon's decision seemed sound, for it would indeed have been hazardous to allow the dozens of newspaper reporters on hand in Luxor into the cramped chamber of the tomb each day and would have seriously jeopardized the progress of the work. But in reality, dozens of reporters would not have trooped into the sanctuary each day. Then, as now, press pools were common.

In any event, it was not the merits of the case that mattered. It had become a matter of appearances and public relations, and it was too late to rectify the error, even had there been the desire to do so. Carnarvon's guarantee of exclusivity to *The Times* planted the seeds for the utter destruction of what he so desired—fame of a high and noble nature, honors for himself and Carter, the burnishing of the British image in Egypt, and a share of the spectacular treasure.

CHAPTER SIXTEEN

A "Renegade" Speaks Out

THE EGYPTIAN ANTIQUITIES Service was almost torn to shreds by the onslaught of the press and the tens of thousands of visitors who rushed to Luxor and the Valley of the Kings. Pierre Lacau was beleaguered on all sides. A flock of Egyptian newspapers, goaded by the foreign press and infuriated by the London *Times,* complained bitterly that they had been refused entry to an Egyptian tomb. Lacau, they claimed, had placed them in a position of subservience by having to accept *The Times*'s dispatches.

Thousands of would-be visitors streamed into Lacau's offices at the Antiquities Service in Cairo or into the local office at Luxor, seeking permits and voicing their outrage that Howard Carter was turning *everyone* away from the tomb, even those who had an official governmental entree. Several politicians of the emerging Nationalist Party were seeking an investigation to find out whether or not Pierre Lacau or any of his associates had secretly arranged to give Lord Carnarvon any work of art from the tomb. A feeling arose throughout the country that no matter what the concession or the Law of Antiquities might have assured the discoverers, and no matter if or when the tomb had been defiled by ancient robbers, none of the unique splendors should ever leave Egypt.

Pierre Lacau met privately a number of times with Howard Carter, beseeching him to give the Egyptian reporters news releases. Carter flatly and arrogantly refused, stating that the Egyptian press already had a preferred position—it didn't have to pay for the *Times* material. Lacau also begged Carter to allow the Antiquities Service to send visitors into the tomb, along with those he was guiding daily through the sanctuary. Carter refused this request too, saying that *his* visitors were all archaeologists and had every right to enter.

Lacau and his aide Rex Engelbach, who had been assigned the task of inspecting the tomb each day, tried to persuade Carter to set aside one day, January 26, for special visitors approved by the Antiquities Service and for correspondents of all newspapers, including the Egyptian dailies, to view the tomb. Carter told them that it would be impossible, for he was too busy with "scientific work." He added that, under his concession, the Antiquities Service had "no rights" for such an event, which would mark "a most serious interruption in the professional undertakings of the tomb."

The harried Antiquities officials tried to bring Carter around by means of gentle humor. Rex Engelbach sent him a hand-delivered message of the most delightful nature:

Please tell me if the journalists can come on the date arranged by Lacau! I seem, in this play, to be between the upper and nether millstones. In the meantime, I am making a corner in all the blunderbusses and rifles, etc. in the district in case I have orders to storm the position and seriously think of asking for some high explosives to demolish that disgustingly strong door by means of which you have locked up the treasures of Egypt's ancestors!

The door—the steel grille that Carter had erected to prevent any modern thievery—had become a malevolent symbol of foreign supremacy. Engelbach's lighthearted letter would appear later to be disturbingly prophetic.

Howard Carter responded to Engelbach's attempt at friendly persuasion by studiously avoiding him and by initiating a vicious campaign to have him transferred from the Valley of the Kings. Lord Carnarvon joined the campaign. Carnarvon tried to persuade Lacau to send Tewfik Effendi, who had been the local inspector at Luxor when the tomb of the Princesses was pillaged, to replace Engelbach, or "Trout." Lacau had not given in, however, and had insisted that Engelbach be present for the first opening and, far from being replaced, be assigned to continue his inspections of the tomb. Carnarvon was annoyed at the decision and informed Carter that he would keep trying to have Engelbach ousted. His campaign never did succeed.

Lacau asked Carnarvon to allow a number of the Press Bureau of the Egyptian newspapers into the tomb on occasion. Carnarvon responded that entry for representatives of any newspapers not covered by the *Times*'s contract would not be possible. But he promised to see to it that an Egyptian representative would receive a communiqué from himself or Carter from time to time. Carnarvon was well aware of the fact that the Antiquities Service was having ferocious arguments with the press, yet he observed to Carter that he was utterly uninterested in helping to smooth matters over. To Lacau's suggestion that there be a special day for all the press, Carnarvon said that he would comply only if the London *Times* concurred! When Lacau lamely protested to Carnarvon that he was being assaulted on all sides, his lordship replied that any change in the status quo could stop the work and would be dangerous to the works of art. Carnarvon took the position that he would be firm for the sake of firmness.

Suddenly, Lord Carnarvon and Howard Carter themselves were besieged on the subject of the special press day. The legal adviser to the Ministry of Public Works sent Carter an outright threat:

Have advised Ministry that it is legally entitled to authorise visit tomorrow. Persistence in your attitude calculated to harm seriously the interests not only of your principal Carnarvon, but of other concession holders. Venture to suggest that in interests of all concerned you should make necessary arrangements.

About the same time that the Ministry of Public Works had entered the fray, Howard Carter received another entreaty for the press day from a man he considered a "renegade"—a thorough disgrace to the profession of archaeology. This was Arthur Weigall, a talented Egyptologist, writer and journalist who had been, over the years, an inspector of antiquities and a colleague with Carter on one of Theodore Davis' excavations. Weigall had left the Antiquities Service under mysterious circumstances. There were rumors, unsubstantiated, that he had been involved in art dealing and for that reason had been asked to leave. A writer of considerable vivacity, Weigall had been retained by the London *Daily Mail* as a special correspondent for "Egyptological matters" regarding the unparalleled discovery. But when he had tried to enter the tomb, Weigall had been turned away by Carter with considerable relish.

Weigall had cornered Carter in the Valley of the Kings. Emotionally, directly, pulling no punches, he spelled out the nature of the hatred Carter and Carnarvon had managed to generate on the part of the world press and the Egyptians. Their argument was summarized in a letter from Weigall to Carter written later that day. He wrote Carter that he found himself in "a rather awkward position," because he had been hired by the *Daily Mail,* under circumstances well known to Carter, and that because of the *London Times* exclusivity, there was little he could do. He reminded Carter that he had been in charge of "some pretty big finds" himself, so he could sympathize with the difficulties Carter was having with visitors and the press. "Since you will not allow me to go down to Cairo and tell Lord Carnarvon what I think," he wrote, "I shall tell it to you and you can tell him—or *should* tell him."

He emphasized to Carter that he was anxious to keep away from "this warfare which . . . looks like becoming big enough seriously to damage British interests in Egypt.

"You, in the depths of Old Tut's tomb," he wrote Carter, "have probably not realised how bitter and dangerous the whole situation is—and what I'm trying to do is to warn both you and Carnarvon of that danger."

He stressed that he had no ax to grind and even though Carter might not believe that now, he would come to see that he, Weigall, was motivated by only two desires—"to maintain British prestige in Egypt and to help Egyptology."

Weigall told Carter very bluntly that, in his opinion, he and Lord Carnarvon had made a terrible mistake in thinking that the perennial British prestige still held in Egypt and that foreign archaeologists could do what they pleased. He pointed out that they had found this special tomb just at the moment when anything could cause the political situation to explode, and added that sensitive diplomacy was key to dealing properly with the natives.

He continued, "You opened the tomb before you notified the government representative and, for all I know, entered it. . . . I believe you when you tell that you respected the rights of entry, but not notifying them of the initial discovery was enough.

"Don't you realise that all the natives say that you may have had the opportunity to steal some of the millions of pounds' worth of gold of which you talked?"

He assured Carter that whereas *he* believed Carter had not stolen anything from the tomb, there was a storm of gossip among the Egyptians that even if not based upon fact, was immensely damaging.

He added: "Anyway, they say that you have insulted their country. You two are being held up to execration of the most bitter kind. Even before I left London I was told of the intense feeling which you had both aroused."

Carter, infuriated, had attempted to cut Weigall off. It wouldn't work. Weigall stood his ground and told Carter that nothing, not even Carter's personal enmity toward him, of which he was well aware, would prevent him from telling his side of the affair. Carter pointed out rudely to Weigall that the Egyptians knew nothing about responsible and "scientific" digs, free from the petty harassments of unwarranted visitors and incompetent government inspections or from government officials who were interested only in playing politics.

Weigall had responded to Carter's insulting words sharply: "You may not like it; it may not be the best or the British way, but it is necessary to let the Egyptians in on this discovery."

To top it all, he reminded him that Lord Carnarvon had given the exclusive rights to *The Times* and that it had caused a tremendous storm on Fleet Street where they had been accused of cashing in on Egypt's "sacred dead," prostituting science for personal gain, and selling rights that in truth belonged to the Egyptian nation and the world. He granted that knowledgeable people would realize that all he had sold to *The Times* was his own personal views, but that he and *The Times* both knew that this involved "shutting out" anyone who might write a word about it.

"Under your system," he went on, "any Egyptologist who came out here . . . would be barred from entering the tomb or getting out a word of information." Not only would science lose his advice or knowledge, "but the public would lose the chance of obtaining first-hand information unless [other newspapers] used *The Times*, which no self-respecting paper could do."

He asserted that all other papers thought that *The Times*, Carter and Carnarvon were disgracing journalistic tradition.

He continued to Carter, "You and Lord Carnarvon say that it is no different from the Everest Expedition. But it is wholly different. Here you found a tomb belonging to the Egyptian government, a tomb in a public place, under the immediate eye of native and foreign tourists, a tomb containing Egypt's 'sacred dead,' a discovery belonging in no way to you, but to the world and especially to Egypt—an Egypt seething with hatred of England. Look what Sirry Pasha, a high government official, said on Sunday—'It is an unheard of thing that the Egyptian papers should have to take all news of an archaeological discovery in Egypt from a London newspaper.' "

Carter attempted to defend his position, citing the difficulty of the work, the incessant meddling of Lacau, the deluge of visitors, tourists and the press, who hovered around the entrance to the tomb or clustered around the Egyptian laborers while they worked. The damage caused by the press, in Carter's eyes, rivaled even the damage generated by the political activity of the Nationalists.

But Weigall answered by saying that he knew Carter's position perfectly well, but that Carter didn't seem to understand the public and press reaction. As for himself, he said: "My attitude is *this*. I will not join the fight by exciting native opinion. I refused to see the Prime Minister in Cairo. I refused to respond to the case before the Minister of Public Works. I even refused to see Lacau. Why? Two reasons. First, I thought in doing so I would help Lacau bring in his law that no antiquities should leave Egypt. Second, I didn't think I had the right to use the power of the *Daily Mail* inadvertently to light the torch which might set all Egypt ablaze.

"Believe me, this is no minor situation. It is of utmost danger to Britain. You don't realise that you have created a storm of sheer hatred by two unfortunate acts: the first by slighting the government at the opening of the tomb of a Pharaoh who from *nothing* has come to be—in the mystical mind of the natives—to be a sort of omen of Nationalism and the second, by making for money, a contract which forces you to shut out press men and Egyptologists and to behave like brigands sworn to secrecy—in fact, to the native mind, like *thieves*."

He begged Carter to take certain measures: First, to get Carnarvon to make a public statement that he would not profit from *The Times*. Second, to let all journalists into his workshop so they could publicize the excellent job Carnarvon was doing to conserve the objects. Third, to hand over to all journalists— particularly the natives—the essential facts at the earliest moment after the opening of the inner chamber, "and *not* one day after *The Times*."

He concluded his letter by warning that it was a bigger problem than a mere excavation, and that patriotism had to be considered, so that Carter and Carnarvon would act with Anglo-Egyptian relations in mind. "You have been ignored and insulted, I know. But I beg of you to keep your temper, and, in view of the strained political situation, to pacify the native press so far as you can."

Carter was stunned by Weigall's emotional outpouring. No one had ever addressed him like that. Carter never realized that he had just been given a rare gift of absolute truth and had received the best possible advice. Instead of thinking about what Weigall had said, he became enraged. From that time on, he did everything he could to belittle Weigall and to damage his reputation both in private and, occasionally, in the public print. But, despite his fury, Carter was chastened. As soon as Carnarvon arrived in the valley to examine the clearing of the Antechamber, he spoke to him of the affair.

Carnarvon felt the sting of Weigall's words. He still refused to issue stories to the Egyptian press on the same day as *The Times*. But he did agree to allow Lacau and the members of his organization to make innocuous visits to the tomb, and he gave in to the demand for a special viewing day on January 26 for all members of the press.

Their change of heart was too late, however, to heal the wounds. They had won a skirmish and lost the struggle, though it was too early for them to realize that.

CHAPTER SEVENTEEN

"Strong Bull, Beautiful of Birth"

WHILE THE CONTROVERSY raged on, Carter attempted to proceed with the delicate scientific enterprise. He obtained as a darkroom for Harry Burton the modest tomb in which Theodore Davis had believed, seasons before, he had discovered the mummy of Akhenaton. The small size of the chamber made it somewhat inconvenient, but its closeness to the tomb of Tutankhamun particularly pleased Burton. When he made an exposure he could rush into the tomb-darkroom and develop his glass plate without moving his cameras out of position. There was another benefit, for Burton's mad dashes from one tomb to the other mollified the crowds of tourists for whom there were few moments of drama the first winter.

After considerable persuasion, Carter finally received permission from Rex Engelbach—who, despite Lacau's assurances, had not been transferred to Giza, and never would be— to use the tomb of Seti II for a conservation laboratory and storeroom. Engelbach, reluctant to give up an ancient tomb for this purpose, had first asked Carter to construct a special building close to the tomb of Tutankhamun instead. Carter

166

acknowledged that the tomb of Seti II was a good distance away, a long haul for the crates that would be used to transport the objects and that had to be guarded by a squad of Egyptian soldiers all the way. But he persisted and eventually won out, pointing out that no new building could possibly be constructed that would be large or secure enough, or insulated sufficiently, to handle the huge array of objects. And so a pillaged pharaoh's home for eternity became the staging area for another pharaoh, in his reemergence to the light of day.

Seti II's tomb turned out to be ideal. It was sheltered by overhanging cliffs so that at no time of day did the direct rays of the sun ever strike its entrance. And there was a large open space in front of its portals that could be used as an outdoor photo studio or as a place where Callender could build the great wooden crates needed to transport the treasures to the Egyptian Museum. On days when the heat reached one hundred degrees or more, Mace and Lucas used the area for a makeshift outdoor laboratory. For security, Carter had erected a great steel gate, weighing over a ton and a half and laden with chains and padlocks, causing Winlock to observe that the Bank of England could not have been safer—or more time-consuming to enter.

The distance between the tombs of Seti and Tutankhamun gave tourists a long space in which to view some of the more spectacular objects as they were trundled down the path. Whenever any object was removed from the tomb and placed on one of the stretchers, a series of excited whoops came from the observers; out came the reporters' notebooks; *click* went the cameras, and a lane had to be cleared through the throng for each trip. Carter wryly observed that "more films were wasted in the valley in that first winter than in any corresponding period of time since cameras were first invented." As he delighted in telling certain privileged visitors to the laboratory, "We once had the occasion to make use of old mummy cloth sent up—it was not Tutankhamun's, nor had anything to do with him—for experimental purposes: it was sent up to us in a stretcher and it was photographed eight times before it got to us!"

Carter continually complained about the spectators, but he was clearly ambivalent about them: though furious at their being there, he tolerantly ordered his workmen to carry the more spectacular finds unwrapped past the spectators lining the path to the laboratory. The lesser objects, all bandaged up and transported with tender care on the stretcherlike trays, looked like casualties being brought out of the trenches.

Carter had also received permission to use another tomb—Number Four, an unmarked and unfinished chamber—for the storage of tools, chemicals, and a quantity of tinned foods and wines from Fortnum & Mason. Occasionally the excavators did not bother to go all the way down to Carter's house for lunch, but picknicked in grand style near the site. Later on, one of the wine crates deposited there would become a bombshell in the escalating struggle for the treasures.

The excavators ached to get through the sealed north doorway between the sentinels—as did Carter, whose first look had been more tantalizing than satisfying. By this time he yearned to discover whether or not the greatest prize of all, the King's mummy, would be intact. But they could not afford to be precipitous; all the hundreds of objects in the Antechamber had to be removed before the large sealed door could be dismantled.

Clearing the objects was "like playing a gigantic game of 'spillikins.' " They had been packed in so tightly or had been thrown about so haphazardly by the thieves that it was a matter of the greatest difficulty to move one without others threatening to come crashing down on something else. The members of the team became experts in jerry-rigging complicated systems of struts and props held up by strings and bandages as they worked their way through the forest of treasures. At times a section of the crowded room gave the appearance of a bridge constructed by a madman, a sight that prompted Winlock to observe that it looked like something deliberately conceived by a committee of the Service of Antiquities.

Winlock had begged the team to set aside for his personal examination anything that appeared to be the dregs of beer. Several years before, he had come across ancient beer paste inside a model brewery from the tomb of Meketra. Intrigued, he had sent the dried-out remains to a friend in the brewery business. His interest had been enhanced by the fact that he had been making beer himself—it happened to be the era of Prohibition. He would tell people with gusto that he had been informed that the yeast organism from Meketra was unlike any known in modern times. Although extinct, it had been given an official, scientific name—*Sacclaromyces Winlockii*.

From the appearance of the objects from the tomb on view today in the Egyptian Museum, it might seem that all Carter, Mace and Lucas had to do was to pick up a pristine work of art, put it in a box and simply carry it away. It was never that simple. Some of the pieces were in near-perfect condition, but others were dangerously fragile. The problem continually arose whether it would be better to apply preservative treatment to an object on the spot or to wait until it could be dealt with in a more complete manner in the laboratory. Carter tried to wait whenever it was possible, but all too frequently the transportation of an object without treatment threatened its destruction.

There were, for example, a number of exquisite sandals fashioned of patterned beadwork. Lying on the floor of the tomb, or wedged into one of the caskets, they looked as if they had been made yesterday. Unseen, the threading had rotted away. When Carter tried to move one of them, it crumbled at his touch and became a handful of loose beads. He soon learned that in such a case it was necessary to provide on-the-spot remedy by melting paraffin and washing it over the whole surface of the sandal. After an hour or two the object could be removed. Once it was in the laboratory the restringing of the hundreds upon hundreds of beads would take weeks.

The funerary bouquets became a conservator's nightmare. They had to be subjected to repeated application by spray gun of a celluloid solution before they could even be taken in hand.

Each object called for a different system of conservation. In most instances, one had to experiment with several techniques before knowing which one would be truly effective.

In this delicate, nerve-wracking work, Carter was fabulous. He felt a heavy responsibility for the restoration work. "Every excavator *must*," he wrote, "if he has any archaeological conscience at all." He spoke of the objects as "direct legacies from the past to the present age." He described himself as the privileged but temporary intermediary through whom they had happened to come. "If, by slackness or ignorance, an excavator diminished the knowledge that might have been derived from the treasures," Carter would observe, "he knows himself to be guilty of an archaeological crime of the first magnitude."

The excavators established an unvarying procedure to record the treasures. First, Harry Burton would take an on-site photograph. Then Carter would make a line drawing on a five-by-eight-inch card and would write a precise description:

Life Size Statue of the King, standing in N.E. corner, magnificently carved in wood, covered with a black pitch-like material in accordance with sacred sepulchral writ. The headdress, collarette, armlets, wristbands, dress, mace and staff heavily gilt and the sandals of gold. On the forehead of the King the Royal Uraeus or cobra of inlaid bronze and gold. The eye-socket and eyebrows of gold. The eyeballs made of arragonite and pupils of obsidian. Note the calm expression upon the King's face.

At the same time Carter would record all measurements, noting the damage or loss of any part of the material. After this, Burton would take a second series of photographs, and this time would place a card printed with a number in front of each object. Following this, the draftsmen Hall and Hauser would locate the object in a set of master line drawings which showed, from above, the juxtaposition of each object to those around it. The conservation spot work was then carried out. After that, the object would be transported to the laboratory, where Burton would take photographs showing the varying stages of repair. Finally, a brief description of each object was made in a preliminary "Journal of Entry" by Carter, who would, at that moment, frequently prepare a new set of notes on his catalogue cards. Each object or fragment was noted, described or numbered at least three times. Never before in the history of archaeology had there been such a precise record made of the clearing of any tomb.

By the twenty-sixth of December the team had removed the first work of art. They had decided they would clear the Antechamber in a counterclockwise manner, starting on the northeast wall with the funerary bouquets. From there they would work toward the chariots. Carter hated the very sight of the chariots, despite their beauty. They were covered with gold plates, highly decorated, with embossed patterns and scenes upon the gold from top to bottom, profusely inlaid with stones or glass. The actual woodwork appeared to be fairly sound. But the leather horse-trappings and reins had become black, damp, viscous glue with the passage of three thousand years, with the result that all the pieces were stuck together. And to add further to Carter's headache, the necropolis attendants who had put them into the Antechamber had simply sawed the axles of the vehicles in half to get them through the doors. The thieves had rummaged among the chariots, eagerly seeking gold, and had casually tossed other objects into the pile. Mixed in with the chassis of the magnificient vehicles were alabaster jars, walking sticks, hunting bows, dozens of reed baskets, and a number of horsehair fly whisks.

As the excavators worked their way around the room, they encountered one marvelous object after another. Just below the lion-headed couch was a superbly crafted wooden chest made of cedar with retractable handles. It was inlaid with ebony strips inscribed with hieroglyphs. On one end, in subtle relief, was a depiction of the King offering a series of ritual vessels to Osiris, the deity of afterlife in his guise as the god of the necropolis. The hieroglyphs, translated by Alan Gardiner, promised the King that his mouth, eyes and ears would be opened, his limbs would be rejuvenated, heaven would receive his soul and earth his body, and he would be granted food, sweet cool breezes and wine—forever.

Gardiner arrived early in January, looking forward eagerly to the work of deciphering what Carter had earlier described to the press as "a number of rolled-up papyri." But on closer investigation, no papyri ever came to light. There had never been any. For, in the first hasty examination, what appeared to be rolls of papyri turned out to be rolls of linen. This came as a major disappointment to the excavators. They had longed for a series of ancient records—letters, journals or archives—that might throw light upon the confused times in which Tutankhamun had lived. As one after another of the "papyri" turned out to be old clothes, the hope that any document would emerge from the tomb became very faint indeed. Gardiner soon stated, "Early on we began to realise that, in the end, the claim of the new tomb to be the greatest discovery ever made in Egypt will rest mainly in the great quantity of objects found and their amazingly high artistic quality; the historical harvest will be of less importance."

Carter was pleased to see that some of the objects were personal possessions of Tutankhamun from the time he had been a child. Tipped back under the lion-headed couch was an ebony chair inlaid with strips of ivory and ebony and, on the sides, panels of gilded bronze showing a recumbent ibex and floral motifs. The chair was only twenty-six inches high and carried no royal insignia. Thus Carter presumed that it had been used by the Prince before he had become god-king at the age of nine.

The world had long known of the grace and beauty of ancient Egyptian furniture from paintings and carvings in tombs, and from some actual examples preserved in the Egyptian Museum in Cairo. But not before Carter's astounding discovery had real examples of such excellence been revealed in such numbers. In front of the middle couch with the head of the cow, the excavators found a folding stool fashioned in ebony, ivory and gold. The stool was covered with an ebony-and-ivory leopard skin—the colors reversed. It even had an ebony tail. And the graceful feet, curving ever so slightly, were fashioned into stylized yet lively duck heads.

Just behind the folding stool, tipped on its side by one of the thieves, lay a ceremonial chair, in cedar and gold, that Carter believed might have been used during Tutankhamun's coronation ceremonies. The superb carving on the chair was, as Alan Gardiner said at the time, in a sense a carved book. The god of eternity, Heh, is to be seen kneeling in the center of the back, on top of the hieroglyphic symbol for gold. In each hand he grasps a palm rib which is surmounted by a solar disc. Hanging from the sun disc is a uraeus, or sacred cobra. From the hood of the serpent hangs a long banner, surmounted by the image of the falcon, or the god Horus, who in turn stands next to another sacred cobra. The banner reads, "Tutankhamun, Strong Bull, Beautiful of Birth." A large ankh, the symbol of life, hangs from the god's right arm. Another solar disc sits on top of the head of the divinity, flanked by two more serpents emerging from two signs for eternity. Rectangular panels on either side of the god Heh spell out the King's personal name, Tutankhamun, and his throne name, Nebkheperura. The inscriptions surrounding the back of the chair exhort a variety of gods to grant the King a life of eternity.

In diaries and letters home, the excavators recorded their sheer joy at discovering object after object of breathtaking beauty, some comparable to objects found in other digs, others previously unknown: a trumpet made of silver with a painted wooden inner form to keep the thin metal intact; the symbols of royal power—the crook, the gentle power of the King as shepherd, and the flail, the harsh power of the King as avenger. There was a collection of elaborately decorated staves, a quiverful of arrows and a number of bows laminated with rare woods. One bow, encased in thin gold plate, was incised with bands of inscriptions and animal motifs, and had been encrusted with gold granulated work of almost incomprehensible delicacy. Another bow had at each end the carved figure of a captive, with the heads of the two so positioned that their chins served as notches for the bowstring. Carter remarked that the King must have been delighted to know that each time he used the bow he was stringing up a pair of captives. There was also a forest of stately alabaster jars—more than fifty of them—that once held perfumes and unguents. Some of the vases even contained traces of their contents; others had been emptied by the thieves.

By the time he had cleared perhaps a quarter of the objects in the Antechamber, Carter was able to deduce how the ancient thieves had carried out their work.

There had been three separate entries. The first had taken place weeks after the tomb had been sealed and before the sloping passageway had been filled with rubble. Carter was convinced that the first intruders had been in league with corrupt necropolis officials. After the first illegal entry had been discovered, the passageway had been plugged with debris.

Some fifteen years after the passageway had been filled, two or more forays were made, by two separate gangs. One group had specialized in metalwork; the other had concentrated upon the oils and perfumes. The first gang made a tunnel in the upper left-hand corner of the blocked passageway and penetrated into all four chambers of the tomb. They had roughly snapped pieces of gold from furniture and chariots, broken the metal heads off arrows and rummaged through caskets, snatching certain pieces of jewelry which were heavily encrusted with gold. Yet they seemed to have avoided whole objects—except for one, a most important one. In a splendid wooden shrine about a foot tall decorated with gold reliefs Carter came across a small pedestal with carved indentations for two tiny feet—empty. There, Carter figured, had been a solid-gold statuette of the King.

After the first gang had gone or had been caught—no one knows which—officials opened the tomb through the thieves' tunnel and attempted to put things in order. Some years later, after the second resealing, the second gang forced an entry by digging out the tunnel made by the first group. This latter group, having found that much of the portable gold had already been taken, attacked the oils and perfumes, emptying them into leather bags. Once again the necropolis attendants discovered their work and tried to put things back in their places, refilling the tunnel and sealing off the doors.

The work of the necropolis attendants had been faulty. They had avoided the Annex altogether. In the Antechamber they merely scooped up the objects scattered by the robbers and jammed them into whatever box or casket happened to be nearby. A long white box at one end of the room had, at the bottom, a group of bows and arrows, above which the priests had thrown a haphazard assortment of the King's underwear. Other bows and arrows from the same box were scattered over the chamber floor. On some caskets and boxes, papyrus labels spelled out a precise inventory of the contents. But only one or two out of dozens had contents which fit the original label.

In several places Carter was amazed to find actual physical traces of the thieves of that far-off age. Several crates in the Annex were marred by the dirty footprints of the tomb robbers. Thrown upon the floor of a box in the Antechamber was a tattered old headband, containing three forgotten gold rings. From this evidence Carter figured that at least one gang had been caught—and instantly slaughtered.

CHAPTER EIGHTEEN

Carnarvon Returns to the Tomb

WHEN LORD CARNARVON and Lady Evelyn returned to the Valley of the Kings in late January, they made their first visit to the tomb in more than a month. This time they did not have to make the trek on the backs of donkeys. The automobile Carter had purchased in Cairo whisked them up in twenty-five minutes. They had feared an unpleasant journey, but it turned out to be relatively quick, easy and fascinating. The first section of the road was a bit hazardous, since it was loose, drifting sand; then, where the road ran parallel with the Nile for about a mile and a half, the surface was hard but exceedingly bumpy. The last half of the journey—slow ascent—had a smooth, hard-packed surface. The sights were splendidly exotic, for the road teemed with Egyptian peasants pulling donkeys, urging on flocks of lop-eared black sheep and goats. Hundreds of women carried huge loads of forage or water bottles on their heads. On all sides was an abundance of wildlife—ground doves, crested larks and painted hoopoes, which barely got out of the car's way, while hundreds of kites whistled and twirled overhead.

Lord Carnarvon and his daughter were greeted warmly by

Howard Carter and the rest of the Tutankhamun team, Mace, Lucas, Burton, Hall, Hauser and Callender. Carnarvon led them at a brisk, military pace to the tomb of Seti II to examine the laboratory and the splendid works of art he had only half looked at weeks earlier in the semidarkness. Carnarvon was mightily impressed with what he saw and congratulated the staff with a few toasts from a bottle of Dom Perignon he had brought with him. (Upon hearing about the champagne, Winlock said that there was nothing more salubrious for the second stage of an excavation than a few magnums.) Carnarvon was "home" again, and, although he was exhausted by the long journey from England, more so than he dared to let on to anybody but Carter and Evelyn, his spirits were instantly lifted by the magnificence of the objects. They seemed to have acquired an even greater beauty than when he had first seen them. And indeed they had, for Mace and Lucas—patiently cleaning, scraping, polishing—had removed, as if by magic, the passage of thousands of years. Every object looked as if it had emerged the day before from the bench of the finest craftsman of the royal workshop.

Mace proudly showed off to Carnarvon the results of his restoration of a series of wooden walking sticks, each about four feet high, each decorated along its entire length with hundreds of beetles' wings. He informed Carnarvon that he had worked for two and a half weeks just on two robes, separating well over three thousand gold sequins nestled among the tangled linen folds of the garments and over twelve thousand beads. Carnarvon asked him how long he thought it would take to repair the sixty objects that had been removed from the Antechamber, and Mace replied, ". . . a little over two years, with *luck*." He told Carnarvon that he had been seriously hampered in his work by continual interruptions from official visitors. And every time he and Alfred Lucas thought they could spend a few hours repairing an object in the laboratory, there came another call asking them to assist in preliminary restoration work on some object in the tomb, just to remove it.

177

After Carnarvon had visited the tomb and the laboratory he was interviewed by Arthur Merton.

What I have to say may, perhaps, be interesting, because the objects are now much more easily examined and appreciated, and no authoritative description of any individual objects has yet been published.

I went . . . first to the tomb of Seti II, which is now used, as is known, as a workshop or laboratory. Here I was able to see and study the results of the labours of Mr. Carter and his assistants. We have to be very careful as to who approaches even the entrance of the laboratory, but admission is not in itself a pleasure. Even from the outside the smell of chemicals is perceptible, and on entering, the odours of acetone, collodion and other unpleasant things which the experts seem to enjoy using are very strong.

The tomb consists of what, in effect, is a long passageway, and all the way down are boxes containing precious objects. There are tables covered with bottles, large parcels of wadding and trays containing miscellaneous objects lightly covered with cloths to keep off the dust, while the door through which you enter has a very ponderous steel gate with four padlocks, which we hope precludes any possibility of theft. Altogether, nothing could be more admirably arranged than the details over which Mr. Carter and his staff have spent so much thought and labour. The passage is a long one, running into the hillside, and the only light comes from the entrance. At the farther end one must examine the objects with an electric torch.

You have already heard of the throne or chair of state. It is even more beautiful than we had imagined; the delicacy of the inlaid precious stone work is quite extraordinary, and the carving and modelling of the figures of the King and Queen, which are in low relief, are really wonderful in power and expression. I believe it is the only example of such a chair of state yet found. Between the seat and the legs were originally figures or decorative work of some kind, probably of gold, because they have been torn away by robbers. From the struts supporting and strengthening the legs jagged ends show where the figures have been roughly broken off. Great care must necessarily be exercised in handling the restoration of this beautiful object, because some parts of it are in a most delicate condition.

Most of the portions of the chair, except the decorated inlaid surfaces, are sheathed in the thinnest gold. Where gold is laid directly on the wood its condition is practically as good as when it was first made. Where, however, the gold is laid over the modelling in plaster, the plaster has deteriorated and extreme care is necessary. When the work of preservation is finished I believe it will reveal itself to the public as one of the most beautiful objects ever found.

Another object, almost more wonderful than the throne, is a box which contained some of the King's clothes. This, as already related, is painted with scenes of the King hunting lions and other animals, and the painting is so delicate as to resemble the finest miniature. At the present moment, the whole surface is thickly coated with a semi-transparent paraffin wax, but even through this the colours are quite bright and the beauty of the work is plainly evident. When the wax has been reduced the box will appear in almost all its original beauty. Mr. Mace and Mr. Lucas already have spent many days work on it, treating it with the utmost tenderness and expert care. When finished it will be recognised as a veritable monument of their patience and skill.

Unfortunately, a certain amount of damp must, from some as yet unidentified source, have entered the tomb at some time, for all the linen is in practically a rotten condition. What once was white is now all chocolate-brown or blackish, and no longer a fabric. Even with the greatest care it is very doubtful if much of it can be saved.

There is, however, one object of this class which would, I imagine, create the greatest interest in Yeovil, the home of glove-making in England. It is a little glove made of some sort of linen. It is of the gauntlet type of glove, and like the rest of the linen is discoloured to a dark brown. In spite of its fragility we hope that, between two sheets of glass, it may be preserved to live many years yet. From its size it appears to be a child's glove. Some suggest that it was the property of King Tut-ankh-Amen when a baby and that it had been tenderly preserved, but nobody knows, nor am I expert enough to say how much linen gloves are in the habit of shrinking in the course of three thousand years. Anyhow, I conjecture that it must be the oldest glove of which there is any record.

For the moment I must content myself with mentioning these few things, but I cannot close without testifying to the magnificent work which Mr. Carter has done in organising the whole procedure for the salvage of these treasures. All of the staff have given of their best, and I believe the result will be commensurate with all the trouble, thought and thoroughness which they have lavished on the work.

In his London *Times* dispatch, Merton stressed that "everything had been handled and removed without any damage whatever." He reported that the most recent object to be taken out of the Antechamber, the Hathor couch, had been slipped out of the narrow passageway and stairs "with a skill which commanded the absolute admiration of the throngs surrounding the entrance to the tomb." Films taken by Harry Burton show that the task had been extremely trying. The couch had been taken out in eight pieces. Only a quarter of an inch separated the top of the curved tail of the mythical creature and the lintel of the outer doorway. It took the excavators a frustrating amount of time to inch it through.

By the time Carnarvon had returned to the valley, the Antechamber contained only the lion and Typhon couches, the chariots, the two sentinels and about thirty smaller works of art. Carter and his associates had begun to be pestered with questions from reporters about how long it would take to clear the first room and the Annex and then open the sealed doorway. Carter had decided to wait to tackle the jumbled mess of the Annex until another season. It was obvious that after the nightmare of moving the chariots, his team needed a rest. He planned to enter the Holy of Holies, examine and record its contents, and close down for the season—except for conservation work.

After Lord Carnarvon's return, Arthur Merton filed some amusing puff pieces. Carnarvon had insisted upon them, apparently in an attempt to balance poisonous publicity issuing daily from the Egyptian newspapers. At times Merton iced his cakes lavishly.

It is impossible not to be impressed here with the extremely friendly, even affectionate attitude of the native Egyptians of all classes towards Lord Carnarvon. Every one knows him and is obviously glad to see him back. It is a refreshing contrast to the attitude of some of the Egyptian newspapers elsewhere, which have been assailing him for political purposes with the greatest of bitterness.

The fact is that the people know that Lord Carnarvon likes them. He likes Egypt and the Egyptians and is their staunch friend. Mr. Carter has also spent the greater part of his life in Egypt, understands the people and likes them and liking, as always, begets liking.

The sugarcoated words did nothing to blunt the attacks. On the contrary, they further enraged one of Carnarvon's most severe critics, a correspondent described contemptuously by the excavators throughout the Tutankhamun affair by his last name only, Bradstreet. He had informed his friends that he was going to "drive C. and C. out of their minds for having sold a piece of the world's ancient history to the London *Times.*" He was the chief Egyptian correspondent for *The New York Times,* and for the Egyptian *Morning Post* as well. Bradstreet seemed to pop up from behind every rock in the valley and appeared to distribute himself simultaneously in *three* hotels in Luxor to track down a hint of a scandal or the most minute nugget of news about a recent discovery. Typical of his prose and point of view was the following "zinger" that Bradstreet had filed for his British newspaper:

Tutankhamun is resting peacefully. Lord Carnarvon has gone to Cairo, allegedly to visit his dentist, while his staff here—including members of the staff of the Metropolitan Museum of Art—are busy preserving and packing the objects when they are not writing special articles for Lord Carnarvon's exclusive service of news and pictures.

There is going to be bitter complaint back in America, for a collection of energetic correspondents have been telling these Americans that while the Met's staff has been loaned to Carnarvon in the interests of archaeology, Carnarvon is capitalizing on the brains of these experts in London, where he has sold information and pictures relating to the tomb to be distributed thence to buyers around the world.

Albert Lythgoe flew into a monumental rage upon reading the story and wrote Edward Robinson that "the contemptible campaign . . . waged against Carnarvon . . . has found its way to some extent into our papers at home." The prime instigator, he stated, was Bradstreet of *The New York Times,* who was now reporting that there were frictions between the English and the Americans in the "perfect machine" working on the Tutankhamun affair. Lythgoe demanded that in light of Bradstreet's articles in the *Morning Post* alluding to "growing frictions," Robinson bring the issue to the attention of the publisher of *The New York Times* himself, Adolph Ochs. "We would appreciate it," he wrote, "if Mr. Ochs would call a halt on Bradstreet's despicable campaign."

Adolph Ochs listened to the complaints and said he would ponder the problem and take the proper action. Apparently he did, for he quietly informed his correspondent in Cairo to "go right ahead." It had not been for the temporary convenience of Howard Carter or his American associates that the great publisher had conceived and caused to be printed with emphatic frequency the basic philosophy of *The New York Times*—"To give the news impartially, without fear or favor, regardless of any party, sect or interest involved."

By early February the work was becoming agony. The heat had already begun to build up, and on some days the temperature reached the nineties. Each day seemed to bring periods of fierce winds, terrifying prognostications of the really severe dust storms that would ravage the valley in March. The eyes of the excavators itched and smarted constantly. Life became hell—particularly for the conservators who might have to pick their way through thousands of beads that had adorned just one royal robe. The objects seemed to have formed a deliberate conspiracy to impede the preservation work.

Every day the team worked against time. Everything had to be repaired, packed and made ready for shipment to Cairo before the brutal heat of April. To pack and crate each object became a back-breaking chore. For each couch, ten thousand square feet of wood had to be carefully crafted.

Their work was interrupted continually. Lythgoe wrote to Robinson of the Metropolitan Museum: "Poor Carter has been simply *buried* under it all . . . and among his other troubles and annoyances, he has seen nearly every Egyptologist one ever heard of." Then, as Lythgoe observed, he would see each one of them rush "into print for his own ends with newspaper

articles" or extensive series about the tomb and the significance of its contents. Percy Newberry, Carter's mentor, contributed what Lythgoe called "a seemingly *endless*" group of
stories to Bradstreet's Egyptian outlet, the *Morning Post*. Professor Griffith of Oxford University wrote weekly articles for
the London *Observer*. Professor Elliot Smith wrote for the *Daily
Telegraph*. Carter was infuriated that they all blithely undermined the exclusive arrangement he and Carnarvon had with
the London *Times*. To top it all off, the venerable James
Breasted had approached Carnarvon and Carter with a direct
request for a complete set of Harry Burton's unique lantern
slides for use on a lecture tour he wanted to launch in England
and America. Carter exploded.

On certain days, when it seemed that the excavators hardly
emerged from the tomb at all or had spent the time cloistered
off in the laboratory, Arthur Merton would be hard pressed to
file an invigorating story. On one of those quiet days he described the restoration of a third pair of royal sandals, ventur-
ing the guess that "probably we shall see our smartest ladies
wearing footgear more or less resembling and absolutely in-
spired by these wonderful things." Within days, Carter's mail
contained dozens of requests seeking world rights for exclusive designs and manufacturing.

The same day Merton filed his sandal story he also reported
that the staff had spent six frustrating and fruitless hours wres-
tling with the chariots which the group had to remove before
the last two couches could be extracted. But "things get stiff in
the joints in thirty centuries," Merton observed. The pole of
each chariot, which originally had been supple enough to
bend when it was introduced to the tomb, had become totally
rigid. The excavators groaned at the thought of having to dis-
mount the four ancient tie poles before extracting the vehicles.
Inside one of the chariots Callender discovered an ancient floor
mat or rug, which he at once christened "the woolly." It was a
sort of deep linen fiber made to look like sheepskin. Getting it
off the floorboard of the chariot consumed four hours of preservation work.

February 1 was a banner day. The lion and Typhon couches

were carried from the tomb. The day was beautiful—cool, slightly overcast, with spectacular shadows passing over the pink-tinged hills. The team made its way to the mouth of the tomb at eight-thirty in the morning. By nine o'clock Callender had filled two large square cases with cotton-wool waste and had covered them with a white sheet. The spectators strained to see each step in these activities, knowing that a special event was about to take place. Harry Burton caused a minor diversion by suddenly showing up lugging a movie camera. Room had to be made for him on the escarpment. A few tourists who had been waiting since seven that morning engaged him in a rather vituperative discussion when they learned they would have to make way.

Deep within the tomb, Carter could be heard issuing orders and giving instructions, his voice booming strangely from the depths. The bed portion appeared, and then the sides. Finally the base of the lion couch was carried out. All the pieces were carried by hand to the laboratory and guarded by the soldiers. As each journey was made, dozens of reporters ran alongside as closely as the troops allowed, trying to catch a glimpse.

And what a gorgeous thing it was, suddenly exposed to the brightness of day—but how barbaric! To the contemporary mind the word "couch" conveys something low, sedate, perhaps even informal. Not so this giant royal piece of furniture. The bed platform alone stood almost five feet off the ground. When the King reclined upon it, he must have been considerably above the level of his audience. The ceremonial bed had a high footboard, but there was no headboard at all so that nothing would obstruct the view of the King. His visage would have been flanked majestically, as if by two heraldic devices, by the two lions. To Arthur Merton the animals' heads were "fearsome, resembling a Cerberus-like piece of furniture." The heads were strikingly gilded, and the mouths of the lions were open in a great roar. Long curling tongues of ivory painted pinkish red stuck out from a dense set of pure-white ivory teeth.

When the Typhon couch came out of the tomb it created a sensation among the spectators. All the mystery of the secret funeral rituals of ancient Egypt seemed to be embodied within it. A group of American tourists who had been waiting on the parapet since six-thirty that morning were overjoyed. At the sight of the strange beast, one of them said, their wait had proven to be "more than worthwhile."

Once the couches had been removed from the Antechamber, dozens of smaller objects that lay underneath them could be lifted from the tomb. Word of the excitement had reached the tour guides in the hotels in Luxor. On hearing this news and the prediction of cool breezes, hundreds of spectators jammed the parapet and the path leading to the laboratory.

Every hour, almost as if a precise schedule had been established, another object would pass by the onlookers. One of the most curious was a tray containing numerous pieces of gilded wood, looking like a bunch of wooden flails or pieces of threshing machinery. They turned out to be parts of a large mobile umbrella provided for the King when on excursion in the desert—a dismountable canopy that could be erected over him as shelter when he rested. The contraption had been discovered underneath the chariots; for that reason, the excavators assumed it was part of the camp equipment used by the King's retinue when in the field or on a hunt. As the pieces came out, Mace picked up one section and demonstrated for the group of tourists how it had been used. One of them pointed out that the diggers could "pay their rent, if they were just to set it up" for the convenience of the tourists.

The chariots came out in pieces: a wheel, then another, then the chassis and the tie poles and at last the bodies themselves. Their removal had been the most difficult work of all. Mace had confided to Carter that the vehicles might prove to be so dilapidated that he was not at all certain they could ever be restored. For weeks he had thought it would not be worth even a try and wanted at first simply to remove the gold reliefs and mount them in frames. But after months of backbreaking labor with Alfred Lucas, he succeeded in a complete restoration. Today they are among the most impressive objects in the Egyptian Museum.

Then the diggers patiently cleared away the tangled debris

from around the chariots. There were fruit baskets, a circular reed tray with partitions which looked like a modern receptacle for hors d'oeuvres, a diminutive wooden figure of the King about eight inches tall, several fly whisks, assorted fragments of jewelry and a superb riding whip. The whip was made of wood covered with leather and had an ivory handle in the form of a supple horse, depicted leaping through the air with legs stretched out so that the curvature of the body fit perfectly into the King's hand. An inscription on the crop described Tutankhamun as "appearing gloriously on horse, even like the rising sun."

Then suddenly the Pharaoh himself seemed to pop up from the mouth of the tomb and walk up the stairs and down the path toward the laboratory. It was a life-sized doll or mannequin without arms or legs. Set on the carrying tray, held by one of the workmen who was partly hidden by its shape, it seemed to be proceeding under its own power. Carter believed it to be the dress dummy of the King. It was exceptionally beautiful, and in almost mint condition. The King's features were finely chiseled and were delicately painted and gilded.

Some people refused to believe that the marvelous image was Tutankhamun's. It seemed too feminine; the colors appeared to be those normally applied to the sculptures of women in ancient times. The crown, which resembled a squat "Turkish" fez, reminded Arthur Weigall of crowns said to have been designed by Akhenaton for his wife, Nefertiti, and her daughters. Weigall told Bradstreet. And Bradstreet reported that the mannequin was unquestionably that of a woman—and an intriguing one at that. He wrote that her face was "wreathed in a glowing Mona Lisa smile—a smile which captivated the few spectators who remained at the tomb after the announcement that the morning's work was finished. The lips are full, the eyes dark and large, but the whites of the eyes are very pronounced. Finally the cheeks are almost certainly those of a young girl."

Carter got word to Bradstreet that the statue was definitely not a girl or a woman of mysterious identity, but simply a model used by Tutankhamun's hairdresser to arrange royal wigs. But Bradstreet ignored the information and wrote that "some observers believe that it is a statue of Tutankhamun's Queen buried with him for company until the Queen died and came to him in the next world." At length, someone on the excavation team remarked sourly to Bradstreet that one would expect a model of an affectionate queen to have been supplied with arms and legs. At that point, Bradstreet offered another theory, reporting that the object might be "a rough sketch of Queen Ankhesenamun made by some sculptor as a model for a portrait statue in stone of Tutankhamun's young wife—who was only seventeen years old when her husband died." Queen Ankhesenamun had become the celebrity of the hour.

The golden throne had been fully cleaned in the laboratory and turned out to be even more beautiful than the excavators had first believed. The figure of the Queen, gently bending over the seated King, was lithe, radiant. The Queen's dress was silver, and the exposed parts of her body were subtly modeled by an inlay of a semi-opaque, glistening light-red glaze. The excavators were deeply impressed by the magnificence of this stunning work of art but somewhat perplexed that the Queen had been given such prominence. Not only was she the same physical size as the King, but her very position seemed to suggest that she was the King's equal.

When Carter and James Breasted examined the throne they were surprised to discover two wholly different cartouches— one with the name Tutankhamun and the other Tutankhaton. To Howard Carter, the changed names upon the throne were closer to historical documents than anything he had yet unearthed. The deliberate alteration of the cartouches symbolized the political and religious ambiguities of Tutankhamun's realm. The appearance of the Amun form of the royal name in some cartouches and the presence in others of the Aton form pointed to the stresses between the competing political parties and religious ideologies at the time. Carter found it curious that such an important object as a throne decorated with such obvious manifestations of the Aton heresy could possibly have been buried in a tomb in the necropolis of Thebes—the very stronghold of Amun. Neither Carter nor anyone else was ever able to explain the phenomenon. He found what seemed to him to be remains of linen wrappings around the throne's legs. These made him think that Tutankhamun's conversion to the religion of the god Amun had not wholly been based upon deep religious conviction. It was possible, Carter conjectured, that Tutankhamun had considered the throne too valuable a possession to destroy and had covered it up and preserved it in one of the more private areas of his palace. Carter also believed it possible that the substitution of Amun for Aton in several places on the object had been sufficient to appease the purists.

The youthful King and Queen had obviously adored each other and had fully enjoyed each other's company. Nowhere was this more apparent than on another spectacular object discovered in the Antechamber. This was a little gold shrine, less than two feet high, in the shape of a pavilion with a gently curving roof, placed upon two sledlike runners—a shrine sacred to the goddess Nekhbet. The shrine is covered by a series of gold reliefs portraying Tutankhamun and Ankhesenamun. In some the Queen is depicted in a formal manner, presenting to her lord official symbols of his exalted rank. In others the relationships between the two young individuals are unusually intimate. On one rectangular panel about eight inches long, the royal couple are represented hunting together. He is seated on a folding stool vigorously pulling back his bow at a flight of ducks thundering out of a dense papyrus growth. She sits on the ground nearby and casually holds an arrow for his second shot, pointing rather languidly at a pair of plovers who are trying to hide in the thick patch of papyrus.

In another scene the Queen sits ensconced on a fluffy pillow at Tutankhamun's feet. He pours some sort of liquid from a small jar into her delicate hand. What does it really represent—a toast to the success of the hunt? No one knows. In yet another golden relief the Queen stands on the pillow and lovingly ties around her husband's neck a distinctive necklace in

188

the shape of a scarab with two large cross-hatched wings. What does it mean? Is it a prize or a medal for an especially successful hunt? Is it a gift? No one has any cogent idea. The only thing that is known is that the scenes are full of humanity, affection, obvious pleasure.

By the first week of February, a number of newspapers that had decided not to become part of the London *Times* syndicate began to criticize the excavators for taking too much time to clear the Antechamber. It was suggested that Carter had deliberately slowed down the pace of the work because of "arguments" with officials of the Antiquities Service over arrangements for the opening of the Burial Chamber. Just prior to Lord Carnarvon's departure for Cairo to meet with representatives of the Ministry of Public Works and the Antiquities Service, he had asked Merton to counter these complaints. So Merton wrote a series of news stories that amounted virtually to editorials. "The criticism," he stated, "that the period which has intervened between the official opening on November 29th and the return of Lord Carnarvon on January 29th should have been more than sufficient for the removal of all the objects is *unfounded*."

Merton praised the "superior talents" of the excavators and the "magnificent quality" of their work. He pointed out that the delays had come about owing to the "wholly benevolent wish on the part of Lord Carnarvon to set aside several special days for government visitors and the press." He observed that no one could possibly have predicted the nature or the extent of the tasks that preserving and removing hundreds of objects required. He vividly described the extraordinary labors of A. C. Mace and Alfred Lucas.

Owing on the one hand to the fragility of the objects and on the other hand to the pressure of the spectators, the transport along the roadway has been necessarily slow, and required, in addition the personal supervision of Howard Carter or one of his assistants. . . . And when I add that all but five objects have now been transferred and that so far not a single mishap has occurred it will, I think, be agreed that Mr. Carter and his staff, which consists, for the purpose of removal, of only five members, have done wonders.

Merton pointed out that their achievement was "even more remarkable" when one considered the "constant interruptions they suffered, not only from official visitors, often forced upon them by the government, but from administrative and other worries which should never have been allowed to take place." Further delays had also been generated by the fact that the excavators had to answer personally a growing volume of mail and cablegrams. Among the more recent communications were requests from seed merchants asking for samples from the sanctuary, textile manufacturers begging for copyrights for Tutankhamun designs, and provision dealers seeking parcels of "mummified foods—apparently they expected them to be tinned." Added to these were telegrams from motion picture people and photographers asking special concessions. Apparently, what outnumbered everything else were requests for autographs. According to Merton, all requests were "being treated with the greatest of respect and courtesy by Carter and Carnarvon, with the result that they had wasted a considerable amount of time." Howard Carter's private comments on the hundreds of requests had been unprintable.

Lord Carnarvon returned to the valley from Cairo on the thirteenth of February and announced that he would open the mysterious sealed door on Sunday, the seventeenth of February. He revealed that Elisabeth, Queen of the Belgians, would be present at the official opening of Tutankhamun's sealed inner chamber. Everyone congratulated his lordship on a brilliant stroke of public relations. Imagine—a living queen to be present at a ceremony that would reveal a king of ancient antiquity!

CHAPTER NINETEEN

The Sealed Doorway

TWO DAYS BEFORE THE sealed door was to be breached, the little town of Luxor had become the center of the globe. Hundreds of press reports clattered daily over the recently installed wire system to Cairo and from there to virtually every capital on earth. An uninterrupted stream of letters and telegrams poured into the hamlet. It seemed to everyone that the eyes and ears of the whole world were focused on this tiny spot. Not since the height of the Eighteenth Dynasty had Luxor achieved such prominence.

Celebrities, notables, lords, sultans and pashas arrived by the trainload. The hotel registries record the appearance of a fascinating variety of exalted personalities: Lord Leigh, Lord and Lady Swaythling, Lady Somerleyton, Sir Philip Sassoon, Sir Louis Malet and Lady Juliet Trevor, and the Raja of Poonah.

The Queen of the Belgians and her son, Prince Leopold, were due to arrive early on the sixteenth of February in their own train from Alexandria. It had been arranged for the Queen to witness the opening with a choice group of twenty specially chosen individuals who would be seated in chairs facing the sealed north doorway. A makeshift theater had been constructed for the exciting event. Howard Carter would open the partition for the select audience, and then he would be permitted to set aside two full days for a detailed examination of the contents—whatever they would be. After that, for two additional days, the world press and "special" visitors would view the discovery.

Fanciful stories began to circulate. The tale of Carter's golden canary surfaced publicly; a number of the natives predicted that the chamber would be full of cobras—all alive. One of the most favored predictions making the rounds was that the excavators would discover a room quite empty but for a French newspaper dated to the time of Napoleon.

Sir John Maxwell, the chairman of the Egyptian Exploration Fund and a personal adviser to Lord Carnarvon, was almost run down in Luxor by an Egyptian boy driving a dog cart. Sir John was convinced the act was intentional. At least the boy had made no visible effort to avoid him, although Sir John had shouted a warning. The young Egyptian apparently overlooked the fact that, as he had the only dog cart in Luxor, there would be no problem in finding him later. The police chief quickly apprehended the lad and sentenced him to a thrashing by his father. He also made the father distribute ten Egyptian pounds to the poor in Sir John Maxwell's name. The coins were distributed at the gates of the Winter Palace Hotel to the great delight of the poverty-stricken. There were, however, those who complained bitterly that once again an Egyptian had received unjust punishment at the hands of a foreigner who had come to see the tomb.

The guest list had been compiled after a great deal of discussion between Lord Carnarvon's representative and those of King Fuad. Through his Chamberlain, the monarch had expressed his deep regrets that his "many present preoccupations prevented his acceptance of the invitation" to appear at the official opening of the sealed chamber. Although the King was a personal friend and had been at Highclere a number of times, Carnarvon apparently was not disappointed. He and Carter had hoped there would be no more than twenty to twenty-five people in the official delegation. But the number finally swelled to forty—or actually forty-one, for there was to be a mystery guest who never actually existed but was present nonetheless.

At the last moment the Queen of the Belgians suffered a mild attack of the flu and was forced to remain in her suite at the Winter Palace Hotel in Luxor. No one knows, but it is possible that, having learned of the growing number of people who would crowd into the narrow confines of that hot, subterranean funerary chamber for hours, she prudently decided to wait until she could obtain a private viewing.

The guest list read like a combination of *Burke's Peerage* and *The Thousand and One Nights*. Protocol was presumably respected, but figuring it out must have produced a number of headaches. No documents have survived regarding the precise seating arrangements. All news accounts of the time vary as to exactly who was there. The most reliable list of visitors was assembled by Herbert Winlock, who apparently compiled it just for his own amusement.

Winlock's list is dazzling. The choice group comprised Lord and Lady Allenby; their highnesses the Princes Kamalel-din, Omar Toussoon and Yusef Kamal; the ministers to Egypt from France, Belgium and America; their excellencies (and all ex-prime ministers of Egypt) Adly Jegen Pasha, Tewfik Nessim Pasha, Hussein Rushdi Pasha, Abdel Khalek Sarwat Pasha and Mohammed Said Pasha; their excellencies Ismail Sidky Pasha and Ismail Sirry Pasha; Lord Carnarvon; Lady Evelyn Herbert; the Honorable Mervyn Herbert; Sir Charles Cust; Sir William Garstin; Sir John Maxwell; the Honorable Richard Bethell; Sir Alan Gardiner; the mudir of Kena, the Honorable Abd-el-Hallin Pasha Suleman; Howard Carter; A. C. Mace; Albert Lythgoe; Herbert Winlock; Harry Burton; Pecky Callender; Alfred Lucas; Arthur Merton; Pierre Lacau; Rex Engelbach; three unnamed Egyptian inspectors of antiquities; an unidentified representative of the Egyptian government; an unidentified "Representative of the Press Bureau"; numerous Arab workmen; James Breasted and his son, Charles.

But there later appeared to have been one more—a George Waller Mecham, under whose name were filed remarkably detailed stories about the opening of the Burial Chamber and every other aspect of the tomb as well. At times, Mecham, who represented the Chicago *Daily News* and the *Christian Science Monitor,* seemed to have garnered information far superior to that provided by Carter to Arthur Merton. But even more remarkable, no one ever recalled having met the deft and knowledgeable Mecham in the flesh, either in the tomb, in the valley or in Luxor. His stories sprouted up as if from magic seeds. It was only years later that Charles Breasted revealed that he had been the phantom correspondent George Waller Mecham, and that when he had informed Howard Carter of his intention to break the London *Times*'s monopoly surreptitiously, Carter had encouraged him.

By a quarter past two the guests had congregated at the entrance to the tomb. A large crowd of journalists encamped around the parapet, among a forest of tripods for the still and moving-picture cameras.

According to the representative of the *Daily Telegraph,* Carter swung open the great "dungeon door," and, after doffing their jackets, the members of the official delegation descended into the gloom. Lord Carnarvon looked back with some anxiety at the journalists but then said, impishly, "We're going to have a concert! Carter's going to sing a song!"

Arthur Weigall was at the parapet, looking on enviously. When Lord Carnarvon had so happily entered the tomb Weigall suddenly turned to another reporter and said half jokingly, "If he goes down in that spirit, I give him six weeks to live." Precisely six weeks later his own remarks would come back to haunt and disturb him.

For the next three hours, the journalist's report continued, "every sound and every incident was noted." There was a great buzz of conversation whenever a block of stone was carried up or when Lady Evelyn could be heard to utter an excited exclamation; at other times nothing could be heard but chisel blows or the sounds of hammering from below. It was reported that "each percussion fomented intense speculation among those who could only sit there in the blinding sun."

As the unseen and tantalizing activities continued, the "opposition Press Combine" grew more and more frantic for any shred of news. One of the native workmen was collared by the "Combine" and stated that three mummies had been found; a few minutes later one of the foremen blurted out that eight had been unearthed. By the middle of the afternoon the word leaked out that a huge statue of a cat had been discovered. There was a mad dash to get these nuggets of information out on the wire. Only late that evening, too late to change the banner headlines about mummies and the cat, did the "Combine" learn that it was wholly spurious information deliberately and specially sent out by Howard Carter. The trick further solidified the outsider press enmity against him.

Below, inside the small chamber, the high-voltage lamps assembled for the viewing made the Antechamber insufferably hot. But no one seemed to care. The crowd was silent, transfixed. The fever was one of anticipation.

Carter recalled later that, as he mounted the low wooden platform he had constructed over part of the partition, he thought how incongruous the throng of modern onlookers seemed to be, sitting or standing in the chamber. But that flashing impression was quickly obliterated by his realization that he was about to wipe aside the passage of centuries and stand before a king who ruled heaven and earth three millennia before.

With a trembling hand, Howard Carter struck his first blow against the plastered stone partition. He took great pains to locate the wooden lintel above the door and chipped gently at the plaster near it, picking away with his fingers the small stones that formed the top layers of the fill. Within ten minutes he had managed to open a hole large enough to insert his flashlight. He directed its beam into the aperture and, for a minute or two, stood there motionless. The spectators nervously watched. There was an unbearable silence. At last Carter blurted out, "I see a wall of gold-and-blue faience!" It was, of course, the side of the first great shrine that he had first encountered months before.

Carter claimed that at first he had no idea of the purpose of

195

the breathtaking golden wall. Painstakingly, utilizing at times his full strength, he loosened the irregularly shaped blocks with a crowbar and gently pried them up, so that Mace or Callender could put a smaller rock underneath to allow him to obtain a better grip. Carter personally hefted out each stone and handed it over to one of his assistants, who in turn gave it to a native foreman, who transferred it to the man at the head of a brigade of workers, who removed it from the tomb.

When about ten or fifteen stones had been broken free, the mystery of the gold-and-blue wall was solved for the onlookers. They realized with a thrill that they were at the very entrance to the actual Burial Chamber of the King and that the barricade was the gleaming side of an enormous shrine.

To Albert Lythgoe it was an absolutely heart-stopping experience: "What a sight it was. I myself felt nothing of nervous excitement—it was all too stupendously awe-inspiring for that. But for the first time in all my experience of looking into and finally entering ancient burial chambers, I felt the presence of the dead."

When the hole was large enough, Carter entered and dropped down into the chamber. Lord Carnarvon quickly followed him. At the threshold, Carter found some pieces of jewelry abandoned by the ancient burglars. Almost half an hour passed as he carefully picked up the pieces. Then, just at the corner of the great outer shrine, Carter came across a superb lamp carved from a single piece of alabaster in the form of a triple lotus growing from the bed of a pond. He had not remembered it from his earlier visit. "My God," Carter later confided to Lythgoe, "how beautiful was this delicate, thin piece of milky alabaster! It was so perfectly and gracefully carved that it appeared almost to be organic, quivering with life gently moving on the water's surface."

Just before they left the inner chamber to allow others to take a look, Carnarvon and Carter examined something Carter had found—a wick lamp with a small mud base bearing some curious hieroglyphs. They fascinated and slightly chilled him: "It is I who hinder the sand from choking the secret chamber. I am for the protection of the deceased."

After about twenty minutes, Carnarvon and Carter emerged. They uttered not a word, but simply lifted their hands in amazement at what they had seen. Then the rest of the party went in, two by two. Pierre Lacau said jokingly to Gardiner, "You'd better not attempt it; you're much too stout." But Gardiner ignored him and entered with James Breasted. They pushed their way through with some difficulty and then turned left, so that they were opposite the front of the shrine. They saw that Carter had already drawn the bolts and that within the great shrine was another, this one with its seal intact.

As soon as he had made his exit, Lord Carnarvon gave an interview to Arthur Merton:

I find it difficult to describe what I felt when I entered that inner chamber, for of a surety, I never dreamt I should gaze upon the amazing sight which met my eyes . . .

With the greatest care I followed Mr. Carter in and whatever emotion and excitement I may have felt when I entered the first chamber were as nothing when I was going into what undoubtedly was the practically untouched tomb of an Egyptian King.

We moved very carefully around to the right and on the East side of the great golden and blue faience shrine found two large doors closed by means of a bolt.

With ominous creakings we managed to open a door, only to find ourselves confronted by the doors of a second shrine. This one was entirely gilt, and between the two structures were some of the most marvellous alabasters it is possible to imagine. One was an alabaster painted pot with a lid fashioned into a reclining cat with a pink tongue which I could scarcely take my eyes off.

It was impossible to open the door sufficiently to be able to see in detail all that lay between the two walls, the outer and the inner wall, but it was possible to see that the whole interior of the outer wall was carved and gilded.

The second shrine was similar and had double doors exactly opposite those we had opened, but a very important point was that the inner doors were sealed with small seals and string, and the whole sealing arrangement was perfectly intact. It was, therefore, almost certain that the body of the King was lying somewhere in this second shrine.

As far as I know, this had never happened before. We have only found royal personages either hidden away or very much plundered. In the case of the tomb of Ramesses IV, if I recollect the papyrus rightly, five of these shrines or canopies figured as surrounding the King's sarcophagus. There is room for as many as that in this tomb, but it is imprudent to venture any prophecy on the subject.

The space is so constructed between the walls of the chamber and those of the outer shrine that it is impossible to pass along on any side but that where the entrance doors are situated; but with the help of a lamp I could discern black paddles or oars for the deceased King's use after death, laid in criss-cross pattern along one side and some kind of large statue at the far corner.

Lord Carnarvon told how he had entered the Treasury, had marveled again at the canopic shrine with its beautiful four goddesses and, with Carter, had opened one of the numerous jewel boxes that stretched from the Anubis shrine back toward the large canopic container. They expected to discover the box full of miscellaneous contents. Instead they found only one object. Carnarvon said at the time:

I believe it is unique in the history of Egyptian exploration. It is an ostrich feather fan. All the feathers are still there, after thirty-two hundred years, looking in perfect condition—but very delicate they are. The handle of this fan is a real joy to look at. It is ivory with a cross-piece set like the letter L. The whole thing is simply but elegantly carved with the King's cartouche in different coloured stones near the top. . . .

And there are also a large number of boats, charmingly painted, some with rigging and linen sails, others like rowboats.

Another thing that attracted me was a box full of jewelry which, whatever the intrinsic value of the solid gold and precious stones may be, might be called priceless today.

I have little doubt that as we remove shrine after shrine, the space between each succeeding set of walls will be found full of articles of the most intense interest, and judging from those already found, probably of surpassing beauty. The work of dismantling will require the greatest care and dexterity and I anticipate constantly increasing interest as we go on, and quickening excitement until we reach the place where, I have no doubt, the body of the King lies undisturbed. This part of the tomb will take months to examine, and I can only hope that that work may be carried on without the constant interruptions which have been the chief feature of this season's campaign.

The members of the official party were stunned by what they saw. As they finally made their exit from the narrow confines of the Burial Chamber and the crowded Treasury through the Antechamber, they seemed unable to speak, so impressed were they by the magnificence of what they had seen—hundreds of unique objects, each one of which, in that emotionally charged moment, seeming to outshine anything discovered in the Antechamber. One of the visitors told Arthur Merton that what had surpassed everything had been the beautiful canopic shrine.

"The four figures are lovely as they stand with their outstretched arms protecting the walls of the shrine and their sweet faces turned to you with a most pitiful and reproachful expression as if begging you not to come near. And to think they have stood so for three thousand years and more—these four goddesses of the protection of the dead King, Neith, Selket, Isis and Nephthys—waiting for the intruder who at last has come. I am not ashamed to say that a lump came into my throat and I longed to tell them we were not robbers or going to hurt them, but would treat their precious charge in a most reverential way. Even now I cannot think of them without emotion."

All who visited that day were enthralled by the beauties of Tutankhamun's Holy of Holies. Some of the members of the official party could hardly tear themselves away from the "Company of the Pharaoh," as one described it. In small groups they emerged from the stifling atmosphere. Weak, weary, they stumbled upstairs to the outer air.

While they had been in the tomb the sun had set behind the Theban hills and the temperature had dropped with it. There was a dash for coats. The guests crowded around Lord Carnarvon and Lady Evelyn and shook hands and whispered warm congratulations in a vain effort to convey their feelings.

Darkness now enveloped the valley. The tomb was locked again, the visitors departed, and the peace of a gentle Egyptian night gradually descended upon the silent landscape.

Arthur Merton later reported that it was as though "Tutankhamun, though dead, yet liveth and reigneth in Thebes and Luxor today."

All the district is his court. He is paid tribute from everywhere. His name is all over the town. It is shouted in the streets, whispered in the hotels. While in the local shops Tutankhamun advertises everything: art, hats, curios, photographs and tomorrow probably "genuine" antiquities. Every hotel in Luxor had something on the menu *à la Tut*. The Queen of the Belgians, though a prominent figure—and she will view the tomb tomorrow—is merely the modern queen of a nation. But to be the thing today in Thebes one has got to show some, any, connection with the ancient King. Slight acquaintances buttonhole one another and tell of dreams they had yesterday of Tutankhamun. There is a Tutankhamun dance tonight at which the first piece is to be a Tutankhamun RAG.

CHAPTER TWENTY

The Queen's Visit

THE VISIT OF THE Queen of the Belgians and Prince Leopold provided a fitting climax to a week of frenzied expectation and profound wonder.

From the first morning light, both sides of the Nile and the road leading to the Valley of the Kings were black with masses of humanity. No fewer than seven motorcars showed up, a phenomenal number for that time and place, and a flashy and exceedingly noisy motorcycle with sidecar sputtered up the valley road at top speed. To one startled observer it seemed that every ancestral horse carriage and donkey cart in the surrounding five provinces of Egypt, along with countless herds of animals and regiments of donkey boys, had been mobilized for the occasion.

A society reporter commented that the Queen was "dressed in white with a broad-brimmed white hat, a stone-grey veil and a grey fox stole," notwithstanding the weather. With fanfare, ruffles and flourishes the mudir, the governor of the province, received her on the west bank of the Nile when she disembarked from her royal felluca. He entered her car and drove with her up to the valley head, all the while recounting the history of the region—rather inaccurately, it was later said.

Extraordinary security precautions had been made along the route, not only to keep tens of thousands of rubberneckers and flocks of animals at bay, but to ward off political demonstrations on behalf of the rapidly growing Nationalist Party. The mudir, the Honorable Abd-el-Hallin Pasha Suleman, pointed with pride to the troops which had been assembled for the ceremony. And impressive they were. Every sixteen yards along the entire five-mile length of the narrow, winding road he had positioned a resplendent *ghaffir,* or guard. Each was dressed in parade uniform of a unique design, decorated with stripes of red, green and magenta, highlighted by a brass plate which glistened proudly on each chest. In the sunshine and the clear blue sky, the magnificent uniforms were radiant. As the carriage of the Queen and then that of her son passed, each *ghaffir* came to attention and saluted smartly with his *nabut,* a long ornamented swagger stick that reflected the sun's rays and appeared to produce a never-ending series of miniature fireworks displays.

Grouped around the low stone retaining wall of the tomb was perhaps the most cosmopolitan and polyglot crowd of individuals that could be seen anywhere in the world—royalty, British peerage, American tycoons and politicians, French statesmen and savants, members of Egyptian officialdom and nobility, and representatives of almost every nation on earth. The notables arrived, Carter said, like waves. One of the earliest was the colorful Dowager Sultana Hussein. Extremely popular with the masses, the Egyptian lady had received an ovation from the throngs at the river and at several points along the road. She "waved prettily" at the crowd and descended into the tomb with other Egyptians of high birth and status. About twenty minutes later she emerged and proclaimed that the find was "extraordinary" and that the work was being carried out with "punctilious care."

Lord Carnarvon and Lady Evelyn Herbert made their appearance. They were followed shortly afterward by the American minister J. Merton Howell, a somewhat frail individual, known for the enthusiasm he displayed for Egypt's long midday siestas. After his tour Howell made a statement to the awaiting press and lost no opportunity to plug his constituency. The sight had been, he averred, "stupendous," far exceeding anything he had anticipated. He was "deeply proud" of his countrymen who, through the Metropolitan Museum, had been "cooperating so wholeheartedly in a great work of science for all mankind."

Promptly at two-fifteen, the Queen's cortege arrived and was escorted into the chambers by Lord Carnarvon, Howard Carter and Pierre Lacau. Accompanying her also were Field Marshal Viscount Allenby and Lady Allenby. The Queen's slight figure easily passed through the narrow opening in the sealed door, and she was able to walk through the narrow space between the wall and the shrine without difficulty. Some of the others had to squeeze through, especially Lord Allenby, who was tall and amply built. He later remarked that "it had been an extremely tight fit."

Despite the heat and the closeness of the atmosphere, Queen Elisabeth was "overwhelmed by the beauty of the treasures." She remained in the tomb for more than half an hour, "asking her conductors many questions and expressing intense interest." When her majesty emerged again into the fresh air she seemed totally overcome. She climbed the last step and sank into a chair, saying with amusement that she was "heartily glad to escape." She refused the lemon squash offered her and asked faintly for a drink of water, which was smartly produced. On her return to the hotel from the valley she graciously received reporters and stated that she was overjoyed to be there. She said that the unique spectacle of the funerary chamber, in which every object still remained where it had originally been placed thirty-two hundred years before, had made an unforgettable impression upon her. She had been "wonderstruck" at seeing the marvelous objects and ventured the personal opinion that the world owed a great debt of gratitude to Lord Carnarvon and Howard Carter.

The dazzling objects and the magnetic aura of mystery surrounding the whole undertaking completely captivated Elisabeth of the Belgians, so much so that she decided to change all her plans and settled in for nearly a month in Egypt. She traveled up and down the Nile and returned three times to examine the treasures in the tomb and the laboratory.

On the Queen's fourth and final visit, in early March, Howard Carter gave her a special treat. In her presence he opened one of the strange black "bituminized" boxes from the Treasury, which resembled a miniature sentry box. Carter removed the mud seal with the impression of the jackal and the nine bound slaves, to reveal inside, swathed in linen, a beautiful gilded wooden snake with penetrating quartzite eyes. To Carter this serpent was "a true marvel, in style and execution, and a most beautiful piece of naturalistic carving." The pedestal carried an inscription identifying the snake as the god of one of the ancient nomes, or provinces. The ancient land of the Nile had been divided into forty-two such nomes, twenty-two for Upper Egypt and twenty for Lower Egypt, each with its own god. When King Tutankhamun entered the "Life of Infinity," he was buried with the emblem of each of these provincial deities to protect him throughout eternity.

People were fascinated by the discovery of the golden serpent. To the local Egyptians, it was the cobra that must have eaten Carter's golden canary. Predictions of impending misfortune were confidently made by some and heartily ridiculed by others.

Albert Lythgoe considered the visit of the Queen of the Belgians and Prince Leopold the most joyful experience of the dig thus far. He had met her in New York two years earlier, when she had been fascinated by the Egyptian galleries of the Metropolitan Museum. As soon as she had been seated at the official luncheon after the visit to the tomb, she turned to him and told him how much she had enjoyed seeing the Egyptian Department.

On the day of the special tour, Lythgoe, true to his talents for working behind the scenes, had seized upon the opportunity to do a bit of politicking against Pierre Lacau's proposed change of the Antiquities Law. He wrote to Edward Robinson soon after the event and said that the threatened change in the law seemed unlikely. "I had," he explained, "a marvelous chance at the official opening and again when the Queen arrived to have a long talk with Lord Allenby concerning the current status." He reported that Allenby had given "definite assurances as to his own friendly intentions" and had said directly to Lythgoe, "If the British and Americans [hold] together, [I] don't think you need worry further about the situation." Allenby had spoken of his great pleasure with the action already taken by the United States Secretary of State, Charles Evans Hughes. Lythgoe wrote another letter to Edward Harkness, telling him that he had received highly confidential information from a government official, whom he did not identify, who claimed that Lacau was "looking for a way out" of the whole matter and would be very glad, at that particular moment, to drop any attempt to secure the change in the law. The political pressure had been effective. He told Harkness that he was planning to go to Cairo as soon as he could in the hopes of talking to Lacau and obtaining his firm agreement to cancel any proposed alteration in the "status quo."

If the visit of the Queen had provided a much needed public-relations boost to Carter and Carnarvon, the boost was by no means an isolated one. For a series of encomiums were now delivered by the Queen's official, personal guide to Egypt. His name was Jean Capart, and he was a distinguished Belgian scientist, a member of the Royal Academy, conservator and secretary to the Musée Royal du Cinquenténaire, and a professor of Egyptology at the University of Liège. Capart, a portly, energetic character, was a legend among Egyptologists for the large size of his family and the prodigious number of books he had authored. He was fond of explaining both by saying, "A child a year, a book a year." The amusing Belgian savant had been overwhelmed by the tomb's contents. He immediately settled into a room at the Winter Palace Hotel and produced a series of exuberant articles on the splendor of the objects, saying among other things that "all things previously discovered in Egypt were rubbish in comparison to those from the tomb of Tutankhamun." But of far greater significance to the embattled excavators, Capart composed several articles lauding Carnarvon and Carter for the way they were carrying out their work. He supported "one hundred percent their sole right to issue exclusive news stories." His statements are extraordinary examples of puffery, and one wonders how Capart was persuaded to issue them.

One of Capart's articles had an ingenious beginning. He speculated that King Tutankhamun would surely have known of an ancient Egyptian proverb that said, "The tongue is the best *and* the worst thing in the world." "Had Tutankhamun lived in our day," Capart asked, "what would *he* have said of the tongue of the press?" That, he said sadly, had been his immediate thought when he first perused the articles attacking Lord Carnarvon. The sacred rights of the press and "its imprescriptible duties toward the public" were, he agreed, most important. But some people said, Capart went on, "that no obstacle at all must be allowed to intervene between examination of the pharaonic treasures and the media distribution of the news to all papers." And they insisted, he wrote, that if Carnarvon did not give way, if he did not cancel his agreement with *The Times*, "the Egyptian Government *must* intervene and the concession must be declared forfeit."

To Capart these people must be dreaming. To him the essential elements of the situation were that the government had granted the right to excavate only after imposing strict conditions, and that Carnarvon had faithfully followed every one of them. Indeed, Carnarvon had done far more than was expected of him or "incumbent upon him" in making the "wise decision to give to the public every day vital information through the greatest newspaper in the world."

Capart then raised the question of whether or not Carnarvon would have aroused any criticism at all had he, like so many other excavators, simply concealed his great discovery from the public and then published the results in volumes produced by a preselected London house. He urged everyone

206

to leave Carnarvon, Carter and their colleagues in peace and to respect the manner in which they chose to communicate to the public the results of their discovery. The final sentence of his article fairly pealed: "We don't say that it is their legitimate reward; it is their *incontestable right.*"

Lord Carnarvon, Carter and Lythgoe were jubilant. And they had every right to be. The find, after all, was miraculous, unlike anything that had ever been discovered in the history of archaeology. Royalty, nobility, professors of Egyptology, scientists in all fields had praised the discovery and the painstaking manner in which the preservation work was being carried out. Carnarvon and Carter fully believed that they had finally begun to overcome the criticisms voiced by the Egyptians, the Nationalist Party and the press. Carnarvon, not wanting to let his advantage slip away, saw to it that not a day passed without some praiseworthy report in the London *Times* on behalf of the operation.

Arthur Merton duly noted virtually everything that might be favorably construed, from the visit of an Egyptian to the receipt of a congratulatory telegram. A cable from the Metropolitan Museum sending "ecstatic congratulations" was commented upon at length, as was a communication from King Fuad sent from the Abdine Palace in Cairo. King Fuad's message had not been anything special, just the customary language of officialdom. It stated that on the occasion of the "discovery of the inestimable treasures with which you enrich science in Egypt, it is exceedingly agreeable to me to address to you the testimony of my warmest congratulations at the moment when your efforts are crowned with success and you have so justly reaped the fruit of your long years of work." The London *Times* seized upon the King's words as being of particular interest at that very moment when certain people conducting a "malicious campaign" were suggesting that friction still existed between Lord Carnarvon and the Egyptian government. *The Times* branded such representations "totally false." The relations were "most cordial," as evidenced by the extremely thoughtful action of the King, which had been "entirely self-initiated." *The Times* also pointed out that the enthusiastic friendliness of the Egyptian public invited to the opening was further proof of good relations between Carnarvon and the Egyptians. Far from there being any disagreement, according to *The Times,* all of Egypt was deeply desirous of showing its regard for Lord Carnarvon and its appreciation of his immense services to the country.

Day after day the London *Times* hammered out the story that every single relation between the excavators and the Egyptians, from those in high office to those on the streets of small villages, was "most friendly." Arthur Merton seems to have spared no effort to confirm this point. He sought and received a statement from Abdel Kahlek Sarwat Pasha, one of the former premiers of Egypt who had attended the official opening, that warmed the hearts of the diggers: "The names of Lord Carnarvon and of Mr. Carter and of their zealous collaborators, whom I was delighted to congratulate on their brilliant success, will remain ever linked with the archaeological splendor of our ancient country, and Egypt will always retain for them feelings of the deepest gratitude."

Arthur Merton was not alone. *The Times* enlisted an unnamed but "eminent Egyptologist" to provide an extraordinarily persuasive argument. It seems to have been good old Jean Capart, plunging on indomitably:

I've just returned from Biban Bimeluk, which is Arabic for "the tomb of the Kings." My thoughts are so disturbed that I have difficulty in collecting them, and in expressing my feelings I should like first of all to testify to the immensity of the debt which the civilised nations must owe to Lord Carnarvon and Howard Carter, whose names will remain linked forever with the greatest archaeological discovery within the memory of humanity. I wish that everyone could realise what self-sacrifice and generosity have been needed for the undertaking, and for the carrying out of the systematic work of clearing which alone has realised the miracle of finding again, intact, a royal tomb so well protected that none of the ancient robbers reached it in spite of the thirty-four centuries during which the hunt for treasure has not been interrupted for a single day. . . .

What is one to say of the hateful and dishonest attacks of which these two men are the object at the present moment? In order to be able to convey rapid and accurate information to the world about their immense discovery, they relieved themselves of the task of drawing up the communiqués, by entrusting this work to a great newspaper. That was their crime. It is much to be regretted that those who write in this campaign neglect to tell what are the motives which prompted them to accuse Lord Carnarvon of converting his unforgettable discovery into a "commercial undertaking" as they have ventured to describe it.

These attacks are abominable; some of them are simply ludicrous.

And the "eminent Egyptologist" did not fail to address himself to another issue, which was just beginning to surface in newspaper articles and in letters to Carter and Carnarvon:

Some people are seized with pity for the hapless fate of poor King Tutankhamen, who finds himself disturbed in his earthly rest by the curiosity of archaeologists. To hear them, one ought immediately to restore the protective walls behind which he has escaped the seekers for treasure.

I readily admit if this tomb brought nothing not hitherto known to the world it would be useless to explore it and useless to devote a minute study to its contents, but it has been said that the advantage which man has over the brute is his faculty of retaining a memory of his past. Today, however, the splendour of a past at first completely lost and then resuscitated in an uncertain manner appears again before our dazzled eyes.

Something more than the groans of neurasthenics and lunatics is necessary to convince me that the Egyptologists are violating the secret of death in a sacrilegious manner. Numerous funerary texts of ancient Egypt give evidence to the anxiety which the dead displayed that posterity should cause their name to live. It was said that he lives whose name is proclaimed. A few weeks ago, Tutankhamen's name was completely forgotten, outside of a small circle of specialists; today he is known throughout the world.

But throughout all the encomiums, Bradstreet of *The New York Times* never relaxed his struggle. He filed story after story suggesting that the problems arising between the Egyptian government and Howard Carter were growing more severe each day.

Dutiful to his task, Arthur Merton would strike back the following day, attempting to unmask the "wantonly malicious campaign that issued from Cairo seeking to spread the false idea that friction existed between Lord Carnarvon and the Egyptian government." Merton enlisted the aid of Abdel Hamid Suleman Pasha, Under-Secretary of the Ministry of Public Works, in his counterattack. The Under-Secretary replied with "considerable bitterness" that the statement was "too ridiculous" to need contradiction. He said that he and his department had been "delighted with the manner in which this work is carried out and the cordiality of the relations which Lord Carnarvon and Mr. Carter and the rest of the staff are maintaining with us and with Mr. Lacau and his department under us."

Even those who had spent a lifetime among the antiquities of ancient Egypt seemed almost to lose their minds over some of the objects in the Burial Chamber and the Treasury. James Breasted, a normally reticent man, remarked, upon seeing the goddesses surrounding the canopic shrine in the Treasury, that the "Greeks even of the age of Pericles are mere hacks when you look at this extraordinary series of sculptures." He praised the way they stood with outstretched arms gently depressed below the shoulder level so that the hands were level with the waist. They were, to him, "absolutely—devastatingly beautiful." One figure was particularly graceful and her features were "most beautiful." This was Selket, whose face was turned so as to face the door while her body still fronted the guarded shrine. Breasted had first believed the figure was nude, "but it's really covered with a film of the finest drapery in gold leaf. She is absolutely marvelous."

As notables, journalists and common citizens poured in to see the great shrine and to have a glimpse of the objects resplendent in the Treasury, some unusual things took place. A number of the visitors said they had grown faint when they confronted the glorious objects. Others said they couldn't sleep for days after having viewed the treasures. The J. Everitt Macys, a wealthy American couple who had been staunch friends of the Metropolitan for years, donating annual amounts of up to twenty-five hundred dollars, saw the treasures and were overwhelmed. Albert Lythgoe reported what took place to Edward Robinson:

The Macys literally took my breath away one day by telling me that they wished to celebrate their twenty-seventh wedding anniversary by contributing twenty-seven thousand dollars to some side of our Egyptian program. It was certainly a wonderful and entirely unexpected gift, and I have thought it could best be devoted to the purchase of that squatting statue, payment for which (if my plans should go wrong in certain respects) has been hanging over me like the sword of Damocles. Mr. Macy seems pleased to have his gift devoted to that and I am going down to Cairo soon to show him the statue and hear his final decision.

Lythgoe's trip was successful, for he was able to purchase sculpture for the Metropolitan Museum on the open market.

Tens of thousands of visitors streamed into Luxor to cross over the great Nile and to climb to the Valley of the Kings for a glance, any glance, at even just the mouth of the tomb. And there were problems. The government persuaded Carnarvon and Carter to let virtually everyone in for one period of four days. Carter became infuriated with some damage that occurred. An "overweight individual" had succeeded in scratching a line right down the gilded façade by trying to squeeze through the narrow passageway between the walls of the shrine and the tomb chamber itself. Carter wanted to close down the tomb for fear that there would be increasing chaos and that more serious damage would ensue. The stream of visitors became turbulent; one group fought its way through a sandstorm to get to the tomb.

Yet, curiously enough, some people rushed to Luxor with little thought of seeing the tomb or, for that matter, ever going near the Valley of the Kings. They came just for the festivities and parties that took place every night. Americans seemed to be particularly eager to partake of the social activities. It was reported in Luxor that, from the distribution of national flags alone, one would have thought a sizable American colony had established itself around the headquarters of the Belgian Queen. Every hotel in Luxor was filled with eager Americans, while the whole riverfront was alive with American flags waving from private boats. There seemed to be an enterprising "cruise director" in every American party. Attendance at the village races—events featuring donkeys, camels and horses—became almost exclusively American. Someone sourly observed that with all the Americans "rolling in wealth," the price of tickets had soared and the natives could no longer afford their own races.

It was said that a few Americans even became interested in Tutankhamun and made a raid on the bookstalls to obtain histories of ancient Egypt. They were thrilled to find a "real live expert" in their midst. Professor James Breasted became the most desired guest at every American function in Luxor.

Before Tutankhamun and the presence of the Americans, it had been fashionable to loll around in the hotel salon after dinner, listening to an orchestra concert. But the Americans had found that entertainment dull and had persuaded or paid the musicians to play only dance music. Each evening a "vivid" scene was enacted in the ballroom of the Winter Palace, a scene extending long after midnight and sometimes to dawn. The new American fashion of ragtime music had completely captured Luxor.

The young males of the British aristocracy found the American girls charming, forthright, and eager for fun. A number of interesting Anglo-American "ententes" sprang up. The spirit of Uncle Sam was exposed in one sentence reportedly uttered by a young American to an English lord: "Luxor is pretty lively all right and there's only one thing wrong and that is the gloom cast around by the death of some character by the name of Tutankhamun."

CHAPTER TWENTY-ONE

Closing Down the Tomb

AT FIVE-THIRTY IN THE MORNING of February 26, Lord Carnarvon and Howard Carter closed the tomb to assure the monarch a peaceful rest until the following season. They installed a massive watertight steel partition for protection against the rare but potentially damaging flash floods that sometimes cascaded through the Valley of the Kings. They prepared a sign in English, French and Arabic, warning anyone who might be tempted to trespass that the gate had been charged with thousands of volts of electricity. No power source of that magnitude existed in the valley, but Carter figured that the warning sign alone—bearing a stark death's head with crossed bones as well as the threat of instant electrocution—might make the villagers of Kurna at least think twice before attempting a foray. A cadre of soldiers and Antiquities guards had been assigned to the site by the government. As if to answer the age-old question "Who shall guard the guards?," Lord Carnarvon paid for his own security force, supervised by the four dedicated *reis*—foremen—who had been on the dig since the very start.

The refilling of the shaft and the stairs was a fascinating spectacle and consumed a full day, a night and much of the next day. Hundreds of little boys and old men, supervised by the foremen, scurried back and forth in an endless chain, dumping thousands of small baskets filled with sand and rubble into the passageway. The activity at night, illuminated by the searchlights, was Dantesque. A huge cloud of white smoky dust rose from the entrance as if from an immense conflagration. The curious spectacle was rendered all the more intriguing because the excavators realized that, though digging out a tomb was a somewhat ordinary experience, this was the first time any of them had ever assisted in the filling in of a sacred funerary sanctuary containing the body of an ancient Egyptian pharaoh.

The last-minute visits to the chambers were poetic experiences. To Lythgoe, crouched alone in the Burial Chamber, it was "all so marvelous, the material so enchanted and beautiful, that my brain could only grasp it in small and easy doses." He wrote his wife in New York that just to *be* there, actually in the Burial Chamber, alone by himself "with the sealed inner doors of the great catafalque still concealing the most gorgeous and amazing element in this succession of archaeological wonders, was to be awed, *awed* by the presence in the still chamber." "I cannot imagine," he wrote, "how I will feel to be back in the busy streets of New York City again within a few weeks. Shall I then be able to convince myself that this had actually been a reality?"

The Antechamber, once jammed like a treasure trove, was bare, bleak and desolate, its modest, undecorated walls of pale pinkish-yellow plaster seeming almost pedestrian without their precious contents. It was hard to imagine that a pharaoh had ever been there. There were only a few objects scattered about—a couple of lovely alabaster vases and a marvelous wooden swan painted black. Nearby lay an indistinguishable heap of blackened and gooey fibrous matter, the remains of a rush basket in which Carter had found some animal bones which he believed had come from some sacrifice.

The hole to the jumbled Annex had been boarded up. Carter left it until the next season. The two black-and-gold statues of the King still guarded the gaping entrance to the Burial Chamber. The lamps shining on the shrine seemed almost to choke the entrance with a light of brilliant turquoise and gold.

As they worked to protect the site, Howard Carter was again moved by "evidence of the scrupulous care and tender solicitude demonstrated in the arrangements for the dead King's life of forever." Carter said that "one could not fail to be affected by the unmistakable proofs of human affection, human conviction and human fidelity to an ideal in these men of thirty-two hundred years before," despite the fact that some people called the ancient Egyptians pagans and claimed they had been motivated only by superstition and slavish observance to custom. He mused that, whatever their effect in modern times, they did "preach a lesson of piety and deep conviction to an age of cynical materialism and unbelief."

Finally all was done. The entrance and the passageway were completely hidden by sand and rubble. The mixture, repeatedly watered down, became as strong as the bedrock of the ancient valley itself.

Once the tomb had been sealed, behind-the-scenes work in the laboratory intensified. It was work of the most arduous kind. Thousands of beads, sequins and rosettes had to be restrung. Linens that had blackened on being exposed to modern air had to be pieced together. Fragile woods surrounded by the thinnest imaginable sheaths of gold had to be repaired. Hundreds of fragments had to be glued together—jewelry, inlays, reeds, pottery, strange petrified balls of crumbled mud and feathers, bits of leather, heaps of iridescent beetles' wings.

The workbenches of the laboratory were covered with the crumbled residue of necessities for Tutankhamun's Life of Infinity—foods, perfumes, oils, unguents, salves, and diminutive farm tools, hoes, axes, hammers, adzes—with which to create the perfect afterlife for the god-King. All sorts of hunting equipment lay about—bows, arrows, staves; and boomerangs in ivory, feldspar, amethyst, wood and golden inlay, to be thrown and always return unerringly to the King's hand. And there were, of course, chariots for hunting, for subduing his enemies; and chairs, tables, couches, beds, pillows and sheets, and blankets of the finest linen; and shrines in gold.

215

But who was he? What had he done? It was a monumental irony that while Tutankhamun's name had become a household word throughout the civilized world, no one knew anything more about the man himself than before the tomb had been discovered. No historical writings, documents or papyri had been discovered. Some specialists thought that the small number of chambers in the tomb had a direct proportion to the years that Tutankhamun had reigned, and that for this reason they proved that the King had accomplished little. Others said that the magnificence of the tomb trappings and the luxuriousness of the objects proved that he had accomplished great works.

The prevailing opinion in 1923 about Tutankhamun was that he had come to the throne in a wholly confused period of history. He had married young, died young—more or less a shadowy and weak puppet king who had danced to the direction of the powerful priests of Amun and to the commands of a soldier of considerable genius, Haremhab, who would eventually assume the throne in his own right after Tutankhamun's death.

According to this theory, all that was known for sure was that his reign marked the close of one of the most interesting and picturesque episodes, not only of Egyptian history but of all of history. Egypt had reached the zenith of its power and glory under the first kings of the Eighteenth Dynasty, kings who were particularly successful in military affairs. The most powerful and enterprising of all had been Thutmose III, a warrior who had extended the boundaries of his dominion into Asia, particularly into the lands of the Matanians, and into Nubia. But even during his reign unmistakable signs of weakness were already becoming apparent along the borders. By the time Amenhotep III died and his son Amenhotep IV came to the throne, the New Empire had fallen on troubled times.

At that moment in history a strong hand was needed, but fate so willed that Amenhotep IV was neither a soldier nor an administrator, but a poet, a man of dreams, possibly even insane. He seems to have allowed Egypt to crumble. Amenhotep IV deserted the religion of his forefathers, dethroned the great god of Thebes, Amun, and the traditional pantheon of deities, and set up in their stead the worship of one god or spirit, Aton, a vital force residing in the sun's creative warmth.

In his zeal for his new religion, Amenhotep changed his own name, casting aside the name of Amun and substituting Aton—becoming Akhenaton. He removed his capital from Thebes and built a capital city devoted entirely to the worship of the new god. He called it "the city of the horizon," what is now known as Tell al-Amarna in modern Arabic.

Upon Akhenaton's death came a period of chaos of about eight years. Then General Haremhab seized the throne and began to rebuild the shattered glories of the kingdom. Most Egyptologists believed that in the eight years between Akhenaton and Haremhab, three weak kings had occupied the throne. The second of the three was thought to be Tutankhamun. The historical data surrounding the period was so meager that there was great uncertainty among historians about what had transpired. Those who accepted eight or nine years as measuring the interval between Akhenaton's death and Haremhab's accession as pharaoh tended to ascribe three of those eight years to Tutankhamun's immediate successor, Ay, and one year to Tutankhamun's predecessor, Smenkhkara. But Tutankhamun may have reigned two, four, six or perhaps as many as nine years. There was speculation, in 1923, that he was not even of royal birth.

During Tutankhamun's short tenure the court had apparently been moved back to Thebes, the city of Amun. This is suggested by the changes from "Tutenkhaton" to "Tutankhamun" on the golden throne. Carter had no doubts that some sort of direct link between Tutankhamun and Akhenaton existed; for he had discovered two intriguing clues inside one of the caskets from the Antechamber. There he had found two small images of King Akhenaton. One was of glass and represented the heretic King himself, crouching or squatting, with his knees up and his fingers in his mouth. The figure was about four inches high, and was apparently intended as a pendant for a necklace. It had been broken and carefully mended in antiquity. To the excavators it was a fascinating little ornament, and they played with the idea that Ankhesenamun had perhaps worn it until the string had broken one day. It had been fondly repaired and worn by the Queen.

But to the historians who were trying to assemble the facts, the changed names on the throne and the presence in the tomb of statuettes depicting the "heretic" Akhenaton were inexplicably at odds with Tutankhamun's own personal words of decisiveness and confidence carved into his stele, which had been unearthed by the French archaeologist Georges Legrain at Karnak in 1907. On the stele Tutankhamun had proclaimed in ringing words that he had restored the Theban gods to their holy places, so that they would bless and support the land that had been brought to destruction. Tutankhamun had boasted that he had erected anew the statues of the old gods, repaired the broken ones, rebuilt the temples and restored the traditional priests. He also claimed that he had revived commerce, trade and industry and built a powerful war fleet.

But if the stele did reflect the truth of history, how should the conflicting evidence in the tomb be interpreted? The throne and the statuettes of Akhenaton might suggest that, perhaps disgusted by the overwhelming pretensions of the newly restored priests of Amun, Tutankhamun once more lapsed into the Aton heresy of his predecessor. This could explain the vindictiveness of Haremhab when, after his accession, he tried to destroy all inscriptions of the recorded deeds of Tutankhamun on any monument he discovered.

It was easy to sink into a quagmire of conjecture. And most specialists did. Everyone hoped that when the mummy was reached, deep within the shrines, solid facts would emerge. Yet if the tomb possessed little for the historian, it was steeped with the aura of Tutankhamun and his time. Almost every object seemed to evoke his presence, almost as fresh as on the day he died. Although Tutankhamun eluded everyone—he was now but a name, a shadow, an object of controversy, conjecture and mystery—he somehow seemed very much alive.

CHAPTER TWENTY-TWO

Sudden Tragedy

DESPITE ALL ATTEMPTS to offset the attacks from the opposition press and the Nationalists, Lord Carnarvon and Howard Carter fell back each week into defensive positions. By the beginning of March their tempers had become dangerously frayed. Several members of the team believed that Howard Carter was about to suffer a nervous breakdown.

The preeminent Egyptian daily, *Al-Ahram*, reported that Carnarvon had made secret arrangements to carry off Tutankhamun's mummy to England as soon as it was discovered. It was a ludicrous statement, issued in all probability to arouse anti-British sentiment among the Nationalist Party, the Wafdists. Yet it was thoroughly believed by a suprisingly large number of Egyptians of all classes.

If there was ever a moment when Lord Carnarvon required the professional press agent he had suggested to Carter earlier, this was it. But the idea had never been pursued. Carnarvon had decided to deal personally with the press. More often than not, his counterattacks simply provoked more assaults by his adversaries. He loathed his critics and seldom bothered to disguise how he felt.

In response to the story about the removal of the mummy, Carnarvon now issued a caustic press release:

I would like to say that at present King Tutankhamun rests where he was originally placed and when the time comes to decide whether it is the mummy of the King, I [have] made arrangements that his body should be left in the sarcophagus in its present resting place for ever. This should be the case unless, in the most improbable contingency, the Egyptian Government and the Government itself insists on its removal to Cairo. I may say I have not yet discovered the point, nor do I view with favour the somewhat unwholesome and morbid taste some people seem to enjoy of looking at mummies exposed in glass cases in museums.

Some Egyptians were infuriated by the implication that Lord Carnarvon himself "had made arrangements" for a tomb they considered their property, not his; others were offended by Carnarvon's suggestion that the Egyptian government might insist upon an "unwholesome" solution. To Egyptians, the mummy of a pharaoh was far more important than any work of art found in an excavation, no matter how splendid. The mummy, preserved in such an extraordinary manner by means unknown, or at least thought to be unknown, not only was royal but was considered by most Egyptians to be their direct ancestor.

The Egyptian press, failing to take Lord Carnarvon at his word, conducted an ongoing debate about his exact intentions regarding the mummy. The debate may have been fueled by a letter that the well-known author of adventure books H. Rider Haggard sent to the London *Times*, harshly criticizing the Egyptians. There were some who believed that Haggard was in some way involved with Carnarvon in a conspiracy to criticize the Egyptian government for its "slovenly" attitude regarding the display of the royal mummies.

In his letter Haggard stated that, years before the discovery of Tutankhamun, he had advised the Egyptian government to "photograph, measure, examine or model in wax the bones of the Pharaohs" and then to remove the bones, lay them in one of the chambers of the Great Pyramid, and seal them there "with concrete in such a fashion that only the destruction of the entire block or acres of solid stone could again reveal them to the eyes of man." Now, Haggard wrote, "the 'minor Pharaoh,' Tutankhamun, is to be added to the long list of more illustrious 'dug-outs.' " He went on to predict that Tutankhamun, too, would be stripped and, like Ramesses and other mighty monarchs of his day, "laid half-naked to rot in a glass case of the museum at Cairo." Haggard did not attempt to disguise his disgust. "Yes, to rot, for thus exposed I doubt whether any of them will last another century; and meanwhile to be made the butt of merry jests of tourists of the baser sort."

As criticism mounted, Lord Carnarvon decided not to read any newspapers at all. But from time to time he would sneak a look at the more virulent attacks against him, and this would send him off into violent tantrums. He raged not only at those who attacked him, but at friends and associates as well.

To compound matters, Carnarvon's health and probably his state of mind were adversely affected by the very climate that was supposed to be beneficial. The heat in the valley had become terrifying; the average temperature in the laboratory was one hundred degrees Fahrenheit; dust storms clogged the air over the site. Carnarvon's physical condition, which had been slowly deteriorating, now began rapidly to fail. Every few days one of his teeth chipped or just fell out. He did not realize it at the time, but this was one symptom of a deep infection exacting a terrible toll upon his body.

Howard Carter and members of the Metropolitan staff became deeply disturbed over Carnarvon's appearance. They were doubtless disturbed by his moods as well. Arguments between patron and archaeologist began to flare up. They clashed over how to deal with the Antiquities Service and with members of the press. The two friends never disagreed on basic viewpoints; sadly enough, they now fought often over insignificant details. Finally, as James Breasted recalls, Carnarvon called upon Carter at his house to try to discuss some of their differences. Bitter words were exchanged, and Carter, in a rage, ordered his patron to leave and never return.

The precise nature of the argument is unknown, but it may have had something to do with Carnarvon's discovery of the infatuation that his daughter Evelyn had developed for Carter. It was no more than a harmless crush of a young girl for an older man, and Howard Carter seems to have done nothing to encourage the "affair." Indeed, it seems clear that he utterly avoided any involvement; he had neither the inclination nor the time. But shunning her may have caused Evelyn Herbert to become even more attracted to Carter. Apparently, during the latter part of February, Eve let slip her feelings about Howard Carter to her father. Without comprehending the innocuous relationship, he flew into a rage.

The details of Lord Carnarvon's argument with Carter have never been recorded, but they are easy to imagine. Carnarvon may have charged Carter with being an inappropriate suitor, thereby bringing to the surface the inferiority complex that Howard Carter had carried around with him for so many years. The argument was surely intense, and although its nature was never explicitly revealed it was commented upon by various members of the American party. Winlock wondered whether or not the disagreement would lead to a permanent rupture between the two friends. The argument was clearly the foundation for rumors persisting to this day that Howard Carter, from that moment on, did not speak to or see Lord Carnarvon again.

But in reality the rupture was short-lived. The anger on both sides calmed down very shortly. Two days after their confrontation—which took place on the twenty-third of February—Lord Carnarvon sent his associate a tender, apologetic note.

MY DEAR CARTER,

I have been feeling very unhappy today and I did not know what to think or do and then I saw Eve and she told me everything. I have no doubt that I have done many foolish things and I am very sorry. I suppose the fuss and worry have affected me but there is only one thing I want to say to you which I hope you will always remember—whatever your feelings are or will be for me in the future my affection for you will never change.

I'm a man with few friends and whatever happens nothing will ever alter my feelings for you. There is always so much noise and lack of quiet and privacy in the Valley that I felt I should never see you alone although I should like to very much and have a good talk. Because of that I could not rest until I had written you.

Yours,

CARNARVON

In early March, Carnarvon and Evelyn left the valley for Cairo to attempt once again to obtain from Pierre Lacau assurances that his lordship would secure his "proper" division of objects found in the tomb. Evelyn wrote Carter every two days, informing him how things were going and inquiring solicitously about his health and state of mind. Then, suddenly, on the eighteenth of March, she dispatched an alarming message. Her father had asked her to inform Carter that he had not been able to discuss the division of antiquities with Pierre Lacau because the Frenchman was suffering from influenza. But this was not the real point of the letter. Lady Evelyn anxiously informed Carter that Lord Carnarvon was looking seedy and was virtually unable to move. He was suffering from a dangerously high temperature and swollen neck glands brought on by an apparently innocuous mosquito bite received in the valley. She had downplayed the seriousness of her father's health to everyone who had asked, so as to avoid flamboyant stories in the press. But she urgently wanted Carter to know the deeply disturbing facts.

Two days later, in Cairo, Albert Lythgoe dispatched a letter to Howard Carter in the Valley of the Kings.

Lady Evelyn says her father's condition is a little bit better today— for which we are all very thankful. Yesterday was a most anxious time for everyone, but his temperature has lessened today and they apparently feel the trouble is more localized or restricted.

We saw Lady Evelyn for a few moments just now in the hall after lunch, and although her anxiety is not as great as yesterday she doesn't feel that the danger is passed by any means.

One feels helpless in such a situation where only nurses and doctors avail, and although my knowledge of the facts is only general I wanted to send you some word as to how his condition stands. Lady Evelyn has been carrying the strain wonderfully, but she has certainly had a heavy burden of anxiety the past two days.

By the next week, on Monday the twenty-sixth, the grave situation had taken another alarming turn. Carnarvon was terminally ill. Richard Bethell, the son of Lord Westbury, who had been acting for several months as Carnarvon's appointments secretary, wrote Carter:

I am sorry to tell you that C. is seriously ill. Eve does not want it known how bad he is, but that poisoned bite has spread all over him and he has got blood poisoning. His temperature this morning was 104. Eve has telegraphed to Lady C. So I suppose she will get out next week. . . . There is hope that he may throw it off in a day or two, but otherwise I am afraid it looks pretty serious.

Carnarvon fought valiantly for his life for three weeks, but it was a losing struggle. Throughout those long weeks of pain and misery, however, he remained his customary gallant self. The daily press bulletins reporting on his illness always emphasized that even during the darkest periods the patient's spirits were good. He himself had no illusions about what was happening to him. With the great courage for which Lord Carnarvon was renowned, he had said to a friend just a few days before the day he died, the sixth of April, 1923, "I have heard the call. I am preparing."

It is ironic that just several days before his death the Egyptian Antiquities Service and the Ministry of Public Works had instructed J. Merton Howell to inform the staff of the Metropolitan Museum and Howard Carter that the Egyptian government had decided to postpone any change in its Antiquities Law until the autumn of 1924 at the earliest. It was understood that the decision of the officials had been greatly influenced by protests from the members of all foreign archaeological expeditions in Egypt and by "a number of diplomatic representations supporting those protests." The dispatch did say, however, that the postponement did not "prejudice the Egyptian government's privilege to promulgate the law after the next season" if it considered that particular act desirable.

Lord Carnarvon's sister recorded that it had been his wish that he be buried on Beacon Hill overlooking his magnificent estate, Highclere. And it was on the summit of that down, overlooking the home he had so passionately loved, that he was laid to rest. Only the immediate family attended the service, with a few workmen and servants, many of whom had been in his service so long that they were virtually part of his own family. No special ceremonies were conducted. There was no organ, no music, no chorister. The simple, traditional ceremony commending "the body of our dear brother to the ground in sure and certain hope" had, as his sister said at the time, something of the stark grandeur of a funeral at sea. But she recounted that the whole air was alive with a springtide song of birds. They seemed to sing with "a passion of ecstasy" which was never forgotten by those who were present. And so Lord Carnarvon was interred in his beloved land. Those who were there felt that his ending had been in harmony with his entire life.

CHAPTER TWENTY-THREE

The Curse

THE DAY AFTER CARNARVON's death, an article written by him weeks before he fell ill was published in the London *Times* as a "memorial to his work." In it, Carnarvon complained bitterly about the "interference from a weekly press day" and stated that the work had been "terribly impeded" by perpetual streams of visitors which increased the fatigue of the professionals a hundredfold. He begged that the workers be allowed by the press, the visitors and the government to continue "without interference and in peace."

The peace that Lord Carnarvon so fervently hoped for was utterly impossible now, owing in part to the circumstances that some said surrounded his death. It was said that at the precise moment of his death all the lights in Cairo inexplicably blacked out and that a subsequent investigation by the authorities could not uncover any explanation for the mishap. To compound the mystery, his son and heir, Lord Porchester, sixth Earl of Carnarvon, claimed that at Highclere at the precise moment of his father's death his favorite dog howled in anguish and dropped dead.

Newspapers around the world ascribed the death to a curse from the tomb. The famous creator of Sherlock Holmes, Conan Doyle, well known for his belief in the occult, announced to the world that a "Pharaoh's curse" could indeed have caused the unfortunate calamity. One newspaper even reported on a specific curse written in hieroglyphs adjacent to the beautiful winged creature on the door of the second shrine: "They who enter this sacred tomb shall swift be visited by wings of death." But there was no such curse on that door; the report was a complete fabrication.

A necromancer, a self-described archaeologist, issued a story to the press saying there had been a curse written on a carved stone at the tomb entrance which Carter had removed and buried. The hieroglyphs, according to this particular individual, were supposed to have read: "Let the hand raised against my form be withered! Let them be destroyed who attack my name, my foundation, my effigies, the images like unto me!"

Another correspondent had apparently learned of a mild admonition on the mud base of the candle in front of the Anubis shrine leading into the Treasury, which reads: "It is I who hinder the sand from choking the secret chamber. I am for the protection of the deceased." But the correspondent embroidered this by adding: "and I will kill all those who cross this threshold into the sacred precincts of the Royal King who lives forever."

Other than this general admonition in the Treasury, no real "curse" had been or would be found in Tutankhamun's tomb. Indeed, curses in any period of ancient Egypt were infrequent. But there are examples of awe-inspiring threats that do appear in occasional tombs. Specialists who have probed the phenomenon emphatically point out that such "curses" are invariably directed against those who seek to embezzle endowments set up to fund guards and maintenance men, seldom against robbers. On occasion one finds admonitions against thieves too.

Perhaps the earliest appears in the Fifth Dynasty of the Old Kingdom, fifty-three hundred years ago: "As for any people who shall take possession of this tomb as their mortuary property or shall do any evil thing to it, judgment shall be had with them for it by the great God." Later on, in the Thirteenth Dynasty, a character by the name of Tety apparently had embezzled part of a tomb's endowment. The priests took steps to see that Tety's name should be thoroughly blackened for his sin against property and endowment:

Cause him to be deposed from the temple, cause him to be cast out from his office, to the son of his son and the heir of his heir. Let him be cast out on the earth; let his bread, his food, his consecrated meat be taken from him. Let his name not be remembered in this temple: let his entries be expunged from the Temple of Min, from the treasury, and from every book likewise.

Along with fabricated curses there was supposition in the press that Lord Carnarvon had pricked his finger or cheek on some sharp object—an arrowhead or some other implement in the tomb—containing a poison so strong that it could have endured for three millennia. Other articles suggested there was a special breed of deadly bacteria within the chambers that had brought about his illness and death. Some newspapers began to publish rosters which tallied the death of anybody who had any connection, direct or indirect, with the tomb. But the speculation went further. It was claimed that Mace was dying of a strange disease. In fact he had bouts of pleurisy, a disease he had contracted long before the discovery of the tomb.

The friend of a tourist who had actually entered the chamber was struck down by a taxicab in Cairo, and this was immediately ascribed to the curse. An unnamed associate curator of Egyptology at the British Museum was said to have died in his bed. An eminent Egyptologist of the Louvre died of old age. These were ascribed to the malevolent effects of the curse.

As the stories spread, there were instances of near-hysteria. Hundreds of people in England, reading the accounts, packed up and shipped to confused members of the British Museum staff every scrap of Egyptian antiquity, mostly of no value whatever, that they had in their houses—including, in one instance, an arm from an ancient mummy. Several American politicians went so far as to call for an investigation of mummies in various museums to determine whether or not these possessed the same medical dangers as those thought to be apparent in the tomb of Tutankhamun.

Herbert Winlock was besieged with questions from the press and received letters from people all over the world about the mummy's curse. For years, Winlock recorded the date and cause of death of anyone who had been to any of the official openings. Virtually every time a newspaper would announce that yet another individual who had attended the "opening" was a "victim of the mummy's curse," Winlock would send a correction. His own tally, entitled "Victims of the Curse, according to the Newspaper Reporters," contained some interesting notations:

George J. Gould: Friend of Lord Carnarvon's, tourist in Egypt, travelling for his health. Was ill before he ever came to Egypt.

Arthur E. P. Weigall, who was not allowed in the tomb except with the public. Had no part in any way with the tomb.

"Prince" Ali Fahmy Bey, murdered in the Savoy Hotel in London by his French wife. If he ever was in the tomb it was as a tourist.

The workman in the British Museum, London, said to have fallen dead while labelling objects from the tomb. But there are no objects from the tomb in the British Museum and never have been.

If Tourists are subject to the curse it should be remembered that a large number of them are elderly people travelling in Egypt for their health.

Sadly and ironically, the "curse" is even today probably as well known as Tutankhamum himself and his unique treasures. When the current Lord Carnarvon was asked about the curse in an interview on NBC Television in New York on July 14, 1977, he replied that he "neither believed it nor disbelieved it," but he assured his interviewer that he would "not accept a million pounds to enter the tomb of Tutankhamun in the

Valley of the Kings." It was reported in the New York *Daily News* by a tenacious reporter of modern manners and mores that that same evening Lord Carnarvon attended a dinner in an apartment high above Manhattan and, as he looked out over the vast expanse of the cityscape, suddenly saw all the lights in the city flicker and then totally black out. He shuddered in the darkness. When candles had been lit he turned to his hosts and said, "It is again the curse of Tutankhamun."

If there was a curse, it was not written in hieroglyphs, nor graven in images, nor placed in the mouth of the Pharaoh. Nor was it uttered by ancient priests or imbued in certain objects in the form of poison lasting forever. It was simply inherent in the human weaknesses that often accompany astounding discoveries of treasures of incomparable proportion. And in this respect the controversy, the chaos and the bedlam surrounding Tutankhamun had just begun with the death of George Herbert, fifth Earl of Carnarvon.

CHAPTER TWENTY-FOUR

The Season Ends

THE DEATH OF HIS patron profoundly affected Howard Carter. For weeks afterward there were days when he could hardly move himself to go back into the valley. He became deeply depressed by the thought that a full month of arduous work lay ahead just to get the objects ready to be packed and shipped to the Egyptian Museum in Cairo and another month to close down the laboratory and storage rooms.

The valley was becoming agony. The wonderful Theban hills were still purple in the sunlight, as they had been two months before, but, as Arthur Merton observed, "they were no longer so restful to the eye, and were partially obscured by haze and quivering heat waves, unmistakable warning of what lay in store in the Valley itself."

The day described by Merton had been relatively cool. It had been only one hundred degrees in the shade. Normally, the heat was "sufficiently trying to cause one to shudder at the thought of what Mr. Carter and his staff have had to put up with during the past fortnight, when the day and night temperature rarely drop below 105°, and often reached 110°."

But Carter and his associates had been "mindful of the urgency of their work and the interests of science, to which they so obviously are devoted," and had "persevered through this ordeal of heat, to which has been added the still more trying ordeal of stifling nights, the effect of which only those who dwell in the East can appreciate, and as a result of their self-sacrifice it will not be possible completely to shut down before the end of the month of May."

On the fifteenth of May, with the temperature above one hundred twenty degrees, the treasures of the Antechamber began their journey to Cairo and to civilization. Originally, when they had been carried up into the valley for burial with the King, their progress must have been surrounded with awesome ceremony. But, as Merton faithfully reported, "the assembly of the priests of those times who were charged with such things could not possibly have taken more care in their transportation than has been displayed in the last two days by Mr. Carter's assistant, Callender."

Carter had first planned to have the objects carried down to the banks of the Nile by Egyptian porters. But most of the cases were too heavy and unwieldy. Another method had to be conjured up.

Although the road had become well traveled and was now relatively smooth, Carter felt that using cars or trucks would be too risky. After lengthy discussions with officials from the Antiquities Service, it was decided that the best means of transport would be to construct a railway.

The principal objects were counted for the first time. The excavators were astounded to discover there were nearly five hundred pieces—just from the Antechamber. These were packed into eighty-nine separate cases, which were reduced to thirty-four large packages by enclosing several small cases in a large crate or by tying two or more cases together. As a result, some of the crates were extraordinarily bulky. The complexities surrounding the packing and shipping were compounded a thousand times by the heat. One of the witnesses to the undertaking wrote:

The nature of the task could hardly be imagined, everything loaded on nine cars in the early hours yesterday morning outside the tomb, everything waiting the order to proceed. To look at them one never would have thought that these matter-of-fact packages contained some of the most valuable and certainly some of the most discussed and published articles in the world today.

The transportation activity began just after five o'clock in the morning. First Callender was the supervisor. At about eight o'clock he was relieved for breakfast by Carter, who labored until lunch, when Callender again resumed control. To their bitter disappointment, the two men discovered that it was hardly possible to lay the light railroad track over any distance at all, much less the five and a half miles down to the river bank from the valley head. The Antiquities Service had managed to collect only ten lengths of straight rail and two or three curved sections, making a pitiful total of only thirty-three yards. Carter was enraged by this information and accused Antiquities of deliberately trying to make the job more difficult.

It was like the punishment of Sisyphus. The rails were laid as far as they could go, and the cars, loaded with packages, were pushed to the farthest point. Then the rails that had been freed in back of the cars were laboriously carried up and placed in front, and the cars were pushed again to the end of the track. The operation was repeated hundreds of times—along the entire five and a half miles from the valley to the riverside.

The press reported this exceptional exercise with baffling sobriety. Bradstreet reported that

the task of directing the running of the cars was not easy, nor, considering the scorching heat and the formation of the country, was the manual work at all light. The first great difficulty was the ancient gateway to the royal sanctuary, a very narrow entrance, with a double curve and an incline of forty-five degrees. One by one the cars had to be guided slowly around and down, and with what was certainly extraordinarily high skill and judgment they were all brought safely to the level below.

The gang that carried out the labor consisted of fifty Egyptian laborers "renowned for their industry and endurance." Most of them displayed marked intelligence in handling and guiding the cars, each of which had three men as a permanent team. The remainder were occupied in raising and relaying the rails, which had to be constantly watered down so that the men could touch them. By noon on May 17, the worst part of the journey, the length of the valley itself, had been covered without a mishap. It was a remarkable feat considering the temperature, which was now well above one hundred twenty degrees.

Carter now hoped that he could complete the transportation of the packages to the bank of the Nile in one more day. But the heat and the physical nature of the valley road proved insurmountable. Much as he tried, he could not make it. After more than twelve hours, Carter had to release the exhausted men. The railway cars with their treasures worth millions of pounds sterling were deposited halfway down the bank of a dried-out canal pointing to the Nile, watched over by a police officer and six men. For additional security, Carter had left his own two chief foremen, who looked upon the night-long vigil with enthusiasm despite the fact that they had exerted themselves far more than any of the workers. Each regarded it as a point of the highest honor not to leave the cases until they could be officially delivered to the government representatives.

The next day, May 19, work was resumed at six. The railroad cars had a dangerous passage down the perilously steep bank of the Nile. The river was low. But within four hours the eighty-nine cases, all of which had to be hand-carried across an intervening stretch of water, had been safely turned over to the Service of Antiquities. They were then stowed in the hold of a barge, which was towed by a tug that afternoon toward Cairo, four hundred miles away.

For seven days the treasures floated down the Nile, coming to a halt finally at a quay a mile from the Egyptian Museum. Early the morning of May 27, the barge was slipped into a wharf on the east bank just below the museum, where porters were standing by on an improvised landing stage. The decision had been made to transport the cases from the riverside by means of a railway similar to that which had been used in the Valley of the Kings. This time, however, all the tracks had been completely laid from the landing to a point two blocks from the museum. There trucks stood in readiness. But at the last moment the inspector general of antiquities, who was personally responsible for transferring these objects to the museum, changed his mind, dispensed with the railway, and gave orders to the museum porters to move the cases by hand the rest of the way.

Carter somehow managed to hold his temper at this turn of events. Accompanied by Pierre Lacau, he opened a few of the cases and examined the condition of the objects. The London *Times* reported that the museum authorities could not restrain their pleasure that the cases gave no appearance of having just completed a journey of five hundred miles.

At the time it was thought that it would not be possible to exhibit any of the objects for six months. But the objects had responded so well to treatment and had been so little affected by the voyage that there was little doubt that some of the treasures could go immediately on view.

A little less than a week later, six showcases had been built and the first objects from the tomb were placed on public view. Thousands of visitors responded with the utmost enthusiasm. Among the first glittering treasures were the King's mannequin, the golden Nekhbet shrine, the painted casket, the King's "wishing cup" and the magnificent golden throne depicting the handsome young King together with his adoring Queen.

CHAPTER TWENTY-FIVE

Collision Course

"ALL WE HAVE TO DO is to peel the shrines like an onion," Carter had told Herbert Winlock at the end of the first spectacular season, "and we will be with the King himself."

From Carter's books about Tutankhamun, one gains the impression about subsequent seasons that, but for a few acrimonious contretemps with the press and the Antiquities Service and the presence of a few too many tourists, the excavation proceeded smoothly, "scientifically," from the glorious outer shrine down through the multiple layers of that "onion." But in reality it would take Carter eighty days to dismantle the shrines before he could examine what lay inside, a delay that often caused Carter's temper to flare with frustration. After that, a full ten months would pass before the mummy was revealed—ten months involving negotiations of the utmost delicacy, outbursts and arguments, lawsuits, a suppressed scandal, riots, and political dissension. The final result of the tumultuous proceedings would alter forever the nature of archaeology, not only in Egypt but throughout the world.

Carter had been confident he would be able to deal effortlessly with the complex tasks involving the dismantling of the shrines. He was eager to get under way and was intrigued with the question of just how many gilded containers he would actually find. He had already penetrated to the doors of a second shrine. From ancient drawings, he knew that as many as five might surround a sarcophagus.

Carter did not expect this phase of his work to take long—perhaps three weeks from the initiation of the second season in October—and he had asked the Metropolitan Museum for the special loan of its staff members for that period. He was certain, moreover, that he would be able to negotiate effectively with the authorities of the Antiquities Service on behalf of Carnarvon's estate. The three executors, among them the late Earl's intimate friend and adviser Sir John Maxwell, were in full accord with Carter's basic philosophy of firmness.

Maxwell and Carter had been invited by Almina Lady Carnarvon to Highclere during the summer months and, while there, had asked her to take over the concession. She promptly agreed and named Carter as the "archaeological adviser" and Maxwell as general adviser for the venture. All agreed on three basic points: they would seek "full rights" as expressed in the original concession; they would sign the exclusive agreement with the London *Times* for another year; and they would insist upon freedom from "harassments or interruptions" from everyone, whether tourist, reporter or member of the Antiquities Service.

The financial terms for the second year's contract with *The Times* was not as favorable as the first, calling for an advance of twenty-five hundred pounds instead of five thousand. The division of net revenues was to be fifty percent for the estate instead of seventy-five percent. The reason for the reductions in the advance payment and the percentage was that *The Times*'s editors believed that the news value of Tutankhamun was bound to diminish in the second season. How wrong they would turn out to be!

Just before departing London, Carter was asked by a newsman whether he was secretly fearful of being struck down by the curse. His response was brusque, rude. He said he had not the slightest inclination to believe the stupid opinions or theories that held that an occult influence had been responsible for the death of the Earl. As to fears for himself, he testily informed the reporter that it was "rather *too much* to ask me to believe that some spook is keeping watch and ward over the dead Pharaoh, ready to wreak vengeance on anyone who goes too near."

He also told the reporter that he thought it would take "four weeks" and no more to reach the mummy of the King. He emphasized his and the late Lord Carnarvon's intention of leaving the mummy in its present resting place, within the tomb and within the royal sarcophagus. "If we disturbed the body," he said, "we would be no better than the tomb robbers of other days." His defensiveness on this particular issue can be excused by the fact that some newspapers had taken up the theme of "modern tomb-robbing" with zeal. "Are we to consider," blustered one English tabloid, "that 'science and archaeology' are anything but the artful and euphemistic substitutions for greed, rapacity and the deep desire to find and seize treasure?" This issue now capped what Carter once termed the "nonsense list" of attacks that the press and others had directed against the excavators. The list had grown long indeed, including domination of an Egyptian tomb and its sacred dead by foreigners; prostitution of science for cash; tomb robbing; selling the tomb; working too fast; working too slowly.

When Carter left for Trieste, to join the Metropolitan staff members and travel with them to the valley, he knew that soon he would gaze for the first time in recorded history upon the majestic coffins that enclosed a pharaoh's body. But he was also profoundly aware that Carnarvon would not be at hand. The Earl's station in life, his easy access to individuals in authority, his ability to discuss disturbing matters amiably and restrain Carter's impetuousness—his sheer brilliance—would be grievously missed, and Carter undoubtedly sensed this.

Carter arrived in Egypt on the eighth of October, fully prepared for the opening of the second season. On the eleventh he attended a meeting in Cairo at the Antiquities Service, where he applied for renewal of the concession in the name of

Lady Carnarvon. The meeting, conducted by James Quibell in Lacau's absence, was cordial. Quibell described himself as being delighted that Lady Carnarvon had agreed to carry on the excellent undertakings that had been effected with such scientific skill and punctiliousness during the first season. He would be *very* honored and pleased, he announced, to grant the renewal. Carter then suggested that the work be officially defined as the "clearing" of a tomb instead of an excavation. Quibell genially agreed.

Then the issue of the exclusivity granted the London *Times* was raised. Carter explained that a sizable number of newspapers throughout the world had signed contracts with *The Times* over the summer, thereby making it even more imperative that Carter's freedom and right to deal with *The Times* be upheld.

To circumvent the demand from certain opposition papers and news agencies, particularly *The New York Times* and Reuters, that all reporters be allowed in the tomb whenever any single member of the press entered, Carter had concocted an astounding plan. He had decided to appoint the London *Times'*s correspondent, Arthur Merton, not as publicity agent but as an official member of the excavation staff! By this means, Merton could enter the tomb any time Carter wished without criticism, Carter explained. But Carter assured Quibell that he would maintain for the Egyptian newspapers their privileged position of receiving, at no charge, a daily report each morning after the *Times* stories had been filed. "It is," Carter argued, "a generous offer. The Cairo newspapers would get free what all European and American papers would have to pay for."

Carter then addressed himself to the problems posed by the flocks of visitors. There was a perfect solution, Carter went on. That was to allow them into the tomb (but never the laboratory) only after a major part of the work had been accomplished—when, say, all the shrines had been removed and the preserved sarcophagus had been revealed.

Quibell was taken aback. Gently, tactfully, he explained that the appointment of Arthur Merton as an "archaeologist" might not placate the opposition press. When Quibell pointed out that Merton was not, after all, an Egyptologist, Carter coolly informed him that Merton's appointment would nonetheless conform to the strict intent of the concession, which unequivocally granted the discoverer permission to publish a find and, indeed, specifically instructed him to do so. Merton, the representative chosen personally by Carter to publish information in the field, was therefore a perfectly legitimate member of the staff.

Quibell registered an objection to the scheme, but appeared to drop the issue. He then turned once more to the question of visitors. He tried to explain his and Pierre Lacau's problem. Each day the Antiquities Service was overwhelmed with requests to see the tomb and observe the work in progress. Many of these requests came, Quibell explained, from natives who considered the tomb purely an Egyptian affair. How could he placate *them?* Carter brusquely told Quibell that he should not bother. He should, quite simply, issue visitation permits only when Carter allowed. Quibell again objected, but he did so in a manner that Carter interpreted as mild. Quibell then said he would have to think about the "solution" proposed by Carter. But Carter prevailed upon him to discuss the matter then and there at length. And finally, according to Carter's recollections, Quibell completely gave in.

The next day, supremely confident and profoundly relieved, Carter made the two-hundred-mile trek to Alexandria to sign the documents confirming his and Quibell's understanding. But, to his intense annoyance, Quibell nervously informed Carter that a host of objections had been raised by certain other members of the Antiquities Service. More time was necessary, he said, to consider the issues and Carter's solutions.

Carter, angered and insensitive to the Egyptian's predicament, pressed his case vehemently. How, he queried, could the Antiquities Service possibly object to an arrangement under which the "native" press alone would obtain free information while, at the same time, undercutting all the other newspapers of the world? He assured Quibell that the courtesy to the Egyptian newspapers had come about only because of his and Lord Carnarvon's "profound fondness toward Egypt." As for the problem of requests to Antiquities to see the tomb, Carter shrugged and told Quibell that the scientific work would be impeded, possibly even stopped, if visitors—and he did not care *which* visitors—besieged the tomb, thereby preventing him from accomplishing his tasks. The majority of visitors, he claimed, came for no other reason than to be able to say they had been there. What good or worth were *they*? Carter demanded.

Quibell tried to calm him down. He pleaded with Carter for time to maneuver politically with his Egyptian associates. *They* were the problem. *They*, not he, were wondering why a member of the Egyptian press should not be allowed into the tomb side by side with Merton. It was *they* who were continually badgering Quibell to arrange for their friends, families and associates to enter the chamber. He urged Carter to give him time, just a few days, only that. This would ease the situation and help him attain a satisfactory solution. Surely Carter could see the logic of that, Quibell suggested amiably. But Carter told him he could not see it at all. He was an archaeologist who could not be bothered with side issues.

Quibell immediately briefed Pierre Lacau on the discussion. Lacau, who had instructed Quibell exactly on how to deal with Carter, was deeply concerned. He recognized that he was on a collision course with Howard Carter. He hated to give way, but he was fearful of the possibility that work on the tomb might be drastically slowed, even halted, if he did not. And he realized that the full force of the London *Times* would be brought to bear against him and the Antiquities Service if there were even a hint of an interruption.

Lacau prided himself on being an excellent administrator. As such, he was tactful and conciliatory, always attempting to establish the "perfect" balance between the parties in every situation. His technique was time-consuming and involved listening to both sides, weighing their words, returning to

241

each side to discuss the question again—a process he was willing to repeat almost endlessly. At every step he would gently and delicately nudge the counterweight on the scales of argumentation this way and that until a precise balance, acceptable to all, had been achieved.

Lacau was, in fact, a near-perfect bureaucrat, blessed with all the strengths and weaknesses of the breed. Yet in the complex relation he was to have with Howard Carter, his weakness overshadowed his strength. For if the main feature of Lacau's personal brand of diplomacy was tact, tact became a frailty now. His inability or unwillingness to be completely frank— attributable in part to his not wanting to offend—would be interpreted by Carter as vacillation, insincerity and, on occasion, outright duplicity.

Four days after the inconclusive meeting in Alexandria, Carter attended another held in Cairo, and to his satisfaction Lacau and his colleagues finally agreed to Carter's proposals regarding Merton and visitors. No one told him, least of all Lacau, that there had been a bitter difference of opinion among the Egyptian members of the group and that approval had been reached only when the Minister of Public Works himself, Abdel Hamid Suleman Pasha—the former Under-Secretary—had forced a decision in Carter's favor. The Minister, a gregarious man and a favorite with the foreign colony in Cairo, particularly with the British, had made up his mind not to entertain further discussions of the matter. The issue was closed. The only problem with this development was that the Minister would resign his post within four months, when the Egyptian Nationalist Party would assume control. Suleman Pasha would be replaced by a man with radically different views on the matter, a man who, moreover, had four years before been brought to trial by the British and imprisoned for high treason.

The talks were concluded ten days after they had begun, with Howard Carter fully believing he had accomplished all his and the estate's objectives. And, finally, on October 18, he arrived in the Valley of the Kings to supervise the removal of more than seventeen hundred tons of fill that had protected the tomb during the off season and to plan for the dismantling of the shrines. The summer-long silence of the valley was broken by the clanking of picks, shovels and hoes—the work force was excavating the tomb of the King for the third time. Carter estimated that this would require no more than a week, and he planned to commence dismantling the first shrine on October 25.

The work was excruciating. Summer refused to relax its fierce grip on the valley; the temperature was pegged at one hundred twenty degrees. Nonetheless, it was reported that the spirits of the boys and the foremen were high. A band of native boys scampered up and down the stairs leading from the mouth of the tomb, clearing remnants of sand, earth and small stones from the door guarding the sloping passageway. At last the day came when all Carter had to do was open the locks and swing back the massive protective partition to find himself thirty-two hundred years removed in time.

Instead, he was forced to wait. A shipment of paraffin and a celluloid substance for the spot conservation of the gilding on the great shrine was still in transit. Moreover, a number of additional electrical lights for the tomb promised by the Antiquities Service had yet to be installed. Carter fumed, for the department had known full well that he was planning to start the operation at an early date. He complained to the local inspector that it was just another example of inefficiency and bad faith. He was particularly annoyed because he had learned that lights for the public had been set up! And the lights inside the tomb—the lights for "science"—would be ready only after the middle of the month, despite the fact that Carter generously had offered to pay all costs for their installation.

Another development added fuel to Carter's anger. He had received a letter from James Quibell asking his personal assistance in unpacking and putting on display in the Egyptian Museum more treasures to help slake the public thirst. It was a reasonable request, one that would be of benefit to Howard Carter in his desire to insulate himself from visitors to the site.

But Carter, who had begun to develop an aversion to Quibell and suspected that Quibell was working against him, complained that Antiquities was attempting to take him away from precious field work.

Privately, Carter had a more troubling reservation. He suspected a ruse. For in the letter Quibell casually mentioned that A. H. Bradstreet of *The New York Times* had visited him the day before and would soon have a meeting with the Minister.

Bradstreet, that alert ferret of a newspaperman, was still pursuing every nuance of the story of the tomb with unyielding determination. He was proud of his position as correspondent for *The New York Times,* the London *Daily Mail,* and the *Egyptian Mail,* as befitted someone whose climb to the top had been hard. He had, for years, been a minor stringer, eking out a perilous livelihood by filing routine stories on the tourist trade, social events, sports like squash and polo, and the dull proceedings of King Fuad's court. When he picked up a lead, he fastened onto it like an iguana, whose jaws even in death remain clenched around its foe. His methods were expedient, tough. It was rumored that one of his favorite techniques was to obtain, by whatever method he might, actual court records from the official stenographer in whatever trial he happened to be covering. From his colleagues he had received the ultimate honor of abiding envy. In a country where one was expected to take life easy, Bradstreet was an eccentric who rushed about, apparently unaffected even by the scorching midsummer heat.

As an investigative reporter, Bradstreet was a fervent disciple of the full freedom of the press, competitive and totally open. Naturally, he particularly resented the exclusive contract that Carnarvon had made with the London *Times,* and after his lordship's death Bradstreet seems to have transferred that resentment to Howard Carter, who became a personal symbol of the intransigence of privilege. Bradstreet's stories on the tomb are filled with editorial remarks about the exclusivity of the contract and the unauthorized use of the Metropolitan's experts as publicity agents for the London *Times.*

Bradstreet pursued Carter daily. No matter what Carter did, there was Bradstreet to comment. He filed several stories downplaying the objects discovered in the tomb, saying that although they were "interesting" they were mute about the precise history of the shadowy era in which Tutankhamun reigned. "The glamour of gold which originally invested the tomb," he wrote, "has been dulled by the lapse of time since the tomb was discovered and the realization that no historical documentation has been unearthed." Such comments did little to endear him to Carter, and the enmity grew.

When Bradstreet met the Minister and his Under-Secretary, Paul Tottenham, he registered a formal complaint against the exclusive contract. Tottenham, a civil servant of retiring demeanor, listened with mounting anguish to the enraged reporter. What did Bradstreet want him to do? After all, the Ministry of Public Works had just reaffirmed its promise to safeguard the contract between Carter and the London *Times*. Bradstreet offered up a simple solution. Knowing that Tottenham's understanding of the newspaper business must be slight, he proposed—in the interests of peace—that Carter be ordered by the ministry to issue a daily communiqué to all newspapers and wire services, not later than nine o'clock each evening. By that hour, the reporter for the London *Times* would have already filed his exclusive report. Therefore no one, least of all the London *Times*, could complain, for 9 P.M. was much too late for the British or European evening papers to scoop *The Times*. Tottenham, obviously confused, agreed to the suggestion. He incorporated it as an official condition into a draft agreement and sent it along to Jean Quibell.

Quibell, who despite Carter's dark suspicions was at this time still sympathetic to him, wrote Carter a letter marked "Confidential":

This is a very private letter. . . . Both Bradstreet and Valentine Williams have been to see me. They want a bare bulletin daily in time for them to send it for the morning paper.

If they get that they will be good, if not they will be naughty. They put this as politely as possible but that is the plain English of it.

The Minister wants to put Egyptian surveillants over your work, not that he doubts your competence or honesty but because he wishes to avoid the criticisms of his compatriots. How this surveillance can be arranged without being intolerable to you he did not know and passed the problem to me!

Quibell then suggested that the Minister's observer, an Egyptian by the name of Mohammed Chaban, be sent "to smoke his cigarettes in the Valley" where he would be no trouble to Carter. He concluded his private communication by asking Carter to consider how far both sides could go to obtain "peace."

But Carter was not in the mood for peace. He was outraged at the suggestion of being watched and was deeply annoyed at what he described as an inherent contradiction in Tottenham's memo, which on the one hand vowed to uphold the London *Times*'s contract and then, by proposing a nightly bulletin, made it "fall to the ground." The following day, when Carter received another letter from Quibell suggesting they get together in Luxor to discuss the draft memorandum before it became final, he demanded that a special meeting in Cairo be scheduled to discuss the ticklish matter with Quibell, Tottenham, Lacau and the Minister of Public Works.

As soon as he sat down with the group and stated that the "nightly bulletin" would never do, Carter sensed a changed attitude. For Lacau was accompanied by a lawyer from the Ministry of Public Works, who insisted that the government had a perfectly "legal right" to issue on its own a bulletin at nine o'clock every evening. Lacau explained to Carter, ever so patiently, that every governmental ministry in Egypt had full and sole authority over such matters and could issue news releases covering a broad spectrum of activities, from the construction of a sewer to the conduct of an archaeological excavation. It was a logical and reasonable "publicity right." Carter challenged Lacau to show him a "single word of documentary evidence" to prove his case. Lacau, commenting that he did not have to prove anything, said that he would nonetheless be pleased to do so. The documentation must have been known to Carter, because it appeared in the official authorization to excavate which had been countersigned by Lady Carnarvon herself weeks before, where it was stated that "the Antiquities Service reserved the right of control over the undertakings to avoid commentaries such as occurred during the preceding season." That, Lacau explained, could mean only the press. Carter, who certainly knew of this document but either had somehow failed to perceive its significance or had hoped it would not surface, was speechless.

Then Carter became a supplicant. He had not traveled all the way to Cairo in stultifying heat to return empty-handed. He beseeched Lacau to waive this right, and ultimately Lacau did! Working with members of his staff, he prepared a simple and direct three-point agreement. The first point stated that "in consideration of the services rendered by the Late Lord Carnarvon and his agents"—and so that all journalistic disputes could be halted and the work facilitated—the government, "as an exceptional case," would "waive its rights" and would "confide *all* duties of publication to the diggers." The second point stated that an Egyptian representative of the Antiquities Service would go every day to the tomb in order to "oversee the investigations." And, finally, the third point stipulated that as soon as the work on the dismantling of all the shrines had progressed to a point where it became "materially practicable for strangers to be admitted" a certain number of visitors, given dated and numbered tickets, would be allowed access.

The Minister himself was delighted, but just before countersigning the memorandum excluding the press he turned to Carter and asked, "Would you, sir, out of courtesy, agree to invite one, just one, representative of the press every day to the tomb?" Carter, in a turnabout that can perhaps best be explained by the fact that he knew that the Minister's wish would not be written into the agreement, quickly consented.

The Minister should have left it at that. Instead he turned to Lacau and the others and said, "Very well, I will look after the Egyptian press, and you, gentlemen, will look after the foreign press."

There was an awkward silence. Lacau, Tottenham and Quibell just looked at one another and then back at the Minister. At length Lacau said that he could not agree, for he felt that he personally could not effectively cope with the members of the foreign press and did not want to do so. Exasperated that the affair had become stalled once more, Carter suggested that all should adjourn, contemplate the problem for a day, reconvene and then, after minor adjustments, finally sign the accord. He appears to have been confident that no real impediments remained.

But at the meeting held the next day Carter was astonished and angered to learn that Pierre Lacau refused to sign any agreement. The obstinate bureaucrat stated that he felt constrained to discuss the whole problem again from the beginning. To Lacau, it came down to the root issue: in what way would the government benefit or be protected against criticism if it waived its right to dispense information, handed that right over to Carter, and refused to give even the briefest daily bulletin to the world at large?

Carter's answer was immediate. After all, he had been ruminating over the matter for weeks. The response he gave— which he committed to a written memorandum and presented to the group the following day—stunned Lacau and Quibell, for it was not really a reply to the question at all. It was a quiverful of indictments. His arrows were aimed directly at the heart of the Antiquities Service and the very men sitting in the room.

"The following remarks," Carter's memorandum began, "are submitted as a reply to your question. But, having regard to the form in which the question is framed, I feel it is necessary to state that the reply must be regarded, in lawyer's language, as 'without prejudice.' "

He went on:

The contract with *The Times* was made to protect ourselves from the importunities of Press correspondents, by enabling us to deal with one organisation for world distribution instead of a large number of individual Press representatives. . . . It was made in good faith, solely with the object of ensuring that the work . . . be carried out with the minimum of interruption and friction. . . .

The contract with *The Times*, accepted by the large majority of the world's Press and approved by scientific authorities, has excited opposition on the part of certain papers, which had, and indeed still have, the opportunity of taking the service, but which for purely personal reasons . . . still refuse. . . .

The proceeds of the contract are entirely devoted to research work at the tomb, and are thus wholly for the benefit of Science, of Egypt and the Egyptian Government. On the other hand, the opposition are entirely self-actuated, their sole object being to break the arrangement of the service and to secure material benefit for themselves. . . .

You have represented to me, though I am not of that opinion, that only scientific publication is my property and that publicity is the Government right. I repeat that there is nothing in the concession to this effect. Neither is there any law existing to cover this case, and such a question could only be proved by legal proceedings, which I should certainly feel myself obliged to take should the Government decide to enforce its alleged rights.

The question of the right of publicity is therefore, in these circumstances, merely a matter of opinion. One would have expected that in such a case the Government would have given the benefit of the doubt to its concessionaire. Instead of this, it is taking the part of those who throughout have tried to do him harm, who have only a material interest in the matter . . .

Again, if the Government says that only scientific right to publication is my property, then why is it, and how is it, that it allows that right to be infringed in this country? . . .

Further, last year, in our desire to meet the wishes of the Government, we agreed to allow weekly visits from newspaper correspondents. So, far from this concession producing peace, it resulted in the attacks and insults directed against Lord Carnarvon and the members of his staff becoming more virulent and continuing to this day.

Again, we acceded to the Government's wish for the installment of a representative in the Valley. This not only proved an utter failure, but also ended in a serious breach of faith. If the Government enforces what it considers to be its rights it will be incurring grave responsibility and grave consequences . . .

To protect myself against any such action as the Government might contemplate, I should feel compelled to defend by all possible means myself and the interests which I represent as agent of the late Lord Carnarvon's heirs. . . .

This would involve making known to the world in the fullest detail the whole of our negotiations from start to finish. The action of the Government, the action of the opposition, and my own action would be clearly revealed, and the world would learn with amazement and disgust of the utter inadequacy of the protection which the Government affords its concessionaires, of its lack of consideration for those working for scientific interests, and of the persistent encouragement which it is giving to the section of the press which last year earned the lively reprobation of the thinking world by the abominable manner in which it attacked this agreement for its own ends.

For all these reasons it is obviously in the interest of the Egyptian Government that the agent should be protected in the matter of this contract. The only way in which he can be protected is by the Government not issuing the proposed communiqué, but relying on him to communicate all information to the world through the medium of the service already instituted.

I sincerely trust that what I have said will convince the Government of the direction in which their best interests lie. I have endeavoured throughout to be conciliatory, and no one desires a peaceful settlement more than I do. But, if the Government persists in its intention, I feel bound to say quite frankly that I shall be compelled to take action against it in the manner indicated, for in this matter I am defending not only the interests of my principals, but also those of the entire scientific world. . . .

Tottenham expressed satisfaction with Carter's words and memorandum and even wrote on one of the copies: "If issue of bulletin means trouble for Carter with the London Times, and consequent interruption of work, this is a valid argument for Carter's 'case.'" Carter waited for an answer. But neither Pierre Lacau nor James Quibell would express a definite opinion either way. Privately, they were infuriated by what they interpreted as an insult and a blunt series of threats.

Carter remained in Cairo a week, expecting to receive the official decision. He repeatedly called the Ministry of Public

Works and, receiving only a vague promise of some definite settlement, concluded that the department was "shilly-shallying." By now he had worked himself up into a fury. He was disgusted that he had wasted nearly eight full days in Cairo in fruitless negotiations, and he desperately wanted to return to the valley. Finally, talking on the telephone to the Minister, who assured him that all would be settled in a satisfactory manner, Carter departed for the tomb. Two days later he received the document at his quarters in the valley.

He was at first overjoyed. He had won all points. But then, after several days of reflection, he began to complain bitterly about the document, declaring it was "practically useless." He put his complaint into writing and rushed it off to Pierre Lacau. His quixotic change of mind was interpreted by Lacau and his associates as one more thoughtless, purposeless demonstration of petulance. As much as any single act in the drama concerning Tutankhamun, it turned the Service of Antiquities fully against Howard Carter.

What had so angered him? When one learns the answer, his rash action becomes even more incomprehensible.

In his letter transmitting the points of each agreement—each one a clear victory for Carter—Lacau had cautioned him that the measures, for obvious reasons, had to be considered "temporary" and were subject to refinement or change depending upon how they worked out in practice. Carter took umbrage at this and demanded that if the government reconsidered any of the proposed measures at any time in the future, it had to consult him before changes were made.

Pierre Lacau in his turn was deeply insulted. He considered Carter's demand to be an unwarranted attempt to meddle with the Service of Antiquities. And he told him so, curtly, in a letter. It was none of Carter's business, Lacau said, to interfere with how the Antiquities Service handled the issue of public access to a part of the State's domain.

Having got that off his chest, Lacau prepared a public announcement which outlined the three points and described, eloquently, the problems of conducting a harrowing archaeological exercise under public scrutiny. The very nature of the work demanded restrictions, so that "permits to visitors must—and will—be ruthlessly limited." The goal would be to remove the canopies or shrines until "the coffin—which, as is supposed, lies untouched in their center—is reached." The announcement explained that "plank by plank the great boxes had to be taken to pieces" without damage to their sumptuous decorations. "With barely room to manipulate the scaffolding, with inadequate supply of air, in the heat of the powerful electric lights," the work, especially if it extended into summer, would become an ordeal. The document concluded with a gracious appeal to "all men of good will not to ask for favours . . . which would compel the diggers to work one more day into the heat."

The Egyptian press assailed the document when it was released to the public, complaining particularly about the waiving of the "publicity right." One columnist put it bluntly: "it is wrong, dead wrong; as it sets a precedent whereby the Egyptian Government must always take second place whenever an important archaeological discovery is made in Egypt."

Carter initially expressed his satisfaction with the text. But then he condemned it, calling it worthless. He began to complain heatedly that the Service of Antiquities was violating the accord, not only in spirit but in word, by attempting to send unauthorized visitors to the site.

The reason for Carter's mercurial behavior is all too clear. His obvious personal feeling that he and the Carnarvon estate really did "own" the tomb was definitely a factor. His personal dislike for Lacau must also have had a bearing. But above all, Carter was exhausted, his mind in turmoil, though the new season had scarcely commenced. In a long briefing letter to Sir John Maxwell on the meetings, Carter had added in one place the words "bored stiff" and in another: "How long, Oh God, shall I be left in peace!" The slightest setback, the smallest irritation, seemed to drive him into periods of rage or brooding silence. He was beginning to crack up.

CHAPTER TWENTY-SIX

The Bastion of Bureaucracy

WHEN CARTER RETURNED to the site to embark upon the removal of the shrines, his vexation began to disappear. Down inside the tomb, surrounded by the treasures, he felt a vitality surging within him and he was at peace with himself and those around him. When he was within the tomb, working on its objects, his mind seemed to clear and his acute sense of deductive reasoning was again fully endowed.

As Carter examined the surfaces of the two visible shrines, he discovered a disturbing phenomenon. The gilding had separated from the wood in numerous places, making dry pockets. When it was tapped ever so gently, a dull reverberation could be heard. Over the centuries, the wood had dried out in certain areas but had maintained its original strength in others. The fragility of the material meant that Carter could not hope to dismantle the great boxes within a few weeks—it would take months. He would have to tear down the entire wall between the Antechamber and the Burial Chamber before lifting out any one of the shrine sections. That would require, first, the painstaking removal of the frescoes on the inside of the wall.

The two life-sized sentinels stationed against the north wall were removed. Carter placed them on special large trays fitted with wheels, after covering them up to their heads with surgical wrapping. The spectacle caused one observer to remark that their "eyes flashed, almost malevolently, uncannily, out of the surgical dressings, and they looked like some severely wounded soldiers after treatment in a casualty ward."

The excavators removed most of the north wall. Once it was gone, visitors could see the entire side of the great outer shrine. It was breathtaking. Bradstreet was moved to comment exuberantly:

Luxor nowadays is just a golden lyric. . . . Yet descend but thirty feet into the earth from the center of the Valley and . . . one will emerge in sepulchral darkness, illuminated by the searching radiance of 10,000 candlepower lamps. This blinding light plays unblinkingly and steadily on the largest area of plated gold in existence. It plays not only on the sheen of gold wrapping the outer shrine in the Burial Chamber of Tutankhamun, but its unwinking effulgence now streams vividly across the front of the second shrine.

A complicated wooden scaffolding was erected around the outer shrine so that Carter and a team of his most able workmen could take it apart. Carter recorded not only the many pieces of the wooden planking forming the roof and the sides of the shrine, but "a certain amount of profanity as well." He told reporters, "We bumped our heads, nipped our fingers; we had to squeeze in and out like weasels and work in all kinds of embarrassing positions."

Carter had to work ten full days just to lift the heaviest of the three sections that formed the roof of the outer shrine. It was first raised by wedges and levers and gently deposited on top of a piece of timber, which would serve as a sort of sled. After that, a scaffolding was placed beneath the timber to shore it up. Then a series of wooden rollers, wrapped with surgical gauze, was inserted underneath the timber sled. It was easy enough to place the rollers and the wedges on the side facing

254

the Antechamber. But how to get them to the inner side? The roof of the shrine was too delicate to support the weight of a grown man, and an adult could not possibly wriggle through the passageway, now almost entirely filled with pieces of the surrounding scaffold. Carter picked out a small, quick-witted boy from the work force, who scrambled nimbly to the top of the golden roof. Stripped to the waist, he sat there on his haunches for hours, slipping the rollers and the wedges into their necessary positions. Finally the massive section of the roof was rolled out and lowered down to rest against the padded inner wall of the Burial Chamber.

The work was unbelievably difficult. But Carter, despite— or perhaps because of—the demanding nature of these tasks, was at his very best. Except for an influx of visitors several days before and after Christmas, he and his associates had been left alone. He was fully in charge. The task was complex, challenging. He was proceeding steadily toward the earthly remains of his King.

The second section of the roof of the outer shrine presented no complications, but the removal of the third, tucked away at the very back of the chamber, consumed a whole day. It took four hours alone to raise it, place it on gauze-covered rollers, and propel it along the top of the shrine to the center, where finally it could be lowered into the Antechamber. Seven additional men had to be brought in just for the operation.

Once the roof sections had been removed it was possible to examine fully the linen pall that covered the second shrine. The pall was supported by a wooden structure with three lintels, the one in the center standing slightly higher than those at each end. Between the wooden supports the delicate pall had collapsed under the weight of the dozens of gilded bronze rosettes with which it had been decorated. Arthur Merton reported that the curious structure, with "its spangled design and gilded understructure, and, underneath, the beautiful inner shrine with its precious contents at once turns one's thoughts to the Ark of the Israelites." And, as a matter of fact, there was a striking resemblance to the Tabernacle of the Covenant described in the Book of Exodus. Carter speculated that the great shrines were probably replicas of the tabernacles in use for thousands of years for local deities in various temples throughout Egypt. It was not unlikely; since the Children of Israel had emerged from bondage in Egypt, they could have known of the common basic shape of the structure and adapted it for their own purposes.

Although he had feared it would take a week or more to dismantle the framework of the pall, it actually was done, safely, in just a day. The wooden framework, painted black, profusely gilded, had, as Merton wrote, "all the appearance of a cage." Carter wrapped the entire structure in surgical bandages. It proved no easy task to maneuver the long, fragile pieces of wood in the confined space at the top of the shrine. But by midday all the beams and the sections had been dismantled and laid in the Antechamber alongside the pole that had supported the pall itself. The wood was olive and persea, both considered sacred in ancient Egypt. The former came from Egypt, the latter from Abyssinia. Carter believed that they could have symbolized Tutankhamun's power at home and over foreign lands.

At the removal of the pall and its supports, the sealed doors of the second shrine could be fully opened to reveal exactly how many others surrounded what had to be, by ancient ritual, a massive stone sarcophagus. Carter was burning with anticipation.

In his bastion of bureaucracy, Pierre Lacau could think of nothing but Carter's continuing intransigence and complaints. He had resolved by now to bring the archaeologist to his knees. By now he had gained the total support of James Quibell, who urgently advised his chief to annul the concession and throw Carter out of the tomb.

But Lacau did not feel quite that confident. The members of the Antiquities Service did not have the expertise to carry out the expedition. If Carter *were* expelled, Lacau doubted that the Metropolitan staff would remain on the job. It was even possible, although Lacau could not be absolutely sure, that the

Americans had arranged to receive, from Carter and the Carnarvon estate, a portion of the discoveries. This, he surmised, may have been why the Americans had already exerted—and were continuing to exert—such powerful diplomatic pressures upon the Egyptian government.

Lacau knew the personality of his adversary well, and he was ready to bank on the fact that Carter, under heavy strain, eventually had to crack. By going by the book, by enforcing his administrative rights to the letter, he just might get Carter to do something rash. It was even conceivable that he could provoke Carter to such an extent that Carter would quit! If Carter did, he reasoned, little criticism could be directed toward the department.

What to do first? Lacau began by instructing Rex Engelbach to drop the word to Carter, casually, that the department wanted a list of his co-workers. James Quibell followed up Engelbach's conversation with a purposefully disarming letter:

The Minister wants a list of your staff—why, I don't know. I could have written it out almost, but not quite, for you may have people coming out of whom I don't know the names, and I'm not sure of Callendar's first name, nor of Mr. Bethell's initials, and so on. So, would you correct and complete this list and send it to me? and I will transmit it. I'm late with it. We have been busy and I'm sadly in arrears. Lythgoe turned up to-day.

Yours as ever,
Quibell

H. Carter
A. C. Mace
H. Burton
A. Lucas
____ Callendar
Dr. Alex. Scott
The Hon.____ Bethell
Sir Archibald Reid
Prof. Derry.

P.S.—Among the things newly put out, an ivory box particularly charmed me. I had not heard of it before. —J.E.Q.

To Carter, this request was "extraordinary, outrageous," so entirely unprecedented in the "whole history of Egyptian excavation" that he was at first at a complete loss as to why he should comply. He immediately responded that he was "thoroughly puzzled as to what the request can mean, for surely in the details of my work I am at liberty to employ whomever I wish, so long as I adhere to the terms of my concession."

Carter dispatched a letter to the London *Times* with a copy of Quibell's and observed, "I am prepared for a hell of a fight, if the occasion arises, and I shall expect you to back me in *full force!*"

A week later, Lacau bluntly replied with a letter as unyielding as Carter's previous communications had been. He informed him that the Minister of Public Works wanted to have the list *"of all your collaborators"* so that he could exercise his right of approval over the presence of any of them. The letter further informed Carter that "no one could visit the tomb without a written authorization from the Government," so as to guarantee that only fully qualified workers would participate in the "scientific research" conducted in the tomb. Lacau also mentioned wanting to avoid having the "scientific undertakings" interrupted by those seeking to satisfy "vain curiosity" alone.

It finally occurred to Carter what lay behind Lacau's move. The "opposition press" had obviously complained to the Minister about Arthur Merton's having been made an official member of the excavation staff. To Carter, the clue to Lacau's real intention was that in Quibell's letter Merton's was the only name that had not appeared.

Because of the extraordinary curiosity engendered by the tomb of Tutankhamun, the letter went on, new governmental measures would have to be invoked. None of them, Lacau smoothly assured Carter, was directed against him personally. But all "the clamor that had surrounded the dig" had forced the government to pursue a course it had never before taken. He was referring, he explained, to the government's decision to revise the concession form.

The proposed form, a landmark in the history of Egyptian archaeology, was tough and explicit. It gave the State total authority to supervise and safeguard all activities involving an excavation, rather than ceding that right to the excavator. And the government reserved the right to approve not only the director but every single member of his staff. Any individual the Service of Antiquities deemed to be undesirable would be promptly removed from the dig.

The government—and only the government—would grant permits for all foreign visitors, Lacau's letter went on. It would supervise *all* activities. The "beneficiary of the authorization," his agents and his staff would have to carry out all instructions without discussion, without complaint.

The right to publish the scientific results would, as before, be given to the diggers, but the government reserved the absolute right to publish, at any time, information of general public interest concerning the excavation. Finally, Lacau announced, any "infraction or contravention" by the concessionaire would lead to the immediate cancellation of the authorization.

The new measures proposed by Lacau raised a furor in the valley. Carter wanted to close down the tomb and walk off the job at once. But Albert Lythgoe and Edward S. Harkness, a member of the Metropolitan's board of trustees, who was visiting the site at the time, urged him not to be impetuous.

There was no question in Carter's mind, or among his associates, that such restrictions would imperil the future of archaeology. For the sake of science alone, they all agreed, Carter could not subscribe to any policy that would establish such an "unfortunate precedent." They further agreed there was little Lacau could do, from either a practical or a legal point of view, if his proposed edict was resisted. Accordingly, Carter resolved to issue a strong protest against all the measures.

On the twelfth of December, Lacau came to the valley to meet Carter and discuss the situation. But Carter was ill that day and unable to leave his house. Lacau visited the tomb and the laboratory, where he came across Arthur Merton and remarked to him that *he* was the major cause of all the difficulties. Unless the *Times* reporter agreed to resign from the staff, Lacau said, a great deal more trouble would follow.

Upon meeting Lacau the next day, Carter told him that he considered Lacau's demands "totally unjustifiable encroachments" upon his rights. Carter refused even to recognize the existence of the resolution. Lacau told him curtly to present his views to the Minister himself.

After his acerbic exchange with Pierre Lacau, Carter went to Cairo to meet with the Minister of Public Works. The Minister stated directly for the first time that the root of the problem was Arthur Merton. Merton was *not* a scientist, and under no circumstances could he ever be disassociated from the London *Times.* In order to resolve "all difficulties," the Minister had made the decision to strike Merton's name from Carter's list of colleagues.

Carter tried to defend Merton as a bona fide member of his staff, on the grounds that every news story emanating from the site thus bore Carter's official approval. But Minister Suleman Pasha informed Carter that he would never accept the logic of that argument and instructed Carter to prevent Merton from entering the tomb except on those days reserved for the entire body of newsmen. Carter argued that were he to do that, or were he to accept such commands from the government, he would establish a fatal precedent. When the Minister persisted, Carter shot back that he would talk with his collaborators and reply formally in writing.

In the discussion with his colleagues, no one attempted to persuade Carter to accept even one of the Minister's proposals. They all seemed to feel that all foreign rights would be terminated forever if Carter gave in to a single demand. Lythgoe stated bluntly that if Carter were forced to capitulate to the Egyptians he would recommend to his board that the Metropolitan close down all archaeological operations forever.

Carter dispatched a cable to *The Times* warning its executives of the drastic new actions:

Government re-makes trouble. Driven by editorial criticism in local press directed personally at Ministry of Public Works and obvious incited by British opposition . . . I have absolutely full backing—financial, otherwise, of Metropolitan Museum and I am told also of backing by American State Department. Please help.

He followed the cable with a lengthy letter, enclosing all documents in the case. "I am," he wrote, "having a very tough fight here and I rely on you to strengthen my hand by generating as wide publicity as possible. I think the publication of all these documents would enlist for us the entire sympathy and support of the thinking world."

At the bottom of the typed letter Carter added a hasty comment in his own hand: "The new Concession formula does not concern us whatsoever—therefore not enclosed here." Why he chose to be deceptive is unclear, but this is further evidence of his unbalanced frame of mind.

The editors of *The Times* had begun to become deeply concerned over the growing controversy at the Valley of the Kings. What had appeared to be an excellent prize—the exclusive contract—was gradually turning into a burden thrust upon them by an increasingly erratic Howard Carter. It was decided by the editors, prudently, not to publish the confidential documents, for fear of adding to the burgeoning conflict. When Howard Carter heard their decision, he bitterly denounced it to Arthur Merton, complaining that he needed *support* in the form of world publicity, not indecision or silence.

Carter sent his formal reply to the Minister on the twentieth of December. Its essence can be conveyed in one simple sentence: "I regret that I cannot see my way to conform to the restrictions you seek to impose upon me."

The very day Carter dispatched the letter he received a telephone call from Paul Tottenham asking him what his decision had been. Lacau's chief aide was shocked to hear the news and begged Carter to retract his letter. The conversation as transcribed by Carter went as follows:

Tottenham: ". . . The Minister is only asking a very small

point from you—that is, in regard to Merton not entering the tomb. We think you should reconsider it."

Carter: "My letter is already written and posted."

Tottenham: "Very well; I can return that letter to you and say nothing more about it."

Carter: "Unfortunately, all my telegrams have been sent to England and various machinery set into motion."

To which Tottenham replied gloomily: "Are you quite sure that you have sent the letter?"

"Yes."

Tottenham pleaded with Carter to recognize that what the Minister wanted was a minor political compromise. It was simply a matter of routine government control and supervision, which might be of benefit to Carter. But Carter abruptly cut off the conversation.

Had Carter been less recalcitrant, more sensitive to human affairs; or had his colleagues from the Metropolitan Museum looked beyond their own special interests; had he somehow managed to give in on what was surely "a very small point"— the outcome of the excavation of Tutankhamun's tomb might well have been quite different.

CHAPTER TWENTY-SEVEN

Dismantling the Shrines

THE WONDER WAS THAT Carter found time to conduct the excavation at all. But on the third of January, after weeks of preparation, he was ready to open the doors of the second shrine, solve the mystery of how many shrines there were, and proceed toward the sarcophagus of Tutankhamun.

He invited Rex Engelbach to come to the tomb at three forty-five that afternoon. But earlier in the day Carter, accompanied by Callender, Mace, Burton, Lucas and Professor Percy Newberry, descended from the dazzling sunlight into the inky shade of the tomb's entrance and approached the second shrine. He slipped back the wooden bolts on the gilded doors, sliced both ends of the entwined ropes with a scalpel, and gingerly removed them. Then he carefully swung back the doors on their ancient hinges and gave the command for the powerful arc lights to be turned on. In a flash, the doors of a third shrine broke into a golden, illuminated blaze.

Carter could see that they, too, were bolted and sealed. The surface of the gilded wood had been carved with hieroglyphs and decorated with the massive figure of a god, its head that of a ram or horse, accompanied by the cow-headed goddess Hathor. When Carter, with surprising ease, opened the doors to the third shrine, he found the portals of a fourth. There he observed more hieroglyphs, surrounded by a series of hawks with wings outspread that appeared to protect, lovingly, the body of the King.

Professor Newberry took only a few minutes to translate a group of hieroglyphs that were placed more prominently than the rest. A silence fell upon the excavators when he finally whispered what they meant. They appeared to be the words of the King himself—"I have seen yesterday; I know tomorrow."

At this point, Carter sliced through the ropes and the seal of the fourth shrine. The arc lights were once again turned on. As the doors of the fourth shrine were gently pulled back, an arm carved on the stone of a beautiful crystalline sandstone sarcophagus stretched out to the gaze of the excavators. It was the arm of the goddess Nephthys, "protecting against all intruders, which symbolised, touchingly and beautifully, as did the goddess herself, the perfect faith and tender solicitude for the well-being of their loved ones which animated the people who dwelt in this land thirteen centuries before our era." For Carter, and for the others, it was a monumental moment archaeologically—and emotionally.

That afternoon Carter showed Rex Engelbach what he had done and cabled Pierre Lacau: "Investigation today enabled me to ascertain that the four shrines contain a magnificent sarcophagus, intact. Regards."

News of the discovery of the superb sarcophagus spread quickly throughout Egypt. Merton stated that everyone in Luxor was "agog with interest" over the smaller inner shrines and the breathtakingly stunning sarcophagus. Crowds of tourists gathered at the site. Everyone seemed sure that something of incomparable beauty would be found within. What would it be? Carter, pressed to make a prediction, would only say, "Something almost unimaginable." He then said he hoped to find a series of golden coffins, possibly three, and the intimate treasures of the dead King—particularly the double crown of Upper and Lower Egypt, the pharaonic regalia and the royal jewels. More fervently, Carter said he longed to discover papyri which might cast additional light on the King who, among all his objects, was still no more than a shadow—an image unchanged since 1913, when Carter and Carnarvon had started their search.

All work came to a halt so that Carter and his associates could photograph the nest of shrines and the sarcophagus inside. As they looked down the sides of each shrine, they could see a number of objects reverently placed there. A delay was required to record the data, and time was needed to ponder and plan the complex job of dismantling the last two shrines.

Paul Tottenham visited the tomb two days after the opening, bringing disquieting news. He informed Carter that the Minister of Public Works had received a sharp complaint from Bradstreet, who accused Carter of having allowed a representative of the London *Times* to enter the tomb at the moment of the opening of the doors of the shrine. He also told Carter that "serious complications" had arisen from the fact that the doors had been opened and the sarcophagus exposed without an Egyptian inspector present. Consequently, the government had decided to take what Tottenham described only as "drastic measures." Carter acidly informed Tottenham that he had indeed invited the chief inspector, Engelbach, to the tomb. He did not mention, however, that he had told Engelbach to come at an hour when he knew the doors would already have been opened. As for the other charge, Carter denied angrily that anyone from the London *Times* had been in the tomb the day of the opening. He had invited no one from the paper. Tottenham accepted Carter's explanations and cabled the Minister his recommendation to cancel the "drastic measures."

While the excavators closed the tomb for several days to record their finds, one of the Egyptian newspapers, the *Exchange Telegraph*, published a penetratingly accurate report. It said that, following Howard Carter's magnificent discoveries of the second and successive shrines, there had come "a sudden slump." The story stated that Carter had been working "under the highest tension" and that the culmination of his brightest hopes had been followed by a reaction—"as he walked through the Valley of the Kings yesterday in the blazing sunlight, wearing a heavy overcoat, his face was drawn with the heavy strain of the last few days." The correspondent wrote that Carter was bowed under the weight of knowing that his relations with the Egyptian government were deteriorating each day.

Despite the implication that Howard Carter, like "mad dogs and Englishmen," ventured out in the noonday sun, on the following day Carter—apparently invigorated—gave a lengthy and enthusiastic interview to the reporter from the London *Times:*

It is really almost ten years to the day since, facing a strong contrary opinion, the late Lord Carnarvon and I undertook to search for the lost King, who I personally was convinced still lay concealed in the valley. Those ten intervening years *have* been years of toil, and two days ago, on Thursday, our hopes were realised.

The results have *indeed* exceeded our expectations, since for the first time in the history of Egyptian archaeology we have been able to discover exactly how a Pharaoh of Egypt was buried.

Our work this season, as you know, has been confined to the sepulchral chamber, and within the first doors of the great shrine has been on wholly untouched ground.

Now, although thieves had entered the Ante-chamber and the so-called Annexe and the store-chamber or treasury and deranged objects there while hunting for portable loot, here within the great shrine were the original seals on the doors to indicate that no one had entered since the King was laid there.

Then through some great piece of good fortune we have at last found what we have been longing for, but never dreamed of attaining—an absolute insight into the funerary customs followed in the burial of an Egyptian King, the earthly representative of the great ancient Egyptian god Ra.

That sight alone is *over-powering,* and the imagination can hardly carry us within the beautiful sarcophagus, for there when the lid is raised—which I hope will be in the course of a few weeks—the contents will solve a problem that has hitherto baffled archaeologists, and for the first time modern eyes will look upon the undisturbed work of men executed three thousand years ago in accordance with the customs of the prevailing religion. . . .

The sarcophagus, which is unusually large, is indeed a superb specimen of its kind. As already mentioned, only the front portions are visible at present, but it has every appearance of being in perfect condition, and the more one looks at its unblemished rose-tinted surface, with its strikingly unostentatious but delightfully elegant decoration the more one realises what a precious addition it constitutes to the world's possession of relics of ancient Egypt.

The contemplation of this magnificent piece of work affords, indeed, infinite pleasure, and with the panelled doors of the shrines opened one behind the other it has all the appearance of a jewel stored within a series of golden safes . . .

After a few days' rest, Carter and the team started in on the backbreaking job of taking the shrines to pieces and isolating the sarcophagus. The atmosphere in the Burial Chamber was tense, and the heat was fervid. Perspiration streamed from the bodies of the men.

Carter gently put his hand to the corner of the outer shrine. The moment had come to attempt to move pieces without damaging the dry, brittle wood. One false move, just a little too much pressure, might mean the destruction of an entire section.

"Well," Carter said quietly, pointing to the great shrine, "there's our patient now on the table; we mustn't breathe yet."

"No," Callender replied, "but I wish we could use the knife."

All fervently agreed.

Carter gave the word. Their hands touched the shrine firmly, yet gently, like surgeons. Some seconds passed, and the wood gave infinitesimally. No one spoke. The woodwork was withstanding the pressure. They exerted more pressure, and the shrine gave another fraction of an inch. In this way, the effort was repeated dozens of times over, always in blistering heat, always with the same anxiety and tension. Amazingly enough, throughout the weeks of exacting labor, nothing was fractured. Not a single piece from a single shrine ever did crack or crumble into dust.

As the excavators proceeded, an unexpected discovery occurred. They came upon a number of clues that led them to an inescapable conclusion: the ancient workers who put the

267

pieces of the shrines together had been negligent!

Each section was inscribed with linear hieroglyphic characters clearly indicating its position relative to the others. But though skilled artists had carefully executed the carving and the decorative work on the shrines, the carpenters who had actually put the pieces in place appeared to have been exceedingly careless. In certain instances, segments were not where they were intended to be placed. The workmen had not taken the trouble to correct their mistakes when they found that the pieces didn't fit; instead, they just pounded them into place.

Carter found a number of bruises in the gilded plaster of the third shrine made by the hammer of a workman who had heedlessly battered it into position. He also found on some pieces a number of hieroglyphic scratches that looked like hurried notes left by the ancient carpenters. These delighted him. One appeared to be a statement regarding the nature of divinity and royalty. On the third shrine Carter found the hieroglyphic sign for "good" or "beautiful," perhaps placed there by the ancient overseer. Beside that, added apparently as an afterthought by a worker wielding a paintbrush when the final assembly was under way, was the hieroglyph for "God" or "God King."

Between the walls of the shrines Carter found objects of rare beauty. One was a golden fan, from which extended white ostrich feathers so fragile that they fell into dust upon being moved. The fan was semicircular in form, with two scenes beaten in gold on the front and the back. On one side the King was depicted in his chariot, hunting ostriches for the feathers of the fan itself. Behind the chariot was the ankh sign, the symbol of life, depicted, amusingly, in human form running on tiny feet, brandishing triumphantly the precise fan on which the scene was represented. On the other side was the denouement of the dramatic hunt. The horses seemed to prance with delight. Bearers carried the bodies of the giant ostriches. But it was the King himself who carried the precious tail feathers, tucked safely under his right arm as he drove his chariot back to the palace.

And among the staves taken from the first and second shrines appeared an ordinary reed, topped by an exquisite gold-mounted ferrule. Why such a luxurious decoration had been attached to a commonplace reed was an enigma to Carter until Mace translated the hieroglyphs delicately inlaid in blue faience, which told the story that the King, as a child, had fancied it and cut it with his own hand.

As Carter carefully peeled his "onion," proceeding toward the splendid pink sarcophagus, a frenzy of expectation and excitement began to build outside the confines of the tomb. News of his progress brought about a fresh influx of tourists to the hotels in Luxor. Chaos ruled. The confusion regarding just who really had reservations for a particular room was solved by the traditional Egyptian technique—baksheesh, the giving of tips.

Antique dealers in Luxor had a field day. Thousands of scarabs emerged from the bottom drawers of virtually every antique dealer and peddler from Alexandria, two hundred miles away, to Aswan, five hundred miles up the Nile, and were hurriedly shipped to Luxor to satisfy the insatiable demands of the tourists for something, anything, associated with Tutankhamun. And since demand by far exceeded supply, local forgers began to produce *antika*s at such a rate that the dean of fakers himself issued a complaint. Although the quality of his *own* work had not deteriorated—since he refused to spend less than a week on a good Tutankhamun scarab—the quality of objects issuing from the workshop of other "artisans" was falling rapidly. He stated that if the situation continued it would give a bad name to his profession. But no matter what other forgers did, he insisted, *his* Tutankhamun scarabs would be fashioned with the same precision as they always had been.

CHAPTER TWENTY-EIGHT

"The Public Domain"

JUST WHEN CARTER's labors were approaching their most critical stage and when Carter himself had become almost totally exhausted, Pierre Lacau launched another move in his series of harassments. He revealed the growing controversy to the Associated Press and informed the reporter that the Egyptian government planned to suspend all work "briefly" at the end of January to permit a thousand visitors entry into the tomb.

The reporter wrote: "One is bound to record the report that the dissension between the excavators and the Department of Antiquities, which is becoming an open secret here, has reached an acute stage." His story went on to say there had been "considerable comment upon the absence of Professor Pierre Lacau, Director of the Department, when first the successive shrines were opened Thursday to disclose the sarcophagus." The grounds of the dispute were said to lie in the question of visitors, the department objecting "to the unrestrained admission to the tomb granted by Mr. Carter to his journalistic associates."

Lacau was shrewdly intensifying his campaign. Just a few days earlier he had sent Carter an official letter on stationery of the "State Legal Department, Public Works and War." The letter was couched in reasonable terms, but the point was emphatic. He told Carter that he "personally regretted deeply his letter of refusal to carry out the Department's reasonable measures" as laid out in the new authorization form. He pointed out that it was the first time "the Government of Egypt had *ever* had difficulties with any excavation." He stated that he found the difficulties conjured up by Carter "surprising," particularly since the preliminary authorization granted to Lady Carnarvon, "no matter how laconic it had been," clearly and utterly assured to the government total supervision over all facets of the work. That incontestable right, Lacau continued, "evolved from its general authority to police all undertakings and from its rights over all objects which were found to be a part of the Public Domain."

Carter was stunned. To him, the words "the Public Domain" signaled a fundamental change over the issue of the division of treasures he had resolved with Pierre Lacau in the first month of discovery. He sent word to the executor of the Carnarvon estate, Sir John Maxwell, and began seeking a lawyer.

Albert Lythgoe considered Lacau's letter the most discouraging piece of news he had received in Egypt in nearly two decades of digging. He saw the total dissolution of all the Metropolitan's excavations in Egypt and he began to lose all hope of continuing to acquire treasures for the museum. He wrote a concerned letter to Edward Robinson, the director of the Metropolitan:

A very serious situation is growing up here between Lacau and Carter. Lacau is clearly seeking to oust Carter and our Expedition from the tomb in order that they may take the work over themselves.

Ever since the work started this October, Lacau, in spite of the right which Carter unquestionably holds under the terms of his concession, has imposed the most petty restrictions of one kind or another—an unending series of "pin-pricks." Now, just the talk about these little issues and the combat over them has halted the work for considerable periods of time and that seriously has interfered with the scientific procedure in the tomb.

Two of the most distinguished (and entirely disinterested) scien-

271

tists in the field, Sir John Marshall, Director General of Antiquities in India, and Dr. Alan Gardiner, one of England's foremost Egyptologists, have expressed their disgust and indignation over M. Lacau's whole attitude towards the work in the tomb. . . .

Now a few days ago, M. Lacau has sent a long demand . . . in which the crux of the situation on their part comes out openly for the first time—their bold claim to all the objects contained in the tomb.

As they have seen fit to legally dispute the right of Lord Carnarvon's Estate to a share of the objects in the tomb, under the terms of his and Carter's concession, and are seriously interfering with the scientific procedure in the tomb, Carter has just called in a lawyer and is preparing a legal defense.

Meanwhile Carter is doing his best, under great distractions and worries . . . All scientific visitors to the tomb are united in their praise of the uniquely admirable manner in which he is carrying out this most difficult piece of work, and in his almost superhuman efforts, in the face of these distractions, to ensure the record through to the actual opening of the sarcophagus and the determination of its contents. . . .

M. Lacau's thoroughly inefficient administration of the [Antiquities] is however soon to present a new and direct issue to our Expedition—with regard to a new form of the concession he intends us to sign and which becomes retroactive to cover the present season. I know the gist of its innovations . . . a series of rights asserted by [Antiquities] might make the procedure of our scientific fieldwork practically unendurable and impossible. . . .

Lythgoe posed two recommendations to the museum's trustees. First was to secure the *"strongest* representations from the Secretary of State Hughes to the new Egyptian Minister at Washington about the utter necessity to continue the Museum's concession and our role with Carter under the same equitable terms as we have enjoyed for so many years. In addition Hughes should get an assurance from the Egyptian Minister that [the Metropolitan] be relieved from these constant and ever-tightening conditions which the fertile but thoroughly impractical brain of the present Director-General of Antiquities seeks to impose upon us."

Secondly, Lythgoe advised that "we should approach" the French ambassador in Washington with friendly representations as to the "complete inefficiency of France's present official appointee as Director-General. . . ."

"In plain words," he wrote, "it has become increasingly apparent to us all during this season that if we don't put an end to M. Lacau, or effectually stop his activities, he will unquestionably put an end to all archaeological work here such as ours and will do it in the very near future."

Carter, who was no less concerned than Lythgoe, answered Lacau at length. He adopted a lofty tone and began by noting with regret that Lacau had consulted the State Legal Department. It would, he said, have been "more dignified as well as the more prudent course" to have postponed all disputes as to the ultimate destination of the treasures until "the continued existence of the treasures should have been secured." He lamented the fact that he was "compelled to turn aside from the scientific work of recording the objects" to consider what he regarded as "a matter of altogether secondary importance, the question of legal rights to which the discovery had given rise."

Carter then went on to reiterate, *ad infinitum,* all the points in his case: the scope of the original concession, the rights of publication, visitation privileges, *and* the division of treasures. He complained bitterly that an enormous amount of time had been wasted on fruitless discussions. Between October 22, when the season began, and December 17 there had been fifty working days. Of these, he had spent fourteen on two journeys to Cairo for discussions and one at Kurna in discussions with Lacau; two days had been devoted to visits by the press. A third of the time had been "frittered away through departmental interference," and additional demands on Lacau's part had caused further and almost equally serious interruption.

Since Lacau had been good enough to articulate his personal feelings, he in turn would articulate his. The work on which he was engaged had not been for gain, but for the interests of science. The discovery of the tomb had produced great benefits for Egypt and for the Egyptian Antiquities Service in particular. It had also produced rights for the Earl of Carnarvon, the author of those benefits.

It was a matter of surprise and regret to Carter that, "whereas every other department of the Egyptian government had shown only good will, kindness and eagerness to help," Lacau's department had, "ever since the death of the late Lord Carnarvon, not only been endeavouring to frustrate the rights of the Carnarvon family," but also had "tried to impede, hinder and delay the scientific work," without which the fruits of the discovery would have been wasted. Carter concluded by declaring he was at a loss to find motives for Lacau's actions, but had "no doubt as to what will be the verdict of the world of science on the issue between us."

Carter was, in fact, convinced he already had "the world of science" firmly behind him. He therefore launched his next attack on Pierre Lacau. It came in the form of a letter indicting not only Lacau but the methods of the entire Antiquities Service, and it was signed by four of the most distinguished Egyptologists in the world—James Breasted, Alan Gardiner, Albert Lythgoe and Percy Newberry. Lacau was informed, in a covering letter, that "after mature deliberation" the signatories had decided to send copies of the indictment to the Minister of Public Works and to High Commissioner Lord Allenby as well.

Lythgoe confided to Edward Robinson, whom he dutifully kept informed of every development, that he hoped the indictment would bring Lacau to his senses. He indicated that the group was prepared to carry the matter even further by sending copies of the protest to the British Academy of Sciences, the National Research Council at Washington and, finally, to the Académie des Inscriptions et Belles Lettres at Paris, the most prestigious archaeological academy in the world.

The letter, like so many documents in the Tutankhamun affair, is unprecedented in the history of archaeology.

DEAR MONSIEUR LACAU:—

We feel it our duty to Science to call your attention, as Director General of Antiquities, to a very serious condition which is affecting the regular progress of the work in the Tomb of Tutankhamun and which is clearly endangering the scientific record resulting from that work.

That unique discovery, with its wealth of historical and archaeological facts, belongs not to Egypt alone but to the entire world. The interest which it has aroused has penetrated into all corners of the globe and has focussed upon Egypt an unprecedented degree of attention among men of all classes and professions.

Moreover, it is universally agreed among archaeologists that Mr. Howard Carter is conducting his complex and very difficult task in a manner beyond all praise. Altogether apart from the collaborators who happen to be among the signers of this letter, it is everywhere recognized that the co-workers assembled by Mr. Carter form a group of scientists of unsurpassed ability and experience such as has never been at the disposition of any other archaeological enterprise in this country before; and you yourself have acknowledged your complete satisfaction with the results they are achieving.

Nevertheless their work has, unfortunately, been interrupted this season, not once but repeatedly, by the demands which you have brought as to the regulation of visitors and other questions of a similar nature—matters which are undeniably inconsequential in comparison with the security of the scientific record of the Tomb and the preservation of its contents.

Besides endangering the completeness and security of the records, the unnecessary delays now being incurred are seriously obstructing and delaying related enterprises of the cooperative staffs. These are irretrievable and totally unnecessary scientific losses of time, ability, and available funds by organisations present in this country to serve science, but in this particular case accomplishing a vast amount of costly work which accrues chiefly to the benefit of the Egyptian Government without having cost that Government a penny.

We feel obliged, therefore, to put ourselves on record at this time, as calling your attention to the serious nature of the present interruptions and to the further fact that unless the unnecessary difficulties now obstructing the work in the Tomb of Tutankhamun are moderated, we can only hold one opinion, namely, that you, as Director General of Antiquities, are failing completely to carry out the obligations of your high office to protect the scientific procedure of this all-important task. It is hardly necessary for us to call attention to the unfortunate effect of such failure of your administration, upon

275

the public and the great scientific world now so eagerly following the progress of the task.

Believe us to be,

Very sincerely yours,

JAMES H. BREASTED
ALAN H. GARDINER
ALBERT M. LYTHGOE
PERCY E. NEWBERRY

Lacau was astounded—and infuriated. But he kept his feelings to himself. Neither Lythgoe nor his cohorts had an inkling of Lacau's true reaction. In fact, Lythgoe was under the misapprehension that their letter had intimidated Lacau, leaving Carter free "to carry straight through the final stages of his work in the tomb." And indeed, for a while, Carter did manage to concentrate again on his work.

The beauty of the sandstone sarcophagus he had encountered with the opening of the doors of all four shrines far exceeded Carter's expectations. It was in every respect, as Merton said, a casket "fit to contain the mortal remains of a King." All the Egyptologists agreed that it was the finest specimen of its kind that the world possessed.

The most remarkable features were the figures of the four protective goddesses, one at each corner, gazing for eternity toward the head of the sarcophagus, with their arms outstretched and wings full spread. They were exquisitely graceful, their beauty accentuated by the tinting of their eyes and the coloring of their jewelry, also carved from sandstone.

Carter had experienced a rude shock when he first examined the entire sarcophagus. He saw to his momentary horror that the lid was cracked completely in half. For one frightening instant it occurred to him that the sarcophagus had actually been penetrated by some ingenious thieves. Then, observing the evidence of ancient repairs, he realized that the massive capstone had actually been *dropped* by the ancient workers. What a furor that must have caused among the priests and the necropolis officials!

Carter also observed that the lid was of a material that differed from the stone coffin itself. It was granite, instead of the traditional sandstone, and constituted a radical departure in the normally rigid Egyptian burial customs. Carter knew that the only other example of the use of granite for a sarcophagus in the entire Eighteenth Dynasty was Akhenaton's, the heretic Pharaoh. Carter personally believed that the granite lid covering Tutankhamun was a reference to the Aton monotheism, indicating that the young King had not entirely cast aside the heresy of his predecessor. It was, he felt, the same type of link with the earlier religion that had appeared on the spectacular golden throne which had been decorated with two royal names, Tutankhamun and Tutankhaton.

While Carter was almost completely preoccupied by the sarcophagus, a political event of tremendous magnitude occurred. Prime Minister Yehia and the members of his government, sympathetic to the British protectorate and to foreigners, were swept out of office in the elections of 1923, and a new regime, under the premiership of Saad Zaghlul Pasha, took its place. The Zaghlul government was profoundly nationalistic. Many of its members belonged to the radical party, the Wafdists, who had proclaimed total independence as their goal and who, incidentally, had also demanded that no antiquity ever leave Egypt for foreign soil.

It was announced that the new Minister of Public Works, replacing Abdel Suleman Pasha, was to be Morcos Bey Hanna, a stolid bear of a man who, in the recent course of his political career, had been tried and convicted for treason. He had been imprisoned four years, an experience which, far from becoming a stigma, had made him a martyr. Thus, under the Nationalists, he became a minister. His knowledge of archaeological affairs was negligible, and he didn't really care that much about Tutankhamun or the tomb. But his suspicion of foreigners, particularly the British and specifically Howard Carter, made him sympathetic to any scheme that might force them out of the tomb, the region and Egypt itself.

As soon as Carter learned that Morcos Bey Hanna would

take over, he asked for a meeting to pay his respects and to discuss the series of events that would take place at the official opening of the great lid of the sealed sarcophagus.

Carter called upon his excellency the Minister at his office in Cairo at five in the afternoon, as requested. On his arrival he was told that the Minister had been detained but would be present in a few minutes. Suddenly he was called into the office of Tottenham, who advised him not to discuss anything with Morcos Bey Hanna but the specific issue of the ceremonies surrounding the opening of the sarcophagus. "In fact," Tottenham said, "it would be better if *all* former negotiations could be forgotten, and the papers about them destroyed."

Carter vehemently disagreed and told Tottenham that *all* former negotiations and documents, if fully revealed to the public, would do nothing but expose the utter weakness of the ministry's case and its lack of faith. Tottenham listened in silence as Carter argued that every scrap of paper regarding his undertakings in the valley would confirm his rights in the tomb. Then Tottenham abruptly handed over a document that, he said, defined the government's policy about the division of Tutankhamun's treasures. Carter examined it and was flabbergasted. For the paper contained a devastating revelation. The legal department of the Public Works Ministry, through Pierre Lacau, had dredged from its files a routine permit for a relatively minor excavation granted by the Antiquities Service to Howard Carter some six years before. It had been so trivial that he had utterly forgotten it. But it was to become a fundamental issue in the argument over any division of treasures.

In 1918 Carter had applied to Pierre Lacau for temporary authorization to dig an isolated tomb, hidden in "a very remote spot in the cliffs of the great Northern Valley—North of the Valley of the Kings." Lacau had complied, but had added a special condition explicitly defining what he considered an intact royal tomb to be—a definition completely at variance with that which had appeared in the original concession.

By the words "intact tomb" employed in this and the earlier authorization, it is understood that it is not a question of an absolutely *unviolated* tomb, but rather a tomb still containing its furniture in good condition and forming an entirety, even if the thieves have already entered in order to take the jewels, as, for example, in the tomb of the father and mother of Queen Tuya.

Carter had signed the document, had conducted his dig, and had found absolutely nothing. And now, as he read the forgotten authorization, he was dumbfounded. It seemed to spell doom to any hope of obtaining a single treasure from the tomb. He could scarcely think.

Just then, Tottenham told him brusquely that the Minister was waiting. Tottenham escorted Carter into the Minister's office. Morcos Bey Hanna at first greeted him cordially, but soon started to complain of a recent visit by Dr. Alan Gardiner, who he presumed had been sent by Carter. Gardiner had vehemently protested the way the Antiquities Service was treating Carter and his staff. Taken aback a third time since entering the ministry, Carter tried to take the offensive. He told Morcos Bey that Gardiner's visit must have been triggered by the fact that he and all prominent archaeologists were indignant at the waste of time and the danger to science brought about by the actions of the Antiquities Service. But Carter vigorously denied that he personally had had anything to do with Gardiner's visit, claiming he had not even known it was to take place. The Minister said nothing, but it seemed clear that he did not believe Carter.

Morcos Bey then asked Carter if he were *"d'accord"* with the members of the Antiquities Service. Carter replied acidly that he was by no means in agreement with their methods of administration. The Minister then told Carter that if he had any concrete grievance against them, he should write to him and he would personally deal with the matter. He urged at the same time that both sides should consider "bygones as bygones."

The Minister then suggested that, although Mr. Carter might have been within his legal rights, he had made a great mistake in having signed an exclusive contract with the London *Times*, "as it had caused a nasty odor with the press."

279

Carter must have sensed the urgent need to be conciliatory with the volatile Minister. He quickly acknowledged that the contract which he had originally approved and so staunchly defended over the tempestuous months had indeed been the cause of considerable friction. Carter made the astonishing statement—without permission from the Carnarvon estate— that the exclusive agreement would be terminated at the season's end. The Minister expressed his approval.

Morcos Bey then asked Carter if it were true he was planning on a lecture tour throughout America in the spring. Carter replied that he was. The Minister abruptly accused him of committing "an error of judgment" by even thinking of leaving. Carter should realize, he said, that "by undertaking the delicate work on which he was engaged, he had become virtually a public servant, and should go straight on until the work was finished." A subdued Howard Carter merely muttered that he begged to disagree.

Then the Minister called for Pierre Lacau. Carter was inwardly infuriated to see that, despite the fact that the Minister had just expressed a desire to bury the past, Lacau entered the room laden with files and dossiers. He began to pick through them and accused Carter of having introduced great numbers of "unauthorized visitors" into the tomb. Carter refused to discuss the subject.

The conversation eventually turned to the ceremonies that would accompany the opening of the sarcophagus. Carter expressed his fervent hope that the Minister and the Prime Minister could be present for the occasion. Morcos Bey asked if he would be able to see the "body of the King." When Carter said he believed that to be unlikely, because there would probably be a series of coffins that would be opened over months, the Minister voiced his disappointment. Why should it not be possible to open the coffins then and there? he asked. Carter patiently explained that to open the coffins rapidly would violate scientific procedures. It was a task which he thought could be accomplished only in subsequent seasons. The Minister dismissed the issue and said coldly that in *that* case he did not consider it worthwhile for him and his colleagues to attend the opening.

Carter suggested that he lift the great lid of the sarcophagus in the presence of Professor Lacau and his immediate staff. If it was agreed that the results were sufficiently interesting, the news would be sent to the Minister, who could come at his leisure. The Minister expressed his satisfaction, told his staff to work out the details, and departed abruptly.

Soon Carter left, too. He was thoroughly mystified about the meeting. What were Morcos Bey and Pierre Lacau up to? The incriminating words in the temporary concession of 1918, which, in Carter's view, had been "disinterred" from the faraway past, were certainly damaging to him, yet at the same time he had been urged by the Minister to regard "bygones as bygones." What would the Minister and Lacau do next?

As Carter was conducting his negotiations in Cairo, Arthur Merton was asking himself a similar question about Howard Carter. What would *he* do next? He wrote his editor in London that he hoped to pull off a major scoop regarding the opening of the sarcophagus—"provided Carter does not take up an attitude similar to what he did in the case of the finding of the sarcophagus." Merton explained that he planned to file a "full description" of the sarcophagus a day before the opening. Then, the next day, Merton would try to obtain a fine statement from Carter, to be followed by impressions from such eminent archaeologists as Professor Newberry, Breasted, Alan Gardiner and Albert Lythgoe. But, Merton observed, "here comes the snag!" When the sarcophagus had first been revealed, Carter had objected violently to anyone else making a statement. Merton had not pushed Carter at that time, hoping to wait for what he believed to be a more dramatic opportunity. "It is quite possible," Merton went on, "that Carter may again object—he is extraordinarily jealous of the others (as a matter of fact, jealousy is one of the strong suits of all archaeologists)." So he urged his editor, *"as soon as you have received my descriptive dispatch,"* to "cable urgent saying that you would like first a statement from Carter and after that impressions from Breasted, Newberry, etc. *mentioning them by name.* This would strengthen my hand and between us we ought to pull off quite a good coup."

CHAPTER TWENTY-NINE

Strike!

THE DAY CHOSEN FOR THE raising of the lid of the King's sarcophagus had finally arrived. Not since the sealed wall between the Antechamber and the Burial Chamber had been
breached just a year before had there been such a fever of
anticipation in Luxor. On February 12, at precisely three in the
afternoon, Howard Carter conducted his special guests into
the tomb and herded them as close to the rose-colored sarcophagus as possible.

Twenty-four individuals were present, including another
Zaghlul, Mohammed Pasha, whom Morcos Bey had just
named under-secretary of his ministry; Edward Harkness,
member of the board of the Metropolitan Museum; Pierre
Lacau; Albert Lythgoe, James Breasted, Alan Gardiner and
Percy Newberry; and of course, the excavating team itself,
along with Arthur Merton of the London *Times*. The atmosphere was tense. But the tension, for once, had nothing to do
with their recent disputes; it was an indication of anticipated
pleasure at what all were convinced would be a magical event.

After an hour or so of prying and wedging the stones, finally
the ropes for raising the lid were strapped around the slabs.
Carter gave the signal. Amid intense silence the two massive
pieces of granite, weighing nearly two tons, rose from the

283

stone coffin. Carter shone a light into the great sarcophagus. At first, he recalled later, he was perplexed—disappointed. Whatever lay there was obscured by fine linen shrouds. With the two pieces of the lid suspended in midair, gently swaying on the great ropes, Carter examined the interior from all sides. With the utmost caution, he began to roll back the covering shrouds, one by one. His hands were quivering as he worked; his head dripped perspiration.

When at last the linen wrapping was removed, a gasp of astonishment escaped the lips of those watching—the sight was so incredibly gorgeous. There, filling the whole interior of the sarcophagus, blazing out in full glory from the reflection of the lights, was a golden effigy of the boy King larger than life. It was of the most magnificent workmanship, fashioned out of wood that had been gilded, decorated with thin gold plates and inlaid with faience, glass and semiprecious stones. The beauty of the image was unsurpassed.

The face of the Pharaoh's effigy was, to Howard Carter, the most splendid feature of all. He was astonished by the luster of the gold, the lifelike impression of the black inlaid eyes and the beauty and delicacy of the crown, which was surmounted by the vulture goddess, Nekhbet, and a sublime image of the divine cobra, so surely crafted that they looked almost alive. Carter was moved, too, by the presence of a delicate wreath of flowers surrounding the head of the cobra. Amid all this regal magnificence, there was something ineffably human about those few withered flowers that still retained a tinge of color from thirty-two hundred years before. To Carter, the passage of those years had never occurred.

Carter's colleagues, and the guests, seemed hypnotized by the shining effigy. The young King, depicted as Osiris, seemed to be gazing steadily, serenely, as if in confirmation of man's ancient faith in immortality. Carter said later that, in those moments of marvelous silence, he could almost hear the "ghostly footsteps of the departing mourners."

Arthur Merton was himself profoundly moved by the experience. Although an immense passage of time had taken place, he was struck anew with the realization that time is transient. While "great empires had risen and fallen and wars and catastrophies had convulsed the universe, invasions had completely changed the face of the land, civilisations had sprung up, developed and disappeared, religions had come into existence and had been superceded by others," he wrote eloquently for the London *Times*, "here beneath the earth within a few inches of where, daily, century upon century, human feet had trodden, unheeded by all the peoples above, forgotten by every one until but fifteen months ago, had lain this King in the peace and grandeur which only death and the grave can give."

Silent and thoughtful, Carter's guests made their way out of the sepulchral hall. The spectacle had struck deep into their hearts. As they emerged from the shadows of the chambers into the light of the outside world, which seemed garish compared to the grandeur of what they had seen within, some of them could not resist asking, "What of the King himself?"

As Carter left the chamber and mounted the sixteen steps, his thoughts still lingered on the splendor of that vanished Pharaoh. There were rounds of congratulations, muted, of course, owing to the emotion of the moment.

Before the officials departed, Carter took the opportunity to settle what he thought to be nothing more than a bit of routine business. He discussed with Pierre Lacau and the Under-Secretary of Public Works, Mohammed Pasha Zaghlul, the arrangements for a press conference scheduled the next day, to be followed by four days of authorized visits. He asked casually if it would be acceptable to allow the excavators' wives to visit the tomb just before the press viewing the next morning. Lacau said nothing. Mohammed Pasha, jubilant over the discovery, said he thought it would be perfectly fine for the excavators' wives to view the golden King, but he would telephone the Minister in Cairo, just to be sure.

Carter, pleased to the depths of his soul by his achievement, humbled and moved by the image in his mind of the serene visage of the young King, was also bone tired. The hours he

285

had worked, the awesome responsibility he had assumed, had exhausted his mind and body. He returned to the tomb for a last inspection of the ropes and tackles that supported the two pieces of granite lid suspended over the golden effigy; then, once again, he mounted the sixteen steps and returned to his quarters, where he slept the sleep of kings.

Next morning Carter was up by six o'clock. The day was extraordinarily beautiful. Carter was refreshed, elated. The image of the beautiful King, sculpted upon his golden effigy, returned time and again to his mind, as did the poignant presence of the withered flowers.

He breakfasted leisurely and planned to head for the tomb entrance at nine to arrange for his colleagues' wives to have their special tour just before the press. During breakfast, he observed someone coming up from the valley to his house on the back of a donkey. Precisely what went through his mind is not known. It is likely that he thought a messenger was bringing news of some last-minute change of plan from Pierre Lacau about the specific number of reporters to be allowed into the Holy of Holies. Over the past three days there had been dozens of such changes. Indeed, the very day before the raising of the lid, Paul Tottenham had told him that, except for the government representatives, Carter could not allow more than twelve people into the Burial Chamber, including his immediate co-workers. Carter had been able to persuade Tottenham to change his mind by pointing out that the embarrassment to the government would be intense if the group of world-famous archaeologists Carter had invited, after already receiving governmental consent, were arbitrarily forbidden entry.

Carter must have complimented himself on his recent handling of the government officials and Pierre Lacau. Despite the trenchant attitude of Minister Morcos Bey and the surprise appearance of the permit of 1918 with its definition of an intact royal tomb, Carter had reason to be optimistic. After all, the 1918 authorization had been clearly designated as "temporary" in its own preamble. Howard Carter had not wavered from his belief that firmness worked. If one held straight to the written agreements, and didn't budge a centimeter, the

Egyptians would invariably have to go along. The Service des Antiquités was lost without him and his staff. Whom else did they have? A few subalterns, minor functionaries or subinspectors of antiquities who were not capable of carrying out an undertaking as complex as Tutankhamun's tomb. Carter thought that his unyielding letters to Lacau and the subsequent indictment from the four archaeologists had blunted any real desire on the part of Lacau to move in on his territory.

The messenger arrived in the courtyard and handed Carter a letter from Mohammed Pasha. Upon reading it Carter was hit, as he said, by a "thunderclap." It stated: "I regret to inform you that I have received a telegram from the Minister of Public Works in which he regrets that the arrangement come to by him with the Ministry does not permit the admission of the wives of your collaborators to the tomb tomorrow, February 13."

Perhaps had Carter taken time to reflect on the letter and considered its ramifications, or had he taken a few minutes to ponder whether or not the direct insult was a snare to entrap him, the events he set in motion might never had occurred.

But nothing in Carter's makeup could possibly have enabled him to hesitate at this particular moment. Throughout his life, when faced with criticism, with any attack, however mild, or any directive from a superior to whom he was not intimately linked in a collaboration of self-interest, Howard Carter had always acted impulsively. In this case he would conform precisely to his life pattern, as Lacau must have expected.

Carter rushed to the tomb and showed the insulting communication to his colleagues. They were as astonished and angry as he. They decided, in a spirit of fairness, to allow the press in for the special viewing. And then they would draft a notice to be sent to Lacau, Morcos Bey Hanna and the public at large, stating that they would close the tomb and walk off the job. It was, they agreed, the only course to take. And they all confidently predicted that in this instance, as in so many others, the ministry would back down. No one else could carry out the excavation. Tons of stones lay suspended over the golden effigy, dangerously so. If there was ever an inopportune moment for the government to deliver such a monumental example of discourtesy, this was it. World opinion would rally to Carter's side. All would sympathize with him over the calculated insult to his co-workers' wives.

How so many intelligent individuals could so grievously have miscalculated their position is difficult to comprehend. If this group of prestigious archaeologists had talked to people outside their closed circle, they might have acted otherwise. Had they discussed their "strike" with Sir John Maxwell, that might have made a difference. Had they consulted with their *wives*, they might have reached a more sensible decision. Had Lord Carnarvon been alive, the issue might never have arisen.

But none of these possibilities had been destined to happen. What did happen was that Carter and his colleagues categorically misread virtually every aspect of the situation. They misunderstood the mood of the new political regime. They failed to realize that the native populace could not care less about, or even comprehend, the genteel necessity of allowing foreign women special entry into the tomb long before any Egyptian. They even failed to perceive the rage of thousands of tourists who had traveled thousands of miles to be in Luxor for the public viewing. They were locked into positions rooted in pre-World War I attitudes, based upon outmoded concepts of colonialism, elitism, and a misguided sense of scientific privilege.

Carter, aided by his colleagues, drafted what may have been his first truly succinct reply to a ministry communication since the dig began:

Owing to impossible restrictions and discourtesies on the part of the Public Works Department and its Antiquity Service, all my collaborators, in protest, have refused to work further upon the scientific investigation of the discovery of the tomb of Tutankhamun.

I therefore am obliged to make known to the public that, immediately after the Press view of the tomb this morning between 10 A M and noon, the tomb will be closed, and no further work can be carried out.

Carter departed for Luxor to post his ultimatum on the bulletin board of the Winter Palace Hotel. He locked both tomb and laboratory and took with him the only existing set of keys. Before leaving, he briefed Merton on the situation. Merton was astounded, but apparently did not utter a word of protest. Carter insisted that Merton publish in the London *Times*, for the entire world to see, the preeminent archaeologists' vehement criticism of Pierre Lacau. In doing so, Carter had taken one more fatal step across the Rubicon. Merton, clearly worried, tried to counsel Carter that if he wanted to carry the day he had to emphasize that the decision to close the tomb was based upon the sanctity of *science* and the issue of the *safety* of the treasures.

Carter demanded that Merton send an emergency cable for him to the London *Times*, which he did. The cable was to the point: "Compelled to shut down tomb. I rely on you to give the widest publicity to the world's service and strongly attack Egyptian authorities."

Carter rushed to Luxor, coldly ignoring a delegation of government officials on its way up to the valley. When he arrived at the ferry slip on the west bank of the Nile, he suffered what he considered the ultimate discourtesy. "Publicly and ostentatiously, in the presence of a crowd of donkey boys and dragomans," as Carter put it, he was presented a letter and an *ordre-de-service* from Pierre Lacau:

I regret to have to inform you that I have just sent to our agents in the Valley of the Kings an order, of which a copy is enclosed. This late misunderstanding is as annoying for me as for you, but the orders of the Minister are formal, and his Excellency the Under-Secretary charges me to transmit them to you.

The order read:

His Excellency, the Minister of Public Works, having replied by telegraph that he regretted not being able to authorise the visit of the wives of the collaborators of Mr. Carter for Wednesday, February 13, his Excellency the Under-Secretary of State has transmitted to me an order to forbid all ladies who have not written authorization. Of course, they must execute this duty with all due courtesy. Mr. Carter has been advised of this measure.

PIERRE LACAU
Director General
of the Service of Antiquities

Luxor, February 13, 1924

Carter marched into the crowded lobby of the Winter Palace Hotel and pinned his startling proclamation to close the tomb on the prominent display board with its information regarding daily tours to the valley. The word spread rapidly throughout the hotel and Luxor. The throngs of tourists were shocked.

Later that day, after he had returned to his quarters, Carter received a confidential phone call from Rex Engelbach, who, throughout the escalating struggle, had always remained sympathetic to Carter. He told Carter that Lacau had just issued an official order to the government guards to prevent Carter and his collaborators from going back into the tomb. The guards were to be augmented so that surveillance could be provided day and night.

Carter sent a telegram to Prime Minister Zaghlul himself, calling his attention to the gross insult inflicted by the Antiquities Service in preventing him from taking his collaborators' wives into the tomb. He stated his conviction that the Prime Minister would "disapprove of this ungentlemanly action which is also illegal and unjustifiable." It was because of this, Carter attested, that he and his colleagues refused to work further. He ended his message with a warning that he planned to take legal action against the Egyptian government.

The Prime Minister's reply was glacial. He pointed out that the government's refusal to allow the wives entry on the day reserved for the press was based upon a procedure which, he claimed, Carter had discussed with Morcos Bey Hanna and had already approved. The Prime Minister admonished him not to blame the staff of the Service of Antiquities, but to respect the agreements he himself had made. "As for closing the tomb," the Minister went on, "I must recall to you that the tomb is *not* your property." The Minister icily observed that Carter's abrupt act on behalf of a group of "private individuals" could never excuse his abandoning scientific procedures "which you forever proclaim . . . are of the utmost interest and importance not only to Egypt but to the entire world."

Howard Carter's impulsive and indefensible gesture became front-page news throughout the world. The London *Times* attempted to defend it and reported that the "crowning insult to Carter" had been the government action to send "special police to reinforce inspectors in the execution of the orders to prevent any lady from entering." That decision was, to the correspondent Merton, the culminating act in "a series of blunders and gross discourtesies on the part of the Ministry of Public Works that had marked its attitude since the tomb had been opened in October." What was also resented, Merton stated, raising a new issue, was that the Egyptian government had assigned a team of special Egyptian inspectors to watch Carter at work. He and the members of his team, "who represented the most prominent scientific institutions in the world, were aghast at the latest uncalled for and grossly discourteous action of the Ministry. It had been an unpardonable affront to archaeological science."

The London *Times* printed a thundering editorial:

There will be a widespread feeling of regret that matters have come to such a pass. The friction which led to the closing of the tomb and the abrupt suspension of work is unfortunately of long standing, and it will seem from Carter's correspondence with the Egyptian authorities that he has been sorely tried. His great discovery was made after nearly sixteen years of indefatigable and for the most part disappointing labour on the part of himself and Lord Carnarvon. Since then, when the season permitted, work has been patiently carried on under extremely trying conditions in a spirit of reverential care, with unremitting energy and a high degree of scientific knowledge and mechanical skill. But for Carter's perseverance, the tomb most probably would never have been found. Its discovery, as he justly claims, has produced great benefits for Egypt and especially for its Department of Antiquities. Every other department of the Government has shown, he says, nothing but good-will, kindness and eagerness to help. It is utterly deplorable that the progress of the work should be hindered by the one department most directly concerned in its success.

But the matter cannot be left as it stands. Departmental jealousy and interference are not peculiar to Egypt. They can and must be overcome. Carter complains that some sixteen of the fifty days during which he might have been at work in the closing months of last year were wasted by unnecessary visits to Cairo and by other interruptions. Recently he and all those concerned with him in the enterprise have been practically placed under surveillance. More than once their right to admit chosen visitors to the tomb or to exclude others at inopportune moments in the interest of their work has been overruled. It is time that the policy of pinpricks to which they have been subjected came to an end. It has reached its climax at the moment when their nerves must necessarily be almost exhausted by the wonderful success which has crowned their efforts.

In the circumstances it is not surprising that they have at last made a forcible and practical protest and we can not doubt that it will be supported by archaeologists, scientists and historians of the civilised world.

And the next day *The Times* published in full the letter of indictment prepared by Breasted, Gardiner, Lythgoe and Newberry against Pierre Lacau.

The Egyptian press vigorously condemned Howard Carter's decision to go on "strike," calling it an act of unprofessional behavior which would thoroughly endanger the nation's treasures. Several articles pointed out that Carter, in stopping the work, had relinquished all rights forever to continue the excavation. It was time, some newspapers claimed, for the government to assert its rights and sovereignty.

The vast majority of tourists in Luxor assailed Carter's precipitous move. They did not give a damn about Carter and his peculiar crusade; they wanted to see the gold effigy.

An English magazine, *The Saturday Review,* published a thoughtful piece on the turmoil in the valley:

When everything was on his side, and judicious action would have gained for Howard Carter the sympathy of all but the most prejudiced, he threw away his case by an unpremeditated act which was followed up by quite the wrong kind of tactics. Where diplomacy would have won, pugnacity was used with failure as the result. In the East, more than anywhere else, it is of no use to threaten your opponent with a stick, unless in the last resort, you are prepared to hit, good and hard. The Oriental calls your bluff—the Egyptian Government has done just that. Mr. Carter, not unnaturally, since he is an archaeologist not an intriguer, has fallen into what looks like a carefully prepared trap.

Deeply hurt by the adverse criticism, Carter attempted to justify the strike. The confused notes of a defense he tried to construct remain in the Metropolitan Museum's files. They suggest his momentary helplessness.

Answer to the accusation that my closing of the tomb has endangered the objects within.

1. The closing of the tomb and the so-called strike was intended as a temporary measure to protest against the insult of the Govt.

2. I fully expected that the Govt. would apologise for this insult, and in that case, I and my staff would have reserved the preparation for visitors and carried out the programme and for this reason I left the lid of the sarcophagus suspended.

3. I was always and now— My staff and I were and are now desirous of doing everything to safeguard the objects until the dispute is settled, but have been prevented from doing so by the Govt. who have refused us access to the tomb.

3 [*sic*]. It never for a moment occurred to me that, if no apology was forthcoming— If no apology was forthcoming I intended at once to lower the lid and make all preparation both in the tomb and the tomb no. fifteen to safe-guard the contents through the summer. It never for one moment occurred to me that I should be prevented from doing this by armed force or otherwise.

4. The action of my staff in striking was taken solely to emphasise my protest at what they and I considered a gross insult from the

293

Govt. They are at one with me in desiring to take every possible precaution to preserve the antiquities.

5. The notice posted in the hotel was drawn up hurriedly and does not make the above points clear.

But, despite all attempts to turn the tide of public opinion in his favor, Howard Carter rapidly lost credibility, as an individual of judgment and as a scientist as well. The question was repeatedly raised: if Carter had really been so solicitous of the protection and conservation of the works of art, why would he lock the tomb and the laboratory with the only set of keys? And so the only set of keys became, as had the steel grilled door a year earlier, a bitter symbol of foreign takeover and intervention.

Morcos Bey Hanna ensured that his side of the argument was represented prominently in Arab newspapers and the English-language dailies in Egypt. He calmly stated that Carter had brought up the question of "certain ladies being admitted to the tomb" long before the official opening, but that the Minister had been forced, with great reluctance, to decline. He claimed he had specifically told Carter that "not even the wives of *Cabinet Ministers* could be admitted to the tomb until after the days set aside for the *scientific* study of the sarcophagus." He said that Carter had persisted in raising the question of "certain wives" right up to the day before the official opening and had eventually sought permission for no fewer than twenty-two women. Again, the special request had to be declined—reluctantly—because the Minister believed it to be "discriminatory" to the wives and families of the Egyptians. He had "begged" Carter to stick to what he had previously agreed. But, according to Morcos Bey Hanna, Carter had refused and had closed the tomb. The Minister reiterated the government's "most sincere interest" in safeguarding the objects in the tomb and in "guaranteeing that unauthorised persons" should be forbidden entry.

Suddenly Carter and his associates began to realize that the hapless "natives" were deft politicians and adroit publicists in the struggle to gain favor with the public. Morcos Bey Hanna had succeeded in redefining for the general populace every piece of the complex puzzle. Foreign "wives" became individuals superior to the spouses of Cabinet ministers. Carter's "modest" list had become a throng. The government "discourtesy" had turned into urgent desire to safeguard the treasures. Carter's protest in the name of archaeology had become a selfish, petulant strike. His concession in the tomb was interpreted as "ownership."

Two days after the strike of February 13, Carter went to the tomb and was refused entry by government troops. He was handed a government order:

The tomb of Tut-ankh-Amen is closed until further orders and neither Mr. Carter nor his collaborators nor any member of the service nor any other persons are permitted to enter. This applies both to the tomb of Tut-ankh-Amen and No. fifteen serving as a laboratory.

A few days after the Minister's public statement, Carter publicly branded him a liar in a newspaper interview. He claimed that no reference to wives of either the excavators or Cabinet ministers had ever come up in any meeting. The only significant issue that had been discussed, Carter contended, was whether or not the body of the King could be seen by the high officials. Carter closed by saying that the greatest opportunity that archaeology had ever had was seriously endangered by the attitude of the Egyptian government.

Just as Carter released his version of the controversy, the Egyptian Cabinet unanimously agreed to approve the action of Pierre Lacau and other government officials at Luxor. The Cabinet ruled that Carter had "infringed his contract" by closing the tomb on his own initiative, and that, therefore, the government was free to continue the work itself. Prime Minister Zaghlul announced publicly that he intended to fix an ample number of days for the Egyptian people to visit the tomb. The news deeply depressed Carter.

And, far away in England, another Prime Minister, Ramsay

MacDonald, made a statement in Parliament that depressed him even more. A member of the House of Commons had asked whether or not special privileges and concessions had been or should be granted to Carter by the British authorities in Egypt. MacDonald, responding curtly, remarked that "no privileges or concessions of any kind had been or would be extended to Carter or anyone involved in the tomb by His Majesty's Government." He stressed that the Tutankhamun affair was purely private and subject exclusively to the provisions of the Egyptian laws.

Meanwhile, as the reporter for *The Saturday Review* observed, "the all too slender rope that holds the cover of the coffin aloft stretches a bit each day towards the point where it may break and destroy the priceless discovery beneath it."

CHAPTER THIRTY

"Bandits!"

A WEEK AFTER THE TUMULTUOUS STRIKE, Ahmed Gurgar, the head foreman, or *reis*, of the expedition, whom Carter had assigned to watch over the locked tomb and keep an eye on the government guards, was making an early-morning inspection. With mounting anxiety he watched a column of armed police, on camels and horses, climb the dusty road leading to the valley head. They halted before him, silent, ominous.

Pierre Lacau approached. He was accompanied by the governor of the province, the chief of guards of the Antiquities Service, the commandant of the police and Mohammed Riad Bey, the director of the legal department of the Ministry of Public Works. The latter stepped forward and formally announced to Reis Gurgar that, upon orders of the Prime Minister himself, the government was officially taking control of the tomb.

Ahmed Gurgar stood his ground and blocked the entrance to the sanctuary. The governor gently ordered him to stand aside. Finally he did.

Two locksmiths equipped with clippers and hacksaws proceeded to cut the padlocks on the steel gates of the tomb and then those of the laboratory. The government forces entered the tomb and gingerly lowered the granite lid back down upon the sarcophagus. Then they entered the lab and made their inspection. When they emerged, the governor ordered Ahmed and his two subforemen to leave their posts. At first Ahmed and his assistants tried to stand guard over the photographic studio. They were told to move on. Reluctantly, they retired to Tomb Number Four, which had been equipped as a storage room. There, finally, they were left alone.

At the very moment the troops were forcing their way into the tomb, Morcos Bey Hanna officially informed Carter that the preliminary concession for the current season had been canceled. Carter thereupon cabled the Minister, informing him that "to safeguard the contents of the tomb" he was "commencing proceedings in the Mixed Courts of Cairo today." But he tried to leave the door open for negotiations by stating that if Pierre Lacau apologized for his insult to the ladies, and if all "vexatious interference" ceased, he would reopen the tomb for the public and would return to work.

With the takeover of the tomb and the annulment of the concession, Prime Minister Zaghlul had won his point. He justified the actions of his troops in forcing open the tomb by saying that, in Egypt as in England, "it is the duty of the government to defend the rights and dignity of the nation. I do not consider that a constitutional government can disregard the opinion of the country." One of his spokesmen publicly announced that the Egyptian government had reestablished its dignity and was now willing to seek "a peaceful solution of the disagreeable episode."

For a while, Carter seems to have been genuinely interested in going to the negotiating table. Then he abruptly turned away, angered by a maneuver executed by Prime Minister Zaghlul. To drive home the point that the Egyptian people were the rightful possessors of the royal tomb, the Prime Minister announced a gala reopening and invited one hundred seventy special guests to the grand affair. Several days before the event, the wily Zaghlul suffered an "indisposition" which "confined him to his room." The Prime Minister perhaps recognized that the event itself would stand as his political triumph and that his physical presence might be going just a shade too far.

The function, held on March 6, amounted to an immense and triumphant political rally. Not a shred of archaeological interest in the tomb was displayed. Instead, from the moment the first special train carrying ministers and members of both houses of Parliament departed Cairo, amid the ringing cheers of a dense crowd of Zaghlulist supporters, the merits of the Nationalist Party were proclaimed. Along the entire five-hundred-mile route, hundreds of thousands of Nationalist sympathizers roared their devotion to Zaghlul Pasha and cried out against the British and Howard Carter. At Luxor, the largest crowd ever assembled in that city in modern times waited through the night for the arrival of the government express. When the train pulled into the station, the throng made what one observer called a "bedlam of political warcries."

Among those present at the reopening were High Commissioner Lord Allenby and his wife. Allenby, who had traveled separately in a special train, was assailed throughout the journey and at Luxor by crowds shrieking for immediate and permanent independence from British rule. Once in Luxor, he proceeded directly to the valley; then he returned straightway to Cairo, avoiding the celebration banquet, which lasted until dawn.

The Antiquities Service had staged quite a show. The lid of the sarcophagus had been removed and placed against the wall of the Burial Chamber. The lighting arrangements had been "admirably carried out." There had been a particularly dramatic moment when Pierre Lacau extinguished the overhead lights, leaving a single spotlight to bathe the golden coffin of the King, which glowed majestically.

The Egyptian press reported that the event was one of the most splendid of the century and demonstrated the deep awareness of the new Nationalist regime for the needs and wishes of the people regarding archaeological matters. It was a curious editorial position to adopt, since it was well known that the average Egyptian citizen's attitude toward his dim and tenuous past was one of indifference bordering upon contempt.

An anonymous correspondent writing for *The Saturday Review*, who may have been Jean Capart, undoubtedly working directly with Howard Carter, took up the cudgels against the Egyptians in a manner that further enraged the Egyptian government.

The unknown writer observed that "some 1,900 years ago Pliny remarked of the Egyptians that they were 'ventosa et insolens natio,' a windy and insolent people." The reporter observed that recent events, including the "fantasia" and "childish tour de force" of the outrageous opening engineered by Zaghlul was proof that the Egyptians deserved the same title today. The article accused the Ministry of Public Works and Antiquities of "petty intrigue," "temperamental weakness" and "pernicious political finagling and persecution." The author blamed press jealousy, rival archaeologists, departmental malice and the political aims of the Nationalists for Carter's "strike." Carter, the writer continued, was anything but the *homme difficile* that his detractors portrayed. He is characterized in the article as the "innocent victim of *The Times* contract," who disapproved of it from the start.

To this blitheringly astonishing statement the anonymous propagandist added another: "Had Carter resisted the first encroachment of the Ministry of Public Works, the disastrous sequel might have been avoided, but obsessed with the scientific aspect of his work he was propitiatory, and it was not till the insidious attacks goaded him beyond endurance that he flung caution to the winds, and displayed in the Winter Palace Hotel at Luxor his gage of defiance, which threw into hysterics half the noisy 'patriots' of the country."

The sentiments of the article and its timing are vintage Howard Carter.

Carter retained a lawyer for his lawsuit to gain the right to reenter the tomb, a certain F. M. Maxwell, an Englishman with offices in Cairo, highly respected for his expertise in Egyptian law. The choice and the timing of the appointment were also vintage Howard Carter. F. M. Maxwell, a morose individual who seemed to be scowling even when he was at his most congenial, was unquestionably knowledgeable. Some years earlier, however, he had acted as public prosecutor for the British protectorate in a notorious treason trial. Maxwell had argued tenaciously—some said viciously—that the defendant deserved the death penalty. Although he failed to secure that verdict, he managed to secure a four-year prison term. The defendant, of course, had been the future Minister of Public Works, Morcos Bey Hanna.

Through Maxwell, Carter submitted two writs to the lower court in Cairo, known as the Mixed Courts, seeking to be appointed "sequestrator" of the tomb and its treasures and to enforce his right to excavate without interference from the Service of Antiquities. Carter also urged the court to confirm that he was entitled to fifty percent of the contents of the defiled tomb or the monetary value of one half of all objects discovered.

Even after Carter had filed his writs to the court, the government continued to be conciliatory behind the scenes, prompting Sir John Maxwell, Lady Carnarvon and the lawyer F. M. Maxwell to urge Carter to secure a settlement out of court. Professor James Breasted was called in by the court to serve as a mediator. He drew up a list of what he considered to be "reasonable conditions under which Carter should be given permission to return to the tomb." But Carter remained obdurate. As Breasted later recalled, Carter was "so overwhelmingly confident of a complete victory that he spurned a compromise, declared the conditions of the proffered authorization unacceptable and, against everyone's advice including his lawyer's, withheld his consent to a postponement of the trial." To Breasted, Carter's decision was beyond reason. He was, Breasted felt, "so overcome by his misfortune as to be incapable of major decisions."

The case would go before a special referee of the Mixed Courts, an American judge by the name of Pierre Crabites.

Under the British protectorate, a legal case involving a foreigner was heard by a court consisting of a mixed panel of foreign and Egyptian judges, with a foreigner as referee and chief judge.

To F. M. Maxwell, the court and the law pertaining to the mixed panel of judges were not mixed law, they were "Confused Law." To Sir John Maxwell, the mixed law of Egypt was hardly recognizable as law at all. Formal injunctions did not exist. But the referee judge could, on his own, take any action he deemed necessary if he thought the matter sufficiently critical. It became Carter's strategy to prove that a dangerous situation did exist and that it was absolutely urgent for him to be appointed "sequestrator" and to start digging. The defendant, the Egyptian government, tried to demonstrate, on the other hand, that no instant action of any kind was required. Thus the government attempted to stall the hearings. But this tactic failed because Judge Crabites became convinced that the tomb and the treasures within were in real danger when he heard of the circuslike reopening.

On the eighth of March the case came before Judge Crabites. The lawyer for the Ministry of Public Works was a suave individual named Rosetti. As soon as the court was called to order, Rosetti jumped up and demanded a mistrial on two counts. First, no plaintiff from the estate was present; Carter, he said, was only an "agent." Second, the Mixed Courts could not deal with a purely administrative measure such as the cancellation of an archaeological concession. Rosetti stated contemptuously that Carter's claim to the "right" to conduct a dig was "nonsense." The right had been derived from a revocable concession that had, in fact, been revoked. And it had been revoked because Carter had "irresponsibly walked off and had endangered Science." Carter's claim to any of the objects was also "nonsense." Lord Carnarvon had allowed Carter to sign the permit of 1918, which clearly defined what an *intact* royal tomb really was, and since Tutankhamun's was technically intact, Carter had signed away any share. Moreover, he added for good measure, Carnarvon had died. Therefore, no concession existed in the valley for anyone.

After Rosetti's lengthy arguments, Judge Crabites adjourned the hearings for a day. During that day, F. M. Maxwell urged Professor Breasted to find out whether or not Minister Morcos Bey Hanna might carry out his earlier suggestion that he renew Lady Carnarvon's concession. Accordingly, Breasted went to see Morcos Bey Hanna in person. The Minister thought about it for several hours, but ultimately refused. But just as Breasted was leaving, Morcos Bey Hanna told him that he would be prone to renew the authorization if Carter signed a renunciation of any share of the objects. Breasted promised to convey the extraordinary message.

Initially, Carter and Maxwell objected violently to the suggestion. Then Maxwell came to the opinion that a renunciation might be a rather impressive move. He believed that a renunciation would burnish Carter's public image. It would confirm that he was interested only in "Science"—not objects—and might make the court more sympathetic to his case.

Maxwell argued that if the government renewed the concession based upon the renunciation, Carter could go back to the tomb at once. Later, when things cooled down, Carter could again raise the issue of a proper share. F. M. Maxwell was convinced that the government would probably in the end come around to "a more generous point of view." If the government refused to renew, even after the written renunciation, Carter would be free to appeal to the higher court, the Mixed Tribunal, for damages, in the form of his rightful selection of treasures or an amount of money.

Carter signed the renunciation reluctantly. But when Breasted took the document to Morcos Bey Hanna, the Minister did a turnabout—he refused to renew the concession until he heard Judge Crabites' decision. Both Carter and F. M. Maxwell were nonplussed. No doubt Rosetti advised the Minister not to rely on the document because he believed Judge Crabites had no alternative but to rule in his favor. It seemed inconceivable that an official representative of the estate could be present in the court—Lady Carnarvon was in England and

Sir John Maxwell in California. If no legal executor of the Carnarvon estate was present, the judge would be forced to rule on behalf of the government. Rosetti, jubilant, was confident he would win.

But the proceedings in the Mixed Court began with a dramatic incident. F. M. Maxwell rose and asked whether or not the government still maintained that the executors of the estate were not represented. Rosetti acknowledged that it did. "F.M." then asked the court to recognize a surprise witness. Judge Crabites, taken aback, asked who that might be. F. M. Maxwell triumphantly announced that one of the executors of the estate was right in the courtroom. It was Sir John Maxwell himself. He had popped up in Cairo as if by a miracle. He had traveled halfway around the world, from California via Cherbourg, Nice and Genoa, when F.M. had cabled him to rush to avoid losing the case.

Rosetti quickly altered his attack and directed his arguments against Howard Carter. He punched out his arguments in a dry, clipped voice. Carter had no right to be in court. He had never had a concession. He had been merely an "agent" for Carnarvon. Only one concession existed, and that had been given to Lord Carnarvon. Even that had lapsed upon his death. Moreover, Rosetti claimed, Carnarvon's concession was only a continuation of Theodore Davis' license for the same area of the valley, and Davis had relinquished those rights by leaving the field.

F. M. Maxwell argued back. He characterized Rosetti's arguments as "circuitous and irrelevant." To him, there were but two simple issues: professional attention to duty, and selflessness. Carter had wanted only to carry out "scientific" work in the tomb. He had never personally sought a share of the objects. Indeed, he was "utterly disinterested" in them. But Carter's other claims to the tomb, F. M. Maxwell maintained, were totally valid. F.M. ridiculed Rosetti's assertion that Carter was merely an agent. He pointed out that Carter's name had appeared specifically as an "associate" on every one of the nine renewals of the original concession.

Maxwell argued further that the original concession had provided that the discoverers of a tomb could "retain possession" until completion of the scientific investigation. That meant, Maxwell went on, that the moment the tomb had been found the concession became more than an administrative permit—it became, in fact, a legal contract. And no administrative act on the part of the government could break a legal contract or deprive the heirs of the concessionaire *or* the representatives of their contractual rights. On that basis, the government had no recourse but to allow Carter back into the tomb.

F. M. Maxwell then declared that he was pleased to be in *"total* agreement" with Mr. Rosetti in pointing out that Theodore Davis once held a similar concession in the valley. He suggested that both concessions—Davis' and Carter's—be dealt with by the government in the same way. Davis had found several tombs, and from every single one of them Davis had received a large number of "unique objects" under an amicable agreement with Antiquities. "It was true," F.M. argued, "that Mr. Davis' actual share had not been half of what he had come across." But that was not due to the Antiquities Law. It had been Davis' own decision. He had wanted to be "generous to Egypt." Nor did the executors of Lord Carnarvon's estate claim half of what had been unearthed in the tomb of Tutankhamun. They, too, wanted to be generous. After all, one unique object might well be worth the entire monetary value of the contents due the discoverers. He suggested that the issue of division be decided when the full contents of the tomb had been explored.

In summing up his arguments, F. M. Maxwell had clearly carried the day with Judge Pierre Crabites, who by the nature of his questions gave every indication that he considered Rosetti's arguments irrelevant. And then, at the end of what seemed a very long day filled with legal flummery, Judge Crabites casually turned to F. M. Maxwell and asked him to clarify just one more minor point. It remained something of an enigma, he said, why Howard Carter had relinquished possession of the tomb *before* he had issued his writs to the court. It was one thing, he stated, for the court to confirm an extant legal possession and quite another thing to give it back after Carter had allowed it to lapse.

F. M. Maxwell was horrified that the judge had overlooked a key element in his case. Heatedly, he explained to Judge Crabites that Carter had still been in legal possession when he closed the tomb and issued his writs, but that the government had come in "like a pack of *bandits* and forced him out of possession by violence."

There was an uproar in the court. Rosetti jumped to his feet, protesting wildly. Even Judge Crabites was stunned. He asked Maxwell whether the word "bandits" was really necessary to his case. Maxwell, uncomprehending, replied that any word would suit him that expressed the violence and illegality of the governmental action—and "bandits" was as good as any.

That did it. In Arabic the word for "bandit"—or thief—is one of the vilest things one can call anyone. The Egyptian press made the most of it, suggesting that not only Maxwell but Carter and everyone involved with him had called the Cabinet Minister a thief and by extension had insulted *all* Egyptians.

The public reaction to the newspaper headlines was wild. Riots erupted in Cairo in which a number of people were injured. It took the police hours to calm down the crowds, and for a while it looked as if military troops would have to be called in.

Morcos Bey Hanna issued a statement announcing that the Ministry of Public Works would never negotiate with Howard Carter, even if directed to do so by the court. It seemed that neither Howard Carter nor his Metropolitan colleagues nor Lady Carnarvon would ever work in Egypt again—surely not in Tutankhamun's tomb.

CHAPTER THIRTY-ONE

"A Malignant Influence"

No one was more discomfited by the public uproar over F. M. Maxwell's insulting remark than Judge Pierre Crabites. He had wanted to rule in favor of Howard Carter and the Carnarvon estate and to instruct the Ministry of Public Works to allow Carter and his Metropolitan Museum associates back into the tomb under an agreement that he hoped Professor James Breasted might work out with Morcos Bey Hanna. After the uproar, Crabites recognized he had to change his plans and would have to proceed more slowly and cautiously than he desired with the enraged Egyptians.

Crabites conducted a private meeting with Morcos Bey and informed him that he would temporarily delay his official ruling in Carter's favor if the Minister would come to the negotiating table and at least attempt a compromise. Morcos Bey Hanna brusquely told him that he would think it over. But Crabites came away with the distinct impression that the government had no desire to settle the case.

Crabites then met discreetly with Herbert Winlock, whom he had known for some years and warmly liked. What was he to do with the tangled affair of Tutankhamun? It was all so ridiculous, so frustrating. Crabites expressed deep concern for the safety of those thousands of treasures still in the tomb. The

Egyptians were allowing hundreds of visitors through the sanctuary each day without proper security. Moreover, the absence of the Metropolitan team meant that no conservation work of any kind was being carried out. The impasse was not only annoying, it was dangerous. Winlock simply had to take on the burden of working out a compromise with Morcos Bey Hanna.

Winlock was in a slightly awkward situation, having an interest in the tomb through his association with the Metropolitan. But Crabites finally persuaded him to try. Straight off, Winlock recommended that Crabites persuade James Breasted to return to the fray to assess the true depth of Morcos Bey Hanna's animosity. It would not be an easy task, Winlock admitted, for Breasted had just about dismissed Howard Carter from his list of friends, so outraged had he become over Carter's obstinacy. Winlock also suggested to Crabites that he call upon their mutual friend J. Merton Howell, the American minister, to support Breasted's dealings with Morcos Bey Hanna. Judge Crabites said these were splendid ideas.

But what could be done about Carter, the judge asked Winlock? He had tried to approach Carter privately through Arthur Merton to persuade him to make a conciliatory move toward the government, but Carter had refused to talk to him. Would Winlock help at least to restrain Carter? Winlock assured the judge that he would try to keep Carter out of any negotiation that might ensue and persuade him, so far as any human being could, to refrain from making inflammatory statements. Winlock confided to Judge Crabites that Carter was planning to seek assistance from the British Embassy, which up to that point had demonstrated a disappointing tendency to ignore the tribulations of one of its most celebrated nationals. But Winlock doubted that his colleague would achieve satisfaction from that source.

Morcos Bey Hanna suddenly found himself in a quandary. When Crabites had asked him to consider a settlement, he had instantly decided against it. Nothing would deter him from keeping Carter out of the tomb forever. But when he attempted to enlist the aid of others to continue the excavation, he was unable to find any takers. Amazingly enough, Morcos Bey Hanna had even sent a message through an aide to Albert Lythgoe, asking whether the Metropolitan archaeologists would take over the dig. When he was coldly rebuffed he was genuinely mystified. And, to his astonishment, not a single foreign employee of his own Antiquities Service was willing to take on the responsibility. Both Pierre Lacau and his second-in-command, Rex Engelbach, politely refused the offer. And no one else in the ministry was willing to risk the responsibility. The Egyptian members of Antiquities and all local superintendents hurriedly admitted that they were ill-equipped for the delicate task. Gradually, public opinion began to turn against Morcos Bey Hanna. Egyptian newspapers that had been entirely sympathetic to him began to comment upon his failure to implement the diggings. Some suggested that perhaps Howard Carter was, after all, the only qualified archaeologist for the undertaking, particularly in view of his "extraordinarily generous" renunciation offer.

When James Breasted paid a call upon Morcos Bey on March 16, his excellency was in a vile mood. Breasted had looked upon the encounter with grave misgivings, and it had taken Crabites and Winlock several hours of persuasion before he agreed to immerse himself again in the discussions. His one condition was that he be permitted to send a personal note to Morcos Bey disassociating himself from the word "bandits." Sir John Maxwell and Howard Carter studied and ultimately approved the note. F. M. Maxwell, the perpetrator of the insult, hesitated for a long time. Finally he, too, agreed and even accompanied Breasted to the door of the Minister's home when the professor delivered his message.

Morcos Bey Hanna had not been performing a political charade when he expressed his anger over the word "bandits." Having been called a thief by the very man who had tried to have him executed, according to Breasted, "roused His Excellency into an apoplectic fury of righteous resentment." With the professor listening avidly, Morcos Bey strode up and down

309

his office, raging against the "haughty injustices of the British, the insufferable behavior of Carter and *Maxwell!*" He uttered his diatribe in Arabic, French and broken English.

When the Minister paused to catch his breath, Breasted happened to glance at him, then beyond to a bookshelf, empty but for a photograph of a group of Egyptian gentlemen, "all clad in suits with the unmistakable design of prison uniforms." The most prominent individual in the photograph was his excellency Morcos Bey Hanna. A smile crept over Breasted's face. Taken aback by Breasted's unexpected levity, the Minister stared at him coldly. Breasted, still smiling, said, "Look here, *there* are the bandits." Morcos Bey Hanna, uncomprehending, studied the picture as if he had never seen it before. Then, as Breasted recalled, "suddenly seeing himself as a common jailbird, rather than the martyr-hero for Independence," he roared with laughter. He became so jovial that Breasted decided it was the perfect moment to urge him to let Carter back into the tomb. Morcos Bey growled that it would be very difficult, and he suddenly asked Breasted whether or not he would take over the concession and carry out the task. James Breasted gently said that the Minister himself knew that he could not do it. But, he beseeched, at least discuss a compromise for Carter with Minister Howell and himself. Morcos Bey looked at him unblinking for a minute, and then calmly said that if he and the Egyptian government were assured of an official apology he would talk about giving Carter a new agreement—*not* a renewal of the old concession, but a new one. As James Henry Breasted left the Minister's office he thought, "Heaven help me from ever again attempting to act as peacemaker over the possession of a royal tomb of ancient Egypt."

Meanwhile, Carter had decided to approach the vice-consul of the British Embassy, in the hope that political pressure might be applied on the Zaghlul regime. Several times in the past three months Carter had privately approached High Commissioner Lord Allenby for advice and support. Allenby had given Carter the impression that he fully backed his struggle against the Egyptian government. Indeed, at least twice Allenby had, according to Carter, urged him to resist the Egyptians. Since the strike, however, Carter had been unable to reach Lord Allenby. Consequently, Carter had come to the embassy annoyed by the cool distance that British officialdom had maintained from the fracas. He was, as the individual who described the meeting later wrote, in a "quarrelsome and cantankerous" state of mind.

Howard Carter strode into the office of the vice-consul to protest the treatment he was receiving from the Egyptians over the "division of trophies" found in the tomb. The relations existing between the British and Egyptian governments were at that time, as might be imagined, extremely delicate, partly because of the surge of Egyptian nationalism, partly because of the growing controversy in Egypt over the issue of establishing a Palestinian homeland for the Jews. The vice-consul had no intention of straining relations further by entertaining grievances of a single British national. And he told Carter bluntly not to expect any assistance.

During the confrontation, Carter rapidly lost control of himself. One hot word followed another, until Carter finally abandoned all reserve. He commented acidly on the inadequacy of the Service of Antiquities and the imbecility of the British vice-consul, exclaiming that unless he received complete satisfaction—"*and justice!*"—he would publish, throughout the world, documents contained in unrevealed papyri he had found in the tomb, documents presenting the true and scandalous account of the exodus of the Jews from Egypt. Recognizing the implications of the threat at the very moment when England was trying to appease both the Arabs and the Jews, the vice-consul lost his temper completely and let fly an inkwell at Carter's head. Carter ducked just in time to avoid being hit. Eventually others calmed the enraged pair.

Carter had, of course, found no papyri or ancient documents of any sort in the tomb, much less documents of a sensitive political nature. The only explanation for his bizarre threat is that, angered beyond toleration by all that had happened to him, he wanted, perversely, to outrage the British vice-consul.

311

Whatever the case, the behavior was yet another vivid example of his unstable and self-destructive state of mind in mid-March of 1924, when he saw the purpose of his entire life ebbing away.

Winlock was profoundly disturbed when he got wind of the story, and he became concerned that Carter might inflict still further damage upon himself. Winlock realized that every day Carter remained in Egypt would be a step backward for his cause and for the cause of the Metropolitan Museum of Art. He decided to get Carter out of the country. But this was not an easy task. Carter had lately been talking about either delaying or canceling his planned lecture tour in America. After days of discussions, Winlock finally succeeded in convincing Carter that he simply had to stand by his commitment. So, on the twenty-first of March, Carter left Cairo for London, not knowing whether he would ever see Egypt or the tomb of Tutankhamun again.

Everyone involved with the tomb was frankly relieved to see Howard Carter leave the Valley of the Kings. Breasted was particularly pleased. As he remarked to Winlock, "When the Egyptians told me I would have to be responsible for Carter, I told them that it would not be so easy, since I have had trouble in the past several years controlling the weather."

Arthur Merton sent out a private and confidential letter warning the editors of *The Times* of Carter's frame of mind:

He has got a bee in his bonnet that *The Times* has not stood by him . . . He declared that the paper had not acted towards him in his trouble as he had expected it to do. He said he considered that you at your end should have defended him more vigorously, particularly as you had all the correspondence and knew what he had to put up with this winter. He added that beyond a short leader on the day after the crisis and an editorial reference to the "Times Agreement" you had done nothing at your end. He was particularly upset at the subheading, "Mr. Carter's Action" in the paper of the 14th Feb. which he said gave the false impression that he and not the Government was at fault and he expressed very bitter disappointment that not a single message of sympathy had reached him . . . I have let the matter drop since then for, from the manner in which he spoke of some of his best friends who have stood by him, I could see that he had become quite unbalanced . . .

Four days after Carter's departure, Breasted and Merton Howell, the American minister, managed to arrange an audience with Minister Morcos Bey. The truculent Egyptian demanded that F. M. Maxwell disavow and apologize for the word "bandits." He insisted upon a written confirmation from Carter that he really intended to give up any right to a division of objects. He also asked Breasted to obtain Winlock's personal assurances that Carter would "cease forever" his criticism of the Egyptian government. Only then would he draft a settlement based upon James Breasted's recommendations. If his demands were met, Morcos Bey told the two negotiators, they could have his unequivocal assurance that he would allow Carter back into the valley. Breasted and Howell promised that his requests would be met. Morcos Bey then amiably suggested that the two Americans return two days later, when, he stated, the settlement would "surely" be handed over, fully signed.

When he heard the favorable news, Herbert Winlock was delighted. After Breasted and Howell returned from their second visit, to pick up the document, Winlock greeted them eagerly. He was shocked to see that both men appeared to be utterly deflated. Howell gave the appearance of having aged years. Breasted was sullen. He told Winlock that Morcos Bey Hanna had broken his word to the American minister himself. He had refused to give them a copy of the concession and rejected any recommendation from Breasted. The excuse, according to Howell, was incredible. Morcos Bey informed them that he had just filed an appeal to a high court against Crabites' impending decision to enforce a compromise. Howell dejectedly went off to tell Pierre Crabites. After that he planned to go home and take to his bed, for he had given up on the whole matter.

Winlock, disbelieving, yet hoping that he could salvage something out of the wreckage, managed to see Crabites that afternoon with Breasted. The American judge was, as Winlock described him, "in a state over the loss of prestige to the U.S.A." Breasted fulminated that finally he believed that Morcos Bey Hanna had been acting in bad faith all along. He swore he would send a personal report to the Secretary of State, Charles Evans Hughes, describing fully how the Egyptians were willing to "diddle a foreign Minister" from America. To himself, Winlock scornfully doubted that Breasted ever would. Although the issues were discussed back and forth at length, Crabites had to admit to Winlock that there was nothing he could do. He advised him to return to his headquarters at Luxor and await the results of the appeal in the Mixed Tribunal. Winlock, who had come to Cairo to pick up the new concession on Carter's behalf, returned to the valley in a state of shock.

Pierre Crabites, infuriated at Howell's ineffectiveness, visited the elderly gentleman at his home. He shouted at him that he could not simply "lie down" under such insulting treatment. But Howell was so badly crushed by the incident that he stated weakly that he would do nothing more and that he planned to stay in bed. Later that evening, Crabites wrote Howell a scathing letter accusing him of knuckling under to the Egyptians and allowing United States prestige to be seriously bruised. He urged Howell to take swift action against the Egyptians so that "the new Egyptian Parliament would not labor under the false impression that having become independent, Egypt's new Ministry could flout America with impunity."

A day after the diatribe, Howell finally left his bed and got himself back on his feet and submitted an official complaint to the Egyptian Foreign Office about his discourteous treatment by Morcos Bey Hanna. Then, accompanied by Breasted, he barged into the Minister's office and demanded the promised concession. But again poor Howell knuckled under. Morcos Bey demanded that Howell read the concession, give it to no one else and put it in his safe. As Winlock acidly observed, "Howell was allowed to save his face before himself" but to no one else.

But Howell did show the proposed agreement secretly to Breasted, who perused it and termed it "disappointing." At that precise moment the Egyptian newspaper *Al-Ahram* published what purported to be an interview with Howard Carter in London stating that F. M. Maxwell had just informed him that the Egyptian government had broken its word three times! Howell, who was just about to meet Morcos Bey Hanna to recommence quiet negotiations, collapsed a second time in his bed.

No sooner had Howell regained his resolve once more than the indefatigable A. H. Bradstreet of *The New York Times* called at his office and asked him to comment upon a lengthy dispatch he planned to submit to New York at once. The story claimed that "a malignant influence emanating from the tomb of King Tutankhamun is held by some here to be responsible for a situation that may cause trouble between Egypt and the United States. . . . a deliberate affront has been offered to the United States in the person of its Minister, Dr. Merton Howell." Howell pleaded with Bradstreet not to run the damaging story. He reminded him that all journalists were "court-bound" to keep off the subject of Tutankhamun until the judgment of the Mixed Tribunal. Bradstreet readily admitted that he recognized the court order, yet he insisted that the yarn was too good to miss and put it out on the wire.

Howell had to issue an official denial to Bradstreet's story, claiming that the Egyptians had all been extremely courteous to him. He said he had used his "good offices in an unofficial way" to arrange an amicable settlement of the dispute. Then, turning his sights on Howard Carter, he stated that "if some of those interested in the settlement of this controversy had been more discreet in their language and attitude toward the Egyptian government, matters would have been less arduous for those of us who are bending our best efforts to effect a compromise."

315

The upshot of Bradstreet's story was that poor old Merton Howell received an official reprimand from the Secretary of State. And the result of the diplomatic storm was that neither the State Department nor Charles Evans Hughes nor young Allen Dulles, who was coordinating the affairs for the State Department and the Metropolitan Museum, ever again applied pressure upon the Egyptians or attempted to persuade the Egyptian minister in Washington to put a halt to the change of the Antiquities Law so that foreign interests could keep, for "scientific purposes," half of the objects discovered.

To Winlock the crowning blow of the disastrous period came the very same day Bradstreet's article appeared in *The New York Times*. On March 31 the Mixed Tribunal at Alexandria declared that the cancellation of the concession to Lady Carnarvon and Howard Carter was a legally permissible administrative act over which the lower Mixed Court in Cairo had no control. Thus the higher court upheld Morcos Bey Hanna's appeal on all counts.

Herbert Winlock confided to his colleagues that he was beginning to believe in the Tutankhamun curse. It seemed to pursue him everywhere—from the valley to Cairo, and back to the valley. The "malignant influence" surrounding the tomb of Tutankhamun had descended like blows from a hammer: "bandits"; Morcos Bey Hanna's refusal to hand over the concession; his insult to Howell; Howell's "going to bed"; Bradstreet's inflammatory article; Howell's reprimand; and the crushing decision by the higher court.

Winlock was at his lowest ebb when yet another hammer blow descended upon him. It came in the form of the final and official draft of the disputed concession.

Winlock read the document in his quarters in Luxor, and, as he put it, his "feet froze solid." To him, the decree was pure nonsense, giving Carter and Lady Carnarvon no rights, no authority, and *all* the burdens of responsibility.

The document was fundamentally an accusation stating that Howard Carter's abandonment of the tomb had been "utterly unfounded" and "constituted a danger to science." There were fourteen provisions in the proposal, fourteen knives pointed at the hearts of the excavators. And some of them were exceedingly sharp. The concession would be granted only on a yearly basis. Carter would be no more than the "supervisor" under the Service of Antiquities, and he would be powerless to appoint a single co-worker without written approval by the government. Five Egyptian "apprentices" would be assigned to the work. (Winlock branded them "spies.") Visitors' permits would be issued by the government alone. Lady Carnarvon could, of course, enter the tomb freely, but every two weeks she would have to make a personal account of how many visitations she or the staff had made. The Countess, personally, had to make a record of all objects and had to guarantee a scientific publication within five years of the termination of the dig. All objects in the tomb were government property. There would be no recourse to the courts. Everyone, including Lady Carnarvon herself, would have to sign yet another apology to the government about the word "bandits." Carter had to state in writing that he would abstain from any further language deemed discourteous to the government. And, finally, Carter would have to make a separate apology for his purported statements that the Egyptian government had broken three promises.

What more could possibly occur in the Tutankhamun affair, Winlock mused to himself. Nothing, he prayed; from now on, matters could only improve. But even in this modest hope he was to be proven wrong.

CHAPTER THIRTY-TWO

"Much Kalaam"

WHEN CARTER LEFT EGYPT, a special commission of Egyptians headed by Pierre Lacau had been formed to make an inventory of the tomb. The group had commenced a leisurely inspection of the contents of the sanctuary and the storerooms. They divided the material into various categories: works of art, laboratory and photographic equipment, furniture, and provisions. Winlock made arrangements with Rex Engelbach for the assistant foreman, Hussein, to be on hand during the inspection and instructed him to send a daily written report on the commission's activities.

On the twenty-ninth of March, Reis Hussein reported to Winlock that Pierre Lacau, accompanied by four aides, including Engelbach, had arrived at the site that afternoon and, with the help of a carpenter, had broken down the doors of a tomb Carter had used for storage and an occasional meal. They entered, made a hasty inspection, then closed the door and resealed it. The next evening, however, Lacau and his party were to return to compile a list of the contents of the storage tomb. Winlock instructed Hussein to keep a sharp eye on the proceedings and to continue sending reports.

Hussein did not have long to wait to make his next report. Startling events in the valley on the evening of March 30 caused him to rush just before midnight to Winlock's house.

318

To be awakened in the middle of the night is a frightening experience. As Herbert Winlock hurried from his bedroom to meet Reis Hussein, a number of fearful possibilities must have entered his mind. The foreman, breathless, awaited him in the sitting room. "Much *kalaam*"—confusion—and great trouble had come about at the tomb, he exclaimed. Had there been a flood or a fire? Hussein quickly said no, but there was great trouble. Mesmerized, Winlock listened to the tale.

Pierre Lacau, Rex Engelbach and the members of the inventory commission had come back to the storage tomb—the "lunch tomb"—that evening. They had inventoried the furniture, then opened some small packing crates containing objects from the tomb. They discovered that all the objects had been dutifully labeled and numbered personally by Howard Carter in three separate places: on the outside of each box, again on the inside, and yet a third time in an entry booklet set on a table nearby. The Egyptians had been visibly impressed with Carter's precise methods.

Then, far back in the storage area, near a stack of empty wooden crates from Fortnum & Mason, they had come across one marked "Red Wine." They almost neglected to open it. But Lacau instructed them to do so. It seemed to be stuffed with surgical gauze and cotton batting. Intrigued, Lacau lifted the layers of wrapping. What he found within caused him to utter a sharp exclamation of astonishment.

Lacau could not believe his eyes. It was a work of art. Hurriedly he removed the object from its nest. Engelbach and the Egyptian members of the commission, who had gathered around when they heard Lacau's exclamation, looked at one another dumbfounded.

What Lacau had come across in the wine case, unlabeled and clearly uninventoried, was a near-life-sized wooden head, covered with a thin coating of plaster and painted so delicately that the figure seemed almost able to breathe. It was a marvel of ancient sculpture.

The face, exceedingly handsome, with sensitive lips and large limpid eyes of the deepest black, must have been that of a boy nine or ten years of age. The head emerged from a small

319

pedestal carved with the petals of the sacred blue lotus of the Nile. The child was portrayed as the Sun God, springing forth from that flower which, according to the ancient Egyptians, was the first of all to grow from the pool of creation. But its strength and confidence marked it as more than a mere child. It was a king as Sun God, illustrating one of the most ancient texts: "He who emerged from the lotus upon the High Mound, who illumines with his eyes, the Two Lands." It was, without question, Tutankhamun.

Winlock listened, appalled, while Hussein described the devastating event. The foreman observed once more that there had been "much *kalaam*" and a babble of simultaneous voices, rising in intensity.

Hussein had told the commission, he said, that the head might have come from one of the chambers of the tomb and been placed in the back of the lunch tomb by mistake. At first his words were greeted by silence. Then a member of the commission raised the obvious question: If that were true, why had Carter neglected to supply the object with notes and numbers as he had done with all the other pieces? Reis Hussein could only shrug.

Hussein reported to Winlock that most "serious views" were taken of the discovery of the head. One of the Egyptians had stated bluntly that Carter had stolen the sculpture from the tomb.

Lacau had attempted to preserve order among his hysterical colleagues, insisting over and over that there had to be a logical explanation for Carter's storing the head in so curious a place. But the Egyptians demanded that a telegram be sent at once to Zaghlul, the Prime Minister himself. Lacau was reluctant, intent perhaps on finding the true facts before the alarm was sounded. Much as he tried, however, there was nothing Lacau could do. The cable was dispatched by special messenger to Luxor. Then the Egyptians demanded that the lovely head be packed up and sent immediately to the Egyptian Museum, as evidence, until the true facts could be ascertained. Lacau had to concur. The majestic carving was to be transported on the morning train to Cairo.

Early in the morning of his rude awakening, Herbert Winlock received another unexpected visitor. It was Rex Engelbach. The Englishman told Winlock that he had visited the excavation the evening before as an *unofficial* member of the government commission in charge of making the inventory. He had been, he emphasized, but a privileged observer. Engelbach then described the discovery of the head, which he referred to as the *"pièce capitale"* of "Tell al-Amarna" style and a superior object of Akhenaton type. The Egyptians, in his words, had gone "completely off their heads," shouting that there was no doubt at all that Carter or *someone* had stolen the sculpture from the tomb—or had intended to steal it. Engelbach assured Winlock that it had been Pierre Lacau who had sent him to help formulate an explanation. He said that Lacau had told the Egyptians that the lotus head had been purchased by Carter on the art market. He was not certain that the Egyptians believed the story, but they seemed to be leaning to it, knowing Carter's "methodical ways." The piece was so splendid, such a truly "capital object" in all respects, that it was inconceivable, Engelbach continued, that Carter, the foreman or a worker could have found it somewhere in the tomb and then simply forgotten it. But he observed to Winlock that if Carter *had* purchased it on the antique market, he had been "incredibly indiscreet" to have brought it into the excavation area and right into a storeroom containing objects from the tomb.

Engelbach paused. Could Winlock obtain confirmation from Carter that he had purchased the carving? That would greatly assist Lacau in reassuring the Egyptians. He begged Winlock to obtain a plausible story from Carter so as to quell the "unjustifiable suspicion" cast upon Carter by the commission. As he departed, Engelbach paused again and looked hopefully at Winlock. Could it be that the masterpiece was one of the treasures discovered by Carter on the stairs or in the passageway before he had entered the tomb? There was, he added hesitantly, only one problem with that. Carter had shown him all the pieces he had found there. And he was positive the beautiful lotus head not been among them.

After Rex Engelbach had gone, Winlock simply sat for a long time and stared at the wall of his sitting room. The truly remarkable thing about the lotus head was not that it had been found hidden in a box but that Engelbach and Lacau were offering Carter several alibis. Why would Lacau want to cover up a potential scandal? It was conceivable that Lacau was laying a trap. But which alibi was the trap? Winlock seems to have had no doubt that Carter had deliberately secreted the head away.

As soon as he could manage it, Winlock sent word to Carter by means of a numerical code that Albert Lythgoe had concocted some years before, in case of emergency, for the members of the Metropolitan excavation team in Luxor. Winlock was convinced that an open cable on such a touchy issue as the lotus head would be instantly relayed to the press. The thought of Bradstreet of *The New York Times* coming into possession of the explosive news dismayed him.

With considerable difficulty, complaining bitterly to himself about the confounded code, Winlock composed the first message:

Transmit Stevens 08716
Company Commission 17642 behind 68509 06262 Fortnum Mason 75826 75821 04804 089 Stop. 19464 Egyptian Committee members Stop. 40762 Marquand immediately and 39864 Cairo Stop. 30816 Severance and Trout 39864 them you 04788 Lord 44856 from Akhenaten. 21422 03627 that actually. 19842 origin 21847. 19974.

The decoded message:

Transmit Carter. To be kept confidential. Government Commission have found behind [tomb] four in case of wine Fortnum Mason "sculpture head, capital piece" unlabeled. Made a bad impression on Egyptian Committee members. It was announced by telegram to Zaghlool immediately and sent by express to Cairo. To protect you Lacau and Engelbach have suggested them you have bought for account of Lord Carnarvon, 1923, last year from Akhenaten. Do not know whether they believe that actually. Send all the information you can relating to origin if possible. Advise us by letter. If any inquiry is made we shall be prepared.

Winlock followed his first coded cable with another, saying that there were three theories as to the origin of the superb sculpture: Carter had bought it somewhere; one of the workers had placed it in the storage tomb by mistake; or Carter had found it in the passageway but neglected to record it.

Howard Carter, still in London, making preparations for his trip to America, quickly answered Winlock by cable and letter, offering an explanation. The "capital piece" was, he claimed, part of the material he had discovered in the debris of the entrance passage. He pointed out that all such objects were noted in "group numbers," but were "not yet fully registered in the Index." He explained that when he first cleared the passage he had collected the discoveries under "group sequence numbers" and stored them for "eventual study, recording and treatment" in Tomb Number Four. That tomb, he went on, had been the only place available for the safekeeping of antiquities at that early stage. It had not been until the opening of the Antechamber that he realized the full magnitude of his discovery. Only then had he applied for and received permission from Antiquities to use Tomb Number Fifteen as a storeroom and a laboratory. Therefore, all objects belonging to the excavation up to the moment of the opening of the Antechamber were put into Tomb Number Four.

Carter asserted that the actual piece in question, "admittedly the most important object found at that stage in the work," had been found in a very perishable condition. It had taken him and Callender a good deal of time to salvage it and retrieve the "fallen fragments of its painted decorations from the rubble and dust." He had carefully packed it and put it into the small storage tomb, along with the fragments, "until the opportunity came for its correct handling."

But Howard Carter's explanation, however profuse, remains unconvincing. His first of three volumes on the tomb of Tutankhamun had been published fully six months before Pierre Lacau and the members of the Egyptian commission discovered the beautiful head in the Fortnum & Mason wine case. In that first volume Carter gave a precise description of what he had found in the rubble of the stairway: "masses of broken potsherds and boxes, a scarab with the name of Thutmose III and other fragments." In the passageway, according to his own text, Carter found only "broken potsherds, jar sealings, alabaster jars, whole and broken, vases of painted pottery, numerous fragments of smaller articles and water skins."

He did not, in fact, mention the superb lotus head at all in the first volume. Nor did he supply a photograph. Nor was the head listed among the articles found in the passageway, in the master copy of the official "Journal of Entry" compiled in Carter's own hand.

Carter himself had previously stated that he showed Rex Engelbach the items from the stairway the day he found them. A few days later he had shown the materials encountered in the passageway to both Engelbach and Lacau in his quarters, where he had taken them for safekeeping. The head was not among them. It is inconceivable that he had overlooked the object as a fragment or something of routine importance. Because of its close similarity to the naturalistic style of Akhenaton, the lotus head is one of the most important clues to the obscure origins of Tutankhamun and a discovery of such spectacular nature that the newspapers would certainly have treated it as a front-page item.

It is, moreover, unlikely that the lotus head had been nestled in the debris of the stairs or the passageway, which could have occurred only had a tomb robber attempted to steal it. For the thieves would not have been interested in the lotus head at all, since there is no evidence that they appreciated objects of beauty or historical significance. A king was to be plundered, not revered as a manifestation of the sun. The robbers were seeking portable gold or oils and perfumes. In their greed for pure gold, the thieves ignored or threw aside exquisite jewelry fashioned only partly in gold. They had snatched a gold statuette of the King from inside the golden shrine, yet spurned the shrine itself, which was made of wood covered with thin panels of gold. They had snapped gold decorations from the ebony-and-ivory stool and left the stool itself. When, in the semidarkness, they had grabbed gold-leaf or gilded material from a piece of furniture and found that it was not solid gold, they had contemptuously thrown the material aside.

The lotus head is made of wood, furnished with a delicate plaster surface, and painted. There is not a shred of gold or anything precious on any part of it. If the large empty holes in the earlobes ever did have earrings, which is doubtful, it is logical to assume that the thieves would have twisted them off, leaving the head itself on the floor. But there are absolutely no marks of violence on those ears. It is difficult to believe that the priests who returned twice to put the tomb in order, after the thieves departed, would have left the magical image of the King as Sun God lying on the floor of the passageway and then callously covered it with rubble.

Miraculously, the story of the lotus head never surfaced. Winlock wrote to Carter that the Egyptian commission had accepted his story and that Lacau "was perfectly delighted with it, partly because it meant there was no question" that the piece belonged to the Egyptian Museum! Winlock also explained to Carter why Pierre Lacau had unaccountably become so sympathetic in helping Carter to cover up the embarrassment over the concealed treasure. Lacau was resentful of Morcos Bey Hanna. When the Minister drafted the final version of the concession, he had failed to consult Lacau or any member of the Antiquities Service. Lacau had been snubbed by his own Minister and had come to perceive that Morcos Bey had seized for himself almost complete control over excavations in Egypt. Lacau, Winlock observed, had become an unexpected ally in their cause. Winlock was convinced that he would be "very friendly and liberal. . . . You've had enough of natives anyway—and I prefer Lacau anytime."

By the middle of April, Winlock had begun to hope that Tutankhamun's malignant aura was waning and that he could persuade "all lawyers to retire and let the only two archaeologists left in the case"—Lacau and himself—resolve the bitter controversy. Only one question troubled him: Would Howard Carter manage to hold his tongue while on tour in America?

CHAPTER THIRTY-THREE

Carter in America

CARTER, RELIEVED TO BE free of the disputes that had plagued him in Egypt, reached New York City on the S.S. *Berengaria* on April 21. His arrival was triumphant. To Americans at least, he was an authentic hero and an international celebrity. His welcome into the United States was in marked contrast to the reception given him in England a month previously. In London, there seemed to be a slight chill in the air—his "strike" was controversial, not being considered quite proper.

While in England, Carter had embarked upon another self-destructive crusade for his rights. Wembley Amusements Ltd. had re-created "in the mud of Wembley" a replica of the four chambers of the tomb with reproductions carved by the "eminent sculptor, Mr. Aumonier." Carter impetuously sought a court injunction to "withdraw from public gaze" any sculpture which had been made with the help of his copyrighted photographs. When Mr. Aumonier proved that he had used other materials for his work, the case was thrown out of court. Once again, Howard Carter appeared selfish, petulant and overbearing.

In New York, Carter was the guest of honor at a dinner given by the board of trustees of the Metropolitan Museum in the grand ballroom of the Waldorf-Astoria Hotel, where it was announced that he had been elected to the exalted post of "Honorary Fellow of the Museum for Life." He was presented the official certificate of membership, which stated that Carter was entitled to all the privileges of the position, including a permanent admission ticket. At the time, the museum's admission price was a dime.

Carter's response was brief but heartfelt: "I beg to thank the Board on making me a life member of this noble institution. It is an honor of which I shall ever be deeply proud. My long association in Egypt with the members of their expedition has been for years a pleasant link between us, and, in that, my election adds an everlasting and much desired bond."

Carter had prepared two lectures for his American and Canadian tours. One was a general discussion of the tomb; the other focused on the most recent discoveries. They were smash hits. Between twenty-five hundred and three thousand persons flocked to Carnegie Hall on the evening of April 23, at five dollars a head, to hear him describe his long years of search, the dramatic discovery and the splendid treasures he had revealed to the world. The audience, which included many "prominent men and women," as the press stated at the time, applauded.

Howard Carter was not only theatrical and ebullient. He was also witty. There were, to be sure, a few surprises. Some members of the audience had the impression that he was an American and a member of the staff of the Metropolitan Museum. That was before they heard him speak. As the New York *Tribune* described the phenomenon:

Just how the belief became current that Howard Carter was an American appears, in the light of revelations at his first lecture, nothing short of amazing.

Mr. Carter spoke to his first public audience yesterday in Carnegie Hall of the "Sa*haw*ra" desert; he "ashuahed" them on "behawf" of his colleagues of various reassuring things about Tutankhamun. Thirty-four years of grubbing about for ancient tombs have intensified his British vocal mannerisms, so that the person who started the report that Carter was an American should be captured, stuffed and placed in a glass case and labeled the most inaccurate of human observers.

Those of the audience who could hear him appeared to enjoy his lecture immensely, but from the rear of the orchestra seats there came one cry of "We can't hear you!" That was about the middle of the lecture. Mr. Carter lifted his voice bravely, but when he had finished those of his audience who descended from the rear of the balconies complained bitterly.

But to most, Carter's performance was dazzling. His lecture was profusely illustrated with a selection of 358 black-and-white slides taken by Harry Burton, showing the works of art in magnificent size and detail.

Howard Carter never once bragged in his lectures about his monumental find. He was reticent about his genius in having mapped out the strategy that led to the pinpointing of the tomb of Tutankhamun. He never talked publicly about his discovery or indulged in self-praise. At times he appeared to be so self-effacing that many listeners came away convinced of his modesty. He rarely revealed to any of his audiences the magnitude of his personal joy over the discovery. Even in the Valley of the Kings he had been reticent, although in one marvelous moment, captured on film by Harry Burton, Carter appears in a suit and vest, wearing a homburg and carrying a cane, walking somewhat stiffly down the narrow footpath leading out of the desolate valley; then he suddenly turns, bows theatrically to cameraman Burton, wheels away quickly and kicks up his heels in boyish pleasure.

Carter's lectures were reported throughout the world. In Egypt, Herbert Winlock scanned the newspapers each day waiting for Carter to criticize the Egyptians once more and thereby undermine the fragile edifice of negotiations he was attempting to construct with Morcos Bey Hanna and Pierre Lacau. But during the first month and a half of his tour Carter devoted himself to his text alone, explaining the circumstances of the discovery, the activities of the thieves, the way in which mummified ducks and other fowl were stored in white ovoid boxes, similar to the "American system of putting food into tin cans." Carter even beguiled his audiences with his description of a cane carved into a woolly-headed captive who resembled Charlie Chaplin: "You see it's all correct, even down to the little bowler he's wearing on his head."

It was all very gripping, particularly the lecture "This Year's Discoveries." With practice, Carter had already developed considerable skill as a lecturer, charming, even captivating, the sympathetic crowds. With his lantern slides and movies, also taken by Harry Burton, he held each audience's attention raptly while, step by step, he led them to the exact second when the lid was lifted off the sarcophagus. "Tears literally came to my eyes when I gazed upon it," he said in a hushed voice to the enthralled crowds.

The audiences were clearly moved when he showed pictures of the sarcophagus itself. Carter relived the moment: "The lid was raised, disclosing a colossal mummy case of heavily gilded wood, carved in the likeness of the monarch. The hands were crossed upon the chest, the right holding the emblematic flail, and the left the crooked scepter, both of gold and faience. The face, a remarkable portrait, was formed of solid gold with eyes of crystal, and on the forehead was the sacred serpent and a vulture of gold and faience, while on each side was the figure of a goddess with arms and wings outstretched."

In every city—Chicago, Detroit, Buffalo, Washington— thousands came and applauded. Carter even met with President Calvin Coolidge early in May and gave a special lecture to a small gathering in the East Room of the White House. Carter said afterward that he was both amazed and flattered by the President's familiarity with his work at the tomb, and that he had been deeply gratified by Coolidge's commendation. When Yale University gave him an honorary degree, he was elated.

In the United States and Canada Howard Carter gave every impression of being confident of his return to the tomb. To everyone who asked whether he really thought he would go back, he would say that he had no doubts at all, only uncertainty about just when that day would come. Below the surface, however, terrible anxieties were consuming him.

He learned that on April 30 the Egyptian Parliament had voted a budget of eighteen thousand dollars for the tomb for the forthcoming season, proclaiming its firm intention to carry on the excavation without Carter or the Americans. Despite his success in America, he was growing more and more morose as the days and weeks slipped by without any positive word from the Egyptian government. The situation looked hopeless. His behavior became increasingly erratic.

Lee Keedick, the president of the lecture bureau handling his tour, who accompanied him throughout the United States and Canada, was pleased with Carter's public posture. But Keedick also saw the darker side and made a few notes about his bizarre behavior:

He was never enjoying himself unless he was in an argument, even over the most insignificant matter, and children could not escape him. Cab drivers, hotel doormen, railroad conductors, Pullman dining car conductors and little flower girls all came in for his invective and acrimonious and irritating comment. He criticized the taxi drivers for their abrupt stops; the hotel porters and doormen for their lack of training. The locomotive engineers did not pass unnoticed. On a long journey he would usually go forward at the first junction stop to the Engine and ask the Engineer who taught him to run it, saying he was getting the worst ride of his life by the inept way the train was controlled. All of this infuriated the Engineer and added to the day's turmoil. Once, on a trip from Montreal to Ottawa, he noticed that the Canadian dining car menu requested comments whether or not the food and service were adequate. The menu was an exceptionally large one, and Carter proceeded to write all over the card on both sides the most exasperating and juvenile protestations over the lack of experience of the Company in pretending to operate a dining car, when neither by nature nor training were they prepared for the job. He took keen delight in neatly folding the card and personally mailing it to the Superintendent of the Dining Car Service at Headquarters.

But complaints on menus were not the only things Howard Carter was writing during his trip. Unknown to anyone, he was patiently compiling a harsh indictment of the Egyptian government, the Service of Antiquities, and his personal nemesis, Pierre Lacau.

Throughout the entire tour, Winlock had briefed Carter several times each week on his efforts in Egypt. In mid-May he sent Carter a letter describing the negotiations he had been conducting with F. M. Maxwell and a new lawyer hired by the estate, an Egyptian by the name of Merzbach Bey. Impeccable in manner, dress and demeanor, Merzbach Bey had been brought into the case at first more as an ethnic presence than as a legal expert. Over the weeks he had begun to urge that the Carnarvon estate reaffirm with Morcos Bey its original letter of renunciation. He also stated his firm belief that the government concession or contract which Winlock and the others had looked upon as so poisonous was not bad under the circumstances. The indomitable Sir John Maxwell, the executor of the Carnarvon estate, thoroughly disagreed. From Cairo he wrote Merzbach that F. M. Maxwell had sent a resume of the new contract the Egyptian government had produced. He stated that he regarded it as "childish" and added that in the interests of science and general peace they were prepared to go a long way to obtain a friendly resolution, but the Egyptian government apparently wished to get "everything for nothing and to treat us as though we had done something wrong." He refused, he said, to accept such treatment and informed him that he had wired his London lawyers to withdraw the letter of renunciation. "Now we will fight for our rights," he promised. The Egyptian government had treated them with "contempt," he concluded, and "Carter may have been tactless, but events now prove him to have been not far wrong."

Both Sir John Maxwell and Winlock decided that the only way to have the concession redrafted and then renewed was to apply pressure upon Pierre Lacau, who now appeared to be sympathetic to their cause. They considered him an untrust-

331

worthy ally but the only one available in government circles.

At the end of one four-hour meeting, Winlock believed that Lacau was "primed and ready" for the "final push." Winlock told him he had decided to recommend that Carter refuse to send a letter to Morcos Bey disavowing the word "bandits." After all, it was not Carter who had hurled the disastrous epithet. Winlock would also urge Carter to refuse the Minister's request that he compose a statement "promising to be good." That, Winlock pointed out, would be admitting that he had been bad. Winlock joked to Lacau that "he would gladly murder [Carter] if [he] weren't good but that was as far as [he] would agree to go." Lacau told Winlock that he thought he *might* be able to persuade the Minister to lay aside his demand that Carter "promise to be good." But he believed that the Minister would never allow Carter to refrain from a personal apology for his lawyer's insulting use of the word "bandits."

Just as Winlock was preparing to depart for New York, Lacau informed him that the Minister had reduced his demands to two: the apology for "bandits" and a formal statement by Carter that he would renounce any share of the treasures from the tomb. Winlock hurriedly dispatched a farewell letter to Lacau stating that he would sincerely try to obtain Carter's agreement on the two points. But in his letter he could not avoid criticizing Lacau. He bluntly informed his colleague that he considered him so completely throttled by the Egyptian members of the department and the Minister that there was little hope that Lacau would ever be able to obtain a concession acceptable to Carter—or to any other foreigner, for that matter. Winlock observed acidly that Lacau's position was not only inconsistent but self-defeating, and wrote: "I find that although you want archaeological work to continue, at the same time you think it necessary to give away on every side to the desires of the Egyptian politicians for the sake of peace."

When he returned to the United States, Winlock sent Howard Carter a letter telling him that despite his desire to start the excavation again without a letter of apology or a total renunciation, this would never occur. It was absolutely essential that Carter make the Carnarvon family realize this. The Egyptian government considered its legal case to be very strong, and Winlock concurred with that assessment. He told Carter there was no use "mincing words or trying to fool ourselves. In Cairo you have the reputation of being difficult. Some of this goes back to the old days and a long series of incidents in which you have not been sparing of the knocks; some of them delivered by you to disgruntled visitors at the tomb in the past two years, some to members of the Service of Antiquities. Winlock advised Carter that if he wanted in again, he must apologize and renounce.

Winlock told Carter that his prime task was to convince the Egyptians that they were totally wrong in "their childish idea" that he liked to "quarrel for the fun of insulting the Egyptian nation." He closed with a pertinent admonition: "As one of your most sincere well wishers, . . . I should advise absolutely no comments of *any* sort to the press."

After Winlock's no-nonsense letter, a despondent Howard Carter responded to both Winlock and Albert Lythgoe poignantly from his lonely room in the Statler Hotel in Buffalo:

All the news is very sorrowful, in fact too sad for contemplation— the more so as I have been, for some unfortunate reason, an upsetting element in the general cause—It was but an endeavour to carry out a duty.

I cannot agree to any action on my part that would in any way prejudice the rights of others. I shall therefore retire—renouncing any claim whatsoever to the Tut-Ankh-Amen discovery, and also from future archaeological research—with a broken heart to find after many years work that all one's alleged faults are dashed upon the scales without one possible good deed used to counterbalance them. The debt of gratitude that I owe to your Trustees, your Director, and yourselves, I fear I can never properly fulfil so, kind Colleagues, take this as a farewell from a retiring fellow-archaeologist who remains an everlasting friend. I look forward to seeing you all in June.

Lythgoe attempted to placate the disheartened archaeologist, writing him that he could not allow his old friend "to wipe yourself off the map" or put himself in a position where his best course "would prejudice the rights of others." He delicately tried to convince Carter that if he cared about ever working again, or was truly concerned about compiling a scientific record of the tomb, he should lay aside his own interests in obtaining a share of the objects and should attempt to persuade his "friends in London" to do the same. Lythgoe recommended that in a few weeks, when Carter had finished his tour, "we'll all sit down to have a fair talk on the possibilities, and we simply won't let you commit hari-kari . . ."

Lythgoe concluded his letter by assuring Carter that his "words of friendliest advice" had been given with the "best of motives" and would "lead through to a completely successful ending." By now, both Herbert Winlock and Albert Lythgoe had almost totally given up on the hope of a single object or treasure from the tomb of Tutankhamun ever coming to the museum. As it later turned out, the Metropolitan would receive part of Lord Carnarvon's share, but in a way that neither Winlock nor Lythgoe foresaw.

Early in June, toward the conclusion of his tour, Howard Carter received from his publishers in London, Cassell and Company, Ltd., the first five copies of a pamphlet he had been writing clandestinely. The secret document had been a labor of love, and when Carter received his initial copies he was tremendously pleased with himself. Printed without copyright, ostensibly for "private circulation only," the booklet was entitled *The Tomb of Tut-Ankh-Amen, Statement with Documents, as to the Events which occurred in Egypt in the Winter of 1923–1924 leading to the ultimate break with the Egyptian Government.*

In a prefatory note Carter explained: "The following pages have been prepared by Mr. Carter with a view to placing before the Scientific Societies, his friends and others interested in the Tomb of Tut-Ankh-Amen, a full statement of the facts which have led us to the present position with the Egyptian

Government." It is a scathing indictment, written in the third person, assaulting the Egyptian government, the Antiquities Service and Pierre Lacau, whose methods Carter described as "a menace to the whole future of archaeology in Egypt."

The booklet mirrors Howard Carter's fanaticism on every page. Only four or five copies have survived, and even those have never been exposed to public scrutiny. His polemic provides a day-by-day account of virtually every single element of the fracas to which he contributed so much. No detail of the complex series of arguments is spared; every episode, incident and nuance is exhaustively analyzed, restated and analyzed again. Throughout the work, Carter emphatically affirms that all he sought throughout the tumultuous contretemps was peace. Yet in its tone, attitude and language the document stands—pathetically—as the product of a tortured man at war with everyone, including himself.

Herbert Winlock received his copy out of the blue on the first of July, 1924, the very morning he was to receive Howard Carter in his office at the Metropolitan. They had not seen each other in months. Winlock leafed through the document rapidly, shocked at the confused, labyrinthine diatribe. What in heaven's name was the "unaccountable cuss" up to now? Then Winlock came across the series of appendices which Carter, apparently at the last moment, had added to give substance to his case. For an instant, Winlock later recalled, he felt like throwing the document right out his window. He was disgusted to see that Carter had included in Appendix Four everything—coded telegrams, confidential letters and notes—which spelled out Winlock's role in suppressing the scandal over the sculpture found in the Fortnum & Mason wine case. It could be a shattering blow to his reputation as an archaeologist. How many of the damned things had Carter sent out?

When Carter arrived, he was genuinely taken aback to find his friend so outraged. Winlock dropped any pretense of diplomacy in the exchange. He informed Carter that, with the appearance of the booklet, he was no longer willing to be associated with him in any way. Perhaps for the first time in

335

his life, Herbert Winlock truly detested another human being. He told Carter quietly and coldly that he believed his conduct throughout the entire affair had been unbalanced and stubborn and that the publication of the confounded pamphlet was the most maladroit act he had ever seen in his life. He spoke of how deeply he resented having been used, and accused Carter of being insensitive and selfish.

Carter was at a loss for words. He did not even attempt to apologize for the damaging appendix or for having printed the confidential papers without permission. It could have been that he was too embarrassed to do so. Instead he attempted to argue with Winlock and told him that the pamphlet would arouse the scholarly world and bring about a reaction that would make the Egyptians think twice about preventing him from reentering the tomb on his own terms. He still believed that firmness would be the most effective way of dealing with the Egyptians. All he had to do was be unswerving and eventually the Egyptians would surrender. Winlock shook his head in disbelief. He expressed his personal view that Carter would never again be allowed to dig anywhere in Egypt, much less in the tomb of Tutankhamun, unless he changed his ways and surrendered to the Egyptians' demands.

Winlock cut short his meeting with Carter and immediately informed the museum's director, Edward Robinson, about the pamphlet and what he thought of Carter's most recent act of impetuosity. Robinson fully agreed with him. Winlock warned Robinson that Carter would undoubtedly give him a copy of the "disgusting" booklet on the steamer—for they were booked on the same ship for England—and would attempt to drag him into a fruitless campaign against the Egyptian government and a new attempt to get rid of Pierre Lacau. In the strongest terms, he cautioned the director not to be taken in. Robinson assured Winlock that he would not allow himself to be sucked into any "propaganda effort" that Carter might concoct and would do everything to avoid a "row of any kind with the Egyptians."

Immediately afterward, Winlock rushed to meet with Edward Harkness, a member of the Metropolitan's board, and warned him of the dangers to the museum of Carter's "temperamental outbursts." Winlock recommended that the museum diminish sharply the scope of its excavations so that it held on to a claim only "sufficient to make an eventual return to Egypt possible." He told Harkness that he thought time had almost run out on the old order of a division of discoveries. In the hope of salvaging *something*, Winlock said, he would try to persuade the Egyptians to accept the proposition of a partition based on one out of every five objects after the Service of Antiquities had first picked its prime choices. Harkness told him to go ahead with the scheme. Harkness asked him what he thought about Carter's idea of trying to oust Lacau. Winlock told him bluntly that he thought the concept was stupid, for the museum would be far worse off with someone else in Lacau's position.

Carter had been profoundly shaken by the resentment and deep anger of his old friend. It had apparently never occurred to him that Winlock would feel betrayed by the publication of the incriminating information regarding the concealed royal portrait head. But he quickly made efforts to halt further distribution of the pamphlet, wrote in his own hand the word "Confidential" on the copies he had, and removed Appendix Four.

Carter made no attempt to see either Harkness or Robinson in his efforts to galvanize the scholarly community against Lacau and the Egyptian government. After his acerbic meeting with Winlock, it would appear that he did not even bother to return to the Metropolitan's Egyptian Department, where he had a temporary office, to pick up his papers relating to the tomb. He remained in his hotel room until he could board the *Mauretania* for his return home.

CHAPTER THIRTY-FOUR

Surrender

AFTER SEVERAL DAYS of wading through museum paperwork aboard the *Mauretania*, Edward Robinson finally found a few hours to peruse Carter's pamphlet. He got "emphatically the impression of a good case badly handled from start to finish." To Robinson, the document demonstrated that Carter had played into the hands of the Egyptian authorities in "a most astonishing manner from the point of view of winning his case."

When the two finally got together, Robinson did not utter a word about his feelings regarding the pamphlet. Howard Carter did not mention the issue, either. Although Robinson was convinced that distribution of the flamboyant publication would cause Carter and the Metropolitan expedition considerable harm, he remained silent so as not to arouse Carter and start a new row. As the two chatted inconsequentially, Robinson could only think to himself, "What a curious and unhappy fatality seems to surround the tomb of Tutankhamun."

A day later, when Robinson met Carter again, Carter brought up the subject of the pamphlet. Robinson disclosed his negative feelings about the pamphlet and Carter's inept handling of the entire Tutankhamun proceedings. Robinson was astonished to discover that Carter agreed with everything he said, admitting "that he had done and said many foolish things which he deeply regretted—some of which were due to bad advice, others to the strain he was under, that had prevented his thinking clearly or calmly." Robinson, seeing that Carter was in an astoundingly receptive mood, advised him to give the Egyptian government "any apology they wanted" so that he could finish his work in the tomb. He also begged Carter not to circulate his pamphlet attacking the Egyptians. Carter muttered his thanks for all that the Metropolitan had done and was doing.

And so, as the ship steamed toward England, Carter finally decided to abandon his long struggle. He returned to his cabin and for hours pondered what he had done over the past year and a half to exacerbate the situation, methodically jotting down notes about his behavior. One can imagine a crushed man, having been spurned by one of his closest friends, thinking that his beloved Egypt would never again be a part of his life, wondering where else he could possibly go. Defeated, exhausted at the age of fifty, full of anxieties, he took Robinson and Winlock's advice and drafted a message of surrender to Pierre Lacau:

I, the undersigned, Howard Carter, definitively renounce any action, claim, or pretension whatsoever, both as regards the Tomb of Tut-Ankh-Amun and the objects therefrom and also in respect of the cancellation of the authorisation and the measures taken by the government in consequence of such cancellation. I declare that I withdraw all actions pending and I authorise the representative of the government to apply for them to be struck out.

When the *Mauretania* had docked in England, Carter met with Lady Carnarvon and Sir John Maxwell and explained the reasons for his complete change of heart, showing them the draft of his capitulation. He was able to convince Almina Carnarvon that she should renounce once again her personal rights to any objects from the tomb and waive her right to go to court for monetary damages. Sir John Maxwell refused to withdraw the estate claims to a share but fully approved Lady Carnarvon's personal action.

So on September 13, 1924, a letter drafted by Carter and Sir John Maxwell and signed by Lady Carnarvon was dispatched to his excellency Morcos Bey Hanna:

I have been carefully considering the terms of the proposed new Concession which have been privately discussed by you with my Representative in Cairo.

The terms as now provisionally agreed are acceptable to me and to my agent, Mr. Howard Carter, the only difficulty remaining being the question of the renunciation by myself, the Executors and Mr. Carter of our claims to a share of the objects found in the tomb to be given to my late husband's representatives as a recognition of his work.

As far as Mr. Carter and I myself are concerned we are perfectly willing to renounce any claim, but Lord Carnarvon's Executors are in a somewhat different position.

I would remind you that my late husband spent over ten years in research work in the Valley of the Kings and that he carried out this work year after year, in spite of many disappointments, entirely at his own expense, the total of which Mr. Howard Carter places at approximately £45,000.

Hitherto all Archaeologists and Scientific Bodies have been granted, in cases where they have been successful in finding objects of interest, a substantial reward, and all that the Executors ask in this case is that they should be treated in a similarly equitable manner.

I cannot express sufficiently strongly my regret at the misunderstandings which arose during the last Winter's Working Season, but I feel quite certain that you will agree with me that in the interest of the Scientific World the work should be proceeded with and carried to a speedy conclusion on the same lines as hitherto and that my friend Mr. Howard Carter is the one man who, with the assistance of his able staff, and the supervision of your department of Antiquities, is able to carry the work to the satisfactory conclusion desired by your Government, myself, all Archaeologists and in fact the whole world. Moreover it is my own earnest wish that he, Mr. Carter, should complete the work in accordance with the intention and wishes often expressed of the late Lord Carnarvon that he should do so.

May I therefore make the suggestion that the renunciation by my husband's Executors should not be insisted upon, but that, when the work is finished, and the actual contents of the tomb fully ascertained, the share of those objects to which Lord Carnarvon's Executors are equitably entitled under the terms of the original Concession should be referred to the arbitration of two independent Archaeologists of recognised standing, one to be appointed by your Government and the other by the Executors, with liberty of course to them to appoint an Umpire should it be necessary.

If you could see your way to accept this suggestion, the work could proceed with all speed, and I feel sure without any further friction, and the outstanding question would when the time arrives be settled in the manner usual between persons who are only anxious to come to an equitable settlement, and to the satisfaction of yourselves, the Executors and the Scientific World generally.

Merzbach Bey, whose advice had been sought by Sir John Maxwell, had suggested the passages relating to a *possible* share of objects, for he believed that the Egyptians would have to offer something or lose face. The canny lawyer had also pointed out that such an arrangement would perfectly suit Sir John Maxwell, the principal executor of the estate. He must never be accused of not having tried to secure for the Carnarvon estate its due rights. It was an admirable idea, and it worked. Soon Merzbach Bey cabled Lady Carnarvon and Sir John Maxwell that the Egyptian government was "willing to give at its discretion to Lady Almina a choice of duplicates as representative as possible of the discovery" wherever the duplicates could be "separated from the whole without damage to Science." He added, "My heartiest congratulations."

Howard Carter waited impatiently in London for official word from Morcos Bey Hanna giving him permission to return to the valley. A month passed. Nothing. What was going on? Was the Minister preparing to back down—again? Messages to his excellency through Merzbach Bey urging a favorable decision met with silence. Two months passed. Morcos Bey Hanna had become the Sphinx.

•   •   •

One of the supreme ironies surrounding the "unhappy fatality" of the discovery of the tomb of Tutankhamun was that just as Morcos Bey Hanna was about to reply favorably, he was thrown out of office. Suddenly Howard Carter was allowed to go back into Egypt, but just as suddenly his utter capitulation became a monumental error.

On November 19, 1924, the British government, waiting impatiently for the opportunity, finally found an excuse to reinstate its full authority in Egypt. Sir Lee Stack, the British commander of the Egyptian Army and governor general of the Sudan, whose position was second only to that of the Lord High Commissioner, was shot down in the streets of Cairo by a group of terrorists.

The British moves against Prime Minister Zaghlul's already shaky governmental structure were immediate and harsh. The British demanded a personal apology from Zaghlul for the assassination; seizure and the death penalty for the murderers; the payment of an indemnity of £500,000; and the imposition of martial law, including a ban on public meetings by more than four citizens.

Zaghlul attempted to bargain for a compromise, pointing out that the murder was an abomination to him and to all civilized human beings. The British authorities would have none of it; government troops moved in and seized virtual control of the nation. Zaghlul and his Cabinet resigned and were replaced by a pro-British regime headed by Ahmad Pasha Ziwar, an old and intimate friend of Howard Carter.

Howard Carter was overjoyed by the turn of events. But he wondered now whether he could somehow withdraw his and Lady Carnarvon's letters of renunciation. As soon as he was able to obtain passage, he went to Egypt. Upon his arrival on the fifteenth of December, he saw a nation shaken by the terrorist acts and eager to embrace a return to British rule. The politically sophisticated were now crying out for total obeisance to British authority—the same people who had denounced Britain when her powers had waned. Now there arose a vigorous outcry against all nationalists and members of the Wafd Party. Great Britain was implored to institute a climate of tranquillity so that tourists would return again to Egypt to visit her antiquities and the tomb of Tutankhamun, the prime antiquity of all.

In his first hours back in Egypt, after so many months of anguish, Carter experienced what he described as a highly favorable omen. On the very morning of his arrival in Cairo Carter met, purely by chance, but as if preordained, the new Prime Minister, Ahmad Pasha Ziwar himself. The head of state brought up the subject of Tutankhamun and vehemently condemned the Zaghlul government for its restrictive policies against Carter. In a letter to Sir John Maxwell's solicitor recounting the negotiations, Carter describes Ziwar as giving every indication that he would be "kindly and co-operative" toward him and was most anxious to come to an amicable arrangement as early as possible. Carter assured his friend Ziwar that he desired nothing more and that, although he was not equipped to start in a day, he could begin again in two weeks—if all went well.

Carter queried Merzbach Bey about withdrawing the letters of renunciation. But the lawyer was hesitant. The suave Egyptian advised him that a complete withdrawal or substantial change of the letter at that moment could be interpreted as bad faith. Despite the fact that the Nationalist Party was on the run, it was probably still powerful enough to initiate a campaign to discredit the new Prime Minister's majority. Furthermore, Pierre Lacau had the letter in hand. Better to leave the renunciation alone for a while, Merzbach counseled, and attempt to change it gradually. Carter agreed. He had become convinced that Ziwar himself would decree that the estate could have part of the treasure in grateful thanks for continuing the clearing out of the tomb. So far, the Prime Minister had appeared to be extraordinarily receptive.

Merzbach Bey urged Carter to approach the appropriate British officials for their help. He was certain that this time the British would support Carter's cause. Their aid would be vital in dealing with Ziwar. If the right pressure came from the

British Residency, and if favorable conditions were granted by the Prime Minister, no one would be able to criticize him, for fear of political reprisals from the British. Merzbach Bey told Carter that they should act as if they were interested in the "scientific" aspects of the excavation alone and, at the same time, behind the scenes deftly work for more favorable conditions regarding a division of objects.

At noon on December 16, Carter visited an official at the British Embassy whose title was Oriental secretary. Luckily for Carter, the individual was not the same embassy official whom he had enraged earlier by his threats to reveal the "secret papyri" exposing the "true facts" about the expulsion of the Jews from Egypt. The secretary asked for Carter's assurances that, if a new arrangement could be worked out, no "private press contracts" would come into being. Carter quickly promised him that there was not "the slightest chance of any press monopoly reoccurring," pointing out that a clause on that precise point could be written into the new concession. Thereupon the official said that he was inclined to support Carter and would place the matter before the High Commissioner himself. In a few days Carter heard the good news that Lord Allenby had decided to throw the full weight of the British protectorate on the scales of negotiation.

Lord Allenby had recognized that the reopening of the tomb would be a significant political and public-relations benefit for Great Britain and might help soften the growing criticism around the world against Britain's takeover of Egypt. In addition, Allenby saw the opportunity to curry favor with Egyptian financial interests embodied in the tourist and hotel companies. He was also well aware that a successful reopening would be regarded as a major accomplishment by Ziwar, the English puppet. The secretary informed Carter that Allenby wanted the tomb opened as soon as possible. Knowing that Carter could not possibly begin full-scale clearing at once, he urged him to make the sanctuary available for the public for just ten days in January for "political reasons." Carter, who had previously struggled tenaciously to keep any tourists out of the tomb, voiced no objection.

344

With the British Residency paving the way, Carter obtained an audience with the Prime Minister at the Council of Ministers' office. While he was waiting, Georges Foucart, the director of the French Archaeological Mission in Egypt, dropped into the office and conversed with Carter freely about how incompetently Pierre Lacau had handled matters. Carter was astounded at Foucart's open expression of his feelings and privately felt that it was most indiscreet.

After an hour's delay Prime Minister Ziwar arrived. But Carter was instructed to wait while Georges Foucart talked to the head of state, despite the fact that Carter's own appointment had preceded his. A few minutes later, when Carter was granted admission to the Prime Minister's office, he was surprised to find Foucart still within. The question of the tomb in all its ramifications was fully discussed in Foucart's presence. Carter noted that Foucart "intrigued against Lacau the whole time."

Carter expressed once more to the Prime Minister his earnest wish to return immediately to the tomb. He was perfectly amenable, he said, to setting aside the issue of the division of duplicates until the tomb had been completely cleared, since no one had seen more than half of the tomb's contents. Carter explained that but for the question of a "rightful division" and a few minor details, he was prepared to proceed at once under the conditions in the proposed concession.

In a letter to his solicitor, Carter noted that the Prime Minister was "most emphatic that . . . the excavator or discoverer should be fairly treated and he even went so far as to point out that Civil Laws of Egypt dictated no other than that attitude." Carter's spirits and hopes were lifted to their highest level in more than a year.

He asked the Prime Minister if he could arrange a meeting between himself, the new Minister of Public Works and Merzbach Bey to arrange an immediate agreement. But the Prime Minister demurred, saying that he far preferred a letter embodying all the details before any meeting. Carter, although unhappy at the delay, drafted the letter.

A week later, on January 4, 1925, Carter received word that

the meeting had finally been arranged by the Prime Minister. The participants were to be Carter, Merzbach Bey and the Minister of the Interior, Sidky Pasha, said to be the most powerful minister in the Cabinet, and, to his anger, two additional negotiators—none other than Bedawy Pasha, who had been the legal adviser to the government when it took over the tomb, and his old enemy Pierre Lacau. He was completely confused, thinking that Ziwar was ignorant of the events that had transpired in the past.

But Ziwar knew exactly what he was doing. He had been fully apprised of the tumult surrounding the tomb. Ziwar was not merely a personal friend of Howard Carter; he was also the Prime Minister. The last thing he wanted was to allow his political flanks to become exposed over the simple matter of the tomb of a dead pharaoh, or be forced into an untenable position between French and British interests. He had deliberately brought both Lacau and *his* enemy Foucart into the discussions so as to forge a balance of power.

The Prime Minister knew that the question of the division was a burning political issue and had made up his mind to avoid a direct confrontation over it at all costs. Accordingly, he invited Carter to a private meeting at the Mohammed Ali Club several hours before the conference in which the negotiations would commence. Gently, smoothly, Ziwar assured Carter that all was going according to plan and that very soon Carter would be able to start excavating anew. But, he confided, there was still "one minute problem" that stood in the way. It was a certain reluctance on the part of the Antiquities Service to proceed with the discussions unless Carter and the estate confirmed in writing their complete and formal renunciation of their rights to any of the treasure, including duplicates, and at the same time agreed to refrain from going to court.

Carter could scarcely believe what he was hearing. "Of course," Ziwar hastened to add, "in time there *would* be objects," and he offered his personal pledge to be "exceedingly generous towards Lady Carnarvon and the estate, in the matter of duplicates which would not interfere with the over-all ensemble."

346

Carter, disheartened by the sham, desperately wanted to remind his old friend of a remark he had made several days earlier, when Ziwar had confidently proclaimed that "all the civil laws of Egypt virtually *dictated* fair treatment to excavators" through an equitable choice of works of art or money. He wanted desperately to speak, eloquently, of the years— those many years—Carnarvon and he had worked, finding nothing, becoming more discouraged each month with such a vast expenditure of funds. He had a great urge to spill out all the reasons why neither the French nor the Egyptians were really capable of carrying out excavations effectively. He must have thought of begging his friend for time so that political emotions could subside. But he simply could not get the words to emerge. Howard Carter had never begged for anything in his life. Pleading was alien to his nature. So he sat there silently, and after the Minister shrugged, implying "What else could I do?," Carter nodded his assent. When he informed Merzbach Bey of the exchange, the lawyer shook his head sadly and muttered that such an action by the Prime Minister was just about what one would expect—particularly in Egypt.

At the negotiating session held a few days later there was, according to Carter, "a decided anti-current throughout the whole discussion," generated by Pierre Lacau. But, he recounted, Merzbach Bey had "brilliantly carried many, many points through: we were to renounce all rights to a division, but we were to receive a letter wherein the Egyptian Government would undertake to give Countess Carnarvon some duplicates *after* the completion of the work. The vital point now rests in the wording of the letter."

On January 13, eleven months after Carter had gone on strike and the government had forced Carter's locks, installed its own guards and closed the tomb, a one-year authorization was granted Howard Carter by the new Minister of Public Works, Mahmoud Bey Sidky, to continue the work of clearing the tomb as the archaeological agent on behalf of Almina, Countess of Carnarvon, and the executors of Lord Carnarvon's estate. The critical parts of the letter stated:

Being sincerely desirous of seeing this work continue I have no objection to grant the authorisation under the condition . . . always that Almina, Countess of Carnarvon, renounces and causes the executors under the will to renounce every action at law, claim or pretention whatsoever, not only in respect of the Tomb of Tout-Ankh-Amoun and the objects originating therefrom, but also with regard to the cancellation of the authorisation and the measures taken by the Government as a consequence of that cancellation.

Anxious to display its gratitude for this admirable discovery, the Government though recognising *no obligation whatsoever* in respect of the objects found in the tomb, proposed—(following the suggestion made by Mr. Lacau, immediately after the discovery) to give at its own discretion to Almina, Countess of Carnarvon, a choice of duplicates as representative as possible of the discovery provided that such duplicates may be separated from the whole without damage to science.

Before he departed for the Valley of the Kings to go back to the tomb, Carter, under instructions from Ziwar, helped Pierre Lacau with the unpacking of a number of crates containing works of art that had been in storage at the Egyptian Museum during the agonizing controversy. He noted sourly that the members of the Antiquities Service had mishandled everything when they had packed the objects at the tomb. They had tried, among other things, to put the wheels of one chariot onto the body of another. Then, muttering to himself darkly about Egyptian incompetence, Carter concluded his long briefing to Maxwell's attorney with a perception he might better have achieved years before: "*This* makes me inclined to quote Goethe: 'The past is fragile, touch it with awe as if it were red-hot iron.' "

CHAPTER THIRTY-FIVE

The Secret Division

ANOTHER IRONY SURROUNDING the ill-fated tomb and the burning question of the partition of its treasures is that Howard Carter and his patron had already made a division of Tutankhamun's works of art long before Ahmad Pasha Ziwar gave Carter his pledge in January 1925. They had made their choice alone, without permission, when they had total control of the tomb.

For five tortuous years, from the day of the Prime Minister's pledge until 1930, five successive Egyptian governments would come to power and disappear. In 1930, the Nationalists once more would gain political control of Egypt. Virtually the first act of the new "People's" government would be to pass a law forbidding the removal from Egypt of *any* object from the tomb of Tutankhamun—duplicate or otherwise.

But, although the Egyptians never did carry through on their pledge to reward the Carnarvon estate with works of art, they did send Lady Carnarvon, in the autumn of 1930, the sum of £36,000, or, at the exchange rate, $173,000. The figure, which came to nearly the exact amount of Lord Carnarvon's expenses for the dig over the years, was arrived at in an ingenious manner. A group of duplicates were identified by Carter and the Antiquities Service and then appraised by Jean Capart "independently." By coincidence, Capart's evaluation came to the figure of £36,000, which was of course precisely the figure desired by the executors of the Carnarvon estate.

Yet, despite the Nationalists' law, a certain number of treasures from the tomb did leave Egypt—through Carter and Lord Carnarvon. Their action has been, for more than fifty years, one of the best-kept secrets in the history of Egyptology.

One group of objects Howard Carter took from the tomb and away from Egypt is described in his own notes. The objects, which number seventeen in all, eventually made their way into the Metropolitan Museum of Art. Some were purchased by the Metropolitan—either from Lord Carnarvon's estate or from Howard Carter during his lifetime or from Carter's estate in 1940. Others were given by Carter to the museum. With the exception of certain unimportant fragments, which have always been in storage, they have been on public exhibition at one time or another since their acquisition. In all the years the Metropolitan has possessed these objects, though, the museum has never publicly acknowledged their provenance.

A handful were apparently taken by Carter for purely scientific analysis: a cupful of dried-out embalming fluid; two fragments of gilded wood from the fourth shrine; a piece of crumbling linen from the majestic funerary pall; other linens from a large sack dropped between the outer and second shrines; fragments of matting that covered the floor of the Burial Chamber; and a piece of quartzite from the rose-colored sarcophagus.

Nine other pieces are far more significant. There are two beautiful finger rings of blue faience decorated with the cartouche of Tutankhamun's throne name, Nebkheperura. These were purchased by the Metropolitan in 1926 from Lord Carnarvon's estate. Carter's note states that they were found on the floor of the Antechamber—just where, he did not say.

Two slender silver nails, one from the Carnarvon collection and the other from Howard Carter's, are described in the catalogue cards of the Metropolitan as having come from the second coffin of the King. Two other royal nails, in solid gold, came from the third coffin. A marvelous rosette in bronze, gilded, from the pall was bought by the museum directly from

Howard Carter in 1935. There is also an elegant broad collar made of blue faience beads described by the museum as coming from the floor of the Antechamber. Finally, there is a splendid little bronze puppy, with its head swung back as if hearing a sudden call from its master—recorded by the museum as also having been removed from the floor of the Antechamber. Although attractive, none of these works can in any way be described as vitally important or unique pieces of Egyptian art, with the possible exception of the broad collar and the puppy. Considering the thousands of masterpieces from Tutankhamun's tomb that remained in the country in the Egyptian Museum, their unauthorized removal amounts to no more than a minor archaeological indiscretion.

There are, however, ten works of art in the Metropolitan's Egyptian collection which are described in the catalogue cards as "probably from the tomb of Tutankhamun, but not positively identified in Carter's list." They are masterworks in any lexicon of ancient Egyptian art.

The first is a solid-gold ring, engraved with Tutankhamun's throne name, presented to the museum as early as December 1922 by Edward Harkness of the Metropolitan's board. Notes in the Egyptian Department's files, compiled by Winlock, state that the splendid gold ring had been on the art market in Cairo since 1915—years before the discovery! No doubt the ring had been given to Harkness by either Lord Carnarvon or Howard Carter as a superb token of their discovery. It might also have been given in gratitude for the "splendid" acts of cooperation demonstrated by the Metropolitan's decision to send the most important members of its Egyptian expedition to assist Carter.

Another superior object at the Metropolitan probably from the tomb is a fragmentary handle of a golden fan or scepter inlaid masterfully with pieces of carnelian, lapis lazuli and green feldspar which are set into a series of horizontal chevrons. The decorations are so minute and delicate that it is difficult to fathom how the ancient jeweler could possibly have fashioned them without the aid of modern eyeglasses or magnifying equipment. The small piece is so close in style and technique to the inlaid portion of the king's scepter found in the Burial Chamber that one can be well assured that it did come from the tomb.

Two delicate cosmetic boxes of ivory, painted and carved in the form of dressed ducks with supple necks curled back right and left to the shoulders, are catalogued as probably from the tomb of Tutankhamun and were purchased from the Carter estate in 1940. In style and aesthetic quality these fanciful ducks are almost identical to a pair of boxes found in the Annex. They are also similar to the ducks carved on the feet of the ivory-and-ebony folding stool, decorated with a stylized leopard skin, which was removed during the first weeks of Carter's work in the Antechamber.

A painted ivory hound, running vigorously, with a movable lower jaw and a collar fitted out for a leash—perhaps a toy owned by the young Prince—was purchased from Carter's estate in 1940. This fine object, frequently on exhibition, has always been linked by the museum in its files to Tutankhamun's tomb, but has never been publicly identified as such.

Another object of beauty in the possession of the museum is a superb alabaster perfume jar about three inches high. This piece, acquired from Carter's estate in 1940, is a masterpiece of carving—almost perfect in symmetry and execution. It has the rare feature of a series of appliqués in carnelian, midnight-black obsidian, purple and blue glass, and gold leaf, features seldom found in Egyptian art outside of the Tutankhamun treasures. The vase is decorated with the image of the most tender of servant girls, standing upon a lotus blossom— her dark-brown skin contrasting marvelously with the translucent creamy tones of the vase itself. The museum's notes assert that the object is of the style of Thebes and is "probably" from the tomb of Tutankhamun.

Two other works of art likely to be from the tomb, according to the museum's files, are a paint palette and an ivory writing palette, from the Carnarvon estate. The latter is furnished with four balls of paint and a pair of reed brushes. On the sliding cover of the slot containing the brushes there is an inscription in hieroglyphs which states: "The King's Daughter of his

Body, his beloved Meretaton, born of the Great Royal Wife Nefernefraton Nefertiti, who lives forever and ever." These must have belonged to the sister or stepsister of Tutankhamun's young wife, Ankhesenamun. In 1926, when Albert Lythgoe was helping Carter pack up the Carnarvon collection for shipment to the Metropolitan, he happened to ask Carter where he thought the pieces had come from. Carter's response was, "The tomb of Amenhotep." But that seems unlikely, since Carter had discovered that tomb, containing only a few objects, in 1915, and the palette and the writing instruments did not come into Carnarvon's possession until 1923.

The final two works of art attributed by the Metropolitan as probably from Tutankhamun's tomb are pieces of surpassing beauty. They have always been considered among the most cherished objects in the vast Egyptian collections of the museum and are generally thought to be preeminent of all masterworks of small scale that have come down to us from pharaonic times.

One is the leaping figure of a horse of painted ivory, with reddish-brown skin and black mane. The eyes of the majestic creature were inset garnets, one of which remains. The horse seems less a horse than a sort of "hippic" bird, flying through the air with an elegant yet strong movement—balanced and sure. The head of the figure is raised at an angle that bespeaks supreme confidence. The forelegs of the royal beast flank an ivory pipe, probably the fitting for a thin whip. The back legs lightly touch an ivory orb. When the horse is turned to an upright position, it seems to transform itself into some sort of heraldic animal, prancing on the surface of the world. Its character changes delightfully as it is turned in one's hand.

The other object is also ivory, painted with a delicacy that reminds one of the talents of a master miniaturist of the Italian Renaissance. It is an African gazelle, or ariel. Barely six inches high, this creature has been endowed with the breath of life itself. Alert—thin strong legs stiff, tail curled up tightly, its head cocked in a position of watchfulness—the diminutive animal stands upon an ivory base painted to look like a desert

353

crag with flowers. The creature seems ready to wheel quickly at the slightest sign of danger and flee to safety. How so much implied motion could have been instilled into an inert piece of ivory is almost incomprehensible. Yet there it stands, quivering with vitality.

The records of the Metropolitan state that these two lovely animals, neither of which has any royal marking, were part of the purchase in 1926 from the Carnarvon collection and may have come from Tutankhamun's tomb. The catalogue of that group of objects, compiled personally by Lord Carnarvon with information supplied by Howard Carter, states that both works are supreme examples of the highest moment of the free, naturalistic sculptural style of the late Eighteenth Dynasty from the royal workshops of Thebes—the style, that is to say, of Tutankhamun. Do these exquisite creatures really come from his tomb? It is entirely likely.

The evidence appears in a private letter from Lord Carnarvon to Howard Carter sent from Highclere to the Valley of the Kings on December 24, 1922—less than a month after the evening the two companions had surreptitiously entered the tomb chambers. When he wrote the letter, Carnarvon was obviously in an ebullient frame of mind; his wry humor was at its best. He described to Carter the variety of people who had come to his estate to congratulate him—heads of political parties, lords, ladies, distinguished individuals from all walks of life, including the most important of them all, the "Jockey Denoghull!" Then he wrote that he had "put the ariel and horse— *bought in Cairo*—into the wall case. They look very well. I have, after mature examination, decided that they are *early* 18th Dynasty and *must* come from the Saqqareh."

It is a purely Egyptological joke. To have said that the two sculptures are, after "mature examination" (in itself a private humorous exchange between the two men), deemed to be *early* Eighteenth Dynasty from Saqqara—a locality which had not been used by Egyptian kings since the Fifth Dynasty, fully one thousand years before Tutankhamun—was akin to saying that one of Carnarvon's prized Vandykes was, "after mature examination," thought to be a portrait of a gentleman painted during the lifetime of Tutankhamun.

The words *"bought in Cairo"* were apparently inserted into the text as a final witticism. In a letter from Carnarvon to Carter two days earlier, his lordship inquired whether or not Carter would find "much more unmarked stuff" in the tomb. Both ivories indeed have no royal emblem. But in style, material and quality they are similar to other objects found in the tomb of Tutankhamun, and only there.

The Metropolitan was not alone among museums where some of the treasures from Tutankhamun's tomb found a home. In the early 1940s, four superb pieces were added to the already excellent Egyptian collections of the Brooklyn Museum: a diminutive ivory girl standing upon a blue faience base; a broad collar in blue faience; a delicate ointment spoon carved from ivory; and a tiny vase of blue glass. They were purchased from a London dealer who had bought them from the estate of Howard Carter.

The Brooklyn Museum has been, since their acquisition, a bit cautious about identifying these gems as positively having come from the Tutankhamun sanctuary. But in the opening paragraphs of an article in that museum's bulletin issued in the fall of 1948, John Cooney, the curator of Egyptian art, mentions the pieces in connection with Howard Carter, Tutankhamun and an important royal tomb of the late Eighteenth Dynasty. When queried in early 1978 as to whether the beautiful objects came from Tutankhamun's tomb, a member of the Egyptian Department's staff remarked, simply, "Where else?" John Cooney, who recommended the purchase of the pieces for the Brooklyn Museum and who is now the curator of ancient art at the Cleveland Museum of Art, is convinced that they were part of the fabulous treasure. Stylistically, the four works of art at Brooklyn possess the exact same delicacy and perfection, similar to but surpassing the finest work of the nineteenth-century Russian master, Fabergé, as the pieces at the Metropolitan and those in the Tutankhamun collection of the Egyptian Museum.

One other Egyptian object at Brooklyn, on loan since 1947 from the Guennol Collection, has always been linked to the Tutankhamun treasures. This is a small ivory carving of a grasshopper so deftly fashioned that the insect seems about to take flight. The splendid grasshopper was sold to the Guennol Collection by a New York art dealer, Joseph Brummer, who had purchased it from the estate of Howard Carter.

In addition to the Metropolitan and Brooklyn, three other museums in the United States possess treasures that may come from the tomb. There is a small amulet in the form of a cat fashioned from black hematite in the Cleveland Museum of Art, acquired less than five years ago by John Cooney, who can trace the provenance back to Howard Carter, who presumably removed it from the tomb. A number of elements of inlaid gold from a royal necklace are today in the collection of the William Rockhill Nelson Art Gallery in Kansas City. These objects were given by Carter to his physician and described by him as coming from the tomb. The physician sold the gold to a London dealer from whom the Nelson Gallery acquired them.

One of the finest objects of Egyptian art in any American collection is a magnificent bronze panther with rock crystal eyes, stalking its prey with its tail up alertly and the splendid head turned to one side. This marvelous creature is today in the Cincinnati Art Museum. It was once in Howard Carter's collection and in all likelihood came from the Tutankhamun sanctuary.

There are at least a half-dozen other objects that appear to have been removed from the tomb by the excavators. One, however, never left Egypt. It is a golden ornament, either an epaulet or a buckle of some sort, showing the young King dashing headlong in his war chariot, fashioned in part with droplets of pure gold, as if infinitesimal golden seeds had been dusted over the object. This ornament was presented in 1952 to the Egyptian Museum by King Farouk, just months before his abdication and flight from Egypt. One assumes that this superb piece of decorative art had been given by Lord Carnarvon to Farouk's father, King Fuad, who then passed it on to his feckless son with instructions that it should eventually go to the Egyptian Museum. King Farouk also appears to have been the conduit to the Egyptian Museum of four or five other Tutankhamun objects removed by Howard Carter and taken to England. His will specified that the pieces—rings in gold and faience—be bequeathed to his niece, Phyllis Walker. When she learned that the cartouches on the jewelry were those of the world-famous Pharaoh, she was appalled and, through the executor of Carter's estate, handed the rings over to Farouk. Just before his abdication, the monarch presented the objects to the Egyptian Museum and was thoroughly criticized for his unauthorized possession of works of art.

Although one can easily understand why the excavators took the objects they appear to have removed from the tomb, their common sense in doing so must be questioned. If their actions had been discovered by the authorities, their concession would promptly have been put in jeopardy. But one must remember that, at the moment of discovery, the excavators, in their own minds, "owned" the tomb.

In 1926, the Egyptian Department staff of the Metropolitan was surprised, and delighted, to learn that the entire Carnarvon collection with its Tutankhamun objects could be acquired. The collection had not seemed a bargain—the price of $145,000 in those years was a fortune. For a while, though, it seemed as if the works of art would never come to the Metropolitan at all, since Lord Carnarvon's will specified that the treasures had to be offered for sale first to the British Museum. But the executors of the estate apparently dealt with that provision in his lordship's will very effectively.

One of the solicitors of the estate arrived without prior word at the office of the director of the British Museum one morning at ten o'clock and offered him the entire contents of the Carnarvon Egyptian collection as a purchase. The director would have been delighted had not the solicitor softly added that the museum had until four o'clock that very day to make the decision and the payment. At the British Museum in those days, and now, a purchase of such magnitude was normally pondered for weeks—even months. And so the Carnarvon collection of Egyptian antiquities came to New York City.

Several years after the purchase, when Herbert Winlock met the curator of Egyptian art at the British Museum on routine business, the subject of the Carnarvon collection somehow came up. "Ah, yes, the Carnarvon collection," Winlock said with a sheepish smile. He paused and suddenly patted his side pocket. "You know—it was really only a *pocket* collection."

When Howard Carter returned to the Valley of the Kings on January 25, 1925, he was ceremoniously handed a duplicate set of keys to the tomb and the laboratory. He immediately made an inspection of the contents of the Burial Chamber with Pierre Lacau. He paused for a few minutes to gaze through the protective glass at the radiant visage of the youthful monarch on the outer coffin, feeling a sense of profound mystery— haunting forces still clung to the tomb. Carter then made a tour of the Treasury. Nothing had been moved, nothing changed. He expressed his satisfaction to Lacau, who quietly nodded and in a low voice told Carter how pleased he was to have him back. It was a brief, private, emotional moment.

From that day on, through eight full years of painstaking work, carried out, as before, in the debilitating heat, wind and dust of the valley, Howard Carter seldom manifested the dark, impulsive side of his character. Now that he was immersed once more in the systematic duties of pure archaeology, his attentive and sensitive nature became dominant. No longer did minor interferences annoy him. And issues which formerly had devoured him seemed not to concern him at all.

Herbert Winlock was pleasantly surprised by the transformation of the former black knight of the valley. In 1926 he wrote Edward Robinson that the most pleasing aspect of the season had been his warm relations with their "friend, H.C." He related how they had "started out chumily" the first day. Despite the fact that Carter had just unwrapped the King's mummy and had been through a considerable strain, "with a mixed bag of natives and French around him telling him what to do at every turn," he had been balanced and in good humor. Winlock, accompanied by his wife and their two children, would see Carter on many evenings for dinner, driving up in the museum's old car, which, as Winlock pointed out, "I can nearly make climb a telegraph pole."

Yet Howard Carter had not suddenly become a saint. As Winlock observed, at times, "of course, he was the same old H.C. . . . and [during] the fear of certain complications, he pulled off some pretty raw things." But, Winlock stated, when the tension had worn off—and it had done so quickly—he had calmed down and "really [became] far more likable than at any time since the finding of Tutankhamun." Working alone or with Alfred Lucas, who was staying with him at his house in the valley, Carter was "incomparable." "He is a wonderfully neat worker," Winlock wrote, "and with his fingers of an artist, there is no better person to whom this delicate stuff could have been entrusted."

Carter's first task upon once again resuming his work was to raise the lid of the gilded coffin he had discovered a year before. It was enormous—seven feet, four inches long—fashioned in wood entirely covered with sheet gold beaten into a magnificent portrait of the King as the god Osiris. Surrounding the deity was a series of feathered decorations in gold. How many coffins, Carter wondered, would eventually emerge? Would the sacred jewelry described in certain ancient texts really be inside? As Carter raised the great lid, it was a magical moment for him—indeed, for the entire world. No one in history had ever embarked on such a journey as the one Carter was just beginning: the patient and scientific probe downward through the undisturbed funerary paraphernalia of a pharaoh.

With great difficulty, Carter carefully removed the lid of the first coffin. He found, within, what looked like a second coffin, covered with fine linen shrouds and decked with garlands of flowers. The shrouds were rolled back, and Carter gazed upon "the finest example of the ancient coffinmaker's art ever yet seen." The lid of the second coffin, like the first, depicted the young King as Osiris. But it was far more splendid in quality. The second coffin was six feet, eight inches long, fashioned of thick gold foil richly inlaid with engraved glass simulating red jasper, lapis and turquoise.

Carter decided to lift all the remaining coffins from the stone sarcophagus so that he could work more easily. When it came time to remove the whole group, Carter was astounded at their weight. It took eight men at full strength to maneuver the pieces out of the sarcophagus.

When the lid of the second coffin was plucked off, yet another human image came to Carter's excited eyes. This, too, was obscured by a film of gossamer linen shrouds. When he folded back the fabric and the elaborate bead and floral collar surrounding the neck, a breathtaking sight came to view. The third coffin, over six feet in length, was fashioned from solid gold—half an inch thick in parts. It was, to Carter, an "absolutely incredible mass of pure bullion."

The resplendent object was covered with the most exquisite reliefs portraying the goddesses Isis and Nephthys and the winged figures of Nekhbet and the snake Buto. The ensemble was superimposed with gorgeous inlays of semiprecious stones and cloisonné work of glass and faience. Carter had expected something rare, but he was completely overwhelmed by such magnificence. "How great," he wrote, "must have been the wealth buried with those ancient Pharaohs! What riches that Valley must have once concealed!" No wonder the ancient thieves had risked their lives to penetrate the tombs of the twenty-seven monarchs who had been buried in the valley.

Carter removed the awesome lid of the third coffin, and there lay the mummy of the King, bound up by a corselet of gold and inlay—impressive, neat and carefully made. Shining magnificently against the somber background of linens was a life-sized gold mask of the King. Gazing down upon the image of the young Tutankhamun, Carter found that his emotions utterly eluded verbal expression. Thirty-two hundred years had passed since men's eyes had looked into the deep, dark eyes of the young Pharaoh. "Time," said Carter, "measured by the brevity of human life, seemed to lose its common perspectives before a spectacle so vividly recalling the solemn religious rites of a vanished civilisation."

The golden mask was inlaid with blue glass simulating lapis lazuli. It was adorned with a ceremonial beard and surrounded by a headdress fitted out with the images of the vulture and the sacred cobra. The King's mask is radiantly—divinely—handsome, but at the same time carries a sad, almost calm expression of youth overtaken by early death. Looked at a dozen times, a hundred times, the mask seems to reveal each time a different character—at times wistful, at times strong, at times serene. It is surely one of the most beautiful portraits in the history of mankind.

A corselet of gold and inlay surrounded the linen wrappings of the mummy and was covered with inscriptions, which consisted of words of welcome from the gods to Tutankhamun as he passed into a blissful, eternal afterlife:

I reckon your beauties, O Osiris, King Nebkheperura,
Your soul lives! Your veins are firm!

Your stability is in the mouth of the living, O
Osiris, King Tutankhamun.

Your heart is in your body eternally.

Once the mummy had been revealed, Carter embarked upon a most unusual journey—a sort of dig within a dig through layer after layer of wrappings. He descended through an abundance of rotted linens lavishly doused with ointments, unguents and natron for mummification. Ironically, owing to their very profusion, the preservatives had brought about a greater degree of deterioration.

With scalpels honed to the sharpest edge, Carter, assisted by Dr. Douglas Derry, professor of anatomy at the Egyptian University, painstakingly sliced through the stiffened linen of the first layer, to reveal a virtual treasure of gold. On the left side of the body lay the royal diadem, decorated with the wriggling body of a sacred cobra. The King's throat was surrounded by a golden pectoral, membrane-thin, depicting the all-protecting god Horus. In the second layer, set in a gold belt, were a knife and a scabbard, both of pure gold. The scabbard is decorated with superb reliefs of a hunt. It must have been one of the King's dearest possessions.

On the two desiccated arms, crossed one on top of the other, lay a treasury of bracelets—thirteen in all. As Carter probed ever more deeply, he unearthed one of the most splendid works of art of the entire tomb, a chest-sized gold-and-glass hawk pectoral comprised of hundreds of pieces of inlay. Below that, he came across another massive enameled pectoral, almost a foot wide, portraying the vulture goddess, Nekhbet, made of hundreds of inlaid stones and glass, surely one of the most beautiful examples of jewelry to have survived from antiquity.

Carter was astounded to find that after cutting through all thirteen layers of wrappings he had unearthed no fewer than 143 magnificent pieces of jewelry, ornaments, amulets and implements.

Finally, the shrunken body of the King himself was exposed. Carter must have been amazed. It was poorly preserved—pitiful. The body was naked but for three decorations: the toes were encased in gold sheaths, as were the fingers and the King's penis.

The removal of the last linen obscuring the face of the King needed the most exacting care. With fine sable brushes the last few fragments of decayed fabric were brushed aside. The face of Tutankhamun himself was finally revealed. To Howard Carter, the royal visage was placid, the features well formed. The King must have been handsome beyond belief. As he held the head in his hands, Carter was suddenly transported to the time when the young, vibrant King still lived. He was profoundly shaken by the experience.

By the end of February 1932, Howard Carter had removed the last objects from the tomb of Tutankhamun and supervised their transfer to the Egyptian Museum in Cairo. A little less than ten years had elapsed from the day he made the most remarkable archaeological discovery in world history. By November of the following year, he had completed the third and final volume of what Lord Carnarvon had, a decade earlier, called "The Book"—*The Tomb of Tut-ank-Amen.* In every respect the best of the three volumes, it describes—with poetic insights into the aesthetic nature of the objects and their religious significance—his technique of clearing the objects from the Treasury and the Annex.

The Treasury was small, measuring no more than fifteen by twelve feet. The very scale and simplicity of the room made Carter feel that "impressive memories of the past" had been preserved in it. When he entered that chamber for the first time, he felt "almost like a desecrator to have . . . broken the eternal silence" hanging over it. "Even the most insensitive person," he wrote, "passing this inviolate threshold, must surely feel awe and wonder distilled from the secrets and shadows of that *Tremendous Past.*"

The Treasury differed markedly from the larger rooms, the Antechamber and the Annex, which had been stuffed with a random sampling of royal possessions. This inner room, Carter decided, was virtually a chapel for the King, containing objects which were almost all fundamentally religious in character.

The choicest object in the Treasury was, of course, the gilded and painted wooden canopic shrine surrounded by the four little figures of Isis, Nephthys, Neith and Selket. To Carter, all objects in the Treasury formed a "coherent and recondite whole" around the shrine. Each one had a mystical potency.

The ominous black boxes that had so intrigued him at first turned out to be filled with statuettes of the King in varying activities. There were also a number of gilded wooden statuettes comprising the entire pantheon of the gods and goddesses of ancient Egypt.

Some of the statuettes of the King are breathtaking. One surpasses all others. It portrays the youngster hunting from a small sampanlike boat. He holds a harpoon in one hand and a coil of cord used to retrieve it in the other. It is an image of such free athletic movement, of such strength and vitality, of such physical, smooth motion that one is amazed to recall that this splendid piece was made some seven hundred years before even the beginnings of Greek art and fully one thousand years before the supreme achievement of Greek art in organic form.

When he dismantled the wooden canopy and chest of the shrine, Carter found a large boxlike object wrapped in a black linen shroud. He removed the covering. There lay a solid alabaster inner shrine carved on each corner with the four guardian goddesses. The glistening surfaces of the stone had been delicately painted. Carter removed the lid and discovered four identical portrait heads of the King, facing each other exactly east and west, where the sun rises and sets. When the heads were removed, Carter beheld a strange apparition: four circular wells, with a small ribbed object inside each. When he extracted the objects, Carter experienced the same thrill as when he had found the three gold coffins. For each turned out to be a miniature coffin, six inches high—fashioned in solid gold, inlaid with colored glass and semiprecious stones, and decorated with a diminutive portrait of Tutankhamun. Inside, each was inscribed with spells and incantations against evil forces, and each held one of the King's vital organs, mummified and swathed in yards of linen.

Carter unearthed some surprising and mysterious things in the Treasury. He found two small anthropoid coffins, clearly intended for individuals of the highest rank. Inside, he discovered the mummified remains of two stillborn children, both girls. The pathetic remains gave Carter much food for thought. He had no doubt they were children of Tutankhamun and Ankhesenamun. Had they died by chance, or by some terrible plan? Carter did not know.

But among all the objects, caskets and boxes in the Treasury,

Carter found not a shred of historical information. By the time he reached the fourth chamber, the Annex, his hopes for finding written documentation casting light upon the murky historical circumstances surrounding Tutankhamun's reign were dashed. From this final room, Carter extracted hundreds of magnificent "bedsteads, chairs, footstools, hassocks, gameboards, baskets of dried-out fruits, every kind of alabaster vessel and pottery wine jars, boxes of funerary figures, toys, shields, bows and arrows, and other missiles, all turned topsy-turvy." But not a single document.

Some of the treasures in the Annex surpassed all else in the tomb. There was a marvelous "chair of state" richly ornamented with a mosaic of ebony and different-shaped pieces of ivory. The chair was fitted out with a footstool carved with the image of nine bound prisoners. But of all works of art in the Annex, the finest to Carter's mind were the alabasters. On the floor of the cluttered chamber, almost unscathed, stood an alabaster boat floating in an ornamented tank, with a princess sitting at the bow. Another alabaster depicted a lion standing upright, phallus erect, his great paw held up in the air as if in salute. The vase which had originally surmounted the lion's head lay some feet away, knocked down by one of the thieves.

It was in the Annex, toward the twilight of his labors, that Carter found one of the most outstanding works of all. It was a chest made of wood, covered with ivory, painted and stained, superbly carved by an unknown master whose achievement stands as one of the most stunning in ancient times. On the chest the King and the Queen are depicted casually, intimately, in a style very much akin to that of the Akhenaton period. Under a banner, richly bedecked in festoons of flowers, the King stretches his hand to receive from his Queen two bouquets of lotus, papyrus and poppies. She is his devoted companion, offering her husband pleasure for eternity. Examining the couple, so elegant, lithe and young, makes it all the more frustrating that so little is known about them.

To Carter, Tutankhamun was a "mere stripling" of eighteen

365

or nineteen when he died, possibly of tuberculosis, who had married Ankhesenamun, one of Nefertiti's daughters, at the age of eleven, and had done little in his nine-year reign. He had been merely a young, possibly frivolous boy king, unaffected by affairs of state, who had simply enjoyed the delights made available to him in his maturing teens. He had hunted and fished on a hundred plains and the length of the Nile. He had gathered around himself the most stunning collection of jewelry that any ruler in history had probably ever accumulated. He had surrounded himself with rare, vivacious works of art, furniture and royal regalia. But to Howard Carter, Tutankhamun's life was an illusion—"the shadows move but the dark is never quite uplifted."

Shortly after he completed his work on the tomb, in the spring of 1932, Howard Carter returned to England. There, early in 1933, he fell sick, and during the next six years he never seemed to regain his health. Although he returned to Egypt several times, he never again embarked upon an excavation. On March 2, 1939, in his mid-sixties, he died. Only a handful of people attended his funeral, among them Lady Evelyn Herbert Beauchamp.

Who was Howard Carter? What had he really done? Dedicated, a man of awesome courage, energetic, obsessed with system, driven by ambition, he accomplished something which no one before him had been able to do or even conceive of doing. Yet, impetuous, stubborn, insensitive, tactless, deceitful and mendacious at times, Howard Carter undermined his achievements and tortured himself and others throughout his entire life.

In more than one way, Carter experienced failure with Tutankhamun. He never completed his work. Aside from his three-volume *The Tomb of Tut-ank-Amen*, written for the general public, Carter never published a serious study on even the most minute part of the extraordinary treasures. In his lack of deep interest in scholarship he was much like his favorite archaeologist, the flamboyant Giovanni Belzoni. Perhaps the

a letter to the King of the Hittites: "My husband is dead. I am told that you have grown-up sons. Send me one of them and I will make him my husband and he shall be King over Egypt."

The Hittite King was cautious: "Where is the son of the late King?"

Ankhesenamun answered: "Why should I deceive you? I have no son and my husband is dead. Send me a son of yours and I will make him King."

At that precise place the tablets are broken. Nothing more is known. The dialogue might signify the last desperate maneuverings of a lonely, frightened queen. But one Egyptologist has observed that in ancient times one simply would never have considered the possibility of initiating such a royal liaison without diplomatic foundations. Is it not at least possible that Tutankhamun, like his illustrious forefather Thutmose III, had conducted a successful campaign against the Hittites and had made a treaty, which his widowed Queen had then tried to build upon? Perhaps one will never know.

Yet, in some unexpected place, hidden in the Valley of the Kings, still to be discovered by an heir to Howard Carter's dream and ambition, on a scrap of linen or upon a fragment of pottery, or perhaps on a few rolls of papyri or the surface of shattered stones, further revelations may emerge. Until then, there will always be doubts, questions, controversies about that "Strong Bull, Beautiful of Birth." Shrouded in silence, surrounded by profound mystery, Tutankhamun has ensured himself a more compelling fascination than most rulers of ancient times. And he has achieved the ultimate victory—a continuing and secure afterlife. His confident words, written upon the last shrine surrounding his great sarcophagus, ring true: "I have seen yesterday; I know tomorrow."

Sources

The primary sources for each chapter are described in brief.

INTRODUCTION
The letters relating to the role of Charles Evans Hughes and Allen Dulles are on file in the archives of the Metropolitan Museum of Art.

CHAPTER 1
For the information on Howard Carter's problems with the Antiquities Service in 1903, and Sir Gaston Maspero's handling of the situation, I am indebted to I. E. S. Edwards, Curator Emeritus of the Department of Egyptian Art at the British Museum.

CHAPTER 2
For Howard Carter's personal feelings about the mysterious valley, I relied upon Arthur Merton's interview with Carter in the London *Times* at the beginning of the first season.

CHAPTER 3
For the material on the thieves of Kurna, I utilized the information in Carter's Volume I of the *The Tomb of Tut-ank-Amen*.

CHAPTER 4
For the information on Jacob Rogers, I am indebted to the Metropolitan Museum of Art.

CHAPTER 5
The primary sources are mentioned in the body of the text.

CHAPTER 6
The briefing paper of January 1922, from Albert Lythgoe to J. Merton Howell, came from the files of the Egyptian Department of the Metropolitan Museum of Art. A copy was sent to Edward Robinson, Director of the museum, and from him to the Board of Trustees.

The information concerning Carter's role as an "advisor on art" to Calouste Gulbenkian comes from a letter from Carter to Gulbenkian in the Egyptian Department of the Metropolitan Museum of Art.

CHAPTER 7
The information about the discovery of the first step came from unpublished notes of 1924, the unpublished memoirs of Lee Keedick, President of the Keedick Lecture Bureau, and was supplied to me by his son Robert.

CHAPTER 8
The primary sources are listed in the body of the text.

CHAPTER 9
The information about the entry into the Antechamber by Carter, Lord Carnarvon, Lady Evelyn Herbert and "Pecky" Callender comes from an unpublished news account written by Lord Carnarvon shortly after November 26, 1922, in the files of the Egyptian Department of the Metropolitan Museum of Art.
The story of Lady Evelyn first seeing the alabaster vases was recounted to me by her daughter, Mrs. Thomas Leatham.

CHAPTER 10
The reference to the entry of Howard Carter, Lord Carnarvon and Lady Evelyn Herbert into the Holy of Holies—the Burial Chamber—appears in an unpublished letter from Evelyn Herbert to Howard Carter in December 1922, in the files of the Egyptian Department of the Metropolitan Museum of Art.

CHAPTER 11
The primary sources are mentioned in the body of the text.

CHAPTER 12
The story on the entry into the Antechamber by Herbert Winlock's daughter Frances was told to me by Herbert Winlock's surviving daughter.

CHAPTER 13
The Treasure of the Three Princesses is mentioned in a letter from Lord Carnarvon to Howard Carter dated December 16, 1922, on file in the Egyptian Department of the Metropolitan Museum of Art.
The information regarding the discovery of the Treasure of the Three Princesses, the role of Carter and Carnarvon, the negotiations between them and the Metropolitan Museum of Art, and the financial arrangements are contained in letters on file in the Egyptian Department of the Metropolitan Museum of Art. The file is sizable, containing over fifty pieces of correspondence, notes and documents. Particularly significant are the following: Mackay's "Interim Report" dated August 1916; a report from Howard Carter to Edward Robinson, 1917; a letter from Albert Lythgoe to Herbert Winlock, June 1920; a letter from Herbert Winlock to Edward Robinson dated March 1920; a letter from Herbert Winlock to Albert Lythgoe dated March 1921; and a letter from Winlock to Lythgoe dated March 1922.

CHAPTER 14
The source for the information regarding Lord Carnarvon's attitude about the discovery was found in a letter from Carnarvon to Howard Carter of December 24, 1922, on file in the Egyptian Department of the Metropolitan Museum of Art.
The information about Albert Lythgoe's dealings with Lord Carnarvon in London appears in letters from Lythgoe to Edward Robinson dated December 20 and December 23, 1922, on file in the Egyptian Department of the Metropolitan Museum of Art.

CHAPTER 15
The information regarding *The Times* of London and its attempts to secure an exclusive arrangement from Howard Carter appears in a letter from Arthur Merton to Sir Campbell of the London *Times* dated December 24, 1922.

The information that Carter was trying to secure the best press offers appears in a cable to Lord Carnarvon dated December 29, 1922, on file in the Egyptian Department of the Metropolitan Museum of Art.

The information that Carter sought to establish an informal auction for press rights appears in a letter from Lord Carnarvon to Howard Carter dated January 10, 1923, on file in the Egyptian Department of the Metropolitan Museum of Art.

The story of Geoffrey Dawson's visit to Lord Carnarvon and Sir Alan Gardiner's reaction to the offer of the London *Times* was recounted to me by I. E. S. Edwards, Curator Emeritus of the Department of Egyptian Art at the the British Museum.

The sources for the story of Lord Carnarvon's interest in the media and film appears in a letter from Lord Carnarvon to Howard Carter dated December 24, 1922, on file in the Egyptian Department of the Metropolitan Museum of Art.

The information on the film treatment was written by a representative of Goldwyn, Ltd., and appears in a draft outline from an anonymous writer of Goldwyn, Ltd., to Carnarvon dated February 23, 1923, on file in the archives of the London *Times*.

The information relating to the offers from the press, the book on Tutankhamun, the issue of the copyright of photographic prints, and the watercolor of the best object in the tomb appear in a letter from Lord Carnarvon to Howard Carter dated January 10, 1923, on file in the Egyptian Department of the Metropolitan Museum of Art.

The references by Lord Carnarvon to Howard Carter's having a difficult time with the press just before the public announcement of the contract with the London *Times* appear in the above-cited letter.

The information regarding Arthur Merton's acceptance of Carter's request to join the staff of the excavation appears in a letter from Merton to Carter dated January 10, 1923, in the archives of the London *Times*.

The story of the opposition press appears in a memo written between January 10 and January 17, 1923, by Arthur Merton to the editor of the London *Times*, on file in the archives of the London *Times*.

CHAPTER 16

The letter from Rex Engelbach to Howard Carter attempting to humor Carter is dated December 24, 1922, and is on file in the Egyptian Department of the Metropolitan Museum of Art.

The information regarding Lord Carnarvon's intention to be firm with the Egyptian Service of Antiquities appears in a letter from Lord Carnarvon to Howard Carter of around January 25, 1923, on file in the Egyptian Department of the Metropolitan Museum of Art.

The reconstruction of the heated discussions between Arthur Weigall and Howard Carter is based upon a letter from Weigall to Carter, dated January 25, 1923, on file in the Egyptian Department of the Metropolitan Museum of Art.

CHAPTER 17

The description of the life-sized statue of the King appears in notes by Howard Carter on file in the Egyptian Department of the Metropolitan Museum of Art.

The information regarding Sir Alan Gardiner's observation on the "papyri" is contained in an unpublished memo in the Egyptian Department of the Metropolitan Museum of Art.

CHAPTER 18

The information regarding Arthur Mace's observation on the restoration work appears in memos on file in the Egyptian Department of the Metropolitan Museum of Art.

The information regarding Albert Lythgoe's annoyance at Bradstreet's stories in *The New York Times* appears in a letter from Lythgoe to Edward Robinson dated February 25, 1923, on file in the Egyptian Department of the Metropolitan Museum of Art.

The source for Albert Lythgoe's observation that Carter was "buried under it all" is a letter from Lythgoe to Edward Robinson dated February 26, 1923, on file in the Egyptian Department of the Metropolitan Museum of Art.

CHAPTER 19

Herbert Winlock's list of the witnesses to the "opening" of the Burial Chamber is on file in the Egyptian Department of the Metropolitan Museum of Art.

The story of Howard Carter's leaking of spurious information about the contents of the Burial Chamber appears in a memo from Arthur Merton to the editor of the London *Times* on February 19 or 20, 1923, on file in the archives of the London *Times*.

Carter's description of the triple-lotus alabaster vase appears in a memo of Albert Lythgoe dated February 19 in the files of the Egyptian Department of the Metropolitan Museum of Art.

CHAPTER 20

The information concerning Albert Lythgoe's discussions with the Queen of the Belgians and Lord Allenby appears in a letter from Lythgoe to Edward Robinson dated February 20, 1923, on file in the Egyptian Department of the Metropolitan Museum of Art.

CHAPTER 21

The observations of Albert Lythgoe about the tomb just prior to its closing appear in a letter from Lythgoe to his wife on file in the Egyptian Department of the Metropolitan Museum of Art.

Carter's quotations on the tomb immediately before its closing appear in stories by Arthur Merton in the London *Times* written on February 26 and 27, 1923.

CHAPTER 22

Lord Carnarvon's comments regarding the mummy of Tutankhamun appear in a story filed by Arthur Merton and published in the London *Times* on February 23, 1923.

The apologetic letter from Lord Carnarvon to Howard Carter is dated February 23, 1923, and is on file in the Egyptian Department of the Metropolitan Museum of Art.

The letter from Albert Lythgoe to Howard Carter regarding Lord Carnarvon's condition is dated March 20, 1923, and is on file in the Egyptian Department of the Metropolitan Museum of Art.

The letter from Richard Bethel to Howard Carter warning him about the ill health of Lord Carnarvon is dated March 26, 1923, and is on file in the Egyptian Department of the Metropolitan Museum of Art.

CHAPTER 23

Winlock's tally of the so-called victims of the "curse" appears in an undated memo of 1934 on file in the Egyptian Department of the Metropolitan Museum of Art.

CHAPTER 24

The observations of the unnamed witness to the awesome problems of moving the contents of the Antechamber appear in dispatches of the London *Times* between May 5 and May 11, 1923.

CHAPTER 25

The reference to the "onion" of the shrines appears in a memo from Carter to Herbert Winlock on file in the archives of the Egyptian Museum of Antiquities, Cairo.

The information regarding Carter's subsequent meetings with the officials of the Department of Antiquities, Carter's speech to Pierre Lacau and his assistants, and Carter's meeting with James Quibell appear in his unpublished pamphlet, *The Tomb of Tut-ankh-Amen, Statement with Documents as to the Events Which Occurred in Egypt in the Winter of* 1923–1924, on file in the Egyptian Department of the Metropolitan Museum of Art.

CHAPTER 26

The letter from James Quibell to Howard Carter asking for the names of his collaborators and Carter's reaction to it appear in Carter's unpublished pamphlet cited above.

Carter's letter to the London *Times* expressing his preparation for "a hell of a fight" dated November 16, 1923, is addressed to Lints Smith and is on file in the archives of the London *Times*.

The proposed new concession appears in full in Carter's above-cited unpublished pamphlet.

The information on Pierre Lacau's visit to the Valley appears in the same pamphlet, as does the report on the telephone call from Paul Tottenham to Howard Carter.

Carter's cable and subsequent letter to the London *Times*, referring to the trouble caused by the Egyptian government, are dated December 19 and 20, 1923, and are on file in the archives of the London *Times*.

CHAPTER 27

The source for Carter's actions in opening the seals on the second shrine is his unpublished pamphlet cited above for Chapter 25.

The information regarding Paul Tottenham's admonition that the Minister of Public Works of Egypt considered that "serious considerations" surrounded Carter's opening of the second shrine appears in the same pamphlet.

CHAPTER 28

The letter from Pierre Lacau to Howard Carter and Carter's response appear in Carter's unpublished pamphlet cited above for Chapter 25.

The information regarding Howard Carter's visit to Minister Morcos Bey Hanna regarding the concession of 1918 and Morcos Bey's conversation are all recorded in the same pamphlet.

The information regarding Arthur Merton's desire to pull off a major scoop on the opening of the sarcophagus appears in a letter from Merton to the London *Times* dated January 28, 1924, and is on file in the archives of the London *Times*.

CHAPTER 29

The information regarding Carter's request for the entry of his collaborators' wives, the so-called strike and Pierre Lacau's messages regarding the strike appear in Carter's unpublished pamphlet cited above for Chapter 25.

Carter's cable through Arthur Merton to the London *Times* informing the editors that he was forced to shut down the tomb is dated February 13, 1924, and is on file in the archives of the London *Times*.

Prime Minister Zaglul's two replies to Howard Carter appear in Carter's unpublished pamphlet cited above.

CHAPTER 30

The information regarding Pierre Lacau's entry into the locked tomb is to be found in Carter's above-cited pamphlet on file in the Egyptian Department of the Metropolitan Museum of Art.

The source for Carter's cable to the Prime Minister is the above-cited pamphlet.

The story in *The Saturday Review* about the dispute over the tomb is dated March 20, 1924.

The information regarding Carter's writs to the Mixed Courts, the proceedings of the hearing, and the use of the word "bandits" appear in a lengthy briefing letter from F. M. Maxwell to the solicitor of the Carnarvon estate, R. H. Molony, and is on file in the Egyptian Department of the Metropolitan Museum of Art.

The source for the proceedings in the Mixed Court of March 8 through March 12 appears in stories filed in the London *Times* by Arthur Merton and his assistant, Moyne.

CHAPTER 31

The information regarding Herbert Winlock's role as Howard Carter's power-of-attorney and negotiator appears in letters from Winlock to Carter dated March 28 and April 5, 1924. They are on file in the Egyptian Department of the Metropolitan Museum of Art.

The source for the meeting between Breasted and Morcos Bey Hanna is Charles

Breasted's book on his father, *Pioneer to the Past: The Story of James Henry Breasted, Archaeologist* (New York: Scribner's, 1943).

The description of the acerbic confrontation between Carter and the representative of the British Consulate appears in notes made by Lee Keedick, President of the Keedick Lecture Bureau, who accompanied Carter on his American tour. These notes were graciously sent to me by Robert Keedick.

The source for Breasted's personal opinion of Howard Carter is a letter from Breasted to Winlock dated March 31, 1924, on file in the Egyptian Department of the Metropolitan Museum of Art.

The information concerning Carter's disaffection with the London *Times* appears in a letter from Arthur Merton to Lints Smith of the newspaper, dated March 22, 1924, on file in the archives of the London *Times*.

The information about the negotiation between Howell and Marcos Bey Hanna, Winlock's role in the affair, the censure of Howell by the U.S. Department of State and the news story by Bradstreet appear in three letters of Herbert Winlock: to Carter dated March 28, 1924; to Albert Lythgoe dated April 5, 1924; and to Carter dated April 5, 1924. All three letters are on file in the Egyptian Department of the Metropolitan Museum of Art.

The proposed new concession appears in Howard Carter's unpublished pamphlet. *The Tomb of Tut-ankh-Amen* . . . , on file in the Egyptian Department of the Metropolitan Museum of Art.

CHAPTER 32

The sources for the undertakings of the Egyptian Inventory Commission, the discovery of the lotus head in the wine case, the report of Reis Ahmed and the communication from Winlock to Carter appear in notes and letters of March 31, April 1 and April 3, 1924, in the files of the Egyptian Department of the Metropolitan Museum of Art.

Carter's replies to Winlock are contained in the above-cited pamphlet in the files of the Metropolitan Museum of Art.

The cables from Winlock to Carter, both coded and uncoded, are on file in the Egyptian Department of the Metropolitan Museum of Art. The uncoded cable appears, in addition, in Carter's above-cited pamphlet.

The source for Pierre Lacau's cooperation in the affair of the lotus-head portrait is a letter from Winlock to Carter, dated April 5, 1924, on file in the Egyptian Department of the Metropolitan Museum of Art.

The information concerning Winlock's discussions with Pierre Lacau appears in a letter from Winlock to Carter, dated April 10, 1924, on file in the Egyptian Department of the Metropolitan Museum of Art.

CHAPTER 33

The letter from Carter to the Board of Trustees of the Metropolitan Museum of Art is dated April 24, 1924, and is on file in the Egyptian Department of the Metropolitan Museum of Art.

The letter from Herbert Winlock to Carter, briefing him in detail about every step of Winlock's negotiations with F. M. Maxwell, is dated May 22, 1924, and is on file in the Egyptian Department of the Metropolitan Museum of Art.

The letter of consolation from Albert Lythgoe to Howard Carter is dated June 3, 1924, and is on file in the Egyptian Department of the Metropolitan Museum of Art.

Winlock's annoyance at Carter's unpublished pamphlet and his statements to Edward Robinson appear in two letters from Robinson to Lythgoe dated July 15 and 18, 1924, and are on file in the Egyptian Department of the Metropolitan Museum of Art.

The letter dated September 13, 1924, from Lady Carnarvon is on file in the Egyptian Department of the Metropolitan Museum of Art.

The information concerning Carter's return to Egypt and his negotiations with Ziwar Pasha and the Service of Antiquities appears in a lengthy briefing letter sent by Carter to the solicitor R. H. Molony in January 1925, and is on file in the Egyptian Department of the Metropolitan Museum of Art.

The letter from the Minister of Public Works, Mahmoud Bey Sidky, to Lady Carnarvon, dated January 13, 1925, is on file in the Egyptian Department of the Metropolitan Museum of Art.

CHAPTER 34

The information about Howard Carter's change in attitude appears in a letter from Herbert Winlock to Edward Robinson, dated April 15, 1926, and is on file in the Egyptian Department of the Metropolitan Museum of Art.

CHAPTER 35

The information regarding the objects from the tomb of Tutankhamun in the collection of the Metropolitan Museum of Art was given to me in part by Christine Lilyquist, curator of the museum's Department of Egyptian Art. Other information regarding the certain or possible provenance comes from the department's catalogue cards on the individual items. The letter from Lord Carnarvon to Howard Carter mentioning the horse and the ariel is dated December 24, 1922, and is in the department's files.

The information about the Tutankhamun objects in the Brooklyn Museum, the William Rockhill Nelson Museum in Kansas City, the Cincinnati Art Museum and the Cleveland Museum of Art was given to me by John Cooney, Curator of Ancient Art at Cleveland. Further information regarding the piece in the Guennol Collection was imparted to me by Alastair Bradley Martin. The information concerning the system utilized by the Service of Antiquities to arrive at the figure of thirty-six thousand pounds for the Carnarvon estate, the story of the visit to the British Museum by the representative of the Carnarvon estate, and the story of Herbert Winlock's characterization of the Carnarvon collection were imparted to me by I. E. S. Edwards, Curator Emeritus of Egyptian Art at the British Museum.

The story of the pieces given by Howard Carter to his niece and, subsequently, to King Farouk was told to me by John Cooney.

Index

Abd-al-Rasul family, 44–45
Académie des Inscriptions et Belles
    Lettres, 274
Akhenaton (Amenhotep IV), 17–18, 55,
    186, 216–18, 368
    style of, 96
    tomb discoveries relating to, 49, 56, 84,
    277, 353
Al-Ahram, 219, 315
Allenby, Lady, 193, 203, 299
Allenby, Lord, 109, 193, 203
    his influence sought, 69, 144, 205, 310–
    311, 344
    and Nationalists, 299
Amarna, see Tell al-Amarna
Amenhotep II, tomb of, 46
Amenhotep III, 84, 216
    tomb of, 39
Amenhotep IV, see Akhenaton
Amherst of Hackney, Lady, 26
Amherst Papyrus, 37, 98
Amun cult, 17, 18, 55, 187–88, 216–18
Ankhesenamun, 50, 55, 188, 218, 353,
    364, 366
    letter to Hittite King, 368–69
Annales du Service des Antiquités de
    l'Égypte, 105–7
Annex, 96, 114, 122, 363, 365
Antechamber
    descriptions of, 88–97, 119–22
    treasures cleared from, 168–74, 180,
    183–90, 214, 232
Antiquities Law, 65–69, 144, 204, 224,
    316
Antiquities Service, 23–25, 47

Carter's career in, 27–29, 40
change in policy of, 64ff.
and Davis, 305
exhibition of, 367
and idemnity to Lady C, 349
"intact tomb" definition, 24–25, 65,
    123, 127–28, 278–79
issue of control over dig, 247, 270ff.
mishandles treasures, 348
and negotiations for concession,
    239–42, 325, 346
new concession form, 258–59, 271,
    272
and opening of tomb, 81–82, 84–85,
    109
postpones changing law, 224
reopens tomb, 299
restoration work, 367
and Times exclusives, 158–60
treasures turned over to, 232–34
see also Englebach, Rex; Lacau, Paul;
    Quibell, Jean
Anubis shrine, 101, 198, 227
Associated Press, 270
Aton cult, 18, 55, 187–88, 217–18, 277
Ay, 217

Bedawy Pasha, 346
Belzoni, Giovanni, 41–43, 366
Beni Hasan, 26
Berengaria, S.S., 326
Bethell, Richard, 193, 224
boats, carved, 96, 102, 364, 365
Bonaparte, Napoleon, 24, 40
Boulos Effendi, Tewfik, 130, 132–33, 160

Brackman, Arnold, 48
Bradstreet, A. H., 186–87, 210, 233, 254
  and London *Times* exclusives, 109
    181, 244–45, 265
  Lythgoe tries to silence, 181–82
  "malignant influence" story, 315–16
Breasted, Charles, 118–20, 193–94
Breasted, James Henry, 116–26, 183, 187,
    193, 197, 212, 283
  on canopic shrine, 210
  on Carter–Carnarvon differences, 146,
    221
  and Carter's lawsuit, 301, 303, 307–10,
    312–15
  letter attacking Lacau, 274–76, 292
  tomb robberies dated by, 123–26
British Academy of Sciences, 274
British Museum, 26, 134, 142,
    357–58
Brooklyn Museum, 355–56
Brummer, Joseph, 356
Burial Chamber (Holy of Holies)
  description of and secret entry
    into, 89, 98–101, 103, 105–7
  official opening of, 180, 189–200
Burton, Harry, 115–19, 183, 193,
    263, 328
  his work at tomb, 141, 166, 170,
    180, 184

Cabinet, Egyptian, 294, 295, 342
Cairo, ferment in, 306, 342
Callender, A. R. "Pecky," 81, 82,
    183, 193, 263, 267
  enters tomb secretly, 88–103 *passim*
  guards tomb, 117, 118
  packs and ships treasures, 167, 184,
    232, 233
  at tomb opening, 83–89 *passim*
  in tour of tomb, 119ff.
canopic chest (shrine), 101–2, 198, 199,
    210, 363
Capart, Jean, 205–7, 208–9, 300, 349–
    350
Carnarvon, Almina Wombwell Herbert,
    Countess of, 22, 60, 224
  applies for concession, 237, 239
  and Carter's lawsuit, 301
  and concession dispute, 316–17, 339–
    341
  preliminary authorization granted to,
    247, 271
  renounces claim, 339–41
  share is pledged to, 341, 346
Carnarvon, George E. M. S. Herbert,
    5th Earl of
  early life, 19–25, 70
  meets Carter, 17, 29

investigations at Thebes, 48–49
gets valley concession, 54
and search for tomb, 57, 58, 60–61, 63–
    64, 69, 72
at Highclere, 69–70, 117
and first opening of tomb, 81, 82, 83–
    89
enters tomb secretly, 88–103, 105–7
stages official opening, 108–9
enlists Gardiner, Breasted, 116, 118
secret Metropolitan arrangement, 116,
    127–28, 139–45, 334
seeks share of "defiled tomb"
    objects, 122–23, 126, 128, 146, 158
and Three Princesses Treasure, 129,
    130, 133–37
failing health of, 136, 221
hailed in England, 138ff.
negotiates media rights, 146–54
plans "Book," 152
and *Times* contract, 154–57, 160, 165,
    181
observes conservation work, 176–80
lauded by Merton, 180–81, 207–8
and Burial Chamber opening, 189, 190,
    192, 193ff.
and Belgian Queen's visit, 202–3
lauded by Caparts, 206–7, 208–9
makes tomb secure, 213
and mummy furor, 219–21
dispute with Carter, 221–23
complains about visitors, 226
final illness, death, 223–25
and "curse," 226–28, 230
secret division of treasures, 349–57
see also Carnarvon estate
Carnarvon, Henry H. S. M. Herbert,
    4th Earl of, 20
Carnarvon, Henry S. M. Herbert,
    6th Earl of, 22, 226, 229–30
Carnarvon estate, 237
  and Carter's lawsuit, 303–4, 307
  division-of-treasures issue, 271, 272,
    331, 339–41, 346
  indemnified, 349–50
  Metropolitan gets treasures from, 353,
    357–58
Carter, Howard
  early life, 25ff.
  works for Petrie, 26–27, 40
  meets Carnarvon, 17, 29
  conducts tours, 29, 31–39
  studies valley records, 40–45
  and Belzoni, 41–43, 366
  investigations at Thebes, 48–49
  disputes Davis' theory, 53–54
  gets valley concession, 54
  searches for tomb, 55–60, 63, 72

and Winlock's discovery, 62, 73
attitude toward Lacau, 65–66
foils Kurna thieves, 70–71
arrangement with Metropolitan, 72–74, 116, 136, 139–40
discovers tomb entrance, 76–82
first opening of tomb, 83–89
enters secretly, 88–107
Evelyn infatuated with, 107, 222
stages official opening, 108–9
problems with visitors, 111–13, 153, 158, 183, 211, 239–41
assembles team of experts, 114–18, 127
shows tomb to experts, 118–22
seeks share of "defiled tomb" objects, 122–26, 140, 141, 146, 270ff., 278–79
and Three Princesses Treasure, 129, 130, 133–37
and media rights, 146–48
and exclusive *Times* contract, 154–55, 159–65, 183, 244–51, 279–80
directs conservation work, 166–71
deduces how robbers operated, 174–175
and Burial Chamber opening, 180, 189, 193–98
and Belgian Queen's visits, 203, 204
lauded by Caparts, Merton, 206–9
makes tomb secure, 213–18
dispute with Carnarvon, 221–23
and Carnarvon's death, 223–24, 231
ships treasures to Cairo, 231–35
and dismantling of shrines, 236–37, 238, 253–56, 263–69
negotiates concession renewal, 237, 239–42, 316–17
reopens tomb, 242–43
and Merton's appointment, 256–62
confronted with 1918 permit, 278–79, 286, 302
examines sarcophagus, 276–77
and opening of sarcophagus, 280–81, 283–85
and excavators'-wives furor, 285–96, 298
closes tomb, 287–95
barred from tomb, 290, 295
sues Minister, 298, 300–316
renounces claim, 303, 309
confrontation with vice-consul, 310–12
and lotus-head scandal, 319–25, 335, 337
American tour, 280, 312, 326–31, 333–337
writes pamphlet, 331, 334–39
returns to England, 337–39
again renounces claim, 339–41
returns to Egypt, 342

and Ziwar government, 342–48
secret division of treasures, 349–57
returns to tomb, 358–59
opens coffins, 359–62
clears Treasury, Annex, 363–65
death of, 366
assessment of, 366–67
Carter, Samuel John, 25–26
casket, painted, 94–95, 235
Cassell and Company, Ltd., 334
"cat with pink tongue," 99, 197
Cecil, Lord Edward, 68
Chaban, Mohammed, 246
chair, ceremonial (in Antechamber), 173
chair of state (in Annex), 365
chariots, 94, 102, 121–22, 171, 183, 185
chest, canopic, *see* canopic chest
Christian Science Monitor, 194
Cincinnati Art Museum, 356
Cleveland Museum of Art, 355, 356
coffins of Tutankhamun, 284–86, 299, 359–60
Colossi of Memnon, 150
Coolidge, Calvin, 329
Cooney, John, 355, 356
Cottrell, Leonard, 64
couches, 93, 94, 120, 122, 172, 180, 183–85
Crabites, Pierre, 301–8, 309, 313–14
Crane, Lancelot, 49
"curse of Tutankhamun," 226–30, 237–238, 316
Cust, Sir Charles, 193

Daily Express, 155–56
Daily Mail, 153, 161, 244
Daily News, Chicago, 194
Daily News, New York, 230
Daily Telegraph, 153–54, 183, 194
Daoud Pasha, 44–45, 70
Daressy, Georges, 49, 54, 140
Davis, Theodore M., 48ff.
    Akhenaton diggings of, 56, 166
    Carter's lawsuit and, 304, 305
    Carter's work for, 27–28, 119, 161
    Tutankhamun findings of, 50, 52–54, 56, 61
Dawson, Geoffrey, 149
defiled tombs, *see* "intact" versus "defiled" tombs
de Forest, Robert, 142
Deir al-Bahri, 27, 31, 44
Derry, Dr. Douglas, 362
Description of the East, A (Pococke), 40
Disraeli, Benjamin, 20
Doyle, Sir Arthur Conan, 226–27
Drovetti, (archaeologist), 42
Dulles, Allen, 316

Eastern Telegraph Company, 153–54
Egyptian Archaeological Fund, 81
Egyptian Exploration Fund, 26, 192
Egyptian Mail, 244
Egyptian Museum of Antiquities, 18, 26, 136, 172
  Farouk gift to, 357
  tomb treasures sent to, 185, 234–35, 320, 348, 363, 367
Eighteenth Dynasty (New Empire), 17, 31, 33–37
Eleventh Dynasty, 118, 140
Elisabeth, Queen of the Belgians, 190, 191, 193, 200, 201–5, 212
Engelbach, Reginald (Rex), 84–86, 166, 193
  and closing of tomb, 290
  and dismantling of shrines, 263, 264, 265
  and lotus head, 318–19, 321–22, 324
  refuses to take over dig, 309
  and secret entry, 104
  staff list requested by, 257
  his transfer sought by Carter, 159–60
Erment, 81
Exchange Telegraph, 265–66

Fahmy, Mohammed Bey, 109
Fahmy Bey, Ali, 229
fans, 198, 268–69
Farouk, King, 356–57
Fifth Dynasty, 227, 355
First World War, 57
Five Years' Explorations at Thebes (Carter/Carnarvon), 49
Foreign Office, Egyptian, 314
Foucart, Georges, 345, 346
French Archaeological Mission, 345
Fuad, King, 192, 207, 244, 356

Gabbanet al-Kurud, 129–30
Gardiner, Sir Alan, 64, 72, 116, 127, 146, 171–73, 193, 197, 283
  complains to Hanna, 279
  letter attacking Lacau, 274–76, 292
  and sale of press rights, 149–50, 152
  and Three Princesses Treasure, 130
Garstin, Sir William, 193
George V, King, 138
Giza, 51
"Golden Bird," 75, 77, 82
Goldwyn Ltd., 151
Gould, George J., 229
Griffith, Francis Llewellyn, 183
Griffith Institute (Oxford University), 367
Guennol Collection, 356
Gulbenkian, Calouste, 73
Gurgar, Ahmed, 297–98

Haggard, H. Rider, 220–21
Hall, Lindsley, 116, 170
Hammad, Mohammed, 131–32
Hanna, Morcos Bey, 277–81, 283
  and Carter's lawsuit, 301, 303, 306, 307–10, 313–16
  concession dispute, 298, 316–17, 325, 328, 331–32, 340–42
  excavators'-wives furor, 287, 294–95
Haremhab, 125–26, 216–18, 368
  tomb of, 49
Harkness, Edward S., 73, 142, 205, 259, 283, 337, 351
Hatshepsut, 17, 26
  temple of, 26, 150
  tombs of, 49, 71–72
Hauser, Walter, 116, 118, 171
Hebrews, 94, 124
Herald, New York, 144
Herbert, Lady Evelyn, 22, 69, 117, 127, 138–39, 202, 366
  enters tomb secretly, 88–103, 105
  and father's death, 223–24
  infatuation for Carter, 107, 222
  at opening of Burial Chamber, 193, 194, 200
  and opening of tomb, 81, 83–89
  returns to tomb, 176–77
  and secret museum deal, 141, 142
Herbert, Mervyn, 193
Highclere, 20, 60–61, 69, 117, 225
Hittites, 94, 369
Holy of Holies, *see* Burial Chamber
Howell, J. Merton, 66, 202–3, 224
  and Carter's lawsuit, 308, 310, 313–16
Hughes, Charles Evans, 205, 272, 316
Hussein, Dowager Sultana, 202
Hussein, Reis, 318–20

Ibrahim Effendi, 104, 108
Ikhenaton, *see* Akhenaton
Illustrated London News, The, 148, 152
Ineni, 33, 34
"intact" versus "defiled" tombs, 24–25, 65, 123, 128, 278–79, 286, 302

Jegen Pasha, Adly, 193
"Journal of Entry," 319, 324, 367

Kamal, Prince Yusef, 193
Kamalel-din, Prince, 193
Karnak stele, 18, 55–56, 218, 368
Keedick, Lee, 76, 330–31
Kurna thieves, 41, 43, 44–45, 70–71, 129ff.

laboratory, *see* Seti II, tomb of
Lacau, Pierre, 203, 264, 367
  appointment of, 64

proposes changing law, 65–69, 204–5
redefines "intact tomb," 65, 128, 278–279
and opening of tomb, 84–85, 109
promises a choice of treasures, 140, 141, 348
and reaction to *Times* contract, 156, 158–60
refuses to transfer aide, 160
at Burial Chamber opening, 193, 197
examines treasures, 235, 348
and Merton's appointment, 241–42, 256–60
and issue of nightly bulletins, 246–48, 250–52
demands list of Carter's staff, 256–57
reasserts right of control, 258–60, 270–276
attacked by Egyptologists, 274–76, 292
and sarcophagus opening, 280–81, 283, 285
and excavators'-wives furor, 285, 287, 289–90, 295, 298
takes control of tomb, 297
at reopening of sarcophagus, 299
refuses to take over dig, 309
and lotus-head scandal, 318–25
and concession negotiations, 325, 328, 331–32, 346, 347
attacked in Carter pamphlet, 331, 335–336
and Carter's renunciation, 339, 343
Foucart and, 345, 346
welcomes Carter back, 358
Lahun, 137
Lansing, Ambrose, 133
Legrain, Georges, 18, 55, 218
Leigh, Lord, 191
Leopold, Prince, 191, 201, 202, 204
Lepsius, Karl Richard, 44
London *Times, see Times, The*
lotus head, 319–25, 335, 337
lotus lamp, 196
Lucas, Alfred, 117, 193, 263
conservation work of, 167, 177, 179, 185, 189, 359
reveals secret entry, 105–6
Luxor, 26, 30
celebrities in, 191–92
tourists in, 111, 211–12, 269
Tutankhamun craze in, 200, 264
Lythgoe, Albert, 207, 283, 322
opposes Lacau's policies, 66–69, 204–5, 271–73
provides specialists for Carter, 117–18
and Three Princesses Treasure, 134, 137, 144
and Petrie purchase agreement, 137

secret arrangement with Carnarvon, 139–45
and *Times* contract, 155, 182–83
tries to silence Bradstreet, 181–82
complains about Egyptologists, 182–83
at Burial Chamber opening, 193, 196, 205
and Macy gift, 211
at Burial Chamber closing, 214
and Carnarvon's illness, 223–24
and Merton-appointment furor, 259, 260
letter attacking Lacau, 274–76, 292
rebuffs Hanna, 309
and Carter's renunciation, 333–34
and secret division of treasures, 353
Lythgoe, Mrs., 141

MacDonald, Ramsay, 295–96
Mace, A. C., 141, 193, 263
Carter team recruit, 116, 118, 139, 140
conservation work of, 166, 177, 179, 185, 189
and "curse," 228
translates hieroglyphs, 269
Mackay, Ernest, 130, 133
Macy, Mr. and Mrs. J. Everitt, 211
Malet, Sir Louis, 191
Maspero, Sir Gaston, 17, 27–29, 49, 54
liberal policy of, 64–65, 67, 68, 143–44
Mauretania, S. S., 337–39
Maxwell, F. M., 300–306, 315, 331
and "bandits" insult, 306, 307, 309
Maxwell, Sir John, 192, 193, 237, 252
and Carter's lawsuit, 301–2, 304, 309
and division-of-treasures issue, 271, 331–32, 339–41
"Mecham, George Waller," 193–94
Meketra, tomb of, 169
Menhet, Menwi and Merti, 129–37
Merenptah, 58, 60
Meretaton, 353
Merton, Arthur, 109, 147–48, 154–57
appointment as "excavator," 239–42, 258–62
and Burial Chamber opening, 193, 197, 200
Carnarvon interviewed by, 178, 179, 197
Carter interviewed by, 266–67
and Carter's lawsuit, 308, 312–13
and excavators'-wives furor, 291
on inner shrine, 255–56
lauds excavators, 180–81, 189–90, 207–208, 210, 232
sandal story, 183
on sarcophagus, 276

Merton, Arthur (*cont.*)
  and sarcophagus opening, 281–82, 283,
    284–85
  on Tutankhamun craze, 200, 264
  on valley climate, 231
Merzbach Bey, 331, 341, 343–47
Metropolitan Museum of Art
  acquires Carnarvon collection, 136,
    141–42, 145, 334, 350–55
  Carter honored by, 326–27
  and Carter's lawsuit, 309, 311
  Davis findings stored in, 51–53, 61–62
  Egyptian digs, of, 51, 68, 117–18, 140
  and Merton furor, 260–61
  Petrie purchase agreement, 137
  secret arrangement with Carter,
    Carnarvon, 73–74, 116, 127–28, 139–
    145
  specialists provided by, 115–18
  and State Dept., 272, 316
  and Three Princesses Treasure, 128–37,
    144
  ultimatum to Egyptian government,
    144
  see also Lythgoe, Albert; Robinson, Ed-
    ward; Winlock, Herbert
Ministry of Public Works, Egyptian, 23,
    109
  and exclusive *Times* contract, 156, 160–
    161, 245–52
  postpones changing law, 224
  see also Hanna, Morcos Bey; Suleman
    Pasha, Abdel Hamid
Mixed Courts, 298, 300–306
Mixed Tribunal, 314, 315, 316
Mohammed Ali, 42
Mohassib, Muhammed, 130–34
Morgan, J. Pierpont, 68
Morning Post, Cairo, 156, 181–82, 183
Morton, H. V., 156

Napoleon, 24, 40
*Narrative of the Operations and Recent Dis-
  coveries . . . in Egypt and Nubia* (Bel-
  zoni), 42–43
Nationalist Party (Wafd), 158, 202, 207,
    299
  assumes control, 242, 277, 349–50
  out of power, 343
National Research Council, 274
Naville, Édouard, 27
Nefertiti, 186, 353, 366
Nekhbet shrine, 188–89, 235
Nelson Art Gallery, Kansas City, 356
Nessim Pasha, Tewfik, 193
Newberry, Percy E., 26–27, 183, 263, 264,
    283
  letter attacking Lacau, 274–76, 292

New Empire, *see* Eighteenth Dynasty
New York Times, The, 144, 239
  see also Bradstreet, A. H.
Nineteenth Dynasty, 33, 34, 37, 38–39,
    123
Nubians, 94, 216

Observer, 183
Ochs, Adolph, 182
Outlook, 152
Oxford University, 367

Palestine, 311
Parliament, Egyptian, 314, 330
Pathé, 150
Petrie, Sir William Flinders, 26–27, 28,
    40, 55, 116, 137
Pococke, Richard, 40–41
Poonah, Raja of, 191
pyramids, age of, 32

Quibell, James Edward, 143–44, 239–41,
    243–48, 250, 256–58

Ramesses II the Great, 18, 60
  bust of, 42
  tomb of, 33–34, 39, 58
Ramesses III, 39
Ramesses IV, tomb of, 198
Ramesses VI, tomb of, 50, 58, 59, 63, 76,
    77, 81, 85
Ramesses IX, 38–39, 122–23
Reisner, George, 51
Reuters, 109, 156, 239
Riad Bey, Mohammed, 297
Richardson, R. B., 67
Robinson, Edward, 82, 133–34, 358
  and Bradstreet, 181–82
  and Carter pamphlet, 336, 338–39
  Lythgoe reports to, 139–41, 155, 182,
    205, 211, 271, 274
  and secret arrangement with Carnar-
    von, 144–45
Rogers, Jacob, 53
Rorimer, James J., 74
Rosetti (lawyer), 302–6
Royal Geographic Society, 152
Rushdi Pasha, Hussein, 193

Said Pasha, Mohammed, 193
Saqqara, 28, 354
sarcophagus, 264–65, 278, 280–82
  descriptions of, 267, 276–77, 329
  officially opened, 283–85
  reclosed, reopened, 297–98, 299
Sarwat Pasha, Abdel Khalek, 193, 208
Sassoon, Sir Philip, 191
Saturday Review, The, 293, 296, 300

Search for the Gold of Tutankhamen, The (Brackman), 48
sentinels (statues of Tutankhamun), 93, 97, 103, 120, 122, 124, 214, 254
Senusert II, 137
Service of Antiquities, *see* Antiquities Service
Seti I, tomb of, 34–35, 39
Seti II, tomb of (laboratory), 50, 166–67, 177–78, 298
shrines of Tutankhamun
  in Antechamber, 188–89, 235
  in Burial Chamber, 98–101, 263–69, 324
  in Treasury, *see* canopic chest
Sidky, Mahmoud Bey, 346, 347
Sidky Pasha, Ismail, 193
Siptah, tomb of, 49
Sirry Pasha, Ismail, 193
Smenkhkara, 84, 217, 368
Smith, Dr. Elliot, 143, 183
Somerleyton, Lady, 191
Stack, Sir Lee, 342
State Department, U.S., 115, 261, 316
  see also Hughes, Charles Evans
stool, ebony-and-ivory, 172–73, 325
Suleman, Abd-el-Hallin Pasha, 193, 202
Suleman Pasha, Abdel Hamid, 210, 265, 277
  and Merton/*Times* issue, 242, 244–48, 251, 257, 258, 260–62
Swaythling, Lord and Lady, 191

Tell al-Amarna, 18, 217
Tety, 228
Teye, Queen, 49
Thebes, 18, 27, 30, 217
Thirteenth Dynasty, 228
thrones of Tutankhamun, 95, 120, 178–179, 187–88, 217, 235
Thutmose I, 17, 31–33, 46
Thutmose II, 71, 84, 128, 129, 216
Thutmose III, 17, 46, 369
Thutmose IV, tomb of, 49, 125
Times, The, London, 122, 126, 220, 226, 235
  Carter gives scoop to, 109
  editorial on excavators'-wives issue, 291–92
  exclusive contract secured by, 146–50, 153, 154–57, 237
  opposition to exclusivity of, 158–65, 181, 239–42, 244–52, 258–62, 265, 279–80
  reproached by Carter, 260–61, 312
  see also Merton, Arthur
Tomb No. Four, 168, 298, 318–23
Tomb of Tut-ank-Amen, The (Carter), 41–42, 62, 69, 152, 363, 366

its account of Carter's first entry, 104–5
its dating of robberies, 126
and lotus-head scandal, 323–24
Tomb of Tut-ankh-Amen, The, Statement with Documents (Carter pamphlet), 334–39
Tombs of Harmhabi and Toutankhamanou, The (Maspero/Daressy/Crane), 49
Toussoon, Prince Omar, 193
Treasure of the Three Princesses, 128–37
"Treasures of Tutankhamun, The" (exhibition), 367
Treasury (of tomb), 89, 101–3, 198, 199, 363–64
Trevor, Lady Juliet, 191
Tribune, New York, 327
Tottenham, Paul, 109, 245–48, 250, 261, 265, 278–79, 286
Tutankhamun
  "curse" of, 226–30, 237–38, 316
  life and death of, 17–19, 55–56, 100, 187–88, 216–18, 364–69
  mannequin of, 186–87, 235
  mask of, 360–61
  mummification and funerary banquet of, 61–62
  mummy of, 219–21, 236, 360–62
  portrait head of ("lotus head"), 319–25, 335, 337
  see also Tutankhamun, tomb of
Tutankhamun, tomb of
  Carter searches for, 55–60, 63, 72
  clues to, 49–50, 61–62
  contents of, *see* Annex; Antechamber; Burial Chamber; coffins of Tutankhamun; sarcophagus; Treasury
  discovery and opening of, 76–82, 83–89, 108–9
  excavators enter secretly, 88–103
  excavators'-wives issue results in closing of, 285–96
  Lacau takes control of, 297–98, 318
  reopened by Zaghlul, 298–300
  return of Carter to, 358
  treasures shipped from, 231–35
Twentieth Dynasty, 33, 34, 37, 39

Underwood, Oscar W., 112–13

Valley of the Kings, description and history of, 30–46

Wafd, Wafdists, *see* Nationalist Party
Walker, Phyllis, 357
Weigall, Arthur, 161–65, 186, 194, 229
Wembley Amusements Ltd., 326
Westbury, Lord, 224
Wilkinson, Charles, 58

Williams, Mrs. Valentine, 156–57
Williams, Valentine, 156, 246
Winlock, Frances, 119, 121, 359
Winlock, Herbert E., 51–53, 81, 82, 167,
    169, 177, 193
  betrayed by Carter, 52, 335–37
  and Carter–Lacau conflict, 64, 66
  and Carter/Metropolitan secret deal-
    ings, 73–74
  and Carter's lawsuit, 307–9, 312–16
  in Carter's team of experts, 118, 119
  on Carter's transformation, 358–59
  and "curse," 229, 316
  discovers clue to tomb, 61–62, 73, 115
  lotus-head scandal, involvement in,
    318–25, 335, 337
  and new concession, 316–17, 328, 331–
    332
  and Petrie purchase agreement, 137

  and secret division of treasures, 351,
    358
  and Three Princesses Treasure, 129,
    131, 132, 134–35, 137
  urges Carter to renounce claim, 332–34
Winlock, Mrs. Herbert E., 119, 359
"wishing cup," 103, 235

Yale University, 329
Yehia, Abd-el-Aziz Bey, governor, 109
Yehia Ibrahim Pasha, Prime Minister,
    277

Zaghlul, Mohammed Pasha, Under-Sec-
    retary, 283, 285
Zaghlul Pasha, Saad, Prime Minister,
    277, 290–91, 295, 297–300, 320, 322,
    342
Ziwar, Ahmad Pasha, 342–48, 349